W9-CES-904

Imperfect

UNION

ALSO BY STEVE INSKEEP

Jacksonland:
President Andrew Jackson, Cherokee Chief John Ross,
and a Great American Land Grab

Instant City:
Life and Death in Karachi

Imperfect
UNION

✷ ✷ ✷

How Jessie and John Frémont
Mapped the West, Invented Celebrity,
and Helped Cause the Civil War

Steve Inskeep

PENGUIN PRESS

NEW YORK

2020

PENGUIN PRESS
An imprint of Penguin Random House LLC
penguinrandomhouse.com

Copyright © 2020 by Steve Inskeep

Penguin supports copyright. Copyright fuels creativity, encourages
diverse voices, promotes free speech, and creates a vibrant culture.
Thank you for buying an authorized edition of this book and for complying with
copyright laws by not reproducing, scanning, or distributing any
part of it in any form without permission. You are supporting writers
and allowing Penguin to continue to publish books for every reader.

Pages 431–34 constitute an extension of this copyright page.

LIBRARY OF CONGRESS CATALOGING-IN-PUBLICATION DATA
Names: Inskeep, Steve, author.
Title: Imperfect union : how Jessie and John Frémont mapped the West,
invented celebrity, and helped cause the Civil War / Steve Inskeep.
Description: New York : Penguin Press, [2020] |
Includes bibliographical references and index.
Identifiers: LCCN 2019030462 (print) | LCCN 2019030463 (ebook) |
ISBN 9780735224353 (hardcover) | ISBN 9780735224360 (ebook)
Subjects: LCSH: Frémont, Jessie Benton, 1824–1902. |
Frémont, John Charles, 1813–1890. | Explorers—West (U.S.)—Biography. |
Women pioneers—West (U.S.)—Biography. | Pioneers—West (U.S.)—Biography. |
Politicians—United States—Biography. | Politicians' spouses—
United States—Biography. | Women's rights—United States—History—
19th century. | Antislavery movements—United States—History—19th century.
Classification: LCC E415.9.F79 I67 2020 (print) | LCC E415.9.F79 (ebook) |
DDC 910.92/2 [B]—dc23
LC record available at https://lccn.loc.gov/2019030462
LC ebook record available at https://lccn.loc.gov/2019030463

Printed in the United States of America
1 3 5 7 9 10 8 6 4 2

Book design by Daniel Lagin

To all those who make possible my own explorations

Contents

It would hardly do to tell the whole truth about everything.

—Jessie Benton Frémont

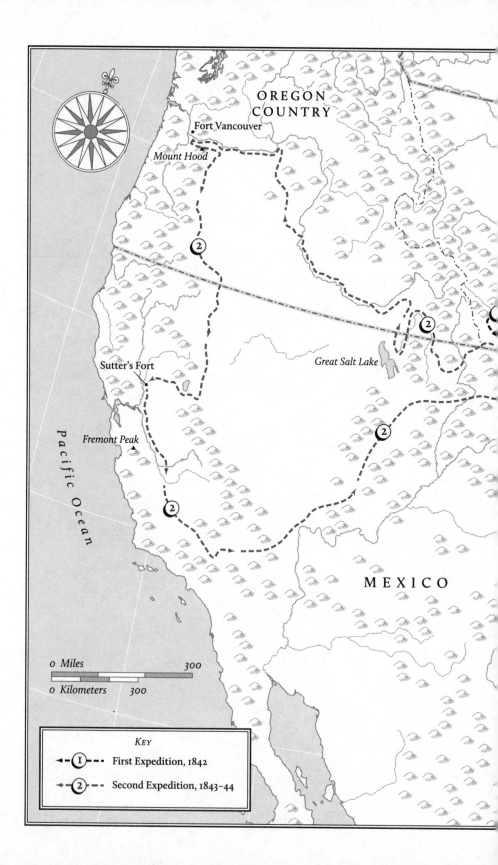

OREGON
COUNTRY

Fort Vancouver

Mount Hood

②

Great Salt Lake

Sutter's Fort

②

Pacific Ocean

▲ *Fremont Peak*

②

②

②

MEXICO

o Miles   300

o Kilometers   300

KEY

◄─①─── First Expedition, 1842

◄─②─── Second Expedition, 1843–44

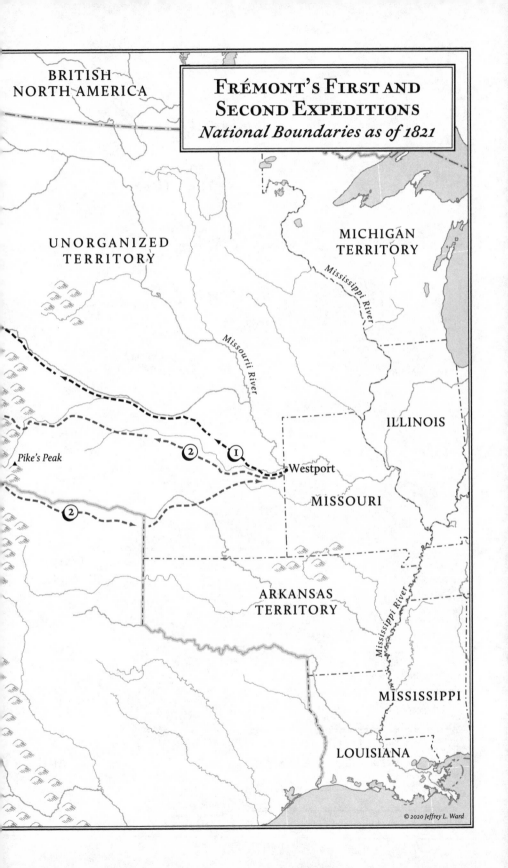

BRITISH
NORTH AMERICA

FRÉMONT'S FIRST AND
SECOND EXPEDITIONS
National Boundaries as of 1821

UNORGANIZED
TERRITORY

MICHIGAN
TERRITORY

Mississippi River

Missouri River

ILLINOIS

Pike's Peak

② ①

Westport

MISSOURI

②

ARKANSAS
TERRITORY

Mississippi River

MISSISSIPPI

LOUISIANA

© 2020 Jeffrey L. Ward

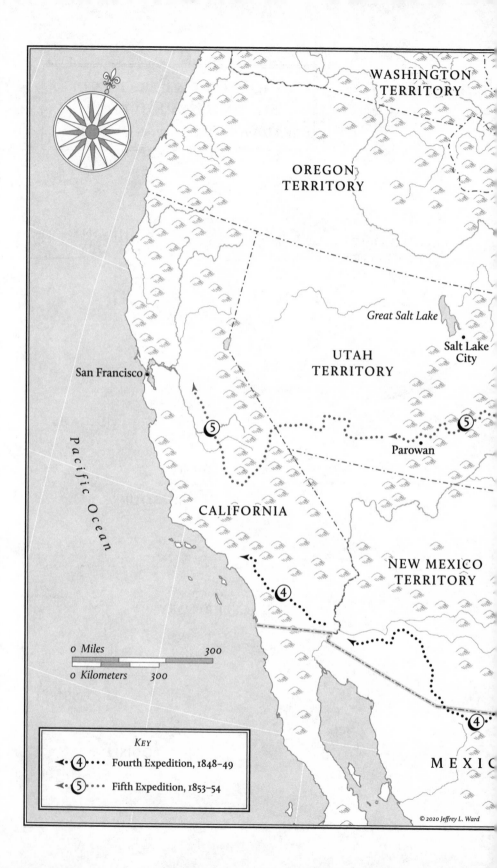

© 2020 Jeffrey L. Ward

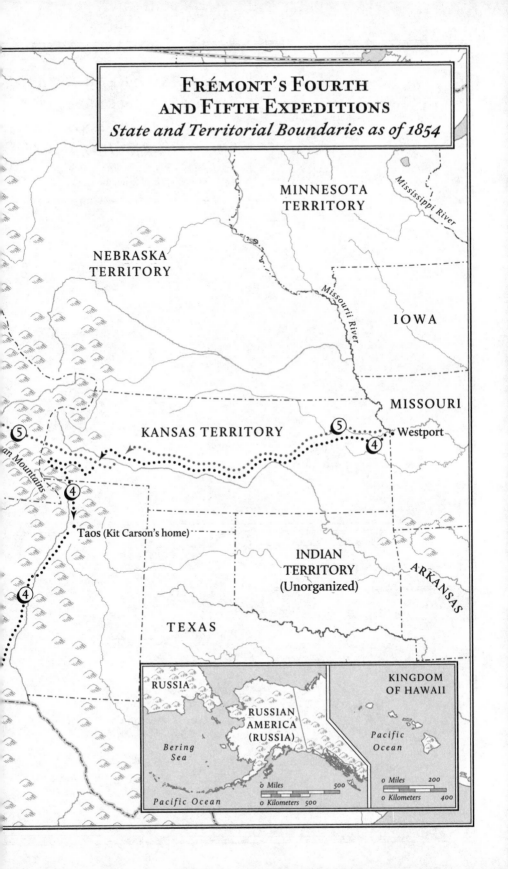

FRÉMONT'S FOURTH AND FIFTH EXPEDITIONS
State and Territorial Boundaries as of 1854

MINNESOTA
TERRITORY

Mississippi River

NEBRASKA
TERRITORY

Missouri River

IOWA

MISSOURI

KANSAS TERRITORY

⑤

④ Westport

⑤

an Mountains

④

Taos (Kit Carson's home)

INDIAN
TERRITORY
(Unorganized)

ARKANSAS

④

TEXAS

RUSSIA

RUSSIAN
AMERICA
(RUSSIA)

*Bering
Sea*

Pacific Ocean

KINGDOM
OF HAWAII

*Pacific
Ocean*

0 Miles   500
0 Kilometers 500

0 Miles   200
0 Kilometers 400

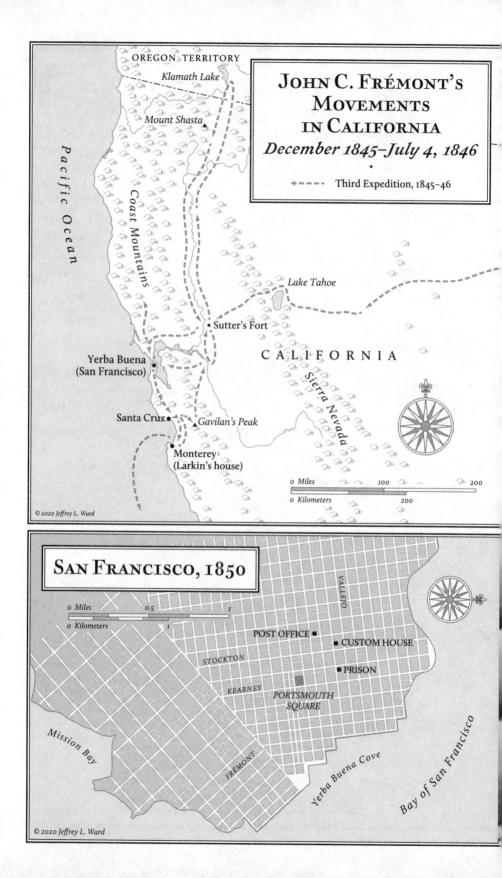

John C. Frémont's Movements in California
December 1845–July 4, 1846

←----- Third Expedition, 1845–46

OREGON TERRITORY

Klamath Lake

Mount Shasta

Pacific Ocean

Coast Mountains

Lake Tahoe

Sutter's Fort

CALIFORNIA

Yerba Buena
(San Francisco)

Sierra Nevada

Santa Cruz

▲*Gavilan's Peak*

Monterey
(Larkin's house)

0 Miles 100 200

0 Kilometers 200

© 2020 Jeffrey L. Ward

San Francisco, 1850

0 Miles 0.5 1

0 Kilometers 1

VALLEJO

POST OFFICE ■

■ CUSTOM HOUSE

STOCKTON

■ PRISON

KEARNEY

PORTSMOUTH
SQUARE

Mission Bay

FRÉMONT

Yerba Buena Cove

Bay of San Francisco

© 2020 Jeffrey L. Ward

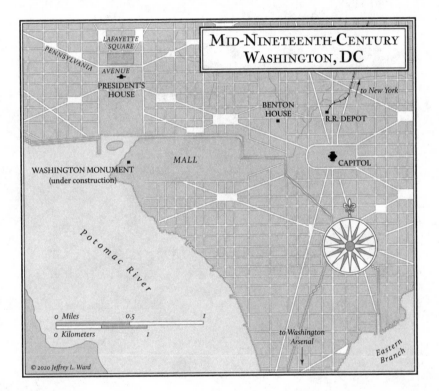

MID-NINETEENTH-CENTURY
WASHINGTON, DC

LAFAYETTE
SQUARE

PENNSYLVANIA

AVENUE

PRESIDENT'S
HOUSE

to New York

BENTON
HOUSE

R.R. DEPOT

MALL

CAPITOL

WASHINGTON MONUMENT
(under construction)

Potomac River

0 Miles   0.5   1
0 Kilometers   1

to Washington
Arsenal

Eastern
Branch

© 2020 Jeffrey L. Ward

Entered according to act of Congress, by Reese & Green

COL. FREMONT
PLANTING THE AMERICAN STANDARD ON THE ROCKY MOUNTAINS.

Introduction

O f the many times John C. Frémont visited St. Louis, the most aus-
picious came in 1845. He was thirty-two years old, a United States
Army captain with shoulder-length hair and a thoughtful expression. Arriving on a steamboat from the east on May 30, he disembarked at
the crowded waterfront with two companions: Jacob Dodson, a son of free
black house servants from Washington, D.C.; and William Chinook, an Indian from the faraway land called Oregon. It was fitting that Captain Frémont reached St. Louis with men from far to the west and east. His mission
was to connect the Atlantic world to the Pacific, surmounting the natural
barriers between.

Frémont served in an army unit called the Corps of Topographical Engineers, which had assigned him to draw maps of travel routes through the
Louisiana Purchase. Twice in the preceding three years he had recruited
small groups of skilled civilians to join him on expeditions that ranged
across thousands of miles of prairies, mountains, and deserts. Each time
their starting point was St. Louis, the commercial hub of Missouri, which

was the westernmost of the United States. Now Frémont was about to command his third expedition, and his preparations in St. Louis should have been routine. He needed to hire men and buy supplies—camping equipment, rifles, food, brandy, and coffee. (The coffee was vital; he had run out once on the prairie, a painful mistake he would never repeat.) But something happened as Captain Frémont made his customary rounds. His arrival was mentioned in a local newspaper, which created an unmanageable situation. James Theodore Talbot, a twenty-year-old aide who joined him in St. Louis, described Frémont's problem in a letter to his mother. "He was assailed by people anxious to accompany him" on his expedition, Talbot wrote. "Wherever he goes he gathers a little train." The job seekers would not let him alone. Declining to stay with Talbot at the Planter's House Hotel, where he might be spotted, the captain "hid himself in some French house down the City." So many men asked for him at the hotel that a clerk vowed to put up a sign reading, "Captain Frémont Did Not Stay Here."

Frémont spread the word that he would meet potential recruits at a warehouse, where he might stand on a barrel packed with tobacco leaves to address them. But when he arrived before ten o'clock on the morning of June 2, he found an unruly mass. "You ought to have witnessed the scene," Talbot wrote his mother. "Long before the appointed hour the house was filled and Capt Frémont found it necessary to adjourn to an open square.... The whole street and the open space was crowded. We could easily trace the Captain's motions by the denser nucleus which moved hither and thither. They broke the fences down and the Captain finally used a wagon as a rostrum but it was impossible for him to make himself heard." Men were elbowing each other to reach him, wanting so badly to talk to him that they would not listen. Frémont, too polite and reserved to command the crowd, gave up and fled. But men found where he was staying and chased him even into his bedroom, forcing his free black servant, Jacob Dodson, to use all his "strength and vigilance" in a vain effort to keep them away. A St. Louis newspaper declared: "This is the strongest manifestation of the Oregon fever that we have yet witnessed."

It was one episode in the life of John Charles Frémont, among the most famous men of his time. He had risen from obscurity just since 1842, when he commanded the first of his major expeditions. After traveling for months at a time on horseback and foot, often through deep snow, he went home to Washington, D.C., to write reports to the army about his adventures—and he told his stories so evocatively that his reports were excerpted in newspapers and published as popular books for the general public. His tumultuous arrival in St. Louis in 1845 marked a new phase in his work: the men he recruited that year deliberately rode outside the territory of the United States, crossing the mountains to reach the Pacific coast near San Francisco Bay. There, his sixty armed men helped to trigger the United States's conquest of the Mexican territory of California. This conquest was not even complete when the once-impoverished young officer began buying many square miles of California real estate, where he afterward struck it rich during the Gold Rush of 1849.

While it was natural that such a life would make him well known, Frémont's fame grew to proportions that were not easily explained; other adventurous people of his era could hardly compare. Newspapers reported his every move. A contemporary journalist called him "the Columbus of our central wildernesses," while a magazine in 1850 went further, listing Columbus, Washington, and Frémont as the world's three most important historical figures since Jesus Christ. He was not even forty years old when Americans began naming mountains and towns after him. Europeans thronged to invest in his gold-mining projects, and followed each step of his adventures: 350,000 people attended a long-running stage show in London that featured paintings of his experiences. His fame made it possible for him to enter politics, lifting him to a seat in the Senate and propelling him

in 1856 to become the first-ever presidential nominee of the newly established Republican Party. John C. Frémont was a social and political phenomenon of a kind we associate with modern celebrity culture.

What brought him such acclaim? Part was earned through genuine
accomplishment. The conquest of California was one of the most consequential acts in the history of the United States. His reports pointed emigrants to Oregon, and helped inspire Mormons to settle near the Great Salt
Lake. His maps were more reliable than earlier charts of the West because
he insisted on mapping only landmarks he had seen himself. While others
had previously walked the ground he traveled, his systematic observations
showed how different parts of the landscape fit together. He collected so
many specimens of previously unrecorded plants that botanists named
many after him, and when he reached San Francisco Bay, he gave the harbor
mouth its name: the Golden Gate.

His achievements were magnified by perfect timing: he explored the
West just as the country was turning its eyes to it. The "Oregon fever" mentioned by the St. Louis newspaper in 1845 referred to excitement about settling the Pacific Northwest, which was matched by an interest in Mexico's
territory to the southwest. That same year the United States annexed the
former Mexican territory of Texas; President James K. Polk took office after
being elected on an expansionist platform; and a newspaperman, John
L. O'Sullivan, wrote of "our manifest destiny to overspread the continent
allotted by Providence for the free development of our yearly multiplying
millions." While O'Sullivan was not the first to talk of a transcontinental
empire, his phrase "manifest destiny" entered the lexicon. It was debated in
Congress and referenced in popular culture. The British performer George
H. Hill, famed as "Yankee Hill" for the uncouth American he played in a
stage show, worked the phrase into his popular stand-up routine in early
1846. He said he favored "a clean fight" for territory beyond the Rocky
Mountains: "It is our 'manifest destiny,' and we cannot help it. Whoop,

Whooray, whar's the enemy?" As Hill spoke, John C. Frémont was in California, about to begin the takeover—manifest destiny personified.

But the most important factor in Frémont's fame may have been the person who made it possible for him to take full advantage of both his talent and the times: Jessie Benton Frémont, his wife. Born when women were allowed to make few choices for themselves, Jessie found a way to chart her own course. The daughter of a senator who was deeply involved in the West, she provided her previously unknown husband with entrée to the highest levels of the government and media. It was no coincidence that his career began to soar a few months after they eloped, when he was twenty-eight and she was seventeen. "I thought as many others did," said one of their critics, "that Jessie Benton Frémont was the better man of the two." She helped to write his famous reports and some of his letters, serving as secretary, editor, writing partner, and occasional ghostwriter. She amplified his talent for self-promotion, working with news editors to publicize his journeys. She became his political adviser. She attracted talented young men to his circle, promoted friends, and lashed out at enemies. She carried on conversations with senators twice her age, offered her opinions to presidents even when they did not agree with her, and was gradually recognized as a political force in her own right.

Her timing was as perfect as her husband's: she was pushing the boundaries of women's assigned roles just as women were beginning to demand a larger place in national life. In the 1840s and '50s, women were holding conventions to call for voting rights and also campaigning against slavery. The Republican Party, founded to oppose the expansion of slavery, captured some of their energy—and when John was nominated for president, Jessie became part of the campaign in ways that no woman ever had. Her husband's campaign literature featured songs of praise for Jessie; it nearly seemed like *they* were running for president. Women attended campaign rallies even though they could not vote. Thousands of Republicans flocked to the Frémont house for a glimpse of John on the balcony, and then refused to leave until they saw Jessie too: "Madam Frémont!" they cried. "Jessie! Jessie! Give us Jessie!" A newspaper said she could have been elected queen. Jessie Benton Frémont achieved a celebrity much like her husband's, with fame out of proportion to her accomplishments—unless we count her husband's fame among those accomplishments.

✳ ✳ ✳

TODAY THE FRÉMONT NAME is imprinted on the American landscape like the crater of some ancient meteor strike, its outlines apparent though eroded and overgrown. A Tesla electric car factory is located in Fremont, California, while vacationers in Las Vegas gamble inside a mall called the Fremont Street Experience. Residents of Seattle live in the Fremont neighborhood, named by emigrants from Fremont, Nebraska, which shares its name with Fremont, Ohio, New York, and New Hampshire. Hikers scramble up Fremont Peak in Wyoming, elevation 13,743 feet, and the smaller Fremont Peak outside Monterey, California. Rivers are lined by a tree called *Populus fremontii*, or Frémont's cottonwood. Readers of the more than fifteen thousand books on Abraham Lincoln often discover both Frémonts, who quarreled with him in the 1860s ("You are quite a female politician," President Lincoln told Jessie when she lobbied him on behalf of her husband). Yet for all the ways that they remain in plain sight, the Frémonts have largely faded from our national consciousness. A relative handful of biographies have been written about them.

This narrative aims to bring the Frémonts back into view through the story of their rise to fame, from their elopement in 1841 to their presidential campaign in 1856. They pioneered a modern path to celebrity in those years. Famous people in earlier times typically were revered because they held traditional positions of authority—kings, princes, clerics, generals, presidents. The cultural elites of Europe also celebrated writers and artists and people of interest. But the Frémonts grew famous in a more democratic way.

They worked through the expanding news media, which never before had reached so many readers or wielded so much influence. They spread their story to an increasingly literate public, and linked their names not to one, but to three great national movements—westward settlement, women's rights, and opposition to slavery.

In attaching themselves to these movements, the Frémonts took part in events that redefined the country. The conquest of California did far more than simply extend the borders of the United States. It created conditions for the rise of a new, more global America. A nation that had been born on the Atlantic—a colonial extension of Europe, with an enslaved population from Africa—became a power in the Pacific with direct trade routes to Asia. The United States also made itself part of Latin America by capturing its northernmost portion, along with the people who lived there. In short, John Frémont's arrival in California signaled the emergence of the United States as *the* nation of the world. There is abundant evidence in these pages that the Frémonts knew what they were doing; John named the Golden Gate not because it was the gateway *into* California, but because it was America's golden portal *outward* to Asia. He advocated a transcontinental railroad to connect that portal to the eastern states. He dreamed of "commingling together the European, American, and Asiatic races."

A careful look at the Frémonts' rise also reveals how their lives were far more complex and ambiguous than their public image. Though John was known as the conqueror of California, he played an erratic and sometimes baffling role in the takeover. And John's global vision of his country clashed with a far more parochial idea, which the Frémonts also embraced. John's reference to Americans as a "race" was a clue: Americans were vaguely described as a new race of people, generally descended from the British but with a distinct character molded by the experiences of the frontier. When Americans captured the Pacific coast, they insisted on the prerogatives of that new race—taxing foreigners and discriminating against Indians in order to keep California's bounty to themselves. Their actions reflected widespread attitudes in the eastern states from which they had come: Indians had been evicted from the East, and a nationwide movement against foreigners was on the rise. Anti-immigrant leaders called themselves Native Americans, by which they meant native-born white people rather than native people who had held the land before them. The Native Americans claimed that immigrants were unfairly swaying elections with their votes for the Democratic Party, and bringing foreign influence through their dangerous and alien religion, Catholicism.

The anti-immigrant movement grew so powerful that when the Frémonts sought political office in the 1850s, they had to decide whether to accommodate it. They did what they considered necessary. They wanted to win, so they wanted the votes of nativists—even though the Frémonts' actual goal was not stopping immigration, but stopping the spread of slavery. They pursued a morally perilous course, crafting words and deeds to win over bigots while trying not to taint themselves. They tried using sleight of hand to enlist prejudiced voters in an essentially progressive cause.

This book contends that the Frémonts advanced the antislavery cause—and also helped to bring about the Civil War that came in 1861. Their role must be properly defined. It would be wrong to claim, as Confederates did, that antislavery zealots such as the Frémonts were to blame for the war. In truth slavery was to blame, and its defenders fired the first shot. But events in which the Frémonts took part—westward expansion and the election of 1856—disrupted the old political order that had protected slavery, and forced a national reckoning with it.

The disruption came during an era that can feel eerily familiar, in that its social and technological change prefigured our own. Then as now, new industries were transforming daily life. Americans had never before seen places like Lowell, Massachusetts, a district of textile mills where eight thousand workers, mostly women, turned spindles and looms that produced fifty-eight million yards of cloth per year. The economy was globalized. Beaver pelts trapped in the West were shipped to Europe to become top hats; ginseng from the Appalachians and lead from Missouri were shipped to China in exchange for porcelain and tea. There was a revolution in communications; never in human history had people been so well connected. New roads, then steamboats, then railroads, and finally the telegraph shrank the world until information that had taken months to spread could travel in days, hours, or even seconds. Upon seeing the first practical telegraph line in 1844, a newspaper writer proclaimed "a new species of consciousness," the unprecedented ability to know "what events were at that moment passing in a distant city." Weekly newspapers became daily papers. They reprinted articles from papers elsewhere, creating a national conversation that the telegraph accelerated. Democratic politics were also transformed: voter participation rose year by year, partly driven by political coverage in the ever more vibrant media. But the increase in voting was, in one respect, ominous. Many Americans went to polling stations out of fear, concerned that the wrong election outcome would cause calamity. The telegraph spread news of political violence, which partisan newspapers interpreted in radically divergent ways. None of the advances in technology seemed to be making the country more stable, more equal, or more just.

Slavery was the great dividing issue. It touched the whole country, even states that seemed free of it; the 1.95 million pounds of cotton fed annually into the Lowell, Massachusetts, textile mills was picked almost entirely by Southern slaves. But Northern states had gradually abolished slavery on their own soil, while Southern states increasingly defined themselves by it. As rivalry sharpened between the sections, some began questioning the political system that held them together. Americans today can relate, for we still question the relative power of politically different states: Why, for example, should California and Oklahoma each have two senators when

California has ten times the population? Why should noncitizens be counted in the census, giving extra House seats to states with more immigrants? The answer is that the nation's founders made the rules when they drafted the Constitution, but in divisive times it is easy to perceive the rules as dangerously unfair. In the 1800s, Northerners resented that the Constitution allowed white Southerners an advantage when apportioning House seats according to population—white Southerners were allowed to count three-fifths of their slaves. Southern leaders resented that the North's population grew larger than the South's. Then westward expansion created the need to organize new states, which must be either slave or free, adding power to one side or the other. For years some parity was maintained, but that changed after John C. Frémont helped to bring the free state of California into the Union. Free states soon seemed powerful enough to elect a president without a single vote from any slave state. This was what John Frémont first attempted as a presidential candidate in 1856, and what Abraham Lincoln tried again in 1860. Southerners, fearing a government that no longer depended on them, prepared to secede from the Union.

Imperfect Union is a story of the American union, as seen through the Frémonts' union. They were early players in America's constant struggles over equality, race, and identity. It goes without saying that the story is set in a time of open bigotry and state-sponsored racism: even outside the South, only five states permitted full voting rights for black men, and none allowed the vote to women. Yet it needs to be said, and is a major theme of this book, that these were also years of American diversity. America as we know it would never have come into being without the work of people who supposedly were not part of it. John, who seemed to define the new race of Americans, was the illegitimate son of a French immigrant. He would not have accomplished as much as he did without his partnership with a woman. When the Frémonts eloped, the only cleric who was willing to officiate was a Catholic priest. The volunteers for John's perilous expeditions included men of numerous religions and backgrounds—a German immigrant mapmaker, French Catholic mountain men, free black men like Jacob Dodson, a Portuguese Jewish photographer, and Indians of several native nations. Numerous languages could be spoken around their campfires. All of these people were creating the nation we have inherited, which is the legacy of all of them.

Part One

NATION
BUILDING

❋ ❋ ❋

Prairie Meadows Burning by George Catlin, 1832.

Charleston, South Carolina, fronted by the Battery.

Chapter One

AID ME WITH YOUR INFLUENCE

C.J. FREMONT, 1813–1840

Charleston and the West

L ong before he was famous for wandering the West, John Charles Frémont grew up in a family that wandered the South. They moved restlessly from city to city, beset by scandal, then tragedy, then poverty. The scandal was John's illegitimate birth.

John's mother, Anne Pryor, was the offspring of an elite Virginia family. She was married when she fell in love with Charles Fremon, a French immigrant and French teacher. Confronted by her husband in 1811, Anne left him and moved with Charles to Savannah, Georgia, where John was born to them on January 21, 1813. Their life in modest rented rooms was a change for Anne from the plantation houses where she had grown up; Charles Fremon made a bare living by opening a "French and Dancing Academy" for elite young ladies and gentlemen, and taking in boarders who wanted to study his native language. But they were not entirely without help. Anne had come from Virginia with a living token of her aristocratic past: a maid named Hannah, a family slave in her midthirties described as having a "reddish complexion." She had an independent spirit. Having accompanied

Anne when she followed her heart to Savannah, the maid tried to follow her own heart, and escaped in 1812 with a free black boatman. But all the rules were different for Hannah; she either returned or was captured, and was on hand to help when baby John arrived.

The family faced trouble from the start. The state of Virginia refused to grant a divorce, meaning Anne could not marry the father of her child. Beyond that, something didn't work for them in Savannah. The baby was only nine months old when they relocated with him to Nashville, where Charles started another French and dancing school. Tennessee also did not hold them long, and they rambled back eastward to Norfolk, Virginia, while two more children, Elizabeth and Francis, were born to them along the way. They no doubt grew poorer with the demands of each new child. Then Charles Fremon died around 1818, leaving Anne with next to nothing, and five-year-old John without any clear memory of his father.

John never said what he felt about the collapse of his family, except indirectly by what he edited out of his life. He did not speak of his father, and was still a youth when he began effacing his father's name. First, he changed Fremon to Fremont. Then his given name went through an evolution. His earliest known signature, from age fifteen, was written J. Charles Fremont—he was going by Charles, like his father. As late as his eighteenth year, some documents called him Charles Fremont or even reversed his initials to make him C.J. Fremont. But he later put the initials back in order, giving John as his first name. Not until his twenties did he add an accent mark, completing his identity as John C. Frémont.

Before his teenage years, when people still called him Charles or C.J., his mother moved the family to Charleston, South Carolina. C.J. sometimes walked to its harbor, lingering at the Battery, a waterfront promenade, where he could "go and feel the freedom of both eye and thought." He felt that "the breast expands" when "the eye ranges over a broad expanse of country, or in the face of the ocean." He could watch white sails on the horizon as ships approached from Liverpool or Boston, along with black smoke from the regular steamer coming up the coast from Savannah. Approaching ships angled past Fort Sumter, a brick pile that was just getting under construction on a shoal in midwater.

He couldn't spend much time looking, because his family needed him to work. At thirteen he interrupted his education to work for a lawyer, serving subpoenas. But the youth's intelligence prompted the lawyer to pay for him to go back to school, the first of many times that Charles would attract an older male sponsor. A schoolteacher became the next sponsor, and recorded a description of his student: "middle size, graceful in manners, rather slender . . . handsome; of a keen piercing eye and noble forehead." The teacher took extra time to instruct him in Greek, passing on a love of Greek plays, and at sixteen Charles was admitted to the College of Charleston, starting as a member of the junior class.

It was a priceless opportunity. The college's brick building was new, its cornerstone having been laid just three years earlier, and though its roof leaked in the rainy climate it was a vibrant institution. Aware that the top colleges were in the North—Princeton, Harvard, Yale—Charlestonians wanted a good school of their own, and leading citizens became trustees. There were three thousand books in the library, and the size of the student body had recently reached a record high of sixty-two. The college president, Jasper Adams, had been recruited from Brown University in New England, and his curriculum blended readings from ancient Athens and Rome with the ideology of the new American republic. That ideology went on display when students performed at a college exhibition: Charles Fremont recited an "Extract from Mr. Crafts' Oration, 4th July 1812." William Crafts was a Charleston politician who in that speech declared, "This country appears to have been created on a magnificent plan, destined for the production of great events, and the display of extraordinary powers." Americans would develop "mental and moral greatness" as they met the challenge of spreading across the continent and conquering the West. "Our rivers," C.J. repeated to the audience, "flowing with boundless velocity—our mountains, rising in awful grandeur—our rocks, braving the fury of the elements, are marked with the characters of independence, and proclaim the residence of freemen."

The faculty member who took attendance recorded the way C.J.'s academic career gradually drifted off course. In the fall of 1830, he missed the first few weeks of class. The faculty understood; attendance records noted that "C.J. Fremont" was "teaching in the country by permission." Probably he was helping to support his family by giving private lessons to affluent families, as his father once had. C.J. returned to college a few weeks later, and his high grades suggested that he caught up with his classmates. But he began missing more classes, sometimes vanishing for a week. His behavior stood out, even in a school with generally spotty attendance ("The whole course of . . . Philosophy," one campus record complained, "will be badly understood by the Senior Class on acc. of the frequent absences!"). His professors gave him "frequent reprimands." His friends were mystified. At last, on February 5, 1831, Charles was summoned to meet the faculty. The confrontation (on a Saturday, after Charles had been absent the previous Tuesday, Wednesday, Thursday, and Friday) could not have been easy for President Adams, for he knew his students well and sometimes visited their parents. He understood that Charles came from a struggling family. Yet the young man gave no explanation for his absences. Adams informed him that he was expelled, and his academic record ended with the sentence: "C.J. Fremont was dismissed from the college for incorrigible negligence."

The young man shrugged. "I knew that I was a transgressor," he said. The punishment "came like the summer wind," for the "edict only gave me complete freedom . . . I smiled to myself while I listened to words about the disappointment of friends—and the broken career."

✳ ✳ ✳

WHAT HAD HAPPENED? Charles eventually confessed a secret. He was "passionately in love," cutting class to visit a fourteen-year-old girl. Her name was Cecilia, and she lived with her family in a house on a Charleston street corner. She was one of five brothers and sisters overseen by their mother and grandmother. They had become his surrogate family; he was part of a "little circle of sworn friends" with the brothers and sisters, and together they explored the woods and islands around the harbor. Sometimes they went shooting or picnicking. Once, in a rowboat, they were nearly swamped by the waves around Drunken Dick, a hazardous shoal on which ships sometimes foundered. Returning to her home, John sat with Cecilia in a side room that had a door opening onto the street, allowing them to flee when the grandmother approached. There is no record of what the grandmother thought of this eighteen-year-old college dropout lounging in her house with an adolescent girl. When Charles revealed this relationship in his memoir, he did not declare whether he'd had his first sexual encounter with her, but he did write: "This is an autobiography and it would not be true to itself if I left out the bit of sunshine that made the glory of my youth. . . . I lived in the glow of a passion that now I know extended its refining influence over my whole life."

Who was the young woman who so affected him? He never gave her family name, and said little of her personality, but described her appearance: she had a "clear brunette complexion" with "large dark eyes and abundant blue-black hair." She also had a compelling family history: her people came from Haiti, in the West Indies, and were Creoles, meaning they descended from French colonists who had once ruled Haiti. The French were expelled by a revolt among Haiti's black slave population, which culminated in 1804 with the massacre of many white residents and the creation of an independent black-led republic. Cecilia's family were refugees.

Notably, John said Cecilia's siblings had the same "brunette complexions," dark eyes, and blue-black hair. Although these words could describe French people who identified as white, they easily suggest people of color. Charles did not state their race, yet the implication of his description was clear enough. One of his early biographers was apparently uncomfortable about this description, and solved the problem by effectively putting the young man's lover in whiteface—rewriting her description to give her "clear ruddy skin" instead of brown. Perhaps the biographer concluded that Fremont misspoke.

A more straightforward explanation is that Charles described her accurately and knew what his description would imply. Haiti had many people of mixed race—and people of all racial identities had to flee Haiti when suspected of aiding the colonizers. And so it's plausible that C.J. Fremont's first love was a person of mixed race, as were all her siblings, his close friends. This would help explain why his classmates at Charleston College were baffled about where he went instead of studying: he could not tell them. An interracial relationship was a greater transgression than missing class. Such relations were common, as was obvious from the city's population of several thousand people of mixed race, known as mulattoes (many of them descended from white slave owners, who did as they liked with enslaved women they controlled). But like Charles's birth out of wedlock, this could not be discussed.

Charles's affair with Cecilia did not last. His mother still needed financial help, and before long his time was taken up with minor teaching jobs, including one in which he and a partner taught French. But he had begun dreaming of the wider world—the world he saw from the Battery, or while roaming with Cecilia by the harbor—and his dreams were fueled by a pair of books he had read. One was a book on astronomy, which awakened his interest in celestial navigation. The book was in Dutch, which Charles could not understand, but he could study the "beautifully clear maps of the stars," and he had the math skills to follow the "many examples of astronomical calculations." The other book collected stories of "men who had made themselves famous by brave and noble deeds, or infamous by cruel and base acts." This book reflected the aspirations and the anxieties that churned within C.J. himself.

✳ ✳ ✳

HE FOUND HIS WAY OUT of Charleston with the help of his next mentor: Joel R. Poinsett, a politician, diplomat, and amateur botanist. Appointed the United States minister to Mexico in the 1820s, Poinsett earned two distinctions: he was the first US ambassador to the newly independent country, and while there he sent home a red flower that became known in the United States as the poinsettia. Returning to Charleston in 1829, Poinsett attended the same church as C.J. Fremont's family and served as a trustee of Charleston College. He was the same age as John's mother, and took notice of her wayward son.

The first and most important thing that Poinsett did was give C.J. a political orientation. Poinsett was a Unionist, meaning he favored preserving the country as it showed early signs of coming apart. In 1831, the year of Fremont's affair with Cecilia, Charleston residents held a "states-rights ball," while other South Carolina towns held "disunion dinners" to promote the South breaking away from the North, and citizens of Beaufort performed a "Disunion Drama." The issue was not slavery, at least not directly. Some South Carolina leaders proclaimed their right to nullify what they called the Tariff of Abominations, federal taxes on imported goods that protected American industries but raised the price of products bought by Southern planters. If Fremont's mentor in these years had been one of South Carolina's radical thinkers—such as John C. Calhoun, who was serving as vice president of the United States yet secretly aiding the nullifiers—his life might have taken a different course. But Unionists such as Poinsett supported President Andrew Jackson and his administration (one South Carolina paper said the idea that the federal government could not enforce its laws was "beyond patient endurance from a people not absolutely confined in their own mad-houses"). Poinsett also held a nuanced view of slavery. In 1832 he told a visiting French writer named Alexis de

Tocqueville that slavery was a disadvantage to the South—that Northern and western states were gaining far more rapidly in population, which meant the South was steadily losing power. It would be a mistake to call him anti-slavery: he said nothing could be done about slavery, a position that allowed him to accept the status quo while deflecting the questions of disapproving outsiders. But as Charles later said, Poinsett "saw the dark spot on the sun," understanding that the divide over slavery endangered the country.

Young Fremont's Unionist associations allowed him to perceive an opportunity when it sailed into the harbor. In January 1833, a US Navy warship glided past the unfinished bulk of Fort Sumter and dropped anchor, sent by President Jackson to signal his determination to enforce federal law. While many Charlestonians saw the USS *Natchez* as a threat, Fremont saw a chance to get away. He learned of a job on board, and Poinsett agreed to recommend him, even though he thought the job—as a shipboard mathematician—was a waste of Fremont's talent. He would spend long, dull days at sea, tutoring poorly schooled seamen to calculate the figures necessary to take navigational readings by the sun and stars. His abbreviated education and his study of the pictures in the Dutch book he couldn't read apparently gave him enough knowledge to persuade the ship's captain that he was qualified.

When the nullification crisis eased (President Jackson's threat of force was followed by a compromise in Congress over the tariff) and the *Natchez* moved on, twenty-year-old C.J. Fremont bid good-bye to his mother and went out into the world beyond the harbor. Never having been at sea, he joined a crew who made their lives on it: one was Lieutenant David G. Farragut, who had served in the War of 1812 at age eleven. Within a few months the ship was patrolling the coast of South America, which was a magnificent adventure, although Poinsett was right that the work did not test the young mathematician. When the *Natchez* returned, John wavered over what to do next. He rejected a permanent position as "Professor of

Mathematics in the Navy," but then wrote Poinsett asking for a mathematician's berth on a ship bound for the Mediterranean.

> *Your kindness to me on a former occasion . . . induced me to hope for it also on this—an excuse which you will think rather worse than none at all, but which was true, and all I had to offer . . . Should it suit your convenience to aid me with your influence, I need not say how great would be my obligation to you . . .*
>
> *I have the honor to be*
> *With much respect*
> *Your Ob't Servt*
> *J. Charles Fremont*

Poinsett didn't get him the job. He had a different journey in mind for his protégé: moving inland instead of out to sea. He was about to give the young man his first experiences in westward expansion.

In the 1830s the major cities on the Eastern Seaboard were competing to become portals to the developing interior. New Yorkers had already opened the Erie Canal, which connected to the Great Lakes. The tracks of the Baltimore and Ohio Railroad were under construction over the Appalachians, and a similar venture was called the Cincinnati and Charleston Railroad. Joel Poinsett of Charleston was among the investors. "The Rail Road will be built," declared a letter published in the *Charleston Courier* in 1836. "Real estate in Charleston will appreciate 100 percent; and our own particular Rail Road Stock will rise in two years 100 per cent. . . . Every dollar judiciously laid out in Charleston in real estate, will double itself in five years." That was just the rosy scenario necessary to persuade men to invest in a plan to lay more than six hundred miles of iron rails over some of the roughest parts of the Appalachians to reach the Ohio River Valley. To find a route, the investors assembled a survey party under the direction of an army engineer, and Fremont was hired to go along. They rode northwestward through South Carolina and into Tennessee, spending long days in the woods and stopping at night at the homes of farmers along the way.

The project was a fateful failure; the railroad was never built. Although Charleston eventually was connected by more roundabout routes to the Mississippi River Valley, it remained a provincial city on its coast, where regional resentments and dreams of independence festered. But for Fremont the railroad survey was a priceless experience, and the army officer who led it later hired him for a second assignment that launched his career as a soldier of the American empire. He was to map Indian country—the Cherokee Nation. President Jackson had imposed a treaty requiring the Cherokees to surrender their land in North Georgia and surrounding states. They were to move west of the Mississippi by the spring of 1838, but because it was an illegitimate treaty, signed by a breakaway faction of elite Cherokees and not the Cherokee government, no one knew if the fifteen thousand Cherokees would go. The army prepared to clear them off the land by force if necessary, and Fremont was assigned to a surveying party ordered to map Cherokee territory in case it became a battlefield.

The men rode into Cherokee country in early 1837, splitting into small groups and moving "hurriedly," as Fremont recalled, through rough mountains. Told to sketch the Hiwassee River, he walked twenty miles along its winding course in a day, climbing huge stones and fallen trees. He woke "so stiff next morning I moved like a foundered horse," and could no longer lift his feet. He had to sit on obstacles and yank his legs over one at a time. But he recovered in the evenings at Cherokee farms. These were his first meaningful encounters with Indians, who had adapted their culture to life among white people: "many of their farms were much the same as those that are to be met with elsewhere on our remote frontier." Cherokees welcomed him into their homes and let him sit by their fires. Nobody threatened him, even though he was working for the government that threatened them. Cherokees were conducting a sustained act of nonviolent protest, simply declining to move west. Their protest would not end until some were rounded up at gunpoint and their leaders at last consented to start along the Trail of Tears in 1838.

Although the young mapmaker accepted the common view that it was "wise and humane" to move Indians out of the way of encroaching white settlers who preyed on them, he grasped that Cherokees were losing more than they gained. "There has been no continuous effective policy by the Government except in the removal of Indians from East to West, and out of the way of the white man," he later said; promises to compensate and support Indians were never fully kept. His ambivalence about his mission did not prevent him from feeling exhilarated by the work. During "this accident of employment," he wrote, "I found the path which I was 'destined to walk.' Through many of the years to come the occupation of my prime of life was to be among Indians and in waste places. . . . There were to be no more years wasted in tentative efforts to find a way for myself." His sponsor was now in a position to help him find more work: Joel Poinsett became secretary of war in 1837, appointed by a new Democratic president, Martin Van Buren. Poinsett helped Frémont obtain a job in the Army Corps of Topographical Engineers, a special unit devoted to surveying and mapping the American landscape. Accepting the appointment, John left Charleston for good. Only his mother remained for him there; his sister, Elizabeth, had died in her teens, while his brother, Frank, had left Charleston for a career in the theater. John moved to Washington and in 1838, at age twenty-five, was one of a group of ten men formally appointed second lieutenant, the newest and lowest-ranking officers in the army.

His qualifications came from life experience rather than formal training. This distinguished him from army officers who had graduated from the military academy at West Point, where cadets were forced to apply themselves in class, master the science of war, and generally grow up. West Pointers were early participants in the national trend of professionalization, which lawyers, physicians, engineers, scientists, educators, and others would eventually follow: raising formal standards, demanding specific credentials, and excluding those who did not measure up. John Frémont represented a different tradition: that of the intrepid amateur who found out how much he could get away with.

✳ ✳ ✳

THE CORPS OF TOPOGRAPHICAL ENGINEERS was filling an enormous gap in the nation's knowledge. The Louisiana Purchase, more than eight hundred thousand square miles west of the Mississippi, was much traveled but little understood; while native people and fur traders knew it intimately, only scraps of their experience had filtered eastward to be recorded. Lewis and Clark's expedition beginning in 1803 had traced the Missouri River more than two thousand miles to its source and continued beyond it to the Pacific, but only a few formal explorations had followed. From the perspective of Washington, the Rocky Mountains were hardly known; the trails to Oregon and California were scarcely mapped; and great mountains and rivers that appeared on maps were merely rumors. The corps was organizing a mapmaking expedition to fill some of the blanks, and ordered John from Washington to the starting point, St. Louis. He reached the city in the spring of 1838 and mingled with army officers posted to a barracks there, among them Captain Robert E. Lee, who had recently finished making a detailed map of the St. Louis waterfront.

Lieutenant Frémont was the sole commissioned officer assigned to the expedition, which would mostly consist of hired civilians. The War Department engaged a uniquely qualified expert to command: Joseph Nicollet, a distinguished French geographer who had previously mapped the source of the Mississippi River. John was to become, in effect, the explorer's apprentice as Nicollet further mapped the northern plains. He was a slight man with an intense focus on his craft; in a letter to his mentor Poinsett,

Lieutenant Frémont described the geographer as "delightful" because of the "almost extravagant enthusiasm in the object of his present enterprise wh[ich] he seems to think the sole object of his existence." He was an immigrant who had fled to the United States for a new start after going bankrupt while speculating in the Paris financial markets. His French background and language made him welcome in St. Louis, where many families had remained since French colonial times. The powerful Chouteau fur-trading family, whose ancestors were founders of the city, supplied Nicollet with provisions as well as with men—*voyageurs*, as they were called—who had learned the rivers and plains while transporting furs.

It was a stroke of fortune that John was able to learn from Nicollet, who had devoted his life to a great mystery of the age: how to study the surface of the earth when so little could be seen at any one time. It required a blend of science, stamina, and systems. Nicollet had brought notebooks, five by seven inches or smaller, in which his tiny handwriting recorded every observation. ("Departed Traverse des Sioux at 11:07 a.m. . . . appearance of rain . . . the heat is overwhelming.") Enchanted by the prairie, he made a note in his journal about "the beautiful lawns we are crossing," and as the expedition followed winding rivers, he sketched the shape of each bend until the river resembled a little snake on his page. From time to time he would halt the expedition and produce a triangular device called a sextant; peering through a lens, he measured the angle of the sun above the horizon at a certain moment of the day. He then stayed up long past dark to measure the angle of Polaris, the North Star. From these and other readings it was possible to determine latitude and longitude. A barometer measured air pressure, which varied with altitude. Once these readings were compared with readings that had been meticulously recorded at other times and places, Nicollet could determine exactly where he stood on the surface of the earth, how far he was from other points, and how far above sea level. He was a master at this craft, a disciple of the great European geographer

Alexander von Humboldt; had Nicollet never emigrated to America, it would have been hard for Lieutenant Frémont to find anyone who had so much to teach him.

The explorer's apprentice learned equally important lessons in wilderness survival from the French-speaking voyageurs. One night, when detached from the rest of the expedition, Frémont and two other men camped on the prairie, and woke in the night to a crackling noise. A prairie fire was sweeping in their direction, swift and unstoppable. The voyageurs understood that the only safe place was on ground that was already burned. They lit a prairie fire of their own, let the wind blow it away from them, and with moments to spare stepped into the blackened area. On another day John persuaded the expedition's hunters to allow him to join the pursuit of a buffalo herd. "This," he said, "was an event on which my imagination had been dwelling." The men approached the herd on horseback, working toward it from downwind so the buffalo would not catch their scent. Topping a low ridge, the men looked down on a "compact mass" of brown creatures making "the loud incessant grunting noise peculiar to them." And then the chase began as the buffalo thundered away in clouds of dust, which was so thick that as the hunters charged after the herd they couldn't see the ground. Frémont learned how green he was: "I made repeated ineffectual attempts to steady myself for a shot at a cow after a hard struggle to get up with her, and each time barely escaped a fall. In such work a man must be able to forget his horse, but my horsemanship was not yet equal to such a proof."

John accompanied Nicollet on a second expedition in 1839, and afterward returned with him to the East. They had grown close, the mentor and protégé. Nicollet, who was Catholic, was living on the grounds of St. Mary's, a Catholic college in Baltimore, and John sometimes visited him there, meeting Nicollet's friends among the Catholic clergy who ran the school. Returning to Washington, the two men set up a workroom near the Capitol and began to produce a map. The periodic celestial readings became dots on paper, the expedition's precise location on certain dates. The men would then use the journal entries and sketches to reconstruct the routes they had taken between these points and the landscape they had seen. It was slow and painstaking work, as Lieutenant Frémont was awkwardly reminded one day when a man appeared in the doorway. He was a man in black, in his late fifties, with a massive body that filled the doorframe, a full head of hair, and piercing blue eyes. He introduced himself as Senator Thomas Hart Benton of Missouri, chairman of the Senate Committee on Military Affairs. He said he wanted to see Joseph Nicollet's map of the northern plains. Frémont gestured with regret to the map projection, which was blank; they were still organizing the raw material.

Senator Benton was disappointed, but the two men made a connection: Benton wanted to absorb Frémont's firsthand knowledge, as he did with every western traveler he met. Though he had never gone west of Missouri, he soaked up so many details from those who had that it could seem he must have walked the ground himself. Frémont began visiting the senator's home a few blocks from the Capitol, where they sat in Benton's upstairs library. Soon John had a new mentor. Sometimes John stayed for dinner at the Benton house, and got to know members of the family. He took an interest in the senator's oldest daughter, Elizabeth, when she came home from her boarding school in Georgetown, the little river port at the edge of Washington.

Elizabeth agreed to attend a school concert with him in Georgetown—and it was at the concert that he noticed Elizabeth's sister Jessie, who was attending the same school. Afterward, John C. Frémont recorded the moment of their first encounter. "She was just then in the bloom of her girlish beauty," he said. "There was no experience of life to brush away the bloom." The "pleasure of seeing her sister" drew her out in "bright talk," he said. "Naturally, I was attracted." He came away thinking of Jessie rather than her older sister.

St. Louis, 1832: the gateway to empire.

Chapter Two

THE EQUAL MERITS
OF DIFFERING PEOPLES

Jessie Ann Benton, 1824–1840

Cherry Grove, St. Louis, and Washington

Jessie Benton Frémont could not have been more different from John in her family ties. While he lost touch with everyone but his mother and could hardly describe his background without risking shame, she came from an intact family. She had multiple siblings and many illustrious relatives. Her mother's family, the McDowells, were a mass of grandparents, aunts, uncles, and cousins, deeply embedded in Virginia since colonial times, with connections by marriage to other leading families and generations of ancestral lore.

Jessie was born at her mother's childhood home, on the McDowell land some two hundred miles southwest of Washington in the Blue Ridge Mountains. It was in Rockbridge County, named for its natural bridge, a stone formation that spanned a river and so charmed Thomas Jefferson that in the 1700s he bought the land on which it stood. If the McDowells were not so famed as the Jeffersons, they did own an expansive estate. A long private avenue led to the house, lined on both sides with cherry trees that had been cut to form a canopy overhead. The estate was called Cherry Grove, and there Elizabeth Benton bore her second child on May 31, 1824.

It is not certain that Jessie's father arrived in time for the delivery. Senator Thomas Hart Benton likely remained at work in Washington until May 27, when Congress adjourned, and then he faced a ride of a few days to reach the home of his in-laws. It was not from any lack of interest in his wife and child that Benton cut it so close; he had been thinking about the baby, perhaps too much. His first child had been a daughter, and he was hoping this time for a son. Although he was disappointed, he never gave up easily on an idea, and he chose for the girl what sounded like a boy's name, a variation on the name of his late father, Jesse Benton.

One of the earliest stories of her childhood illustrated Jessie's bond with her father. When Jessie was three, she received a new dress—purple, with chinchilla trim that she could run her fingers through. Her five-year-old sister, Elizabeth, received a matching outfit, which so excited the girls that they put on their finery and raced through the house to show their father. Finding him absent from the home library where he usually worked, they noticed piles of paper there. Jessie seized some of the pages and began scribbling with a red pencil and scattering them about the room. Elizabeth followed her example, though Jessie thought she was "timid and nervous" about it. Not until their father returned did they discover that they were defacing one of Senator Benton's speeches. "Who did this?" he demanded when he returned.

Jessie stalled for time. "Do you really want to know?"

He said he did, and she came up with an answer that melted his anger: "It's a little girl who cries, 'Hurrah for Jackson!'" Andrew Jackson was the candidate her father was supporting in the next presidential election. The ploy worked: her father embraced her.

This family story, as Jessie wrote it down much later, suggested the way she viewed herself. She was assertive and self-confident, leading her older sister rather than being led. She made her own rules and sometimes got away with it, even though men ruled her world. She was politically astute— knowing Senator Benton's candidate preference and sensing that she could disarm him by endorsing it. Above all, she was devoted to her father, and he to her. "Catching me up in his strong arms he held me close," Jessie wrote. "By what flash of instinct did I go straight to the hidden spot in my Father's armor? Did he even then feel the germ of that instinctive sympathy which made us one?"

Part of their connection involved her name. She felt as if he had assigned her a different gender. "My father gave me early the place a son would have had," she said, and when a third daughter arrived without a son, Jessie embraced the role of his boyish sidekick. When he went hunting at the McDowell estate, she followed him through sloping wheat fields covered in stubble after the harvest. "Especially he liked autumn shooting," she said. "I stuck to him like a pet doggie, and trotted everywhere with him. . . . It tried my young feet but I trudged on, proud to carry the game bag, and presently when my Father shot a quail I had the honor of carrying the limp warm thing." At midday, resting under a tree, he produced biscuits and a book from his shooting jacket, and she leaned against him while he read aloud in French, challenging her to follow along.

She remained beside him as he moved about Washington, and this assured her a special view of the world. Their house, at 334 C Street Northwest, was just off Pennsylvania Avenue, the city's main street and the center of life. Although Pennsylvania was an unattractive ribbon of dirt, it offered amenities to the elite of an aspiring nation: the Foreign Book Store was selling works in French, Spanish, Italian, and Latin, while a few doors down one could visit a carriage dealership or even buy a used chariot, "very little worn." Many kinds of people appeared on the street—lawmakers from every state, diplomats from European countries, visiting chiefs of Indian nations, free black servants, and slaves. The Capitol rose just a few blocks from the Benton house, topped by a green copper dome; Jessie sometimes trailed her father to work in the Senate, and he would deposit her at the Library of Congress for safekeeping.

Sometimes she even followed when he called on the president. Andrew Jackson, the candidate for whom Jessie had strategically cheered as a toddler, won election in 1828 and was inaugurated shortly before Jessie's fifth birthday, in 1829. Her father was a leading figure in Jackson's political movement, which came to be called the Democracy and then the Democratic Party, and Jessie was in tow when Senator Benton climbed the stairs inside the white presidential mansion. They found Jackson in an upper room, "where the tall south windows sent in long breadths of sunshine; but his big rocking-chair was always drawn close to the large wood-fire." Jackson needed the warmth. He suffered constant digestive attacks and was shockingly thin, with a hatchet face and a mass of gray hair. His wrecked body was the consequence of a life of exertion and moments of rage. He had once been shot during a pointless gunfight with Thomas Hart Benton when both were living in Tennessee, though they later reconciled. More recently Jackson had survived the first assassination attempt on a president, which suggested the passions he stirred as he destroyed the national bank and painted political rivals as aristocrats and elitists. Jessie, of course, did not yet know his politics, only that he was an old man whose wife was dead. She thought she perceived "sadness and loneliness" in his haggard face.

Jessie said afterward, "I was to keep still and not fidget, or show pain, even if General Jackson twisted his fingers a little too tightly in my curls." The near-skeletal president "would keep me by him, his hand on my head—forgetting me of course in the interest of discussion—so that sometimes, his long, bony fingers took an unconscious grip."

✳ ✳ ✳

JESSIE'S FATHER IMPOSED HARD ROUTINES ON HIMSELF, and his family had to follow them too. Having been stricken with tuberculosis as a youth, he believed it was better for the lungs if he slept with the windows open even in winter, so everyone else had to burrow as deeply as they could under their covers. He dictated a simple diet for himself, and thus for everyone at his table. Above all he was a nomad, who moved back and forth between several homes and often brought his family. In addition to the house in Washington, he had a house at his political base in St. Louis. He spent long periods with his wife's family in Virginia, owned a farm in Kentucky, and sometimes made business trips to New Orleans. Rotating between homes every few months depending on the work of the Senate, he left behind a trail of notes asking newspapers to forward subscriptions to his next address. The Bentons moved so much—when travel was so difficult—that Jessie said her life was seen "almost as a reproach and a matter of sympathy among the stay-at-home friends and relations." Of course, constant travel also gave her a more expansive view of the nation than her "stay-at-home friends and relations," who, when a crisis came many years later, felt less attached to the nation than to their state.

In 1832, when Jessie was eight, the family made one of its journeys from Washington to St. Louis. The trip was eight hundred miles, so far beyond the Appalachians that the family did not get there every year, although the pace of travel was growing faster. In 1800 the journey had required up to six weeks, but now steamboats and better roads made it possible to arrive in well under three. The first leg of the journey led over the National Road, a smooth ribbon of crushed stone called macadam, which the Bentons traveled in style, hiring a "reserved" stagecoach that the family had to itself. Senator Benton liked to sit outside with the driver, and even took the reins. Elizabeth Benton sat inside with the children—there were five now: Elizabeth and Jessie; another sister, Sarah; and two boys at last, an infant named James and his older brother, Randolph. Randolph was about two years old, meaning that in the jolting vehicle Mrs. Benton faced the eternal struggle between a toddler's desire to stand and the parent's desire that the child should sit. Stables operated every ten miles or so, and the Bentons used them to change horses. Sometimes when they stopped, Jessie asked to sit up with her father for the next ten miles, and when they started off she saw "the four eager horses dash away as the black stable-men jumped back when they loosed their heads and cheered them off."

At the Ohio River the family transferred to the first of the steamboats that would relay them downriver to its junction with the Mississippi. There the boat would swing northward, churning against the current toward St. Louis. On its final approach the craft angled toward the west bank, making a left turn just before Bloody Island, a fabled spot where men fought duels; then the crew tied up at the waterfront. Looking up the slope from the gangplank, Jessie saw the tightly packed houses of the city, topped by the rising facade of a cathedral under construction—a Catholic cathedral. It served the population left over from French colonial days, who could be heard speaking their ancestral language as they moved about the town. The Benton family had a short walk along streets lined by locust trees to reach their house, which occupied its own city block amid more locusts. Here Jessie's father liked to sit on an upholstered sofa on a long covered porch, drinking his coffee outdoors even on a rainy day. When Jessie came to the porch and looked out at the street, she saw a "kaleidoscopic variety of figures" passing by, including "long files of Indians," Catholic priests, "hunters and trappers in fringed deer-skins; army officers in worn uniforms going by on horseback," and poor residents in French "peasant dress." Her time in the West, she wrote later, "rubbed out many little prejudices, and fitted [me] better than any reading could have done to comprehend the necessary differences and equal merits of differing peoples, and that although different, each could be right."

The most recent census showed only 4,977 inhabitants, who, according to the map drawn by Robert E. Lee, were packed into a street grid covering less than a square mile. The town seemed larger than it was because it was an imperial outpost, the main portal to all that lay beyond. It was near the confluence of the Missouri and Mississippi rivers, which were the main highways through the West. It was an army headquarters and a crossroads for global trade. Trappers and traders shipped beaver pelts from all over the West to St. Louis, and they were shipped onward to become top hats in New York, London, and Paris. (Jessie's father was close to the fur traders, having borrowed money for his house in Washington from the fur magnate Pierre Chouteau Jr.) Almost anyone who traveled the West might pass through St. Louis, and during Jessie's stay in 1832 a famous visitor appeared: Washington Irving, author of "Rip Van Winkle" and "The Legend of Sleepy Hollow." He was researching a nonfiction book called *A Tour on the Prairies*, intended to satisfy public fascination with the West, and in his notebook he made descriptions of the town: "St. Louis—old rackety gambling house—noise of the cue and the billiard ball from morning till night—old French women accosting each other in the street." He also rode just outside town to visit the farm of St. Louis's most famous denizen, William Clark of the Lewis and Clark expedition. The gray-haired explorer treated his visitor to a fried chicken dinner, and Irving inquired what it was like to own the slaves who prepared their meal. Clark replied a bit defensively that he had freed several slaves, including York, a man who had accompanied his expedition to the Pacific.

Clark now served as federal superintendent of Indian affairs, a kind of ambassador to native nations. Likely as not some of the "long files of Indians" Jessie saw from her porch were in St. Louis to see Clark, who regularly hosted them at a building near the Benton house. It was known as his "Indian museum," a long, low brick structure filled with pipes, arrows, and other artifacts from tribes he oversaw. He used the building for tribal councils and treaty negotiations, sitting with native leaders, who, according to one observer, wore a "profuse and almost gorgeous display of ornamented and painted buffalo robes," along with "porcupine quills, skins, claws, horns, and bird skins." According to Jessie, Washington Irving was invited to watch one of Clark's Indian councils—and eight-year-old Jessie also appeared, doubtless trailing her father. As Jessie recounted it, the Indians were persuaded to perform "a war dance" in the yard outside for Irving's benefit.

Jessie became disturbed. "I was very young," she said, "and the whole horrible thing, as they grew excited, threw me into a panic." Fortunately someone noticed the terrified girl—a soldier who was on hand. "A tall strong kind-faced young officer, married to a favorite cousin of my mother, carried me off and comforted me." The kindly relative was Albert Sidney Johnston, a rising star in the army.

Jessie would have been too young to fully understand that the natives she saw were slowly being displaced. Some of Clark's treaty negotiations were aimed at securing rights to their land for the United States. Their removal triggered sporadic resistance—Albert Sidney Johnston was just back from an Indian war. He had been part of a force that chased down and captured Black Hawk, a Sauk leader. The old chief had led his people eastward across the Mississippi into land that had once been theirs, causing panic among white settlers. United States troops killed many of his followers before the survivors surrendered. Black Hawk was now in semidignified captivity, allowed to stroll the grounds of the nearby army post with two sons. Washington Irving saw him there, carrying the iron ball that was chained to him, and clutching the tail feathers of a black hawk.

✳ ✳ ✳

IF HER VISITS TO ST. LOUIS let Jessie learn the diversity of the West, they also helped her grasp her father's ambitions for it. Senator Benton was a western visionary, who had moved there enamored of its possibilities. He had grown up in North Carolina and then Tennessee, studying law and volunteering for the War of 1812 as an aide to General Andrew Jackson. But after his quarrel and gunfight with Jackson ("the most outrageous affray ever witnessed in a civilized country," Benton declared with characteristic bombast), Benton was repeatedly transferred away from combat assignments, giving him no chance for distinction. He left Tennessee after the war, crossing the Mississippi to start anew in the Louisiana Purchase. Practicing law in St. Louis, he advertised that he would take any case in "any part of the Territory of Missouri," which had been formed from part of the Purchase land. He also ran for political office and lost, but found a different sort of political perch, hired in 1818 as editor of the *St. Louis Enquirer*. "Newspapers," he declared, "are the school of public instruction. They are in America what the Forum was in Greece and Rome." His move to journalism was well timed. Voting rights were expanding to include virtually all white men, and the way to reach the newly empowered masses was through the media. Jackson shrewdly surrounded himself with talented newspapermen who became advisers in his famous kitchen cabinet; Benton, self-reliant to the point of arrogance, became a newsman himself.

The new editor had hardly taken the job when he gazed out over the Louisiana Purchase and decided it was even larger than it seemed. It did not merely reach west to the Rocky Mountains, but extended beyond to the Pacific, through the distant region called Oregon. Benton was outraged when US diplomats, failing to support his view, agreed in 1818 to a "joint occupancy" of Oregon with Britain, allowing both to exploit the country without annexing it. Benton proposed that the United States should seize full control and establish a Pacific seaport. Trade could then flow from St. Louis to Oregon to Asia and back again.

Benton's vision had so much influence over Jessie's and John's lives that it is worth noting how grand it was. He was anticipating, by almost two centuries, the central role that trade with Asia would come to play in the United States's economy. "I looked across the Pacific Ocean," he said later, "and saw eastern Asia in full sight. I traced an American road to India through our own dominions, and across the sea." St. Louis, he said, could "find herself as near to Canton," the international trading port of China, "as she now is to London, with a better and safer route." His town of a few thousand could grow into a great city fueled by globalized trade.

He was drawing on a centuries-old idea: the quest for the shortest route to Asia, which had driven European exploration of the New World from its earliest days. It was the very idea that inspired Columbus to sail westward from Spain in 1492: he wanted to improve upon the long and dangerous eastbound routes from Europe. After Columbus found the Americas blocking his way, other sailors tried to go around or through them, exploring American bays and rivers or risking their lives in Arctic ice. Though no one found a northwest passage to the Pacific, its potential value only grew as the British colonies in North America began importing goods from Asia. This trade was significant enough to factor in several famed episodes of early American history: The Boston Tea Party of 1773 protested a tax on tea carried on British ships from Asia. Soon after gaining political independence in 1783, several Founding Fathers confirmed American trading independence by importing their own tea, sending a ship called *Empress of China* to bring it back from Canton. Before long, men engaged in the China trade had collected some of the United States's first great family fortunes. But the round trip to and from China could take more than a year. In 1803, the dream of a faster route to Asia motivated President Thomas Jefferson's decision to send Lewis and Clark across the Louisiana Purchase. He was hoping they would find that the Missouri River reached so far west that it came near the Columbia River, which emptied into the Pacific. In this respect, Lewis and Clark disappointed him. But Benton was certain in 1818 that *some* combination of rivers and roads could work well enough. And he held on to this dream even though it won little support at first.

A Pacific seaport was just one of the schemes for national expansion that Benton embraced. When American gunmen tried to seize the Mexican province of Texas in 1819, he noisily approved ("success will attend" these "adventurers," his newspaper proclaimed, and "Liberty" would "continue her march to the Pacific"). Here, too, he was ahead of his time; American settlers would not capture Texas until 1836. A vision that became reality more quickly was Benton's support for the Missouri Territory to become the first state entirely west of the Mississippi. When statehood arrived in 1821, the legislature chose Benton as one of Missouri's first two senators. He quickly grew into the legislator Jessie would always idolize, a scholar-politician. Representing a state that traded with Mexico, he learned to read Spanish, and when he spoke on the Senate floor about Mexico he translated Mexican newspapers aloud. He conducted his Senate business without the aid of a clerk and wrote out copies of documents himself. He represented values of the West: hard work, frankness, and egalitarianism.

But there was another aspect of her father's life in the West that Jessie talked about much less: his ownership of slaves. His family had controlled more than twenty African slaves when he was a boy, and by his own account he had "never been without" at least a few as an adult. He owned several when he came to St. Louis, which contributed to a deadly dispute: a fellow lawyer repeatedly insulted Benton, in part by questioning whether he had paid property taxes that were due on the human beings he owned. To settle this quarrel, the two men rowed out to Bloody Island, that dueling ground on the Mississippi, and shot and wounded each other. Later they returned for another round and Benton killed his opponent. Benton never renounced dueling, saying it was "deplorable" but expressed real human passion, and "there is at least consent on both sides." He also never fully renounced slavery. In the fight for Missouri statehood, he was slavery's advocate. He spoke in 1819 at a grand public meeting for statehood at the St. Louis courthouse, which was filled to overflowing: "Many remained at the doors and windows" to listen as Benton spoke, according to an article in his paper. Benton spoke against proposals that Missouri should be forced to abolish slavery before joining the Union.

He seemed to grasp that slavery was wrong ("dishonorable to the United States," his paper was willing to admit in passing in 1820), yet he rationalized. Without evidence, his paper claimed that slaves had an easier life in Missouri than elsewhere, so why keep them out of Missouri? The same article in Benton's paper whipped up the racist fears of white readers: if Congress had the power to free slaves in Missouri, it would also have the power to invite "free negroes" to *move to* Missouri, where they could vote and "intermarry with the whites." The Missouri debate grew so intense that it ignited the first national crisis over the expansion of slavery into new territories. Congress resolved the impasse with the Missouri Compromise of 1820, drawing a line through the Louisiana Purchase. Slavery could exist south of the line, but nowhere north of it—nowhere except Missouri, which was north of the line but was allowed to establish its own slave laws. Slavery, too, was a global trade, and produced products that were traded globally. Benton didn't want Missouri missing out.

* * *

JESSIE GREW UP MORE SKEPTICAL OF SLAVERY. She credited this view to her mother, Elizabeth, whose family had a history of questioning it. Although the McDowells built their fortune as other prominent Virginians had—importing enslaved workers to farm the land they had taken from Indians—they occasionally pondered whether their way of life made any moral or practical sense. One such occasion came after a slave uprising known as Nat Turner's Rebellion, which was savagely suppressed in 1831 but provoked Virginians to consider how badly it could all go wrong. Virginia's legislature soon debated ending slavery through gradual emancipation. And the legislators who spoke in favor included James McDowell, Elizabeth's brother and thus Jessie's uncle. He argued that the state could justly interfere with the property rights of slave owners because of the danger slavery posed to society.

Uncle James's side lost: rather than free slaves, the legislature voted to tighten control, blocking antislavery messages by making it a crime to teach any black person to read or write. Uncle James, wanting to run for governor, stopped talking about abolition. "When the South grew stormy," Jessie said, "he grew silent, and took refuge in fine sentences about [protecting] his native State [against] Northern aggression"—finding grounds to defend slavery indirectly when he knew it was indefensible. Jessie wished afterward that he had shown as much "courage in the cause" as her mother, who was "of a more enduring nature." Elizabeth's ideas were born of personal experience. As Jessie learned the story, her mother's family was Presbyterian, moralistic and judgmental, and Elizabeth grew up to quietly rebel against "the grim Scotch Puritan atmosphere that dominated her own home." She developed "a generous spirit of broad resistance to any form of intolerance and of active sympathy with the oppressed." She resolved that when she inherited enslaved people she would free them, and she kept her word. She brought up Jessie "to think it good fortune to be free from owning slaves," because slavery degraded both the enslaved and their masters. It warped the minds of white children, "making them domineering, passionate, and arbitrary."

After Elizabeth married Senator Benton, it was certainly at her urging that their house servants "were all freed, or born free," even though her husband apparently still used slaves outside the home in business ventures. Census records from 1840 listed a "T. H. Benton" of St. Louis with six slaves, whose spare description made them seem like a family: a man and woman between the ages of twenty-four and thirty-six, and four children, three of whom were under the age of ten.

✳ ✳ ✳

JESSIE WAS NEARLY FOURTEEN when she had to separate a bit from her father. During one of their winters in Washington, D.C., her parents sent Jessie and Elizabeth to a boarding school in Georgetown. She considered her enrollment "a great misfortune," though it should have been a joy. The school, where about a hundred girls lived and others came during the day, had a Danish woman as principal and a cosmopolitan flavor. Her classmates were the daughters of lawmakers and military officers, Jessie's social peers—but she could not stand them. There was "no end to the conceit, the assumption, the class distinction." She felt "miserably lost." She felt that nobody measured up to her father, who had been cured of snobbery by his experiences in the West.

One event brought her feelings about Washington society to a boil. It was a wedding scheduled for April 9, 1840, shortly before Jessie's sixteenth birthday. One of her classmates had caught the eye of the much older Russian ambassador, and their union became a major occasion, even attended by President Martin Van Buren, Andrew Jackson's close adviser and successor. Jessie was a bridesmaid, and though she liked the dress chosen for her ("very long; of white figured satin, with blonde lace about the neck and sleeves"), the event began to feel oppressive. The bridesmaids and groomsmen differed in age as much as the teenage bride and fortysomething groom, which became apparent when they were paired off. Jessie walked into the ceremony on the arm of Senator James Buchanan of Pennsylvania, a bachelor in his late forties. He was the Bentons' neighbor and family friend, which should have eased the oddness; but Jessie was revolted by the scene. The more she looked at the Russian groom, Baron Alexander de Bodisco, the less she liked him. She saw him talking with Senator Benton: "Contrasted by my father's superb physique—his clean, fair, noble presence, his steady blue eye and firm mouth—the curious ugliness of Bodisco came out painfully. He was a short and stout man . . . with rather projecting teeth. . . . and restless little eyes," which made Jessie wonder how happy her classmate would be once the newlyweds were alone.

After the wedding, Jessie cut off her hair. She thought a boy's haircut would make it easier to keep following her father around as she had for years. She meant to stay with him and turn her back on conventional society. But Senator Benton was "horrified" when she showed him the haircut, and even more so when she informed him that "I meant to study and be his friend and companion. . . . I really meant it. He was really displeased. Then I learned that men like their womankind to be pretty, and not of the short-haired variety."

It was a few months later, as her hair was growing back, that she decided to attend a concert at her school. She saw her older sister, Elizabeth, in the crowd—and Elizabeth was not alone. She was accompanied by an officer in the army. He was handsome and clean-shaven, though he let his dark hair grow long in a fashionable style. He looked dignified and reserved. Jessie came across the room to talk, and Elizabeth introduced him. He gave his name as John Charles Frémont.

He didn't talk much about himself. He did not, for example, mention his age. In the months that followed, when they encountered each other again at the Benton house, he still did not get around to saying how old he was. He surely could not be nearly as old as the Russian ambassador, but probably was older than some of the teachers in Jessie's school. His reticence drew her in. He was intriguing. At this school where so many students seemed to be the daughters of somebody important—the very feature that Jessie disliked even if she was the ultimate example of it—*this* man didn't seem to have a name that anybody in Washington knew.

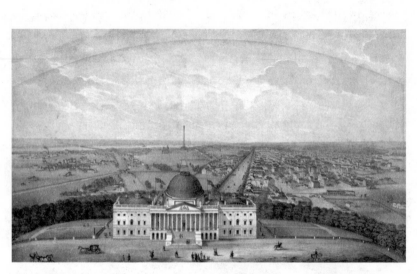

Washington before the Civil War. Pennsylvania Avenue angles to the right.

Chapter Three

THE CURRENT OF
IMPORTANT EVENTS

JESSIE AND JOHN, 1841–1842
Washington

John and Jessie's courtship peaked in Washington's most crowded season, the time of a new presidential administration. Martin Van Buren had been defeated for reelection, and Democrats gave way to an opposition party called the Whigs, whose nominee, William Henry Harrison, was sworn in March 4, 1841. He mounted a white charger for his inaugural procession, riding down Pennsylvania Avenue near the Benton house. Without doubt Jessie and John were in the crowd as the sixty-eight-year-old delivered his address in front of the green-domed Capitol, speaking in a "clear, strong and harmonious" voice, according to a Whig newspaper, displaying an "erect and manly form." One month later he was dead. His doctor blamed pneumonia, giving rise to a myth that he had caught it in the cold of his inauguration, but researchers later identified more likely causes, such as an infection from sewage dumped in marshland near the White House.

It was said that all of Washington was thrown into mourning, but this was an overstatement. Lieutenant Frémont did not lose sight of his priorities, and asked to be relieved of his duty to march with hundreds of other men in uniform in Harrison's funeral procession April 7. The work-room where he was mapmaking, on 4½ Street near the Capitol, had an excellent view of the procession, which he wanted to watch with invited guests: the family of Senator Benton. From the windows they saw the presidential coffin pass on a horse-drawn wagon, draped in black velvet and decorated with two crossed swords and a scroll of the Constitution. John wrote later that the event "was something to see and remember," but did not write down anything about the procession that he saw or remembered. He was paying attention to Senator Benton's second-oldest daughter, his true reason for wriggling out of his marching duty: "The funeral occasion proved, as I had hoped, my red-letter day," a day to cherish.

These were the lengths to which they had to go to see each other, since Mr. and Mrs. Benton did not fully approve of the penniless lieutenant as a suitor. The young couple's path grew even narrower in early June: John's commanding officer, Colonel J. J. Abert, ordered him to spend the summer conducting a survey of the Des Moines River, one thousand miles west of Washington, beginning "without delay." Jessie, too, left Washington, attending a wedding in Virginia, near her grandparents' house in Rockbridge County. It was a last moment of childhood for her: in a house that was jammed with relatives for days, she climbed with cousins to an upper floor, rummaging through closets and changing into "old uniforms and gowns." One cousin was a young man on leave from West Point, whose features resembled Jessie's, and she persuaded him to trade clothes to see if anyone noticed—the second time that something about attending a wedding prompted Jessie to try looking like a man. "Go to your room and dress properly," one of the uncles barked when they emerged.

John and Jessie both returned to Washington at the end of the summer, each unchanged in their feelings. "The survey was a health-giving excursion," John said, "but it did not cure" his "special complaint." Jessie, too, was in love—and overcome with the fear that her father would marry her off to someone else. As closely as she had clung to him, she rebelled; the grand wedding to which her family's status entitled her was not anything she wanted. She decided to elope with John in October. Seeking a pastor who would agree to marry them without telling Senator Benton, John approached his mentor Joseph Nicollet, and the Frenchman referred him to a Catholic priest. The cleric agreed to marry them even though neither bride nor groom was Catholic. The simple ceremony "was in a drawing room," Jessie said afterward, with "no altar lights or any such thing."

For weeks afterward they continued their lives as before. If they consummated their union, it could only have been done desperately and in secret, since Jessie was still living at home. Only a few people knew the truth, including a friend of John's named F. H. Gerdes, who warned him on November 7, "Any delay of an open declaration, which some time or another must follow, makes your excuse less well, as this declaration itself, more difficult." A few days later the young couple finally told Senator Benton, who was enraged. According to the family story, he ordered John to leave the house. Jessie held her ground, or rather held her spouse: she took John's arm and quoted from the book of Ruth, "Where you go I will go also." Her threat to leave with John melted her father's heart.

There is another, less romantic account of this confrontation. In this story, Benton was enraged not only at John but also at Jessie. According to a relative, the senator was so angry that he "would not let her remain in his house," and ordered them both to go away. Mrs. Benton tried to make peace, proposing a second, Protestant ceremony to make the union seem more proper; the senator refused, fearing it would amplify the scandal. But within a few weeks he surrendered, acknowledging his daughter's free will and placing a brief notice of the marriage in a newspaper. Because John could not afford the lifestyle to which Jessie was accustomed, he moved out of his boardinghouse and into Jessie's room in the Benton house. John adopted the whole family much as he had once folded himself into his girlfriend Cecilia's family in Charleston.

Not long after they married, John wrote her a letter. "Fear not for our happiness," he said. "If the hope for it be not something wilder than the Spaniards' search for the fountain in Florida, we will find it yet." It was a curious choice to compare their quest for happiness to Ponce de León's fabled search for the Fountain of Youth in Florida in the 1500s. In the apocryphal story, the explorer never found what he was looking for, plunging into the American wilderness in search of a goal that did not exist. But the metaphor suggested the way John and Jessie's marriage was intertwined with both ambition and exploration. John's work mapping the West served Senator Benton's goal of establishing a trade route to Asia; the two could be of great use to each other. Jessie's choice of John had its own logic: while she refused to let her father dictate her life, she wanted to be close to him. The gender roles of the time would not allow her to become Senator Benton's assistant—so she married a man who was certain to assist him.

✳ ✳ ✳

ON NEW YEAR'S DAY 1842, a newspaper announced a civic ritual. "The President of the United States," a brief note read, "will receive the visits of his fellow-citizens this day, between the hours of 12 and 3 o'clock." It was customary for the president to begin each year by throwing open his home to shake hands with all comers. Top officials and diplomats attended— someone spotted the Russian ambassador Baron de Bodisco and his teen-age bride—and so did many others, "the dashing dweller of the city, in fashionable array, and the hardy farmer, proud of his homespun costume," as a newspaper described the crowd that filled the ceremonial rooms of the presidential mansion. Mr. and Mrs. Frémont took their place in the receiving line for what amounted to their public coming-out as a couple. Jessie wore a blue velvet gown with a blue cape and lemon-colored gloves, topped with a hat adorned with ostrich feathers. John's Army Corps of Topographical Engineers uniform was at least as eye-catching—his hat decorated with the image of an eagle, topped by a plume, and twice as large as his head. He would have to make sure he had space around him before removing the hat in the crowd.

The president at the front of the receiving line was John Tyler, who had assumed office after Harrison's death. If his conversation with the Frémonts resembled holiday encounters with presidents in later eras, then John and Jessie each said something brief and awkward, which the sore-handed president received as gracefully as possible before moving on to the next guest. The point of the encounter was not the words but the face time: the president of a republic must expose himself to the people, who were his employers. Perhaps John was nervous to meet him, but seventeen-year-old Jessie would have been less so—Tyler was a Virginia aristocrat who'd turned to politics, the sort of man she had known since she was born.

After the republican ritual the Frémonts returned home, where Senator Benton asked to have a word with his son-in-law about the year to come. He reminded John that there was money available for the Corps of Topographical Engineers to mount another expedition in the West. Now that Joseph Nicollet, with John's aid, had mapped much of the region east of the Missouri River, the next expedition would range west of it. The Frenchman was in declining health and could not command this time, so Benton suggested that John should succeed him—and the senator had confidence that he could persuade the army to give him command. Even if his Democratic Party was out of power, he remained on the military affairs committee and had ties to key military officers. Whatever lingering anger he may have felt about the elopement, he set it aside—for practical politics demanded the channeling of passion, the suppression of anger. If Benton could reconcile with Andrew Jackson, who had tried to kill him, he could reconcile with the young man who had stolen his daughter's heart.

"I felt I was being drawn into the current of important political events," John said. For the senator was not simply planning a mapping expedition. He had larger ambitions. He wanted to use John's mission to advance his long-standing plans to capture the Oregon country—or rather recapture, since he felt the United States had given up its rights to that territory by sharing it with Britain. As long ago as 1825, he had introduced a bill titled "An Act to Authorize the Occupation of the Oregon River." By this he meant the Columbia River, which emptied into the Pacific: he wanted his American seaport to be established there, ready to trade with China. Senators rejected the idea, unwilling to risk war with Britain. In 1842, President Tyler was no more inclined to take up Benton's notion than the Senate had been in 1825; his administration was negotiating away conflicts with Britain, not creating new ones. But Benton was about to develop his own foreign policy.

Benton had learned of a route through the Rockies to Oregon, crossing the Continental Divide at a gap in the mountains called South Pass. Fur traders, a few settlers, and missionaries had used it. If more Americans emigrated on this Oregon Trail to the Pacific, they would alter the facts on the ground: a significant population of Americans in Oregon would make it a de facto part of the United States. Emigrants would form a constituency demanding that the United States give them protection and formally annex the territory, and if it came to war with Britain, hardy and well-armed settlers could be turned into a military force. As Benton well knew, this was how the United States commonly expanded—not by overt invasion but through settlement. It was the way Benton's onetime home of Tennessee became a state: white families carved out farms on land belonging to Indian nations and went to war when natives resisted. It was the way the United States captured the eastern portion of the state of Louisiana: American settlers seized this Spanish-controlled territory in 1810, and the United States swiftly annexed it. In 1836, American settlers in northern Mexico rose in revolt (as Benton had long wanted them to do) and declared the independent Republic of Texas. The Texans immediately requested annexation to the United States, which had not happened by 1842 but still seemed possible. Surely American settlers could work similar wonders in Oregon.

To encourage emigration, Benton wanted to use the media. The one-time newspaperman had so much influence over the *Washington Globe*, the leading Democratic paper, that a critic claimed its editor, Francis Preston Blair, allowed Benton's "undried copy" to be placed "directly into the hands of the compositor" to be set in type. Now Benton wanted to make John C. Frémont the leading character in a news story. He would send his son-in-law beyond the Missouri River, and Lieutenant Frémont would plan his expedition so that he was mapping the approaches to Oregon. His maps would define the trail more clearly. His advice on the availability of wood, water, and supplies would make travel safer and more practical. His story, well publicized, would make the route better known. The mere fact of a government-supported expedition up the Oregon Trail would imply federal support for settling Oregon. When they discussed this after dinner on New Year's Day, John grasped it all. "Daily intercourse under [Benton's] own roof had given me a familiar knowledge of Mr. Benton's plans," he said afterward. "I gave henceforward to him . . . unstinted devotion."

John received his appointment to command. Next Benton lobbied the army to send him on a route toward Oregon, though he did not mention Oregon by name. "I think it would be well," Benton wrote Frémont's commander, Colonel Abert, "for you to name, in the instructions for Mr. Frémont, the great pass through the Rocky Mountains [South Pass]. . . . It is the gate through the mountains . . . [and] will be a thoroughfare for nations to the end of time." If John set his course for South Pass he would naturally be on the Oregon Trail. Abert was opposed: he wanted John to survey the Kansas and Platte rivers, two major waterways of the Great Plains that were ripe for settlement, and felt that sending him to the mountains was too much for a single season. But knowing Benton's influence, Abert reluctantly told Lieutenant Frémont to visit South Pass if he could do it without jeopardizing the river surveys. That was enough for Benton, who knew he could count on John to ride for South Pass no matter what. "Upon its outside view," Benton said, the expedition was "the conception of the Government," but in reality it was "conceived without its knowledge and executed upon solicited orders, of which the design was unknown."

* * *

JOHN BEGAN ASSEMBLING EQUIPMENT. He borrowed a sextant and surveying instruments (to the annoyance of Colonel Abert, who said Frémont was not following procedure), and when spring arrived he made a shopping detour to New York. The transportation network had improved so dramatically in the past few years that it was possible to move the 230 miles or so from Washington to New York without ever riding a horse or carriage; it took a day or two on a relay of steam trains and ferry crossings. A boat carried John across the Hudson to the New York City docks by May 4, 1842.

The New York weather was unpleasant ("Fickle, changeable, cold, and uncomfortable," one of the newspapers complained) but the city was soaring. Trinity Church was under construction on lower Broadway, with a spire that was projected to rise nearly three hundred feet. Its builders looked down on a city of more than three hundred thousand, most jammed into lower Manhattan Island within a mile or so of the church. While John was in town, the American Temperance Union held a meeting that drew more than six thousand people, a crowd hard to imagine in any other place he had seen. He passed near the Broadway meeting hall, where spectators filled every seat, according to a newspaper, with additional "hundreds and hundreds standing all down the four broad aisles," including "young, lovely, and most beautiful women." The streets crackled with the energy of migrants from the countryside and immigrants from different corners of the world.

In shops that lined the crowded streets, the twenty-eight-year-old lieutenant spent more money than he ever had, writing drafts for merchants to be reimbursed by the government. Ducking into a store off Wall Street, he paid three hundred dollars for a "first-class" chronometer, a precise clock that could go two full days without winding. Knowing the exact time would allow him to make navigational readings based on the position of the sun at certain hours. He paid ten dollars for a carrying case "with extra pillows, cushion, &c" to insulate the clockworks from bumpy rides. He bought a barometer in a leather case, and thermometers encased in mahogany. Strolling up Broadway, past the white stone city hall in its triangular park, he discovered a district of camera sellers. The "daguerreotype apparatus" was a popular new invention—a new form of art, it was said—which made images from life by exposing chemically treated metal plates to light. "It is sun-painting," proclaimed an ad for a daguerreotype portrait gallery at Broadway and Chambers Street. John was convinced. He found a doctor selling cameras on the side, and paid $78.50 for a set with twenty-five plates. He planned to be the first western explorer who was known to try to illustrate the landscape with this new technology.

He failed to follow army procedure, neglecting to obtain advance approval for his purchases. When his commander discovered these irregularities, he sent an angry letter down the road after him, but it was too late. Leaving New York, John struck out directly for St. Louis, and by the time the letters went in the mail he was far to the west and beyond recall.

In Washington, Jessie knew John would be absent half a year. They had been married barely half a year, and she understood that his separation from her was a choice, not his fate. "It would have needed only a request from my father," she said, "to obtain for Mr. Frémont duty which should keep him in Washington . . . but self-renunciation lies at the root of great work, and this was to be my part in being of use to my father." So she bid John good-bye. "Mr. Frémont was gone into the silence and the unknown, how silent how unknown it is impossible to make clear." He would pass beyond not only her touch and sight, but beyond even the reach of the mail.

It would be especially hard because Jessie, not quite eighteen, was pregnant. Maybe he would be home for the baby's birth and maybe not. All the hazards of the West lay ahead of him, and all the hazards of childbirth lay ahead of her. Death was common in labor or soon afterward, and the joy of pregnancy was mixed with foreboding. Medical science was baffled by the complications of childbirth, which killed so many that almost anyone could name a lost neighbor or relative. "Young women," a scholar said after studying women's letters from the era, "perceived that their bodies, even when healthy and vigorous, could yield up a dead infant or could carry the seeds of their own destruction." Jessie had to contemplate whether the struggle might signal her final hours on earth.

Realizing that his pregnant daughter needed some distraction, Senator Benton put her to work. He led her to his home library, telling her that he needed some "translations from Bernal Díaz' Conquest of Mexico, and this occupied my mornings." Diaz was a Spanish conquistador, one of the men who invaded and took over the Aztec empire beginning in 1519. Jessie lost herself, as much as she could, in the story of the badly outnumbered Spaniards who approached the Aztec capital built on islands in a lake.

> *Our number did not amount to four hundred and fifty, we had perfectly in our recollection the accounts we had received on our march, that we were to be put to death on our arrival in the city which we now saw before us, approachable only by causeways, whereon were several bridges, the breaking of one of which effectually cut off our retreat. And let who can, tell me, where are men in this world to be found except ourselves, who would have hazarded such an attempt?*

Jessie translated such drama while thinking of John's even smaller force. The story was as close as she could come to joining his adventure.

The pleasure of the story could not distract her for long. Her mother, Elizabeth, began suffering "an intolerable headache." She summoned a doctor and submitted to the old-fashioned medical treatment of bleeding, and when it failed, allowed herself to be bled again. Jessie blamed the treatment, rather than the disease, for what happened next: Elizabeth suffered a "paralysis of the throat" that made it impossible for her to eat, and lay for days "looking dead." Her condition improved, but she was never entirely right again, and wandered the Benton house with its English-made mahogany furniture, sometimes disoriented in her nightclothes. All this Jessie bore without her husband by her side. He was away on a prairie, or in the mountains, or dead—she had no way to know.

John C. Frémont scaling "the highest peak in the Rocky Mountains."

Chapter Four

MISERIES THAT ATTEND
A SEPARATION

LIEUTENANT AND JESSIE ANN
BENTON FRÉMONT, 1842–1843

St. Louis, the Oregon Trail, and Washington, D.C.

O
n stagecoaches and steamboats to Missouri, John was accompanied by two people. One was Jessie's brother, twelve-year-old Randolph, who was brought along for a priceless life experience. (He was also given a job: John assigned him to wind the chronometers.) The other was Charles Preuss, a mapmaker who had knocked at the Bentons' door seeking work. Preuss, a German immigrant with "a shock of light curly hair standing up thick about his head," had no wilderness experience. He would have preferred to stay home and draw maps from the information John gathered, but John said the German must see the ground that they would map together.

Walking through the little river town of St. Louis—not so little anymore, for the 1840 census had found nearly seventeen thousand people, more than triple the number from a decade earlier—John sought out the Chouteau fur-trading family, who identified voyageurs to transport equipment and hunters to feed the party. (The Chouteaus also advanced him credit for supplies, although John again disregarded army procedure by failing to secure permission first, which triggered another protest from Washington.) About twenty men set out westward, taking the first leg of their trip by catching a commercial steamboat up the Missouri. On the boat, John hired one more man, a passenger on the same vessel by chance. "He was a man of medium height," John said, "broad-shouldered and deep-chested, with a clear steady blue eye."

Kit Carson was thirty-two, not far in age from twenty-nine-year-old John. He said he could guide Lieutenant Frémont wherever he wanted to go, and his background suggested it was not a boast. For sixteen years, ever since he had run away from his youthful apprenticeship with a Missouri saddle maker, Carson had been crisscrossing the West, mainly as a fur trapper and hunter. He climbed mountains and crossed deserts. He bought a house in Taos, in the Mexican province of New Mexico, and even accompanied a trading expedition that went all the way to Alta California, the Mexican territory on the Pacific. He battled Apaches, picked up Indian languages, married an Indian woman, and had a daughter by her. He was famous in the fur trade for both his knowledge and his ruthlessness, as a story about him illustrated. In January 1833 he was traveling in a group of trappers when men from the Crow nation stole some of their horses. Vowing to find the thieves, Carson joined eleven other men and tracked the Crows through the snow. Finding them asleep in a camp late at night, the trappers silently liberated their horses—a bloodless triumph, after which most of the men wanted to slip away. But Carson wanted "satisfaction for the trouble" of his hours in the snow. He persuaded his comrades to open fire on the much larger group of Crows, killing several and triggering a battle that lasted the rest of the night.

With Carson on John's payroll, the party disembarked from the steamboat at a fur-trading outpost called Chouteau's Landing, at the western border of Missouri. From the trading post and surrounding settlements they gathered horses, mules, and more supplies. John made celestial observations to fix their starting point, and they rode across the prairie, a line of men and animals and carts who sometimes spread out to escape one another's dust: the army officer from the East with his shiny instruments and nephew at hand; the quiet, watchful westerner Carson; and the immigrant mapmaker Preuss, who struggled to make sketches on horseback, slowing down the party until John ordered him to ride in one of the horse carts instead. The carts were driven by the French voyageurs, who included a black man named Johnny Auguste Janisse.

John began the journey by following Colonel Abert's instructions, surveying the Kansas River, which led them westward; but he was not hiding his true intention. Behind him in Missouri, a newspaper ran an item about him on June 14:

> IMPORTANT EXPEDITION.–Lieut. Fremont, of the corps of Topographical Engineers, left here under orders from the War Department, about ten days ago, with a party of 20 men, on a tour of the Rocky Mountains.

The article said John was traveling to South Pass "with a view to the establishment of a line of military posts from the frontiers of Missouri to the mouth of the Columbia River." His survey of domestic rivers had been redefined as a phase of the occupation of Oregon. It was even said that the survey was being made in support of the latest proposal in the Senate to authorize that occupation. This article also introduced the public to the dashing man at the head of the vanguard: Lieutenant Frémont, who, "though young," had "much experience in surveys of this kind." While the source of the story was not named, the timing and location suggested it was John, who had just passed through St. Louis, or his father-in-law, who knew St. Louis editors. The story quickly spread beyond Missouri in the way news items commonly did: newspapers in different parts of the country exchanged copies with one another by mail, and reprinted any articles they found of interest. Multiple papers printed John's news until it reached the East Coast on June 26, in the New York Herald, the most powerful and widely read daily of the moment. Senator Benton's goal of occupying Oregon was being advertised as if it was already in motion. This seeming fait accompli might encourage potential settlers to occupy Oregon. The act of saying it could make it come true.

✳ ✳ ✳

THE EXPEDITION TRAVELED IN STYLE, thanks to the supplies John had purchased outside army rules. He had bottles of brandy. He had six pounds of "Dresden chocolate," along with 148 pounds of tobacco. He had enough food supplies that on Independence Day, 1842, he halted his men on the prairie early to prepare a celebratory feast: "Our friends in St. Louis had provided us with a large supply of excellent preserves and rich fruit cake; and when these were added to a macaroni soup and variously prepared dishes of the choicest buffalo meat, crowned with a cup of coffee, and enjoyed with a prairie appetite, we . . . sat in barbaric luxury around our smoking supper on the grass." Coffee was vital to the commander's peace of mind. One day, while the group was fording the Kansas River, disaster struck: two men were nearly drowned and lost 150 pounds of coffee, almost the entire supply. The lieutenant mourned "a loss that none but a traveller in a strange and inhospitable land can appreciate."

In mid-July, after turning northward to leave the Kansas River Valley, they picked up the course of the Platte and followed that river westward until they camped outside a fur-trading post called Fort Laramie. There they heard stories of Indian war parties in nearby mountains, stories that were serious enough that Kit Carson made out his will. John culled his party, ordering twelve-year-old Randolph to remain for safety at Fort Laramie, which was surrounded by adobe walls; the boy would wait until the expedition returned from South Pass. John also asked if any voyageurs wanted to be relieved of duty, and learned that one did. But having made this gesture, John treated the man as a coward: "I asked him some few questions in order to expose him to the ridicule of the men, and let him go."

Just as the remaining men were striking their tents to move ahead on July 20, a group of elderly Indians approached, appealing to John to wait a week until their village's war party returned home. Otherwise their young men might attack the expedition by mistake. "The observations of the savage appeared reasonable," John said, but having shamed another man, he could no longer take counsel of his own fears. He refused to wait, demanding instead that one of the Indians travel with them for several days to avoid any misunderstandings with the war party. Making their way forward through the mountains, they saw apparent signs of recent battles: the mapmaker Charles Preuss reported finding "a bloody pair of trousers pierced by a bullet; a pipe was still in the pocket."

Despite this disturbing sign, the danger to the well-armed expedition may never have been that great. Throughout the journey natives never harmed them, instead inviting the army lieutenant to dinner and approaching to ask curious questions about his "numerous strange instruments applied to still stranger uses," especially the sextant and chronometer he used in "talking with the sun and stars." Native people also traded with John; it was a mixed-race Indian who relieved the expedition's most desperate shortage by selling them a fresh supply of coffee. The land was not as empty as it seemed: it had an economy, trade routes, and connections to the world. The coffee John bought had certainly come from some other country. The Indian who sold it to him may have obtained it in trade for furs that were shipped to yet another country.

In August the men reached South Pass. It was anticlimactic. A rough wagon road ran through the pass on the way to Oregon, as if to emphasize that they were finding nothing new. The Continental Divide was so subtle, John said, that "we were obliged to watch very closely to find the place at which we had reached the culminating point." He compared it to the modest slope of Capitol Hill back in Washington—the very point, some nineteen hundred miles away, toward which he was now obliged to return. But on all sides lay snowcapped peaks, and John decided on a more dramatic finish. Although the pass marked the limit of the expedition under his orders, he would continue.

Leading his men northwest, he made for the nearby Wind River mountains: "A great part of the interest of the journey for me was in the exploration of these mountains, of which so much had been said that was doubtful and contradictory." Old maps suggested the mountains were the source of several great river systems. John first thought he should survey the streams that flowed down the slopes, a project that would call for him to circle the entire mountain range, but he abandoned this quest for knowledge in favor of a quest for altitude. The tops of the Wind River Range rose alluringly above pine forests and lakes, and their jagged outlines were irresistible. "The air at sunrise is clear and pure," he wrote of waking in camp on August 10. "A lofty snow peak of the mountain is glittering in the first rays of the sun, which has not yet reached us." He resolved to climb the highest mountain in sight. Leaving men behind to guard the horses and supplies, he began the ascent in a group of fifteen, who mounted more durable mules. The mules picked their way through the forest and up sloping fields of broken rock, as John made note of torrential streams, hidden lakes, and "scarlet flowers" that "everywhere met the eye." They arrived at a valley the mules could not cross—"a gigantic disorder of enormous masses, and a savage sublimity of naked rock"—and left the animals to graze while the climbers proceeded on foot. Thinking they were near the summit, they brought scientific instruments to calculate the altitude but left behind their food, blankets, and even their coats.

It didn't take long to understand that they had misread the ground ahead of them. What looked like a direct ascent concealed more valleys that they needed to navigate. They were reaching altitudes where snow covered the ground even in August, and one of the men nearly slid off a snowy slope and over a precipice to his death. He saved himself only by dropping flat on the surface to gain traction. Exhausted in the thin air, the party stopped for the night just below the tree line, around ten thousand feet above sea level.

They tried to hunt a mountain goat for dinner and failed. They tried to sleep without their blankets on a slab of bare granite. Lieutenant Fremont began to experience severe headaches and to vomit.

His leadership grew erratic the next day. He let his party lose cohesion as they clambered uphill across broken ground. They split into ones and twos, taking divergent routes through the rocks and snow, which meant they could not easily help one another. The mapmaker Preuss was walking alone at the top of a snowy slope when he lost his footing and began sliding. There was no way to stop. He continued some two hundred feet before he crashed into rocks at the bottom, and was lucky to somersault over the first rock in a way that broke no bones. Afterward Preuss was found by Johnny Auguste Janisse, the black voyageur, who brought word that Lieutenant Frémont was vomiting again, as were at least two others. The doubled-over Frémont had sent a message telling Preuss to try to reach the summit; Janisse had brought the barometer, expecting that he would accompany Preuss and help him determine the altitude.

Preuss refused. He took a barometric reading where he was, and the two men descended to where Frémont was resting. Other men straggled into camp, and the party prepared to spend another night near the tree line. The day's only success came when a few men went downhill and found a route to bring up mules laden with dried meat, blankets, and coffee. Refreshed by their first meal in nearly two days, the men rolled into blankets around their fires. Preuss expected that in the morning everyone would descend the mountain, but he woke to discover otherwise. John reminded him that they had brought a bottle of brandy: "Well, Mr. Preuss, I hope we shall, after all, empty a glass on top of the mountain." That was the sick and dehydrated lieutenant's way of saying that he intended to keep climbing.

His men were exhausted. They had been in the saddle for more than a thousand miles. Their clothes were ragged and torn; Preuss sometimes wore two pairs of pants so that each would cover the holes in the other. Much of their equipment was a mess: one of John's two chronometers was broken, and the barometer had cracked during a river crossing a few days before, forcing him to make an improvised repair. John had never been able to make the daguerreotype camera work, placing metal plates into the camera only to have them come out blank ("That's the way it is with these Americans," Preuss groused in his diary. "They know everything, they can do everything, and when they are put to a test, they fail miserably.") For weeks the men had been eating whatever they could kill along the way: prairie chicken, turtles, buffalo, and polecat. The food they had brought from St. Louis was running low, and the coffee they drank that morning was some of their last. John acknowledged their haggard state, releasing some men to stumble down the mountain while he continued up with a few volunteers. Some who volunteered had mixed feelings. Preuss was writing cutting descriptions of the lieutenant in his diary—"foolish," short-tempered, "childishly passionate," and far too prone to headaches when under stress—yet the mapmaker did not take his opportunity to flee. Others who joined the attempt included Johnny Auguste Janisse, who was lugging the fragile wood-and-glass barometer. (Preuss assumed Janisse was not entirely a volunteer, saying that as a "mulatto," he "had no privilege to choose.")

They ascended slowly, with frequent rest to make sure they were not sickened again. Though snow crunched beneath their feet, the summer air was above freezing, warm enough for the men to sweat in the sun from the effort of the climb. John put on thin-soled moccasins so that he could use his toes to help keep his footing. He chose to climb a steep rock slope that, thanks to its high angle in sunshine, was clear of snow. Near the top he was stuck beneath an overhanging shelf of rock before pulling himself up to level ground, where he discovered members of his party who had climbed by a less perilous route. Soon their goal was in sight:

> I sprang upon the summit, and another step would have precipitated me into an immense snow field five hundred feet below. . . . I stood on a narrow crest, about three feet in width. . . . As soon as I had gratified the first

feelings of curiosity I descended, and each man ascended in his turn, for
I would only allow one at a time to mount the unstable and precarious
slab, which it seemed a breath would hurl into the abyss below.

Raising his spyglass, John believed he saw the distant tops of the Grand Tetons, beyond which streams led toward the Columbia River and Oregon. Janisse brought up the barometer, and Preuss took readings of the air pressure and temperature. John later used them in a mathematical calculation to show an altitude of 13,570 feet above sea level. He decided that it must be the highest point in all of North America.

They were not long on the summit, wanting to make it back to camp by dark. No doubt the drink of brandy was hurried, and Preuss grumbled that the lieutenant was rushing him before he could properly finish his work. But they took time for a gesture, planting an American flag on the summit that had been specially designed for this journey. Among the twenty-six stars was the image of an eagle clutching a peace pipe, which was thought to be effective symbolism when encountering Indians. They let it "wave in the breeze where never flag waved before," then furled and carried it down the slope.

His party had not lost a single man.

* * *

ON THE LAST DAY OF OCTOBER 1842, when John returned from the West and stepped back into the Benton house in Washington, he still had the flag he'd hoisted atop the mountain. He carried it to Jessie, who was resting in bed, and she watched as he unfurled it and spread it over her. "This flag was raised on the summit peak of the highest point of the Rocky Mountains," he said. "I brought it to you." For Jessie it was a moment of joy, and of anticipation. When he draped the flag over her body, she was swollen and uncomfortable, her baby almost to term.

She went into labor in mid-November 1842, barely two weeks after his return, and emerged from the ordeal without complications. But when the baby was delivered, the mother suffered a blow: the child was a girl. Jessie had been hoping to present a boy to her spouse, just as her father had once expected a boy when Jessie arrived. There was no evidence that John desperately wanted a boy, or that he especially wanted children at all—but she wanted to make an impression. He had just returned from a life-altering, horizon-expanding experience that did not include her. Sons were prized, and she was devastated not to have one. She was also beginning to have dark thoughts about a girl's prospects in life. She had just experienced the limitations imposed on her gender in an especially galling way: she would have loved to travel westward with her husband, but her twelve-year-old brother went instead. Now she was bringing another girl into a frustrating world.

She could console herself that John's work was entering a phase in which she could participate: generating publicity for his achievements, of which there were many, including the mapping of the Oregon Trail, the journey to South Pass, and the scaling of "the highest point of the Rocky Mountains." Jessie cared for her baby through the holidays—the girl was named Elizabeth after Jessie's mother, and would come to be called Lily—and then, with a nurse to help, freed up time for work. John was supposed to write a report of his expedition. Army officers usually wrote such documents to be read by their superiors, but the Frémonts had a grander concept. They wanted to create an adventure story for the public. It was to be less bloody than Bernal Díaz's tale of conquering Mexico, but infused with the same spirit.

The story took the form of an ordinary bureaucratic document, and did not have a snappy title.

A Report on an Exploration of the Country Lying Between the Missouri River and the Rocky Mountains on the Line of the Kansas and Great Platte Rivers

Nor did it have an arresting opening line.

Washington, March 1, 1843.

To Col. J.J. Abert, Chief of the Corps of Topographical Engineers:

Sir: Agreeably to your orders to explore and report upon the country between the frontiers of Missouri and the South Pass in the Rocky Mountains...I sat out from Washington city on the 2d day of May, 1842.

But it was the beginning of a chronological narrative in which the drama gradually built. John framed his journey evocatively, saying it began "on the verge of civilization," as the men prepared for "the nomadic life we were about to lead." Or maybe this was how Jessie framed it, because the opening pages of the report were written in her hand. She later explained that her husband was not in the right state of mind to work alone: "The horseback life, the sleep in the open air, had unfitted Mr. Frémont for the indoor act of writing." He inexplicably began suffering nosebleeds. Because he was stymied, "I was let to try, and thus slid into my most happy life work." She would write while John paced the room, dictating. He confessed that he wrote most easily this way; when writing by himself, he would dwell too long on each word, but "in dictation there is not time for this." As he told the story he would study her face, "and get there at times the slight dissent... or the pleased expression which represents the popular impression of a mind new to the subject."

Eventually John's condition improved, and Jessie became a more conventional editor of a narrative that constantly gave the reader the feeling of standing next to Lieutenant Frémont. On one page, John was fording the Kansas River through water so swift that two men were nearly swept away—this was the moment when they lost nearly all their coffee. On another page, John was waking to an inspiring view at dawn: "The long mountain wall to the east rising two thousand feet abruptly from the plain, behind which we see the peaks, is still dark, and cuts clear against the glowing sky." Elsewhere, he was greeting curious Sioux who visited his camp:

> *Now and then one would dart up to the tent on horseback, jerk off his trappings, and stand silently at the door, holding his horse by the halter, signifying his desire to trade. Occasionally a savage would stalk in, with an invitation to a feast of honor, a dog feast, and deliberately sit down and wait quietly until I was ready to accompany him. I went to one; the women and children were sitting outside the lodge, and we took our seats on buffalo robes spread around. The dog was in a large pot over the fire.*

This was typical of his encounters with Indians—he was often diplomatic and frequently made friends, but wrote unflattering descriptions when he returned home. He was civilized and they were "savage," amusingly ignorant of his world. He seemed unconcerned that he was mostly ignorant of theirs.

The mountain climb was described in dramatic detail, without hiding his decisions that exceeded his orders and put his men at risk. He even reported his own headaches and vomiting. This apparent humility made the narrator seem honest and relatable, even as he was making the extraordinary claim of having climbed the highest point on the entire continent. The Frémonts qualified the claim, indicating to the careful reader that it was a guess, but they still made the guess, instinctively grasping how meaningful that claim could be. Later exploration eventually revealed how wrong they were: close to a hundred Rocky Mountain peaks rose higher.

On the return journey, they wrote, John stopped at Independence Rock, "an isolated granite rock, about six hundred and fifty yards long, and forty in height." Past travelers to Oregon or California had carved their names in it, and John carved a cross in the stone, which he covered with "a black preparation of India rubber, well calculated to resist the influence of wind and rain." Weeks later, reaching the Missouri River where it took in the waters of the Platte, he heard a sound that symbolized his return to civilization: "I rose this morning long before daylight, and heard with a feeling of pleasure the tinkling of cow-bells at the settlements on the opposite side of the Missouri." As described in *Report on an Exploration*, western travel was noble, brave, romantic, and practical. The plains on the way to the Rockies, which had at times been described as a great American desert, had water, grass for animals, even trees. South Pass was a gentle slope. Oregon beckoned. Within weeks of its completion, the *Report on an Exploration* was bound for a printer and for the newspapers.

✷ ✷ ✷

JESSIE DID NOT HAVE MANY MONTHS to keep her little family together in Washington. John had hardly submitted the report when it was time for him to say good-bye again; Senator Benton had arranged for him to command a second expedition. It was to be longer than the first, and more blatantly centered on Oregon—continuing through South Pass all the way to the Pacific. The official plan was simply to fill a gap in the military's survey work, connecting past surveys of the interior with a recent US Navy survey of the Pacific coast. But no one could doubt the real purpose. Jessie of course supported the mission, but did not want to lose her husband again, and when he started westward in late spring, she resolved to accompany him as far as St. Louis. They brought an entourage: baby Lily, and likely a female servant to help with her; Mrs. Benton, who had recovered some of her strength; and two men who would join John for the expedition: the mapmaker Charles Preuss and Jacob Dodson, the eighteen-year-old free black son of Benton family servants. Jacob was eager to go west, and took on a role as John's personal servant.

In St. Louis the family had their evenings together while John spent his days filling out the expedition's roster. He was forming a group "of many nations," as he later said: "American, French, German, Canadian, Indian, and colored—and most of them young, several being under twenty-one years of age." He was celebrating the polyglot nature of his young country, although his phrasing reflected a particular way of thinking about nationality and race. He described "colored" people as distinct from Americans, even though Jacob Dodson was American. The French were probably also United States citizens, even if they were of European descent. "Americans" were hazily regarded as a new "race"—white people, mainly of British descent, creating their own identity as they chased their destiny across the continent. A closer look at John's own expedition would have given him a broader concept of Americans, including his trusted French companion Basil Lajeunesse; Kit Carson, who had married an Indian wife; Dodson; and two Indians. Both were Shawnees, "a fine-looking old man and his son"—with names showing their attachment to the new nation sweeping over their ancient one: the father, James Rogers, had named his son Thomas Jefferson Rogers.

Jessie bid her husband and his men good-bye at the waterfront, where they caught a boat to meet their horses at the western edge of Missouri. John said he would be gone about eight months, and she said she would wait in St. Louis. She took it upon herself to open her husband's mail there, becoming his stateside representative and gatekeeper—and also, for the first time, his defender. He had left St. Louis with a howitzer, a short-barreled cannon on wheels, which he had checked out from the nearby army arsenal. It was an odd armament for a small party in Indian country. While artillery might have some intimidating effect, Indians were unlikely to charge in a densely packed mass that could be blasted by a cannon shot. It was more likely that the howitzer would endanger the party by slowing its progress. Was John dreaming of more than exploration? He seemed to provoke such suspicions in his superior officers, who were startled when they learned what he was doing. Shortly after the expedition departed from St. Louis, a letter arrived for John, from his commander Colonel Abert in Washington:

Sir

. . . I fear the discretion and thought which marked your first expedition will be found much wanting in the second.

The limit placed upon your expenditures . . . indicated the kind of expedition which the Department was willing to authorize. But if reports be true you will much exceed this amount [and will] involve yourself in serious difficulties.

I hear also that [you obtained] a Howitzer. Now Sir what authority had you to make any such requisition, and of what use can such a piece be in the execution of your duties[?]

Abert said John was to lead a "peaceable expedition" to gather "scientific knowledge," and if he really believed he faced threats so grave that he needed a howitzer, then he was to "immediately desist in its further prosecution and report to this office." In another letter he said the howitzer was so cumbersome that John would likely have to abandon it somewhere. Worse, it would make his little force seem like a "hostile expedition" to Indians, risking an "Indian war."

Colonel Abert's letter to John amounted to an order—but when Jessie read it in St. Louis, she made a defiant decision: she refused to try forwarding it to John on the frontier. She suspected a political plot to break up the expedition so important to her father and her husband. It was probably too late to stop John anyway, but she did not try. She also nursed a grudge against the commander who had spoken so critically of her husband, and a few months later she had an opportunity to lash out. In the fall of 1843, a member of the expedition broke off to return home, and brought the latest news to Jessie in St. Louis. He said the expedition had encountered Sioux warriors, and John had the cannon rolled out to impress them. Jessie seized on the story—the howitzer had proven its usefulness! She wrote a letter to her father in Washington, who took the letter to the *Washington Globe*, the leading Democratic newspaper. The editor, Benton's friend and ally Francis Preston Blair, printed it:

> . . . *Mr. Fremont caused the famous howitzer to be drawn to the front, and his little party arranged in battle order; when the Sioux, seeing the brass piece, changed their plans, and made a peaceful salutation, leaving them unharmed. . . . A week after, [the Sioux] met a trading party, and robbed them—taking every horse they had! Tell that, with my compliments, to Colonel ****.*
>
> . . . *Your affectionate daughter,*
> *JESSIE ANN BENTON FREMONT*

The howitzer wasn't "famous," of course. Most readers could not have known what Jessie meant or who "Colonel ****" was—it was a blind item, in newspaper parlance—although Colonel Abert was sure to read Jessie's jab, along with an added jab from the newspaper complaining that the Tyler administration had sent John westward with inadequate supplies. Jessie's letter was reprinted in papers from Massachusetts to New Orleans. Most editors could not have fully grasped the half-told story, but were intrigued by the idea of a woman who had something biting and political to say. In Little Rock, Arkansas, one reader wrote a newspaper in protest: "The parading of a lady's name before the public is rarely warranted; and this case is by no means an exception. The great *Globe* did it for political effect, and the 'Jessie Ann Benton Fremont' proves the why and wherefore of its publication."

In her new role as her husband's spokeswoman, Jessie was sometimes cutting and other times reassuring. In mid-September she began corresponding with a Washington, D.C., woman whose son had joined the expedition. Theodore Talbot was just eighteen—and though Jessie herself was only nineteen, she offered Theodore's mother emotional support.

To Adelaide Talbot

St. Louis, Sep. 16th, 1843.

My dear Madam,

Knowing the anxiety you must feel on account of your son, I take great pleasure in sending you the news which we received a few days since. They had gotten on very prosperously as late as the 26th of June, at which time Mr. Frémont found an opportunity to write by two Indians who brought the letter in. . . . By the middle or end of December they expect to be in this place [St. Louis] & at the New Year's rejoicings Mr. Talbot will I hope be again with you. . . .

Jessie B. Fremont

The hope of a New Year's reunion lasted deep into the fall, but then Jessie met the man who left the expedition and told her about the howitzer. Based on his information, she wrote Mrs. Talbot with updated timing: "Mr. Fremont says that early in January 1844, he will be here." Having promised a return in January, she was obliged to write Mrs. Talbot again on February 1, 1844.

Your letter has remained unanswered my dear Mrs. Talbot because it found me prostrated by sick headaches occasioned as you will at once conceive by "the sickness of the heart." It made me sorry to see the note to your son for he is not here yet. . . .

My own Mother says I am too young and too perfectly healthy to know all the miseries that attend a separation, & if I were older and in a nervous state of health this incessant disappointment would wear me out. It is very fortunate for us all that I have elastic spirits for being here I hold a very responsible place. . . .

> *Mr. Fremont may come in any conveyance but a steam car & from the moment I open my eyes in the morning until I am asleep again I look for him.*

On March 3 Jessie wrote Mrs. Talbot again. Having consulted with a man who knew Oregon, she decided that John must be spending the winter somewhere west of the Rockies: "He cannot be here until the middle of April." After the middle of April had passed, she was required to write Mrs. Talbot once more.

> . . . *He will not be here until the middle of May—so you see dear Mrs. Talbot I can say nothing to comfort you—but only repeat—patience patience.*
>
> *Jessie Benton Fremont*

She wrote Mrs. Talbot a sixth time on June 15, 1844, rambling through various subjects and signing the letter before she realized that she had left out the only pertinent information, adding in a postscript that she had no information about the expedition's whereabouts.

"The old whaling days of Nantucket," Jessie once observed, "have these experiences as legends among them, where absence and silence lasted for years," and now she knew "the same unbroken silence with its fears and anxieties, and its useless hopes." She was beginning to realize that her husband's absence was the normal condition of her marriage.

Part Two

DESTINY

✳ ✳ ✳

The Sierra Nevada depicted by Albert Bierstadt.

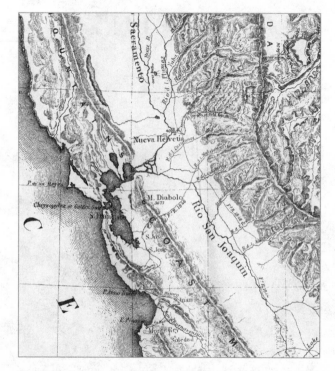

From John C. Frémont's 1848 map of California.

Chapter Five

I DETERMINED TO MAKE
THERE A HOME

JESSIE B. AND JOHN C. FRÉMONT, 1843–1844

St. Louis and the Pacific

Jessie had one consolation during her months of waiting: she was able to witness her husband's spreading fame. Even before he departed on his second expedition, their report of the first was generating publicity. The Frémonts themselves could not have written a more flattering description of John's unauthorized mountain climb than one in a Pennsylvania newspaper:

> *Leaving the valleys to indulge a laudable curiosity, and to make some useful observations, [John] climbed the loftiest peak of the Rocky Mountains; until then untrodden by any known human being. . . .*

Coverage accelerated as the year went on. By September 10, the powerful *New York Herald* reviewed the report ("romantic and thrilling scenes of life . . . sublime scenes of the Wind River chain of the Rocky Mountains") and reprinted a passage ("we cannot forego an excerpt or two") and then, two weeks later, printed more. ("Considering the universal interest," the paper explained, "which has been awakened . . . we are induced to give some further selections from the narrative of our enterprising officer.") Multiple publishers eventually put out editions ("a little book . . . in which [Frémont] details many amusing and exciting adventures," said a newspaper in Ohio). Jessie observed it all with delight. "It is very flattering," she wrote in one of her letters to Mrs. Talbot, "to see him remembered and praised as he has been although I am so unreasonable I constantly want to hear more." She alone knew the role she had played in his success.

Americans were moved by the Frémonts' literary style—and so were some people in the country jostling with the United States for control of Oregon. A magazine in London, *The Athenaeum*, published a perceptive review, noting that "the country gone over by Lieut. Fremont is certainly not the most interesting in the world, nor is it quite new; yet he is evidently not the man to travel two thousand miles without observing much which is worthy of being recorded." His writing had "so much truth and spirit" that the West became "fresh and tempting." Knowing that John was bound for Oregon, the reviewer predicted he would do good work there, and if British engineers could match his efforts, "we may be able to calculate, on safe grounds, the exact amount of blood and treasure which may be prudently expended in the conquest of it."

Senator Benton's plan, of course, was to expend neither blood nor treasure and instead to rely on settlers. Anyone inspired to head for Oregon found in the *Report on an Exploration* a step-by-step template—and people *were* inspired, for the report was well timed. Oregon had been working its way into the national consciousness for years. In 1836, Washington Irving had followed up his *Tour on the Prairies*—the book that brought him to St. Louis when Jessie was a girl—with a book on Oregon. *Astoria: Or, Enterprise Beyond the Rocky Mountains* was based on the journals and letters of fur traders that the New York fur magnate John Jacob Astor had sent there. In 1842 a news event brought Oregon further attention. President Tyler's administration completed talks with Britain, resolving a border dispute with

British Canada—but failing to settle possession of Oregon, which remained under joint occupation. Some Americans spread suspicions that the British might snatch control, and the fear of losing Oregon triggered stronger feelings than the desire to have it. Public meetings were organized in Missouri, Illinois, Iowa, Indiana, Kentucky, and elsewhere demanding that the United States occupy Oregon. The growing public interest in Oregon both fed and was fed by the publicity for John's travels, and it was surely not coincidental that the number of emigrants to Oregon increased.

In the spring of 1842, before John completed his expedition, only about one hundred pioneers were believed to have hitched up their wagons and made the months-long summer journey along the Oregon Trail. Then came news of the unresolved Oregon border, and the first newspaper reports of John's trip. In the spring of 1843, the number of emigrants increased tenfold, to about one thousand. During 1843, the *Report on an Exploration* spread across the country—and several thousand emigrants hitched up wagons over the next few years. In the spring of 1845, Independence, Missouri, alone was hosting about a thousand people preparing to launch two massive wagon trains; a report said "all the houses" in town were filled with emigrants, "and a large number were encamped in tents in the vicinity." Hundreds more were staging from St. Joseph, Missouri, where their belongings filled 220 wagons. In the spring of 1846—by which time a second Frémont report was circulating—the writer Francis Parkman arrived in St. Louis to find that "the hotels were crowded" with emigrants, "and the gunsmiths and saddlers were kept constantly at work providing arms and equipments." To see the Oregon Trail for himself, Parkman headed for the frontier on a steamboat, which was so overloaded with emigrants that "water broke alternately over her guards." Of course the writer had with him the one essential travel book for the journey, which he put to novel use when he reached the Rocky Mountains. Invited to spend an evening with Indians, Parkman entertained them by setting off little fireworks called "squibs and serpents." He had fashioned them out of "gunpowder and charcoal, and the leaves of 'Fremont's Expedition,' rolled round a stout lead pencil."

Frémont's critics later minimized his importance in spurring the Oregon migration. He had not discovered the Oregon Trail, which was used before he saw it. This was true, but it hardly slowed the growth of John's legend. His true achievement was the thoughts of the West that he inspired in the minds of emigrants and easterners, such as Horace Greeley, who had recently founded the *New York Tribune*. At age thirty-two, just two years older than John, with an intense gaze and thinning hair, Greeley was making his paper an essential read, combining colorful reporting with his own memorably worded opinions. "We have generally thought of the Rocky Mountains," his newspaper said in October 1843, "as some nearly impenetrable barrier . . . frowning at the onrushing tide of civilization." But after reading the Frémont report with its description of the gentle slope of South Pass, "the mind is involuntarily filled with new and vast ideas"—so vast that they enlarged Greeley's idea of America. "The nineteenth century will set open a whole continent peopled by freemen."

✳ ✳ ✳

WHERE WAS JOHN AS HIS STORY WAS SPREADING? He didn't know without careful study. On clear days he would unsheathe his sextant and chronometer, and at a precise time measure the location of the sun. At night he might wake at three o'clock in the morning to gather information from the stars. He noted his experiences. On July 17 he was near the 38th parallel, eight hundred miles or so west of St. Louis, watching as the immense bulk of Pikes Peak faded from sight: "The clouds, which had been gathered all afternoon over the mountains, began to roll down their sides; and a storm so violent burst upon me, that it appeared I had entered the storehouse of the thunder storms." Farther north, he took notes about deposits of coal, visible in rabbit burrows, and recorded signs of Indians and emigrants. One evening they found a cow that had strayed from an emigrant party, "and as she gave an abundance of milk, we enjoyed to-night an excellent cup of coffee." He savored these moments of urbanity, and unlike on the last journey, he had packed enough coffee that he would never run out. At some point came the incident in which John allegedly used the howitzer to intimidate a group of Sioux, although there may have been less to the incident than it seemed. In his diary, Charles Preuss cast the howitzer in an entirely different light. "Our cannon caused unnecessary alarm" among a group of Indians, Preuss reported in August. Another diary entry contained this brief remark: "Shooting buffalo with the howitzer is a cruel but amusing sport."

Reaching South Pass in August, John released eleven men who wanted to return to their families for the winter, then angled southwest to explore the Great Salt Lake. His men boiled down lake water to replenish their supply of salt. They unfolded a boat made of India rubber and used it to sail across the lake to one of its islands, where John accidentally left behind "the brass cover to the object end of my spy glass, [which] will furnish matter of speculation to some future traveler." He assumed his voyage was "the first ever attempted on the interior sea." This was as mistaken as his assumption that he had climbed the highest of the Rocky Mountains in 1842: a fur trader had made a similar journey by canoe almost twenty years before, not to mention Indians who might have attempted it before him.

But John was gathering material for an informative account of the Salt Lake region. Legends, and even some maps, suggested that rivers flowed out of the lake and all the way to the sea, but John concluded the stories were "highly exaggerated and impossible." He grasped that much of the region between the Rockies and the Sierra Nevada was a bowl—so hemmed in by mountains that no rivers found outlets to an ocean. The rivers flowed into the Great Salt Lake or sank in the desert. He gave the region a name, the Great Basin. It was so immense that the men spent weeks exploring just one corner of it before emerging on the far side. They spent a few more weeks pushing onward through Oregon, following a trail that led to the Columbia River, then riding parallel to the river. On November 1 they glimpsed snowcapped Mount Hood "glowing in the sunlight this morning." Eventually John took to the water, leaving most of the party to rest and refit while three of his men joined him in a hired canoe with an Indian crew. "We were a motley group, but all happy," John said. "Three unknown Indians; Jacob, a colored man; Mr. Preuss, a German; Bernier, creole French; and myself." Drifting down the Columbia at night, when it was said the wind blew less fiercely, he encountered people his work had been enticing across the continent. "On a low broad point on the right bank of the river . . . were pitched many tents of the emigrants." His canoe continued past them to Fort Vancouver, a British trading post on the river, which was near enough to its mouth to allow navigation from the Pacific. A sailing ship was at anchor.

This was the end of John's westward journey, and as with the first expedition, the conclusion was an anticlimax. British traders welcomed Lieutenant Frémont and gave him a place to spend the night; they commonly offered shelter to Americans on the way to "their land of promise," the broad and fertile Willamette Valley just across the Columbia. John never had a look at the Willamette Valley, and didn't even get a chance to float the last hundred miles down to the Pacific. Those miles were already mapped, and it was so late in the season that he couldn't justify spending the time. Within two days he was in a boat being rowed back upriver to his men.

They regrouped in late November at The Dalles, a rocky bend in the Columbia, site of a Methodist mission to Indians. A man asked to join them there, a nineteen-year-old named William, who wanted to see the white man's world. (Misidentified by the missionaries and others as Chinook, he would become known as Billy Chinook, although he was believed to have come from the related Wasco tribe.) John agreed to take him east and help him find a way home. The travelers bought fresh horses and culled their equipment, giving away the wagons and carts, stripping down because they planned a route home that followed no known trail. John meant to strike out southward from the emigrant route before turning east again, discovering some new way through the mountains. That was the hope when they set out on November 25.

In a quiet moment as they left the Columbia River behind, he might have recalled sending a message to Jessie, promising that he would be home in January. John would probably miss that deadline even if he stuck to the emigrant trail. Now that he was deviating from it, he was sure to miss it by months.

✳ ✳ ✳

UNTIL HE LEFT THE TRAIL FOR OREGON'S MOUNTAINS, John had never experienced winter in the West. As a southerner who'd grown up in coastal cities he had little experience with winter at all. Still he should have realized that attempting a winter crossing of high mountains, at high latitudes, was close to insane. Doing so on an unknown path was even closer. Had the men returned on the emigrant trail, they would at least have traveled a well-worn route, with an occasional fur-trading post where they might find help. (Jessie understood this as she agonized over his fate, and assumed her husband understood too, reasoning that he must be safely spending the winter at a post with "every comfort that fire food and shelter could give.")

Instead John was starting into a region where the map was mostly blank. Unknown lands held "a charm for me," he said. "It would have been dull work if it had been to plod over a safe country and here and there to correct some old error." It may have seemed reasonable to assume his wilderness veterans were a match for nature, and apparently his men agreed, because they followed him into the unknown, even those like Kit Carson, whose experience would have warned them of the risks. The mapmaker Charles Preuss did record dismay in the privacy of his diary. "God only knows what we shall still have to go through on this winter journey," he wrote on December 1. "We still have two thousand miles back to the States." He had time to write while dismounted from his mule, sitting on a fallen fir tree in the snow, because he was waiting on the remainder of the caravan to catch up. Even after discarding every other wheeled vehicle, John insisted on keeping the heavy howitzer. "Unless he presents it to someone as he did the wagon, we shall move ahead slowly."

No feature of the landscape was quite so distinctive as the immensity of it. Forests covered thousands of square miles. Between mountains lay mysterious plateaus, as flat as a coastal plain but at elevations higher than most of the Appalachians in the East. One day they stood on the shore of Klamath Lake, which was the size of an inland sea with mountains lining the far shore. The next day they rode on without any idea what lay ahead. Days became weeks. The party could not locate a clear way eastward. They traveled through woods so thick that they struggled to maintain a straight line; and at sunrise on December 13, Lieutenant Frémont managed to get his stiff fingers around a pencil to record a temperature of 0 degrees Fahrenheit. On other days the temperature climbed into the 30s, but that could be worse than extreme cold: the sun softened the crust of snow, causing the feet of horses and mules to sink. On December 16, the horses were thrashing through three feet of snow and ice that cut their feet, while "the air was dark with falling snow, which every where weighed down the trees," John said. Around midday, "the forest looked clear ahead, appearing to terminate; and beyond a certain point we could see no trees. Riding rapidly ahead . . . we found ourselves on the verge of a vertical and rocky wall . . . At our feet—more than a thousand feet below—we looked into a green prairie country." A lake lay in that green valley, so much lower in altitude that it seemed to be summer down there rather than winter.

It was "a magic view from above," Preuss told his diary, but there were "great difficulties to get into the promised land." They had to pick their way down the slope, and then a mule lost its footing and rolled downhill some five hundred feet before standing up. The howitzer was stuck on the slope and had to be manhandled the rest of the way. Reaching the waters of what John named Summer Lake, the men luxuriated in the higher temperatures— 52 degrees Fahrenheit at sunset the next day—and passed thousands of rabbits clustered on the shore. But this was a brief respite, not relief. A forbidding landscape lay to the east, and the look of it told John not to go there. He led the expedition farther south. Two more weeks of effort found them back in snowy mountains on the far western edge of the Great Basin, having traveled 571 miles since the Columbia River, but most of it southward rather than eastward, meaning they were effectively going sideways and not much nearer home. They had drifted out of the Oregon country into Mexico—east of the Sierra Nevada, in an area toward the western side of modern-day Nevada.

Around New Year's Day 1844, John ordered the men to dismount from their exhausted horses and walk. On January 5, when they woke to a temperature of 12 degrees, the mapmaker Preuss wrote that the party had lost momentum: "We have been sitting here for three days, wrapped in fog, on a miserable plateau surrounded by bare hills. The animals are dying, one after the other. Very little grass, snow instead of water." Aside from the dead animals, some horses and mules had gone missing—stolen, the men believed, by Indians watching the party from places unseen. It was becoming apparent that the men could no longer make it home as planned. If they turned eastward, the next location where they could be sure to find safety and supplies was Bent's Fort, a trading post on the Arkansas River—across the deserts of the Great Basin, over the snow-covered Rockies, and roughly eleven hundred miles away.

Survival demanded that they find fresh animals and supplies—but where? They could have tried to retreat northwestward to Oregon, but that would force them to retrace the hundreds of miles that had nearly killed them. They knew nothing inviting about the land to the south. The remaining choice was to turn westward. Moving that way would take them even farther from home, and force them to confront the snow-choked Sierra Nevada, of which there was no recorded crossing in winter. But if the men could thrash over a mountain pass they would descend into the warm central valley of Mexican-controlled Alta California. Many miles back in this journey, the men had spent the night beside a train of emigrants bound for that valley, their wagons loaded with "furniture and farming utensils" as well as "an entire set of machinery for a mill," which they intended to set up near the Sacramento River. Kit Carson had been to California fifteen years ago, and recalled "plenty to eat" and "grass in abundance" where the rivers flowed into San Francisco Bay. So they knew shelter lay that way, though it was an excruciating decision to change course. As early as January 5, the men grasped that they "probably" would have to turn westward to survive, but their leader delayed giving the order for nearly two more weeks. Giving up the eastward crossing would be admitting failure. John's strength was his persistence—but it also took strength to confront defeat, and at first he could not summon it. By the time he relented on January 18, his men were more than ready to change course: "My decision was heard with joy by the people, and diffused new life through the camp."

Scouting for a route to California, they discovered that someone was scouting them. Members of the Washoe tribe watched warily from a distance before inviting the strangers to their nearby village. They were a humble people, wearing clothes woven out of bulrushes and cloaks made of furs. They lived on fish, rabbits, and pine nuts, and they offered nuts to the hungry visitors. Lacking any common language, the two groups had to communicate through gestures and pantomime, which was how John asked for help. He said he would give them "scarlet cloth" if they would provide a guide to lead them over the mountains to "the country of the whites" to the west. The Washoe men were troubled. They "pointed to the snow on the mountain, and drew their hands across their necks, and raised them above their heads, to show the depth; and signified that it was impossible for them to get through." Any passable route must be farther south. Lieutenant Frémont moved on after trading for more pine nuts to supplement the expedition's "now scanty provisions"—the mules were carrying the last of their peas, flour, rice, and sugar, though the coffee supply was holding out.

Another band of Indians urged the travelers not to cross the mountains until spring, but when John declined to wait, one young Indian agreed to serve as the explorers' guide. They called him Mélo, a word they had heard the Indians use, which appeared to mean "friend." "He was thinly clad," John said, "and nearly barefoot; his moccasins being about worn out." They gave Mélo animal skins so that he could make a new pair, and spent time mending their own clothes. They at last abandoned the howitzer, burying the gun in hopes that no one hostile would find it. They had the heartiest meal they could manage, slaughtering, among other things, one of the dogs that had been traveling with them for months. And then, just before they started, snow began to fall. They moved out in blinding weather, feeling their way. "We still do not know where we really are," wrote Preuss on January 26.

High on the slopes, the snow was so deep that some horses and mules thrashed about half-buried. The men had to make a road. Walking on improvised snowshoes, one would beat down snow with a maul until he was exhausted, then fall back to let another take the lead. Behind the maul, other men laid down branches to provide traction. Kit Carson said the snow at one point was "six feet deep on the level for a distance of three leagues," or about ten miles. Behind the road crew waited animals that Carson found in a desperate state. "Driven by hunger, they had eaten one another's tails and the leather of the pack saddles, in fact everything they could lay hold of. . . . We would frequently kill one to keep it from dying, then use the meat for food." Needing a campsite while the road was being cleared, the men set immense bonfires: two "old tall, thick fir trunks were set afire," as Preuss recorded, "and the eight-foot-deep snow soon melted all around. Two snow-free holes are now our living quarters and our kitchen." The challenge was keeping the kitchen supplied. Another dog, named Clammet, was slaughtered to supplement the horses and mules.

The travelers discovered people in the mountains. They lived in huts so nearly buried in snow that the passing men almost overlooked them. Some residents came out to talk; one Indian traded them for a block of salt, which the men needed to help choke down the animals they were eating. Two Indians approached Lieutenant Frémont one night as the men camped beneath an enormous tree. "One of them, an old man, immediately began to harangue us," warning that they would never make it over the mountains. By now the travelers had begun to understand a few words of the local language, and between words and gestures they grasped the man's message: "Rock upon rock—snow upon snow," he said, adding that even if the men survived the snow, their horses would slip on the narrow trails ahead, tumbling over precipices. Billy Chinook, the youth from Oregon, covered his head with a blanket and wept. He said he had been curious to see white people, not die among them. John studied his companions. "Seated around the tree, [with] the fire illuminating the rocks and the . . . pines round about, and the old Indian haranguing us, we presented a group of very serious faces."

The thermometer that night read 10 degrees Fahrenheit. It was the end of an unproductive day. John was marking the distance traveled each day, which in earlier parts of the journey was typically between ten and thirty miles—but on this day, February 4, the men had traveled three miles. On February 8 they made one mile. Later, during a period of road building, came a full week with no recorded progress at all. On February 16, John and Jacob Dodson scouted the route ahead, one black man and one white man in the vastness of the mountains in the snow. Crossing through a gap in the mountains, they were relieved to discover a stream that flowed in a westerly direction toward the Pacific: they had made it over the divide. But they were still far from safety. That night, he recorded, "was clear and very long. We heard the cries of some wild animals, which had been attracted by our fire, and a flock of geese passed over during the night. Even these strange sounds had something pleasant to our senses in this region of silence and desolation."

The main party did not make it over the divide until February 20, working through the snow beneath looming rock walls and evergreen trees. As men and animals staggered through that gap, their commander paused for a scientific ritual. He lit a fire. He brought water to a boil and dipped in a thermometer, knowing that the boiling point dropped as altitude increased. He calculated that they were 9,338 feet above sea level. (As precise as he made his number seem, it was a rough calculation; the elevation would later be measured at 8,574 feet.) The next morning they spied several ridgelines, purple in the morning light, and beyond them lower, snow-free ground that seemed to be California's central valley. In the valley was the zigzag line of a river. But for the moment the view merely tantalized them.

A week later, they were still in the mountains. "We had with us a large kettle; and a mule being killed here, his head was boiled in it for several hours, and made a passable soup for famished people." Some men seemed to be losing their minds from hunger and exhaustion; one "became lightheaded, wandering off into the woods without knowing where he was going." Jacob Dodson followed, found him, and brought him back, but a few days later, having "not yet recovered his mind," the man leaped into a cold mountain stream and swam "as if it were summer." Some of the men may have thought John himself was slightly deranged as he continued to pause for random observations: "On a bench of the hill near by, was a field of fresh green grass, six inches long in some of the tufts which I had the curiosity to measure."

At the start of March, John rode ahead with Jacob Dodson and a few others. In the warmer air of a lower altitude, they encountered a waterway that a local Indian identified for them as the Rio de los Americanos, the American River. "Never did a name sound more sweetly!" the American explorer declared. The Indian told them in Spanish, "I am a vaquero," or cowboy, "in the service of Captain Sutter." John Sutter was a European who had established a settlement east of San Francisco Bay. "He is a very rich man," said the vaquero, informing the travelers that they were already within Sutter's empire. Catching his horse, he led the men over a hill to

Sutter's two-story house, made of thick adobe walls. Here they met the man himself—short, solid, balding, and mustached, seemingly in command of all he surveyed. He welcomed Frémont and his men to spend the night "under his hospitable roof." It was March 6, 1844, nearly three and a half months and 1,142 meandering miles since they had ridden away from the Columbia River.

In the morning John rode back uphill to find the rest of his men, who "were all on foot—each man, weak and emaciated—leading a horse or mule as weak and emaciated as themselves." They were arriving in the valley in a season when the daytime temperatures regularly exceeded 60 degrees Fahrenheit and once even hit 75. Reaching Sutter's land, they turned out their animals to graze, and pitched their tents, and ate Sutter's food, and slept.

✳ ✳ ✳

IN THE TWO AND A HALF WEEKS THAT FOLLOWED, John bought supplies from Sutter, negotiating a price for 130 horses, 30 head of cattle, and items such as a "silver plated bridle." He paid with drafts, or checks, which he hoped the United States government would honor. He paid on his own account for new clothes, including "buck-skin pantaloons & moccasins" for Jacob Dodson. While doing business and dining with Sutter he learned a little of his host's past, although Sutter apparently kept the story vague. He said he was a Swiss man, who was known as Captain Sutter because he had served in the Swiss militia. He apparently did not mention that he was on the run from Switzerland. While operating a dry-goods store there, Sutter had lost so much money that he fled to avoid debtors' prison, leaving his wife and children behind. Catching a ship to New York, he spent several years moving westward in search of opportunities—to St. Louis, then Santa Fe, then Oregon, then Hawaii before turning back eastward to Alta California.

He arrived in California with his own workforce—eight Hawaiians, known as kanakas, contract laborers who were rented out to him. They accompanied him inland when the Mexican authorities granted him 48,400 acres to develop, and he supplemented the Hawaiians by putting California natives to work. The natives tended his wheat fields. They built his ranch house. They made sun-dried bricks and stacked them to make the walls of a fort for defense against less cooperative Indians. Frémont learned that for all their work, the Indians received "a very moderate compensation—principally in shirts, blankets, and other articles of clothing." Sutter was often given these laborers by Indian chiefs as payment for his help in battling rival tribes, and he had forced them into serfdom. Once he rented thirty Indians to another landowner, saying in a letter that he would "take payment in dried meat," and that the laborers were "innocent" and must be kept isolated so they would remain that way. Frémont noticed that from the chief of a nearby village, Sutter "obtains as many boys and girls as he has any use for." He probably did not know of a rumor that Sutter sexually abused the girls he employed, but Sutter was open about using children for labor. Girls at the fort were in training to be put to work in a planned wool factory. He apparently obtained some of the children after killing their parents in war.

Celestial observations told Frémont that Sutter's empire was near the 38th parallel, almost directly west of both Washington, D.C., and St. Louis. They were near 121 degrees west, which meant he had traveled 44 degrees west of Washington, nearly one-eighth of the circumference of the earth. He was nearer the kingdom of Hawaii than Washington. He was nearer Mexico City than Washington. He was in Mexico illegally, a US Army officer who had appeared without papers or permission. While he had an explanation, authorities would have been within their rights to question or even expel him. Sutter had a duty to report Frémont's presence: he had taken an oath of citizenship to Mexico and acted as a local government official. But he took his time notifying the departmental authorities nearly two hundred miles away in the coastal town of Monterey, waiting until Frémont had completed his purchase of animals and supplies and ridden away.

Frémont had risked his men's lives with little need, much as when he climbed "the highest point in the Rocky Mountains," except on a grander scale. Again he got away with it, as persistence and endurance overcame his erratic decisions. The experience shifted the orientation of his life. Fate had momentarily brought him to California, a great stage where he sensed there would be more acts for him to play.

The men had hardly started home on a warmer, more southerly route when Frémont began thinking about returning to California. He no doubt recognized in Sutter a self-invented wanderer like himself, who seemed to have made his own prosperous world. The appeal of the landscape was apparent: the expedition was a little smaller as it started east, because several of his men chose to resign and take positions working for Sutter. Frémont himself was "inspired with California," he said. "Its delightful climate and uncommon beauty of surface; the great strength of vegetation and its grand commercial position; took possession of my mind. My wish when I first saw it settled into intention, and I determined to make there a home."

James K. Polk's inauguration, said to be the first depicted in a newspaper illustration.

Chapter Six

THE MANIFEST PURPOSE
OF PROVIDENCE

Thomas Hart Benton and the Frémonts,
1843–1844

Washington and St. Louis

The country palpably changed while John was away from May 1843
to the summer of 1844. Prophetic events pointed toward a new
phase of American history—beginning with the National Convention of Colored Citizens.

On August 15, 1843, as John camped on the Green River in the Rockies, about forty people arrived for the convention in Buffalo, New York. They gathered in a public hall at the corner of Washington and Seneca streets, and Henry Highland Garnet called the meeting to order. The principal subject of the convention was the abolition of slavery, and Garnet had escaped slavery in Maryland. This meeting was not unprecedented; free black Americans had organized other such conventions in past years, and some white people had long campaigned against slavery. But the meeting in Buffalo took the dramatic step of discussing violent resistance. Describing slavery's inhumanity in terms that left the room "infused with tears," Garnet called upon slaves to demand freedom from their masters, and "if the master refused it, to tell them, then we shall take it." It sounded like a call for revolution, though Garnet did not say precisely how slaves should take their freedom.

The crowd roared its approval—until another former slave rose to object. Frederick Douglass was only twenty-five, but he'd had enough life experience to speak with authority. He had been born enslaved in eastern Maryland around 1817, and was separated from his mother as an infant so she could be made to work in the fields. Sent as a youth to serve a family in Baltimore, he learned to read through a flaw in the slave system: it was run by people susceptible to human feelings. His new master's wife, he said, "at first lacked the depravity indispensable to shutting me up in mental darkness," and helped the boy learn the alphabet and basic spelling. Her husband discovered the lessons and ordered her to stop, fearing that education would ruin the youth for slave work, but the boy covertly enlisted white schoolchildren to give him lessons. Later he met a free black woman, Anna Murray, who aided his escape to the North and then married him. And he began a life as an antislavery activist, a disciple of the radical white newspaper editor William Lloyd Garrison of Boston, turning the words he had learned into weapons.

Douglass told the convention that they should continue to rely on words. He warned that if slaves demanded their freedom in the way that Garnet proposed, it would lead to a futile "insurrection," and Douglass "wanted emancipation in a better way," through peaceful moral persuasion. Douglass prevailed. The convention called for the establishment of an antislavery newspaper, and for traveling lecturers to make the antislavery case. Afterward, Douglass and two white men followed up on their commitment to moral persuasion by beginning a speaking tour of western states, including an event in Pendleton, Indiana. Thirty stone-throwing white men drove the speakers off the stage, and one chased Douglass and broke his hand with a club.

Brutal as their actions were, the attackers' underlying sentiment was no different from official federal policy: slavery was best not discussed. Talk was dangerous. Neither major party had an interest in raising the issue, because both sought votes from the North and South by emphasizing less divisive issues. It required selective vision for Abraham Lincoln, a lawyer and former state lawmaker from the free state of Illinois, to join the same Whig party as Alexander H. Stephens, a slave owner elected to Congress from Georgia in 1842. The House of Representatives imposed a gag rule blocking discussion of antislavery petitions. But agitation was growing harder to contain. Improving transportation meant that like-minded people could gather for events such as the Convention of Colored Citizens, and activists could range more widely giving speeches. Increasing numbers of newspapers meant that dissident voices could be heard. Antislavery papers covered antislavery politicians, such as former president John Quincy Adams of Massachusetts, who had been elected to Congress and was campaigning to end the House gag rule. As the abolitionist movement grew, Southern leaders were becoming more extreme in defense of their institution. Slavery was a barrel of gunpowder waiting for a fuse—and that slow-burning fuse was lit accidentally by the next prophetic event while John was away.

In February 1844, a navy warship turned into the Potomac below Washington. The river was choked with ice for forty miles below the capital, but the ship cracked through the white sheets easily, leaving behind a trail of clear smooth water the width of the hull. The USS *Princeton* resembled a standard three-masted sailing ship, but its wooden hull hid features that made it unlike any warship seen before. A steam engine was churning belowdecks. It burned smokeless coal called anthracite, and had a funnel that could be retracted out of sight in order to surprise enemy sailing ships with its mysterious speed. Rather than the vulnerable paddle wheels of most steamers, the engine turned a screw propeller below the waterline. Each cannon on deck was mounted so it could swivel to fire to either side, rather than poking from a gunport on one side, and its two main guns were so massive they had been given names: one was the Peacemaker, while the other was named for a territory over which the ship might someday fight: Oregon.

The *Princeton*'s commander, Captain Robert F. Stockton, had designed the ship in collaboration with John Ericsson, a brilliant engineer who was an immigrant from Sweden. Calling his ship's innovations the most important "since the invention of gunpowder," Stockton had championed the big guns over the objection of the army's chief of ordnance, who warned that such huge iron barrels might contain imperfections and come apart when fired. Now he brought the ship to Washington to show off his creation, anchoring within sight of the Capitol's green dome. On February 16, President Tyler boarded the ship for a short exhibition cruise. On February 28 the president returned with other officials, including Secretary of State Abel Upshur and Senator Thomas Hart Benton. Had Jessie not been away in St. Louis, she surely would have come: Dolley Madison, widow of President James Madison, was one of several women on board as the *Princeton* cruised downriver past the grave of George Washington at Mount Vernon. The crew demonstrated the big guns several times, and late in the voyage, the secretary of the navy announced a final blast of the Peacemaker. President Tyler was delayed belowdecks, but other dignitaries gathered. Captain Stockton—stern-faced, with a full head of hair and boundless energy— stood near Senator Benton and took hold of the lanyard. "I saw the hammer pulled back," said Benton, "heard a tap—saw a flash—felt a blast in the face, and knew that my hat was gone: and that was the last I knew of the world, or of myself, for a time, of which I can give no account." He regained consciousness a moment later to see "Stockton, hat gone, and face blackened, standing bolt upright, staring fixedly upon the shattered gun." The left side of the barrel had come apart, showering the deck with shrapnel. The deck was strewn with bodies. The secretary of state was killed. The secretary of the navy was killed. Others of the dead included a black man, a slave who worked as President Tyler's valet.

The disaster had a notable aftereffect. Tyler had to choose a new secretary of state, who would face an especially sensitive task. The late Secretary Upshur had been negotiating for the United States to annex the independent Republic of Texas. Mexico still claimed Texas and threatened to go to war over it, while Texas's admission would face domestic opposition because the Texans permitted slavery. It would take great subtlety for Upshur's successor to avoid disaster, but President Tyler nominated John C. Calhoun of South Carolina, who threw aside all subtlety. As soon as the Senate confirmed him as secretary, he demanded the annexation of Texas as an essential move for the protection of slavery. American politics soon began to fall apart. David Lee Child, an antislavery journalist, voiced astonishment that Calhoun could ever have been entrusted with Texas when the stakes were so high: "It is almost as if [Calhoun] had been appointed cannoneer to fire off the 'Peacemaker' after the evil genius of another had contrived and charged it."

✳ ✳ ✳

CALHOUN WAS THE FORMER VICE PRESIDENT who had been in league with the South Carolina nullifiers when John was growing up there. He was also a political theorist and a stiff, stern-faced, brooding tribune of slavery, who persuaded himself that it was "a positive good." Discarding the thinking of men like Thomas Jefferson, who called slavery an inherited evil that he wished he knew how to end, Calhoun declared in 1837 that slavery was no more unfair than any other economic system: "There never has yet existed a wealthy and civilized society in which one portion of the community did not, in point of fact, live on the labor of the other." Northern free laborers were also exploited by the rich, he said, and Northern capitalism was less orderly. Revealing the paranoia of a white man who represented a majority black state, he alleged that Northern abolitionists wanted not merely to free black slaves but to turn them into masters and their masters into slaves.

Now it fell to Calhoun to justify the annexation of Texas. Although he could have chosen arguments that downplayed slavery, he embraced a conspiracy theory that was popular in proslavery circles. The United States must seize Texas, he said, because the British empire was plotting to take it and abolish slavery there, with destabilizing effects on the American South. When the British ambassador in Washington denied any such conspiracy but expressed a general wish to end slavery around the world, Calhoun took the bait and responded with a letter defending slavery. He argued that Southern slaves were better off than free black citizens in the North, who suffered from high rates of "deafness, blindness, insanity, and idiocy." It was on these terms that the administration sent a treaty of Texas annexation to the Senate.

Calhoun's attitude triggered another prophetic event: Senator Thomas Hart Benton rose in opposition to annexation. He set aside his lifelong support of national expansion, including the acquisition of Texas, and argued that taking Texas would be wrong. An about-face of this magnitude called for an explanation, which Benton gave in a speech on the Senate floor beginning May 16, 1844. Working from a stack of items on his desk—books and newspapers in multiple languages, documents obtained from the Tyler administration, and even extracts from his own old speeches—he delivered a speech that eventually spread across portions of three days. He said *northern* Texas should belong to the United States, but Texans also claimed the Rio Grande Valley to the south, which they had never controlled. The Rio Grande was simply part of Mexico, and seizing it would be a "sudden, reckless, and monstrous course." Mexico prohibited slavery, which meant the land along the Rio Grande was free soil and should remain that way: "I shall not engage in schemes for [slavery's] extension into regions where it was never known . . . where a slave's face was never seen!" Seizing Texas would lead to "the crime and infamy of unjust war."

Every senator must have appreciated the irony: Benton himself was still a slave owner. It was likely that his view of African Americans had evolved slightly: because he used free workers in his home, he had come to know Jacob Dodson, the son of family servants who had volunteered to take risks in the West by John's side. Benton respected the young black man enough that he would later find him a job in the Senate, asking his colleagues to vote Dodson "the same extra compensation" paid to other workers. But Benton's stand on Texas was not based on racial equality. He was defending the Union. He suspected that Calhoun and the slave interests wanted Texas in order to make the South large enough to declare independence.

When it came time to vote on the treaty of annexation, Benton's side appeared to triumph. He peeled away several Democrats to join nearly all the Whigs to crush it. Yet the debate was not over. The presidential election was looming. Taking Texas was broadly popular, and the election could turn into a referendum on it.

✳ ✳ ✳

DURING THE SAME DAYS IN MAY that Senator Benton made his Senate speech, a prophetic activity was taking place beneath his feet. Below the semicircular Senate chamber was the semicircular chamber of the Supreme Court, a vaulted red-carpeted room where the judges' bench backed up against a row of windows. The court was out of session that May, but the lamps were lit, and passers-by could be forgiven for wondering what was happening. Men had run copper wires into the room and attached them to a Grove battery, made with nitric acid in a ceramic container. The wires also connected to a device made of wood and metal, small enough to rest on one of the tables. A man sometimes pressed a lever on the device, which pro- duced a clicking sound. Other times the device appeared to click on its own, and the man paid strict attention, as if the clicks were some kind of language.

Samuel F. B. Morse had been working on this project for years. Jessie Benton Frémont had seen him around Washington; he visited the patent commissioner, a neighbor of the Bentons, and she noticed his desperation: "He was so worn-out that his dead-white face and brilliant hollow eyes startled one." He was a clean-shaven New Englander in his fifties, deep into a life of frustrated ambition. In the 1820s he was a painter, who created an epic scene of the House of Representatives in session but failed to interest Congress in buying it. In the 1830s, he became a political activist in New York, and wrote newspaper essays under headlines such as FOREIGN CONSPIRACY AGAINST THE LIBERTIES OF THE UNITED STATES. He alleged without evidence that European powers were using the religion of Catholic immigrants as a way to control the country. His career as a conspiracy theorist ended when he ran for mayor of New York as an anti-immigrant candidate and the city of immigrants defeated him. Next, in the 1840s, Morse asked Congress to help fund a long-distance test of his "electro-magnetic telegraph." The hollow-eyed man "was laughed at in Congress," Jessie said. One representative mockingly suggested that if subsidizing telegraphy made sense, Congress should also subsidize mesmerism. But lawmakers narrowly approved Morse's thirty-thousand-dollar payment, and by May 1844, crews under his direction had hung cable from chestnut poles, with the bark still on, that marched some forty miles alongside the railroad tracks from Washington to Baltimore. He arranged for the Washington end of the cable to terminate inside the Capitol, which was how the Supreme Court chamber became the nation's first telegraph office.

On May 24, as two dozen people stood watching, the fifty-three-year-old used the code that would bear his name to tap out "What hath God wrought," a phrase from the book of Numbers. It had been suggested to him by a young woman he liked, the patent commissioner's teenage daughter, Annie Ellsworth. Morse was elated when confirmation of his message arrived from Baltimore, and on May 27 he began a more ambitious demonstration. The Democratic National Convention opened that day in Baltimore, where delegates from every state gathered to choose the party's nominee for the fall presidential election. Morse made arrangements for news updates from the crowded convention hall to be raced to his telegraph set at the Baltimore railway station. His operator tapped out each update for the benefit of those in the capital city.

9¾ o'clock. Buchanan stock said to be rising

That was the Bentons' neighbor James Buchanan, one of numerous presidential contenders. Former president Martin Van Buren was considered the favorite.

10¼—A Van Buren cannon in front of the Telegraph office with a fox tail
attached to it

Runners shuttled to the Baltimore telegraph office, bringing bits of color from the crowded convention hall.

6¼—Senator Walker is speaking in favor of the two-thirds rule—was
cheered by many—hissed by some

The crowd in Washington was cheering and hissing too. The dozens of spectators who'd come to watch Samuel Morse became hundreds. He read each news bulletin aloud. A correspondent for a newspaper called the *Whig Standard* declared: "Those attending *at the Capitol* may almost be said to have been *in attendance at [the convention in] Baltimore!*" At some point the crowd undoubtedly included Senator Benton. A correspondent wrote to the *New York Herald* that there was no news in Washington; nobody was doing anything important except following the latest burst of information from elsewhere. People sensed that they were witnessing a profound change in the human condition—"the annihilation of space," as more than one person called it. Who could imagine the possibilities once people could learn about any event anywhere, instantly? "Professor Morse's telegraph," the *Herald* correspondent said,

has originated in the mind . . . a new species of consciousness. Never
before was any one conscious that he knew with certainty what events

were at that moment passing in a distant city—40, 100, or 500 miles off. For example, it is now precisely 11 o'clock. The telegraph announces as follows—"11 o'clock—Senator Walker is now replying to Mr. Butler upon the adoption of the 'two-thirds' rule." It requires no small intellectual effort to realize that this is a fact that now is, and not one that has been.

The arcane updates about a "two-thirds rule" contained the key to the presidential nomination. Van Buren needed two-thirds of the delegates and fell short. To avoid an impasse, delegates began coalescing behind another candidate: James K. Polk, a former Speaker of the House and former governor of Tennessee.

Mr. Saunders declares it is necessary to have a candidate in favor of annexation

And Polk, unlike other contenders, wanted to annex Texas. Delegates chose him unanimously. When Morse read out the news, cheers went up from the crowd at the Capitol, along with "mutterings" from those opposed. A runner hurried across town to the office of one of the newspapers, which in an unprecedented feat was able to rush the news of Polk's nomination into print on the same day it happened.

Polk's supporters exulted—and not all were from slave states. George Bancroft, a noted historian turned politico, attended the convention from Massachusetts, and turned toward Polk; he wanted both Texas and Oregon, and soon wrote in a public letter that it was "the manifest purpose of Providence that the light of freedom should be borne from our fires to the domain beyond the Rocky Mountains." But Senator Benton felt his own expansionist goals had been hijacked. If Polk won the election, a second effort to annex Texas would be inevitable. Days after the convention, he rose at his Senate desk and told his colleagues that war with Mexico loomed: "Senators say this is a small war—a little predatory war—a war between weak powers—and, therefore, it is nothing to engage in it. I tell them that is nonsense, and worse. War is war, whether great or small!" But party unity forced Benton to stifle his own doubts as the election neared.

An empire was available for the taking. Democrats were for Texas; Democrats were for Oregon; and grand as these ambitions were, their presidential nominee held a grander one: Polk wanted California. It was his biggest goal. He did not publicize this; few if any of the delegates who voted for him would have known it. No word of it came down the telegraph line from Baltimore, so it was unknown to the members of the public who crowded around Samuel Morse at the Capitol as he translated the telegraph clicks and read out the news. They listened, rapt, to the clattering sound of the future, but Morse's translations were not enough to tell them what the sound really meant.

✳ ✳ ✳

JOHN CHARLES FRÉMONT HAD NO WAY of knowing any of this before he at last crossed the frontier that summer, reaching St. Louis on August 6, 1844. It was after dark. His men who lived in St. Louis headed home, and John walked through dim streets to the Benton house, only to find the lights out. Gabriel, the Bentons' coachman, explained that Jessie was not home, having gone to care for a sick relative. John crossed town to the relative's house, only to find it also dark. Unwilling to wake anyone, he sat in a public square beneath the stars, then checked into a hotel, sleeping long past daylight. Another man might have pounded down doors to find his wife and child, knowing the household would forgive the intrusion; John's reserve would not allow it, nor did he seem in a hurry to step back over the threshold into ordinary life.

Not until later in the day did Jessie see her husband, when he came to the relative's house "in his uniform and thin as a shadow." They did not have much time alone. As soon as word of John's arrival spread, the house "was thronged with welcoming friends." The throng apparently included a reporter, to whom John described his exploits. And then they were packing. Within days the Frémonts were moving toward Washington, the shoreline passing them as they stood on the deck of a steamboat, wheels churning the water and Jessie doubtless trying to restrain the curiosity of twenty-one-month-old Lily as she once had seen her mother restrain little Randolph. John had an entourage: Jacob Dodson was still with him, as was William, the Indian from Oregon who wanted to see the white man's world. There was also a Mexican youth, one Pablo Hernandez; the expedition had rescued him when he was separated from a Mexican trade caravan that was attacked by Indians. At first John intended to arrange for Hernandez to return home, but having been borne eastward by fate, the young man wanted to get an education, and was on his way to become part of the crowded Benton household.

By August 21 the party was in Washington, D.C., and John and Jessie were fending off visitors. John's knowledge of the West made him a source for anyone with questions about Oregon or, as Jessie noticed, about California. So many people called at the Benton house that the Frémonts had trouble beginning their report—and there needed to be a report, for as with John's previous expedition the purpose was not only to explore but to publicize. "We were forced," Jessie said, "into leaving home every day. There was a good small house within a square from us," a square being the way she referred to a city block, "and this Mr. Frémont rented." They developed a routine. Each evening John organized his notes for the next day's writing. In the morning, John said, Jacob Dodson "kept up the camp habit and very early brought me coffee," and then John and Jessie went to work upstairs in the rented house, which they used as an office. "Nine o'clock always found me at my post, pen in hand," Jessie said, "and I put down Mr. Frémont's dictation." John would talk, "pausing only for a more fitting word, for the whole of the four hours—walking about. The freedom of movement was essential to his freedom of expression—it was my great reward to be told that but for me the work could not be done."

"The narrative," John said, "will be strictly confined to what was seen." They decided "to present nothing, either in the narrative or in the maps, which was not the result of positive observation." Maps would show only the expedition's lines of travel across the countryside, with white spaces to either side. In this way they avoided information from unreliable sources and ensured that the narrator John C. Frémont would always be at the center of the story. He was present in every scene, like the first-person narrator of a novel. He described his actions straightforwardly. His plunge into the unknown on November 25 was simply a decision he made, and he did not reflect on the wisdom of it. He admitted to abandoning the howitzer as his commander had predicted, although he still said it was good to have brought it. And just as his first report described him vomiting at a crucial time, the second report confessed to unheroic moments. On February 23 in the Sierra Nevada, he was walking with Kit Carson and came to an icy creek: "Carson sprang over, clear across a place where the stream was compressed among rocks." John tried to copy him and fell in. He was a democratic everyman waging civilization's fight against nature—often in peril, at times over-matched, but never giving up.

Their writing ended each day at one o'clock, and they had lunch with toddler Lily before "going off for a long brisk walk," as Jessie said. "A slight rain, we did not mind—only a rain storm." At last she was alone with him. Walking south, they crossed a bridge over a canal and reached the National Mall, an expanse of green space that stretched westward from the green-domed Capitol. They made a handsome couple. Tested by motherhood, her mother's illness, and John's absences, the "girlish beauty" John had first met at sixteen was now a poised and experienced woman of twenty. John was lean and formal in his uniform. Their walks would have been a chance to get to know each other, because for all they had been through, they had not been through much together. When they reached their third anniversary in October 1844, she might have counted the thirty-six months and noted that he had been absent for twenty. Her desire to be near him made her especially grateful to help him write about the experiences that occupied more of his time than she did.

It was only human that she would wonder what her place really was in his work and life. The report they produced included a timeline of dates, locations, and miles traveled each day, so it was easy for her to compare chronologies: What was *she* doing on this or that day? At the start of December 1843 she had received his message that he expected to be home in January, news she passed on to Mrs. Talbot in a reassuring tone. Now she knew her reassurance was out of date before she had given it. Her husband had changed his plans, delayed his return, and condemned her to extra months of agony. If she said a word to him about how she'd felt, no trace made it into the report.

She at least could think of her suffering as the price of fame. When he had given his story to the reporter in St. Louis, it had been picked up by other papers so rapidly that the news had reached Washington before the Frémonts did; many people in the capital had read of his exploits battling snow that was "from five to twenty feet deep" on peaks that rose "seventeen thousand feet above the sea." (The highest peaks in all the Sierra Nevada were closer to fourteen thousand.) One day a Washington paper contained a remarkable phrase: "Fremont's Peak beyond the South Pass." His name was being given to "the highest point in the Rocky Mountains," the summit he had taken such risks to ascend in 1842. His name was also attached to more modest items: He'd returned with hundreds of plant specimens slipped into envelopes or pressed into books, and while most had broken apart during the journey home, they included a shrub that John's botanist called *Fremontia vermicularis*. Its leaves, John informed the botanist, "have a very salty taste which perhaps you do not know." James Hall, a paleontologist, wrote an appendix to the report describing "fossil ferns" that the expedition had brought back; he named one *Sphenopteris Fremonti*. In the spring of 1845 the Convention of American Geologists and Naturalists, meeting in New Haven, Connecticut, held an extended discussion of the meaning of fossils John had found in eastern Oregon, which some scientists viewed as evidence that the region must have contained some vast lake in the distant past.

Before the report was even complete, the secretary of war sent a message to Congress, declaring that John's mission had been "peculiarly arduous and dangerous." The description of John "and his bold adventurous party in situations and perils the most critical, and requiring the utmost fortitude to encounter and overcome" was enough to make any truly modest officer blush. It was reprinted in the *Daily Madisonian* in Washington, and then on the front page of the *New York Herald.* The army was promoting him by brevet—rewarding him for meritorious service—not once but twice: from second lieutenant to first lieutenant, and then from first lieutenant to captain. A brief Senate debate emphasized John's growing celebrity. The Senate ordered ten thousand copies of the still-unfinished report, and then considered a proposal to meet demand for it by printing "five thousand extra copies," bound up with the report of John's 1842 expedition to make a single volume. The Bentons' friend and neighbor, Senator James Buchanan, disagreed with this proposal and successfully shepherded through a change: Why five thousand extra copies? Make it *ten* thousand extra copies.

People across the country were waiting for their copies—not least the people of Nauvoo, Illinois, a Mormon settlement on the Mississippi River. The Mormons were considering migration farther west and had been eager for John's report ever since news accounts of his expedition had appeared in the Nauvoo paper in January 1845. In September, after the full report arrived, the Nauvoo newspaper reprinted three long excerpts describing John's explorations. That December, church officials gathered in the attic of Nauvoo's Mormon temple while one of them staged a reading of sections of John's report. Brigham Young climbed the stairs to the reading and sat quietly, listening to the descriptions of the Great Salt Lake.

The young explorer.

Chapter Seven

A TASTE FOR DANGER AND
BOLD DARING ADVENTURE

THE FRÉMONTS, 1844–1845

Washington, St. Louis, and Alta California

W hen the presidential nominating conventions were over, the 1844 general election pitted James K. Polk, the advocate of territorial expansion, against Henry Clay, a skeptic of it. Clay was a gray-haired former senator from Kentucky, the Whig party founder, and a brilliant orator who had walked the national stage even longer than Thomas Hart Benton. Much like Benton, Clay had spent his early career promoting visions of empire, but had lately grown to fear the consequences. New territories would provoke conflicts over slavery, he said, so it was "better to harmonize what we have than to introduce a new element of discord." Clay's difference with Polk presented the country with a fateful choice, which would also have great influence over the future of the Frémonts.

It was not, however, an absolutely clear choice, since the election touched on many issues at once. In the key electoral state of Pennsylvania that year, the big news was neither Texas nor slavery but a dispute involving immigrants. They were Irish Catholics, who were seen as a threat because of their religion. Philadelphia's Catholics called attention to their faith when they asserted an equal right to practice it. Pennsylvania mandated the use of the Bible—typically the Protestant, King James Version—for students to practice reading in the public schools. Catholics used a longer version of the Bible and said using the King James Version violated the separation of church and state. Shocked Protestants formed a new nativist party known as the Native Americans or American Republicans, and in May 1844 organized a rally provocatively located in an Irish Catholic neighborhood. Irishmen violently broke up the rally. Nativists then burned two Catholic churches, saying they were upholding the right of free speech.

Weeks later, crowds of nativists came from out of town to march in Philadelphia's Independence Day parade. Some reserved their own railroad cars to travel down from New York. A nativist mob formed outside a Philadelphia Catholic church, alleging that weapons were hidden inside and saying they feared a terror attack. When the sheriff and the state militia arrived to protect the church, the mob wheeled a cannon up from the waterfront and opened fire. A local resident, George S. Roberts, reported "watching the flashes of artillery against the sky." It took four days to end the battle, in which a number of people were killed, and the *New York Herald* declared that Philadelphia was "the scene of riot and bloodshed—of civil war." When news of Philadelphia's violence reached the telegraph office in Baltimore, it was wired to Washington, where Samuel Morse was still demonstrating his invention. He found the information so important that he rushed the latest updates to Secretary of State John C. Calhoun.

Philadelphia's "civil war" fed into nationwide resentment of immigrants. The Democratic Party actively courted immigrant and Catholic votes in hotly contested New York and Pennsylvania. The Whigs had brooded for years on what they perceived as an unfair Democratic advantage, and in 1844 some talked of suppressing the immigrant vote. Joseph T. Buckingham, the Whig editor of the *Boston Courier*, published a signed editorial (addressed to "Native Americans!") at the end of October, saying that he was willing to grant newcomers every privilege except political power:

"domestic demagogues" must be stopped from winning office with the votes of "factious foreigners." Immigrants should be treated with "generosity and justice" and paid "liberally" for their labor—but adult immigrants should be required to wait twenty-one years before becoming eligible to vote, the same period that newborn native children had to wait. It was the sort of rhetoric that might bring out the nativist vote—or drive immigrant voters to the polls to resist. Because the presidential election was close, the Frémonts' fate, and the nation's fate, could depend on which side of the immigration debate prevailed.

It took many days through October and November for the election results to become clear. Not all states voted on the same day, so instead of an election night there was an election season, from late October to mid-November, during which the Frémonts followed each day's vote tallies in the Washington papers. On November 3, the compositor of the *Whig Standard* in Washington was typesetting county-by-county results from Pennsylvania when fresh information came in. Rather than start the story again, he interrupted himself for a late-breaking news bulletin:

Half past 2, p.m.—We have received, by Professor Morse's Electro-Magnetic Telegraph, the following additional returns....

Henry Clay was on his way to losing Pennsylvania, the second most populous state. The most populous state, New York, went for Polk by a mere five thousand votes. The Democratic coalition, with its important immigrant vote in those two states, narrowly prevailed; had New York instead gone to Clay, so would the election. The Democratic-leaning *Daily Madisonian* crowed on November 6 that Clay would be "shamefully defeated," and when Polk won Michigan a week later a headline proclaimed, THE DEMOCRACY GLORIOUSLY TRIUMPHANT. By November 16 the *Whig Standard* surrendered, announcing not only that the election was lost but that the newspaper was closing: "We have no regrets, personally or otherwise, except that our cause has not been triumphant." The paper acknowledged that some Whigs had additional regrets—especially a fear that the coming conflict over Texas would split the Union.

Although Senator Benton had formally supported the winner, everyone knew his feelings. He grimly gathered evidence that the incoming administration planned to punish him. On January 12, 1845—it was a Sunday, but no day of rest for him—he wrote his friend and ally Francis Preston Blair, editor of the *Washington Globe*, and in his carefully indented handwriting began listing evidence of conspiracies against them, seventeen numbered points in all, including:

> *3. The design to send you on a foreign mission,* [and thus remove you as editor of the *Globe*] . . .

> *5. The design to destroy Benton through newspaper denunciations . . .*

> *11. Prostitution of the Post Office to all the schemes . . .*

> *. . . These, and other points of inquiry, will confirm, & extend your knowledge of the plots against us.*

> *Yours truly, Thomas H. Benton*

Benton was not wrong. Blair was removed as editor of the main Democratic Party paper, neutralizing one of Benton's channels of influence. Benton himself was harder to dislodge, since Missouri's legislature, which chose its senators, elected him to a fifth six-year term; but his home-state opposition was growing.

✳ ✳ ✳

LAWMAKERS READ POLK'S VICTORY as a popular mandate for Texas, and even before the inauguration considered an annexation measure, which Senator Benton could no longer stop. He even helped the process in hopes of uniting the party. President Tyler approved the measure hours before completing his term at the start of March, leaving Polk with only a few more steps to complete the transaction. The evening before Polk's inauguration a crowd held a "Texas Torch-Light Procession" down Pennsylvania Avenue, their cheers surely audible a block away at the Benton house. A pro-Polk newspaper reprinted an article on Texas under the headline LAND! LAND!

The next day guards blocked the streets near the Capitol, keeping the crowd away until the hour of the inauguration. When the guards stepped aside, a newspaper reported a "fearful" rush: "No limbs, happily, were broken, though injuries both to clothes and persons certainly were sustained." Thousands filled the lawn in the rain. The Frémonts doubtless had walked the few blocks to attend, while dignitaries including Senator Benton joined the incoming and outgoing presidents on a platform erected over the eastern Capitol steps. Although it was still raining as Polk took the oath (John Quincy Adams quipped that the ceremony was witnessed by "a large assemblage of umbrellas"), a reporter said Polk delivered his inaugural address "in a firm tone of voice, with the air of a man profoundly impressed by it himself." He celebrated the annexation of Texas, and acted as if Oregon was already won ("our domain extends from ocean to ocean"). Stiff and formal, his gray hair combed back straight from his forehead, he also called for the preservation of the Union, which he said was endangered: "It is a source of deep regret that, in some sections of our country, misguided persons have occasionally indulged in schemes and agitations, whose object is the destruction of domestic institutions existing in other sections." Listeners understood that "domestic institutions" meant slavery, and that the "misguided persons" in "some sections" were Northern abolitionists. Their "schemes and agitations" were the problem, not slavery—and Polk went to some lengths not to say "slavery" or "slaves." His euphemisms invited his audience to consider the situation in the abstract, without thinking of the human beings affected. He ended the speech by asking for the aid of God, and then he was done, and out of the rain, and governing.

He agreed to meet Senator Benton after the inauguration. If he ever had supported his allies' "design to destroy Benton," the president set it aside; he needed his fellow Democrat's power in the Senate. They shared broad goals: Polk wanted Oregon along with California and Texas, and Benton didn't object to these goals so much as the manner in which they were being sought. Benton, too, grasped the need for accommodation, and brought an offering to the presidential mansion: his famous son-in-law, who had seen as much of California as anyone in Washington. Polk had not articulated his California ambitions in his inaugural address, but Benton, having gathered intelligence from men around Polk, could perceive what those ambitions were.

John told the new president that official Washington did not yet know much about the land west of the Rockies. "I mentioned that I had, shortly before, at the Library of Congress, drawn out from the map-stand one giving the United States and Territories, and found on it the Great Salt Lake represented as connected with the Pacific Ocean by three great rivers." John said the map was wrong, that no rivers flowed from the Great Basin to California, but the president gave the impression that he believed the maps. It didn't matter. Whatever California was, Polk wanted it while there was still a chance. He was thinking of geopolitics, not geography: Mexico's hold on that distant territory was tenuous, and he worried that Britain, already in competition with the United States for Oregon, might seize California first. Benton believed that Americans could take California the way he wanted to secure Oregon, by encouraging emigrants to settle there in such numbers that the result became inevitable. Polk favored more direct measures: he wanted to buy California from Mexico.

The president's interest did not come from nowhere. California was a part of the national conversation. The *New York Herald* published a steady flow of articles that mentioned it—fifty-nine stories during 1843 and fifty-three in 1844; in other words, more than one article per week. Although the

Herald naturally paid far more attention to Oregon and Texas, its interest in California was consistent. Some of the articles were letters from an anonymous correspondent in Monterey, California's capital, who went by various aliases—"Americano," "Paisano," or no name at all—and promoted the appeal of California. Other papers printed their own California stories, including some from the same anonymous correspondent, and this subject of interest to news editors became of interest to public men. Daniel Webster, the great senator and former secretary of state, invited Captain Frémont to dinner to discuss California, and wrote in a letter in March 1845 that he regarded the excellent harbor at San Francisco Bay to be "twenty times as valuable to us as all Texas." Webster opposed territorial acquisitions—he meant his remark to disparage Texas as much as praise California—but it was all the same to Polk, who wanted both.

Polk's new secretary of state was James Buchanan of Pennsylvania— the Bentons' neighbor and friend, the recent presidential aspirant, and the groomsman who'd had Jessie on his arm at the wedding of the Russian ambassador. In the spring of 1845, Buchanan began bringing documents to the Benton house relating to Mexico. He was a distinctive character in Washington, regarded with a mixture of respect and derision. Some found him fastidious and almost effeminate; Andrew Jackson called him Aunt Fancy. He was cautious and noncommittal, avoiding strong stands that might harm his later prospects. Yet this weakness was a kind of strength: he was a survivor who arrived in Washington in 1821, the same year as Benton, and had spent all the years since moving in and out of Congress and prime administration posts. Buchanan, a bachelor, had dropped by the Benton home for dinner for years, and it was politically savvy now for Buchanan to seek Benton's counsel as a way of showing the administration's respect. The two climbed the stairs to Benton's third-floor library, sometimes joined by another senator who lived in the neighborhood, as well as by John and Jessie. Some of the papers Buchanan placed on the table were in Spanish, and at her father's request Jessie wrote out translations as the men tried to guess the mood in the distant Mexican capital they'd never visited.

The plans for John's next expedition began to change. He was already under orders to arrange another trip, and before the inauguration those orders ruled out California: his commander, Colonel Abert, told him to scout the upper reaches of the Arkansas and Red rivers, which were east of the Rockies. He was to work near Bent's Fort, twelve hundred miles or so short of San Francisco Bay. Even if he was to contemplate a detour to California, his instructions allowed no time: he was to return within the current year, and hire no more than forty men. It would be his least ambitious expedition. John's letters to Abert suggested that he was planning an ordinary scientific survey; he requested permission to hire a "Botanical Colourist" to make drawings of the plants they encountered. Then the Polk administration took charge. On April 10, John was told he could increase his party by ten or more if desired, and he should also note "the military peculiarity of the Country which you shall examine." He was given extra months to explore before he returned, but should still come back as soon as possible so that "if any operations should be required in that Country, the information obtained may be at command." He was, in other words, gathering information of military use in the event of war, in an area near the US border with the Mexican province of New Mexico.

There was still no mention of California. There was nothing in the orders—at least nothing in the written orders—to justify the description published in *Niles' National Register*, an influential newspaper, on May 3:

> *EXPLORING EXPEDITION. Lieutenant Fremont is now . . . organizing an exploring company of young men to form an expedition to the waters of the Pacific. He desires none but young men of intelligence and good character. The expedition will last for three years, and its operations will probably extend from the Black Hills to the Western ocean, and from California to the northern limits of Oregon. Those*

who have a taste for danger and bold daring adventure, may now have a chance.

It was hard to imagine the *Register* printing the story unless John or someone close to him was the source. He was by now comfortable describing his mission in different terms than his chain of command, and this was different enough to attract attention: "What we do not understand," a Boston paper said, "is how, or for what purposes, an expedition is sent from the Government into Mexican territory, nor why our engineers are employed in surveying rivers and harbors not belonging to us. We have no objection to the survey; we only want to know by what right it is ordered."

When asked directly, John said he was seeking a better and shorter route to Oregon, and thought the route might lead through California. Because his objective was incompatible with his orders to hurry back with information from the border with New Mexico, he planned to divide his force at Bent's Fort. Some of his men would survey the eastern slope of the Rockies and head home as ordered, while most would journey with John into Mexican territory.

Did President Polk, his commander in chief, really mean for John to go to California? At least Polk did not mind, since Frémont's destination was publicized before he departed and the president did not object. Polk also did not object when, after John's departure, his destination was discussed in the presidential mansion. Senator Benton had a long talk with the president, and Polk made a vague entry in his diary: "Some conversation occurred concerning Capt. Frémont's expedition, and his intention to visit California before his return." The phrase "his intention to visit" framed it as Captain Frémont's choice, which Polk could disavow later if necessary.

✳ ✳ ✳

JOHN SAID GOOD-BYE TO JESSIE IN MAY 1845. They had been together nine months this time, their longest period yet without a separation. If he'd told the newspapers that he planned to be gone three years, he surely had to face his wife and tell her something; Lily was two and a half, having had her first real chance to know her father, and if he really did stay away three years, he would by the end have missed more than half her life. Like many a spouse with bad news, John may not have spoken with perfect clarity; Jessie came away with an impression that he would use the summer of 1845 traveling to California and the summer of 1846 returning, reaching her after an absence of fifteen months or so. They would not have to be entirely out of touch, because letters could be sent to and from California by sea.

Jessie would not accompany him to St. Louis this time; her mother was ill in Washington. Charles Preuss would not be coming either; the German mapmaker decided to skip this expedition to spend more time with his wife. Other familiar faces would be coming: Jacob Dodson, the son of the Benton family servants, was ready to go west again. So, too, was William Chinook, the young native man who had come east with John in 1844 and was now desperate to return to Oregon. John and Senator Benton had arranged for him to spend the previous nine months with a family in Philadelphia, but nine months was too long. William was so depressed that his hosts summoned a physician, who reported that "he seems drooping & anxious about his return," and "eager to join his old friend Captain Frémont to whom he seems much attached." Informed that it was time to go, he came down the coast to Washington bearing a Bible he'd been given by his hosts, and said that he had "been a Quaker all winter." Doubtless he was also wearing white men's clothes, although his "old friend" Captain Frémont was unimpressed, later writing a patronizing description of William speaking pidgin English and unchanged in his Indian ways. William would travel with John as far as St. Louis, where an Indian agent would help connect him with travelers bound toward his home along the Oregon Trail.

A steamboat glided up to the St. Louis waterfront and deposited John with his companions on May 30, 1845. The publicity of the expedition had

preceded them, and when John organized a meeting for potential recruits, he was mobbed. The crowd overflowed the warehouse where he had
planned to speak, forcing him to adjourn to a nearby park, where men were
so frantic to catch his attention that he could not get a word in. He escaped
the meeting, only to have men follow him back to his lodgings. In the days
afterward he managed to interview men who wanted to work for him even
though he offered miserable wages. Thomas S. Martin of Tennessee nearly
turned down the job when he learned the pay was just fifteen dollars per
month, but the captain proposed a compromise: he would "name no wages
at present," but if Martin went along he would "make everything satisfactory." So alluring was the work that Martin agreed. More than ninety men
enrolled, and in June they started west on a Missouri River steamboat, aiming to pick up animals at the Missouri border as John had done before.

Enthusiasm for American empire was peaking that spring and summer
of 1845. This was the season when a thousand emigrants to Oregon departed from Independence, Missouri, with many embarking from other
points. In Washington, President Polk was preparing his first diplomatic
proposal to divide Oregon with Britain, with the southern part attaching
to the United States and the northern part to British Canada. He faced
public pressure to take it all ("Fifty-four forty or fight!" was the slogan, re-
ferring to the Oregon country's northern border, surely one of the few slo-
gans in American political history that turned on a popular interest in
latitudes). When the British rejected his proposal due to an apparent mis-
communication, Polk withdrew his plan, demanded all of Oregon, and
began making preparations for war; perhaps the new ship *Princeton*, with
its powerful gun Oregon, really would prove itself on the Oregon coast. It
was possible that the United States could be fighting *two* wars, because the
annexation of Texas was proceeding. The Post Office was establishing service from New Orleans to the Texas port of Galveston. Captain Robert F.
Stockton, creator of the *Princeton*, sailed into the Gulf of Mexico for an

ostensibly friendly visit at the Mexican port of Veracruz. He then steamed up to the Texas coast and plotted, unsuccessfully, to raise a private army of Texans to march against Mexico.

In his essay that summer declaring "our manifest destiny to overspread the continent," journalist John L. O'Sullivan began picturing the United States after that destiny was realized. The Pacific coast would be connected to the East by a transcontinental railroad. Alongside the tracks would march a long row of wooden poles bearing copper wire. "The day cannot be distant," he wrote, when congressmen would travel to Washington from the Pacific coast in less time than it once took from Ohio. Just as soon, "the magnetic telegraph will enable the editors of the 'San Francisco Union,' the 'Astoria Evening Post,' or the 'Nootka Morning News,' to set up in type the first half of the President's Inaugural before the echoes of the latter half shall have died away beneath the lofty porch of the Capitol." Once they had a fully connected continent, Americans' "yearly multiplying millions" would dominate the world; Europe would never be able to compete against "the simple solid weight of two hundred and fifty, or three hundred millions—and American millions—destined to gather beneath the flutter of the stripes and stars, in the fast hastening year of the Lord 1945!"

The new secretary of the navy was the historian George Bancroft, the man who, after Polk's nomination, had written that territorial expansion was "the manifest purpose of Providence." He was a New England minister's son who became a teacher and then the author of a multivolume history of the United States, which began with an epigraph: "Westward the star of empire takes its way." He'd gone into politics in 1837, when Martin Van Buren appointed him the federal collector of customs in Boston. His power of patronage (the men he hired included fellow writer Nathaniel Hawthorne, appointed a "measurer of coal and salt") and his power of the pen had given him influence when he swung his support to Polk at the Democratic convention. Polk brought him to Washington, where he could nudge the star of empire on its way. Around the time of the inauguration, according to Bancroft, Polk sat with him and, slapping a hand on his thigh for emphasis, named four main goals. Two were standard Democratic priorities: low tariffs and an independent treasury system, a predecessor of the Federal Reserve. The third was settling possession of Oregon. The fourth was California. Bancroft ordered extra navy ships to the California coast, and made plans to assign a new, aggressive commander to the Pacific squadron: Robert F. Stockton of the USS *Princeton*.

✳ ✳ ✳

THE MORE THAN NINETY MEN Captain Frémont assembled in St. Louis included some reliable old hands. Theodore Talbot was with him again. Basil Lajeunesse, John's favorite companion on two previous journeys, signed up for the third. Alex Godey, another Frenchman, joined the party as he had the last. Kit Carson would be summoned to join the expedition on its way west, and he would bring a friend, Richard Owens, who was as experienced as Carson. John thought of Godey, Owens, and Carson as the elite of his party, and his most recent report included an anecdote illustrating what he admired about them. Returning home from the previous expedition in April 1844, the men encountered a Mexican trading party that had been victimized by Indian horse thieves. Though they had no stake in the matter, Carson and Godey volunteered to track down the thieves and punish them. The two rode back into camp a day later, driving a band of recovered horses and bearing "two bloody scalps, dangling from the end of Godey's gun." Frémont considered this a "disinterested" act of justice performed by this diverse pair of his countrymen—"the former an *American* . . . the latter a Frenchman, born in St. Louis." The mapmaker Charles Preuss witnessed the same scene and found it revolting: "The more noble Indian takes from the killed enemy only a piece of the scalp as large as a dollar. . . . These two heroes . . . brought along the entire scalp." Preuss thought that John simply admired the men for drawing blood: "I believe he would exchange all [his scientific] observations for a scalp taken by his own hand."

Although Preuss's dark commentaries would be missing on the latest expedition, the "botanical colourist" Edward M. Kern was also skilled as a topographer and could carry out both roles. John filled out the force by recruiting twelve men of the Delaware Nation, mainly as hunters, though he appreciated their skill in a fight. Two of the men were chiefs, who gave their names as Swanok and Jim Sagundai. The Delawares were dressed and equipped in a fashion similar to that of the white men; a drawing of Jim Sagundai showed a mustached man with strong features, wearing a buckskin coat. He had a knife tucked in his belt and another hooked on his chest, and a rifle at hand; the only hint of a different tradition of warfare was the spiked war club he rested comfortably on his knee as he took a seat. The presence of so many Frenchmen and Delawares ensured that English would be just one of several languages spoken on the trail.

They were getting a late start, moving out in June rather than May, so he set them sweeping across the prairie, not taking the trouble to stop for scientific observations for the first few hundred miles. The "principal objects of the expedition," he knew, "lay in and beyond the Rocky Mountains." As they hurried forward, some of the men chafed under John's command. Several quit the expedition, saying the captain was imposing conditions to which they had not agreed. Later, a group of men shot at prairie dogs for sport and accidentally shot a mule; as punishment the captain decreed that they must walk instead of ride for ten days, leading their horses. A few days later the men on foot shot a buffalo, and Captain Frémont relented, saying they could remount as a reward.

On the high plains approaching the Rockies, the travelers "encountered a Cheyenne village which was out on a hunt. The men came to meet us on the plain, riding abreast and their drums sounding. They were in all their bravery, and the formidable line was imposing." His men fingered their weapons. The approaching Cheyennes proved to be friendly and rode alongside the explorers for several days, but John's men remained watchful and tense. One night a man posted as a sentry let an ember from his pipe get in his powder horn; the explosion startled the camp, and even the pipe smoker, into thinking they faced an Indian attack.

One day an animal strayed from camp. Basil Lajeunesse took a companion to look for it, and they too vanished. A day and a night passed. Captain Frémont ordered most of the men to remain in camp and went out with a group of searchers. It was open countryside, sometimes offering vistas for miles, but not as flat as it seemed; subtle dips and rises obscured much of the landscape from view, and it emerged that Basil and his companion were only a few miles from camp. John spied the missing men and decided to play a prank. "Throwing off the greater part of our clothes we raised an Indian yell and charged. But there was no hesitation with them. They were off their horses in an instant and their levelled pieces brought us to abrupt halt and a hearty laugh." He could have been killed by friendly fire, but so enjoyed playing Indian that he decided to try it again when returning to camp. His group charged their comrades with "the usual yell. Our charge gave them a good lesson, though it lasted but a moment. It was like charging into a beehive; there were so many men in the camp ready with their rifles that it was very unsafe to keep up our Indian character. . . . Still, like all excitements, it stirred the blood pleasantly for the moment."

Reaching Bent's Fort a little east of the Rockies, he bought supplies and divided the party. Two junior officers separated from John at the head of thirty-three men, following John's original orders to map the rivers in the area before turning back to St. Louis. On August 16, 1845, John started west again with the bulk of his force, a "well-appointed compact party of sixty; mostly experienced and self-reliant men, equal to any emergency likely to occur and willing to meet it." He paused briefly on August 20 to read the sun and the stars. He was once again near the 38th parallel, about 1,600 miles almost due west of Washington, D.C. He was about 1,200 miles due east of Sutter's Fort; it was just a bit farther to San Francisco Bay.

They spent the autumn traversing little-known parts of the Great Basin, naming landmarks as they went; John had realized that a mapmaker could claim that privilege. One of the Delaware leaders, Sagundai, found a spring where they camped one evening, so John decreed it Sagundai's Spring. Encountering a river, the captain declared it the Humboldt after the geographer who inspired his mentor Joseph Nicollet. Reaching the western lip of the Great Basin, he confronted the Sierra Nevada, and here he divided his force of sixty, sending most men and supplies well south to outflank the highest and coldest of the mountains and enter California by a comparatively safe route. The captain said he would meet them on the far side after his smaller party of fifteen pushed directly over the mountains west of Lake Tahoe. It was a gamble to cross the mountains this far north so late in the season, and it created the risk of a desperate struggle like that of 1844; but he wanted the pass to form part of his new route to Oregon, so he started upward, scanning the sky as he went. At 5,900 feet above sea level the riders passed a glittering lake, eleven miles of water tucked between rock faces and smooth as a mirror. It would someday be called Donner Lake, after the party of emigrants who took a similar late-year gamble there in 1846 and got trapped in the snow—but for John's men in 1845, the weather held. The sky stayed clear as they crossed the divide at 7,200 feet and followed westerly streams down to John Sutter's land near sea level. The crossing was easy—it had taken only a few days—the sort of anticlimax that tended to start John Charles Frémont looking for new chances to prove himself.

✳ ✳ ✳

THE LAND THEY WERE ENTERING was a world apart. Geography had made it so: California's great Central Valley, stretching 450 miles north to south, was deeply isolated by mountain peaks, deserts, and ocean. Although it was alluring country, temperate in all seasons and watered by the annual snowmelt from the mountains, the difficulty in reaching it meant that California had been settled by Europeans much later than other parts of the Americas. Spanish conquistadors, who controlled the Aztec empire to the south by 1521, failed to seriously penetrate California for almost two and a half centuries afterward. It was so hazy in the European mind that early maps displayed it as an island, and its great anchorage at San Francisco Bay went undiscovered for generations. All the British colonies on the Atlantic coast and all the Spanish and Portuguese dominions of South America were established before the colonization of California. Not until 1768 did the landscape meet its match, in Father Junípero Serra, a Spanish cleric who walked much of the way from the Baja California peninsula to San Francisco Bay, founding a string of Catholic missions as he went. Clerics sought to teach the arts of Spanish Catholic civilization to the native population— several hundred thousand people who, until then, had enjoyed California's plenty for many centuries undisturbed. Alta, or Upper, California became a department separate from the peninsula of Baja, or Lower, California.

The northernmost of all the missions was in a valley above the Bay of San Francisco, at a settlement called Sonoma. By the time John's men were approaching California in 1845, this mission, like the others, was closed, its adobe buildings dilapidated; the government of independent Mexico had secularized the missions, seizing the vast lands the clerics controlled. In theory the land should have reverted to the Indians, but in reality colonial administrators made immense land grants to settlers, who developed ranchos, vast farms alive with cattle. The land was worked by Indians, poorer settlers, foreign migrants, and anyone else the owners could find in their sparsely populated world. At Sonoma the largest landowner was Mariano G. Vallejo, the son of a Spanish soldier, who built an enormous house and military barracks near the mission, on Sonoma's central square. He was called General Vallejo, for he had once commanded Alta California's scanty armed forces. He now held a less expansive post, overseeing affairs in northern California, which gave him responsibility for dealing with American settlers as they came over the Sierra Nevada into the Central Valley. Several hundred had done so in recent years, usually following the California

Trail—crossing the Rockies at South Pass, then angling southwestward across the Great Basin toward San Francisco Bay, mostly settling near the bay or at points north.

In December 1845, a messenger arrived in front of Vallejo's house, which had a balcony stretching the full width of the second floor, a sloping roof of red Spanish tile, and a kind of castle tower looming over one corner. The messenger pounded on the wooden door and delivered a letter to General Vallejo, who settled down to read it. He had a youthful face, with dark hair and thick sideburns that reached almost to his lips. Although not yet forty, he was known for his dignity and patience, and commanded the respect normally accorded an older man. He was tied by blood or friendship to many of California's leading figures, as well as to some of the foreigners who settled there; American migrants to California had married two of his sisters. General Vallejo favored immigration, knowing that foreigners brought skills and boosted the population in ways that Mexico's central government did not—Californians sometimes felt so abandoned by Mexico City that they talked of attaching themselves to Britain or France. Vallejo had been thinking that California's destiny lay with the United States. But for the moment he had duties as a leading Mexican citizen, and when the message arrived at his house at the end of 1845, he did not like what he read. The letter came from John Sutter at his fort on the Sacramento River. It said that a small number of Americans had arrived—a US Army officer at the head of a few men. They were purchasing horses and other supplies. They seemed to have been in the country for several weeks already. Vallejo was troubled to have been notified so late, and wrote instructions on the back of the letter for his secretary.

> *Charge [Sutter], in the quickest way possible, to send detailed information about the new immigrants, a thing which has always been done in similar circumstances, even in case of small parties, which he inopportunely failed to do when it was most necessary and, even, urgent.*

Everyone knew that American settlers had seized Texas in 1836, leading to fear of a repeat in California. In 1840 a few settlers had talked up a Texas-style revolution, prompting the government to temporarily deport them. With the US annexation of Texas beginning to make war seem likely in 1845, Mexican authorities tightened restrictions for migrants, insisting that new arrivals ask for passports in order to remain in California. Because the newly arrived party of men had yet to do so, they were undocumented immigrants. Vallejo wanted more information, though he also hesitated to raise a military force to hunt down the interlopers. He waited for clarity on who they were and what they intended to do.

Frémont's campsite near snowcapped Mount Shasta.

Chapter Eight

THE SPANIARDS WERE SOMEWHAT
RUDE AND INHOSPITABLE

CAPTAIN FRÉMONT, 1845–1846

California and Oregon

The newcomers at Sutter's Fort were John Frémont's fifteen men. They soon rode away, searching for the larger party of their comrades who had taken the southerly route. They passed through groves of enormous trees. They moved alongside hundreds of elk, which at one point made "a broken band several miles in length" along the route. They didn't find their comrades, but encountered groups of natives—"horse-thief Indians," as John called them. These marauding bands were said to be "mission Indians," who had been educated by the old missions in the ways of white civilization. Cut loose when the Mexican government secularized the missions and took the land—perhaps the cruelest lesson that civilization taught them about itself—many retreated into the mountains, descending to annoy the settlers who had taken from them. Indians tried to steal the expedition's spare horses, and John's men opened fire, killing several. John came upon one of his men facing a lone Indian. The Indian had a bow and arrow; the American shot him with a rifle.

Returning to Sutter's Fort without finding his men—he was confident they would turn up eventually—John decided to visit authorities in Monterey to obtain a passport. Sutter had sailboats that he used for trade on the rivers, and John caught a ride with eight men, gliding through the delta where the Sacramento River met the San Joaquin. When the boat emerged on San Francisco Bay, John thought it resembled "an interior lake of deep water, lying between parallel ridges of mountains . . . crowned by a forest of the lofty cypress." On the water, he saw a knob of rock known as Alcatraz Island, and beyond it the misty channel that led to the Pacific. Daniel Webster had been right when he told John over dinner of the bay's value; *this* harbor could become the American gateway to Asia, the seaport Senator Benton had always envisioned in Oregon. John began thinking about what to name the harbor entrance (the Mexican landscape, in his mind, was already his to name), and as a student of Roman and Greek literature he remembered the Golden Horn, the name of the harbor at Constantinople from which the ancient Roman empire conducted trade with Asia. He named the entrance to his harbor Chrysopylae, or the Golden Gate.

Near the harbor mouth was a dilapidated Spanish presidio, or military base. Its old cannons protected a little town called Yerba Buena. Coming ashore, John found a local merchant named William Leidesdorff, who served as the American vice-consul and who welcomed John into his home, "one of the best among the few" in town, where he lived with his "girl-like" Russian wife in "a low bungalow sort of adobe house with a long piazza facing the bay for the sunny mornings, and a cheerful fire within against the fog and chill of the afternoons." Leidesdorff was originally from the Caribbean, a man of mixed race—the son of a Danish father and a mulatto woman. He had emigrated to the United States and had become a US citizen when living in New Orleans. It was said that his appearance suggested "considerable Negro blood," which limited his ability to pass as white; but he had found ways to escape the strict racial categorizations of his adopted country. He had managed to be appointed a ship's captain, who made a port call in California in 1841 and then settled there when the ship was sold out from under him. In this remote location he was able to rise according to his ability. He became a merchant. He obtained thirty-five thousand acres in the countryside from the Mexican government, which was comparatively open to people of mixed race. When he accepted the job of vice-consul at Yerba Buena, he apparently became the United States's first-ever diplomat of color. He was hired by the consul, who was based in Monterey, while the slave-owning president in far-off Washington surely did not realize his background. Now John settled by Leidesdorff's fire. He learned that he could send a letter from California's coast—ships regularly sailed down the coast to Mazatlán, Mexico, from which letters were carried overland to the Gulf of Mexico and placed on boats to the United States—and it was possibly the sight of Leidesdorff's young Russian wife that reminded John of the person he needed to write.

What could a man say after eight months away from his wife? He tried to summarize what he had been doing. He reported crossing a new part of the Great Basin, and finding the landscape "so at variance" with previous descriptions of it that "it is fair to consider this country has been hitherto wholly unexplored, and never before visited by a white man." He said he had been correct that no rivers escaped this interior zone: "I find the theory of our Great Basin fully confirmed." He said he had found a better route to California, and seemed anxious to get the credit, sensitive to the criticism that he mostly explored trails that were previously discovered: "I wish this [new route] known to your father, as now, that *the journey has been made,* it may be said this too was already known." In its list of accomplishments and points subtly scored, John's letter resembled a newspaper opinion article. He probably knew that Jessie, without being asked, would arrange for a newspaper to publish it. Only toward the end did his tone grow personal.

I am going now on business to see some gentlemen on the coast, and will then join my people, and complete our survey in this part of the world as rapidly as possible. The season is now just arriving when vegetation is coming out in all the beauty I have often described to you. . . . So soon as the proper season comes, and my animals are rested, we turn our faces homeward, and be sure that grass will not grow under our feet. . . . Many months of hardships, close trials, and anxieties have tried me severely, and my hair is turning gray before its time. But all this passes, et le bon temps viendra [and the good time will come].

Vice-consul Leidesdorff escorted John to Monterey, 110 miles down the coast, riding through the cattle-grazing lands of ranchos in the San Jose Valley and over low mountains to Monterey Bay. The hillsides were covered with pines and free of undergrowth, so elegantly organized by nature that one visitor said the landscape had "the appearance of an extensive park." Monterey lay on the sweeping curve of the bay shore, a town of only a few hundred people. A tiny cathedral stood there with a white sandstone front and curving roofline of a sort that was familiar throughout Latin America. Red-roofed adobe houses were scattered around. Cannons at the presidio guarded the town, though the guns were so old and the soldiers so few that it was indefensible. In 1842, when a US Navy captain received a mistaken report of war between the United States and Mexico, he had sent sailors and Marines ashore and captured Monterey without resistance, departing only when he was persuaded there was no war after all. Captain Frémont surely knew this, and just as surely studied the defenses when he arrived on January 26, 1846.

The vice-consul led him through town to the home of Thomas O. Larkin, the American consul—a trim man in his forties, with a cleft chin, thoughtful eyes, bushy sideburns, and graying hair. He was a New Englander by birth, as Frémont could have guessed as soon as he arrived at

Larkin's house. On Calle Principal, the main street, Larkin had built a two-story home with features that drew more from New England than from Mexico. Although the adobe brick walls were the same material as most houses in Monterey, the nine-pane windows, central staircase, and upstairs fireplace all spoke of the North Atlantic coast. Instead of a Spanish tile roof he had paid workmen to nail down redwood shingles. The New Englander had connections to California's elite: his half brother had come to California before him and was one of the two Americans who married into the family of General Vallejo in Sonoma. Larkin himself, after thirteen years in California, was a successful merchant and a player in local politics, sometimes lending money to California officials. In his role as consul he didn't receive much support from home—he complained that the State Department was regularly rejecting his expenses, even refusing to reimburse $31.34 he paid for a United States flag and staff—but he saw his future in a California that was part of the United States.

John had never met Larkin but probably had seen his work. The New Englander was the source of some of the stories about California that were appearing in eastern newspapers. A man like Larkin in some remote place could write a letter to an editor such as James Gordon Bennett, who controlled the *New York Herald* with its nationwide circulation—and if Bennett judged the information credible and entertaining, or at least entertaining, he might publish the letter as an article. Larkin's letters were the ones describing California as paradise. He wrote of sailors from visiting American warships who "spent their leisure time ashore hunting wild deer or dancing with the tame dear, both being plenty in and about Monterey." Beautiful women were just one of the attractions: "What do you think of a salmon weighing sixty pounds, and other fish every day in the year?" In 1844, as the looming annexation of Texas raised the prospect of war with the United States, one of Larkin's dispatches suggested that Mexicans would not defend Monterey. The same year he extolled the raw but healthy state of the country: "We have . . . no elections, nor political mobs; no doctors nor much sickness; no surgeons, nor those with amputated limbs; no lawyers, therefore no court-houses nor prisons . . . Solomon, in all his glory, was not more happy than a Californian." California was a dreamland—sunny, abundant, whimsical, undeveloped, and available to the first nation that came to take it.

✳ ✳ ✳

LARKIN WAS AN EFFECTIVE CONSUL. "I never make to the Government an unreasonable request, therefore never expect denial, and have for many years found them well disposed toward me," he told John. After the captain had a night's sleep in Monterey, Larkin took him around town to have his visit to California properly authorized. They could not meet the governor of California, who had temporarily moved to Los Angeles, so Larkin sought other officials, of whom the most important was José Castro, the commander of the department's military forces.

General Castro was in his late thirties, a man of John's generation, solidly built, with bushy hair and sideburns connecting with his mustache. He owned a magnificent uniform but had few troops to command. Whenever Castro needed an army he had to raise it from the colonial population, recruiting men to meet this or that Indian war. But he was capable of making trouble, and John set out to pacify him. He said he was a lone US Army officer, and that his men were civilians; he was simply exploring the best route from the United States to Oregon. He said he would keep his men away from Mexican settlements, except when they needed to purchase supplies, and that he would leave for Oregon as soon as his men had rested and refitted. In response, General Castro apparently avoided ordering Captain Frémont to leave, while also not quite authorizing his visit. He was finessing the situation—he knew Mexico's government would view the captain's appearance with alarm, but did not want a confrontation. For the record, Castro wrote out a formal request to Larkin for information about the expedition. Larkin then wrote out a formal explanation, and Castro did not reply.

Returning to the interior, John at last united the two wings of his force and moved them to an abandoned rancho on the far eastern side of the Santa Clara Valley, well east of Monterey. Curious Californians came to meet them. John said the locals showed off their horsemanship, and "very friendly relations grew up with us," but not for long. The captain learned that three of his men had gone off drunk and insulted Californians. For this he apologized. But he responded differently when a Californian came to accuse the expedition of stealing horses, a charge John indignantly denied. He followed up with an intemperate letter to a Mexican civil official, declaring that the accuser was not only wrong but offensive, and should have received "a severe horsewhipping" for opening his mouth. Forgetting that he was a visitor whose problematic presence was barely tolerated, he had swiftly become an entitled local who imagined he had every right to be where he was. He demonstrated more of this attitude in late February, when the expedition broke camp and moved out. Traveling to Oregon required John to ride north—yet he did not. He moved westward, across the Santa Clara Valley and over a chain of coastal mountains. He camped near the summit, studying groves of two-hundred-foot redwood trees, then drifted even farther westward, down to the Pacific, aiming for the coastal settlement of Santa Cruz.

This was a fateful provocation. It was impossible to pretend that he was keeping his promise to stay out of settled areas. Was he trying to trigger a Mexican attack that would justify a war? Probably not; this would require Machiavellian strategic foresight that he did not demonstrate elsewhere. Did he have a vague intention to kill time until news arrived of a declaration of war? This was plausible. In a letter that spring he wrote that a declaration of war was "probable," and he sent a note to Larkin in Monterey, asking for "any intelligence you may have received from the States." He may have thought his mission was simply to wait and see what came up. But if it was his plan to wait for news, he could have done it safely in the interior. Why wander to the settled coastline where he had promised not to go? Usually when he defied authority he had a reason that made sense, at least to him. In later years he would give several explanations, most of which could be disproven by surviving documents. But there was one explanation John gave that was plausible and fit his increasingly entitled frame of mind. He said he was shopping for real estate.

"I had before my mind the home I wished to make in this country," he explained. "First one place and then another charmed me. But none seemed perfect where the sea was wanting, and so far I had not stood by the open waves of the Pacific. . . . [Only the coastline had] the invigorating salt breeze which brings with it renewed strength. This I wanted for my mother." He had loved the sea since he was a boy. His happiest moments had been spent in places where "the eye ranges over a broad expanse of country, or in the face of the ocean," walking the Battery alone or exploring the shore with Cecilia. Now he sought to recover that feeling on the western coast, and had heard that Santa Cruz was especially beautiful. John Charles Frémont risked war between the United States and Mexico because he wanted to shop for beachfront property to share with his mother.

After inspecting Santa Cruz he drifted southeastward, farther from Oregon and nearer Monterey. He camped a few miles outside the capital at the start of March, and messengers began passing between the camp and Thomas Larkin's New England house in town. In a letter to Larkin, he suggested that he was passing time until the snow melted in the mountains. He also suggested he was technically following his promise to stay away from settlements because he was not bringing his main force into the center of Monterey: "I therefore practice the selfdenial which is a constant virtue here and forego the pleasure I should have found in seeing some little of society in your capital."

The day that Captain Frémont sent this letter was the day California's

General Castro lost patience. Apparently someone disturbed the general's breakfast with news of the wandering Americans. He wrote a letter and gave it to Larkin to translate for Frémont.

At seven o'clock this morning [I] was given to understand that you and the party under your command have entered the towns of this Department, and such being prohibited by our laws I find myself obligated to advertise you that on the receipt of this you will immediately retire beyond the limits of this same Department.

Larkin wrote a letter in reply, trying to smooth over the dispute by urging General Castro and another official, the Monterey prefect, to avoid any "unfortunate" clashes based on "false reports, or false appearances." The prefect responded with mounting anger that there was no false appearance: Frémont was right there, and "must now either blindly obey the authorities or on the contrary experience the misfortunes which he has sought by his crime." Larkin watched with alarm as General Castro began summoning armed men. Sixty men went up the road toward the Americans, then another forty, and Larkin expected that Castro might gather another hundred. The general also issued a proclamation warning of "a band of robbers commanded by a Capt. of the U.S. Army, J.C. Frémont," and calling for all citizens to report to his headquarters to help him "lance the ulcer."

Outside town, Captain Frémont was defiant. When a Californian delivered Castro's demand to depart immediately or face the consequences, John said it was an insult to the United States and that he would not retreat in shame. (His subordinate Theodore Talbot summarized John's position in a letter: "Captain said that he wd leave the country, but wd not be driven out.") His men broke camp, but only to move to higher and more defensible ground, a mountain called Gavilan Peak. They raised an American flag while John used his spyglass to watch California troops and artillery gather below. Soon a courier from Larkin arrived bearing a letter, which John did not take time to read before replying, scrawling a note in pencil so that the same messenger could carry it back down to Monterey. "I am making myself as strong as possible," he told Larkin, "in the intention that if we are unjustly attacked we will fight to the extremity and refuse quarter, trusting to our country to avenge our death." He added:

> *I thank you for your kindness and good wishes and would write more at length as to my intentions, did I not fear that my letter will be intercepted; we have in no wise done wrong to the people or the authorities of the country, and if we are hemmed in and assaulted, we will die every man of us, under the Flag of our Country. Very truly yours,*
>
> *J.C. Frémont*

The captain envisioned himself a martyr. He might have imagined his struggle would win California for his country: his words echoed an earlier letter from a confrontation between Mexicans and Americans. In 1836, when Texas rebels were surrounded at the Alamo by thousands of Mexican troops, the Texan commander William Travis slipped a messenger through enemy lines with a note: "I am determined to sustain myself as long as possible & die like a soldier who never forgets what is due to his own honor & that of his country. Victory or Death." It was said that Travis's sacrifice inspired other Texans to victory. But it was also true that Travis and his men died in a pointless effort to hold an indefensible position from which he had been ordered to retreat, and in 1846 Captain Frémont had wiser second thoughts. He finally opened and read Larkin's letter to him. It was a sober warning that if John did not have orders from Washington authorizing his incursion, then he was in trouble, because he was violating Mexican law. Even if John's force could defend itself, warfare with the Mexicans would "cause trouble hereafter to Resident Americans." American settlers, already under pressure, could face collective punishment. That night John's men broke camp and slipped away. It was a good time to head for Oregon.

✳ ✳ ✳

THEY RODE NORTH PAST SAN FRANCISCO BAY, past Sutter's Fort, and through the flatlands at the heart of the Sacramento River Valley. By the first of April they were almost three hundred miles north of Monterey. One night the captain brought out his sextant and calculated that he was near 40 degrees latitude, a little less than two hundred miles from the Oregon border.

Two men asked permission to quit the expedition and return to the United States. Captain Frémont agreed, realizing that he could give one of the men a letter to carry home to Jessie. He took out some paper to write by the fire. Informing his wife of the confrontation and retreat from Monterey, he put the best face on it. "The Spaniards," he told her, "were somewhat rude and inhospitable."

> My sense of duty did not permit me to fight them, but we retreated slowly and growlingly before a force of three or four hundred men, and three pieces of artillery. . . . Of course I did not dare to compromise the United States, against which appearances would have been strong; but, although it was in my power to increase my party by many Americans, I refrained from committing a solitary act of hostility.

The letter was revealing, and not only because he probably inflated the size of the Mexican force at Gavilan Peak. By saying he could have increased his party "by many Americans," he meant that he could recruit the American settlers of California just as Castro had called out the Californians. He still had this option. He was moving among settlers in the Sacramento Valley, stopping at some of their ranchos. One offered to raise a force of "hardy warriors," an offer John declined for the moment. Another settler had already served under his command: Samuel Neal, who had come to California with the expedition in 1844, and dropped off at Sutter's Fort to start a new life.

John was acting like a settler himself, allowing himself to be drawn into local disputes. Some said they feared attack by Indians, and the captain responded by vowing to protect them. It was not clear what disagreements—over control of land or resources—might have led to this fear of war. But having made a grandiose promise, John had to keep it, and he decided to strike the Indians a crippling blow. It was a significant change in policy. In all his travels he had never fought a full-scale battle with natives, despite occasional episodes such as the fight with the "horse-thief Indians." He normally came among Indians while carrying the lamps of science and reason. Not all had responded well to him—in early 1844 one of his men had wandered off alone and had been killed—but John's men rarely fired first, instead keeping well armed and on guard. Why would he now take the side of white settlers he had just met, by launching an armed conflict the origins of which he did not understand?

Captain Frémont said he could not leave the settlers defenseless. They suspected California's General Castro was sending messengers to rile up the Indians against white people. John embraced this fear, taking up a racial stereotype of natives at odds with his experience: "An Indian let loose is of all animals the most savage. He has an imagination for devilment that seems peculiar to him, and a singular delight in inflicting suffering." But on this occasion it was white men who took a "delight in inflicting suffering." His scouts found a village where men had "feathers on their heads, and faces painted black, their war color," as if preparing for combat. The main body of John's men charged, killing some natives and driving others into a nearby river. The horsemen rode on to several more villages, whose inhabitants scattered. One of the Americans, Thomas S. Martin, later declared in an oral history that the attackers killed 175 Indians. Martin's guess was probably high—all the numbers in his oral history were unreliable—but there was no reason to doubt the visceral statement of Kit Carson: "We found [the natives] to be in great force. . . . We attacked them, and although I do not know how many we killed, it was a perfect butchery. The survivors fled in all directions."

∗ ∗ ∗

PUSHING NORTH TOWARD OREGON, the expedition rode past Mount Shasta, a snowbound volcano that loomed over the valley and blended into the clouds. They departed the Sacramento Valley and climbed into mountains and high plains, a land of extinct volcanoes and lava fields long since grown over with forest. By early May they were in Oregon and riding past Klamath Lake, its waters ringed by mountains. They had seen this landmark during their wanderings of 1843–44, and John had a hazy idea to track down a friendly native chief he'd met. But the first Klamath Indians he saw this time were not welcoming. "Our arrival took them by surprise, and though they received us with apparent friendship, there was no warmth in it, but a shyness which came naturally from their habit of hostility." Captain Frémont did not understand why Indians who'd been living safely beyond the range of white settlement might be concerned by the explorers' sudden appearance. One day a group of Klamath men walked into the explorers' camp, asking for food and possibly sizing up the visitors.

A few evenings later the men of the expedition had settled around their fires when they "caught the faint sound of horses' feet." The men waited quietly, listening, hands near their guns. "There emerged from the darkness—into the circle of the firelight—two horsemen, riding slowly as though horse and man were fatigued by long traveling." John was surprised to recognize both men—two California settlers, including his former subordinate Samuel Neal. They said they were the vanguard of a small party that had been looking for John, escorting a messenger from the United States. In the morning Neal and Frémont rode back down the trail to meet the messenger, accompanied by ten chosen men including Carson and Basil

Lajeunesse and a few Delawares. Late that day they found him, a white man accompanied by a black servant and two more California settlers. The messenger and his servant had come all the way from Washington, D.C., which he had departed the previous autumn.

It was too late in the day to ride back to the main force. John decided to spend the night in a cedar grove, where the messenger told his story by the fire. His name was Archibald H. Gillespie, and his servant was Benjamin Harrison. Gillespie was a marine lieutenant traveling undercover in civilian clothes. He was thirty-three, the same age as John; the firelight showed a man who was lean and weary, with a distinguished-looking Vandyke beard. He was a man of the world. In 1845, having finished two years on a navy vessel that circled the globe, Gillespie asked for an easy shore assignment that would restore his health, but was chosen for the mission to California; the government prized his fluency in Spanish. The exhaustion he felt from sea duty was overcome by the thrill of the new assignment. He visited Washington to receive instructions from Secretary of State Buchanan as well as President Polk. He caught a ship bound for Mexico, then traveled overland across the center of the country, boldly making observations about Mexico's preparations for war and mailing letters back to Washington. He told Mexican customs officers and anyone else who inquired that he was a businessman traveling for his health, and offered papers to back up this cover story. He had other, more incriminating papers that he memorized and burned, intending to write them out again once he reached California.

At Mexico's Pacific port of Mazatlán, he caught up with a visiting US Navy ship, whose captain obligingly welcomed him on board and set sail for Monterey as if on a regular patrol. On arrival, the traveling American paid his respects to the American consul Thomas Larkin. Revealing his true identity, he delivered a letter that he had since restored to written form—a letter from Secretary of State Buchanan. It informed Larkin that he had been appointed to a new position as a "confidential agent" of President Polk, authorized to conduct certain covert operations and paid six dollars per day. Larkin was to use his influence to conciliate Californians to the United States, peacefully preparing the way for eventual American rule. "The future Destiny of that Country," Buchanan said, "is a subject of anxious solicitude for the Government and People of the United States." The letter specifically said that the United States should *not* take California by compulsion. But President Polk "could not view with indifference the transfer of California to Great Britain or any other European power." Polk was betting that if Europeans could be kept away, California would fall peacefully into American hands.

Seeking Frémont next, Gillespie slipped out of Monterey with Benjamin Harrison and a guide. The American settlers in the Sacramento Valley welcomed their countryman and organized the party that brought him onward to Oregon. Now, sitting by the fire, Gillespie produced more correspondence—letters addressed to Captain Frémont. There was a note from Jessie, the first words he had seen from his wife in almost a year. There was also a letter from Senator Benton. And there was an official letter from Secretary of State Buchanan, though it was merely a greeting and gave John no particular instructions. Gillespie verbally repeated the instructions he had delivered to Larkin—that the consul was to ensure warm relations with Californians and keep European powers out.

The exact nature of John's instructions would prompt generations of controversy. Was he secretly told to conquer California? Neither Gillespie nor Frémont ever said so, though John asserted that he was given a message in a kind of elaborate code. He combined Buchanan's seemingly innocuous letter with Gillespie's words, then mixed in hints and suggestions from Senator Benton's letter, along with John's own memory of past conversations about California in the Benton home. Weaving it all together, John C. Frémont alone understood that he was being given a mission: "The information through Gillespie had absolved me from my duty as an explorer, and I was left to my duty as an officer of the American Army with the further authoritative knowledge that the Government intended to take

California. . . . It was with thorough satisfaction I now found myself required to do what I could to promote this object of the President." So he said long afterward. Benton, also years after the fact, asserted nearly the same.

Their assertions were not quite true, according to the only shred of contemporaneous evidence that suggests what really happened. Although the letters John received did not survive, he wrote a note soon afterward to Senator Benton: "Your letter led me to expect some communication from [Secretary of State Buchanan], *but I received nothing.*" In other words, Senator Benton really did offer his son-in-law a hint that Buchanan's letter would tell him something—but the secretary of state's letter had to complete the thought, and the cautious James Buchanan didn't. Buchanan, the only one who actually held a responsible post in President Polk's administration, either did not want to order John on a covert mission or did not want his fingerprints on it. The attempt to send a signal was botched. It would be easy to imagine Buchanan in the Benton home, assuring his friend that he would of course write a letter with instructions for his son-in-law, and just as easy to imagine that Buchanan thought better of it afterward.

The one unmistakable sign John did have was Gillespie's presence: the Vandyke beard at his campfire was enough to show that John was part of the grand design, whatever it was. Gillespie had come directly from the president, who had given clear enough instructions to Larkin and apparently wanted John to know them so he could assist the consul if needed. John momentarily lost track of himself that night as he considered the prospects. He did not organize the camp as he normally would. He forgot to post guards overnight, and failed to turn in to sleep at a sensible hour. By eleven o'clock that evening the camp had settled down, the men rolling into their blankets while John alone remained awake. "I sat by the fire in fancied security," he said, "going over the home letters. I had about thought out the situation when I was startled by a sudden movement among the animals."

The animals had been left near the lakeshore a hundred yards away from the fires. The captain rose and walked in that direction. He had acquired an innovative new weapon known as a revolver, which would fire several shots without the need to reload; he now drew this weapon and crept through the cedars to look around. Finding nothing amiss, he returned to the fire and resumed his reverie. He resolved that he would halt his exploration of Oregon and plant himself on California soil, even if he was not sure what to do there. The captain at last fell asleep under a cedar.

He was awakened by Kit Carson's voice: "What's the matter over there?" No answer came back. And then Carson shouted, "Indians!" He had been stirred by a noise in the darkness, a sickening sound from within the camp, the sound of an ax chopping.

✳ ✳ ✳

THE MEN HAD TAKEN at least one security precaution. Most slept shielded by darkness, just outside the circles of light from the embers of the fires. Now, alerted by warning cries, they rolled to their guns and watched for targets. Some draped their blankets over tree branches to block flying arrows. When Klamath men ran into the firelight, Carson and several others fired. Their leader went down. The other Klamaths silently withdrew; they used axes, tomahawks, and arrows and never fired a gun. John's men stayed alert the rest of the night, listening to every sound in the bushes, but the Klamaths never returned.

At daylight the captain looked upon the remains of Basil Lajeunesse. The Frenchman had been the first to die; it was the sound of an ax blow to his head that had alerted Kit Carson to the attack. Basil had been John's best companion through three expeditions, a man with whom he had spent much more time than he'd spent with his wife the past four years. A Delaware named Crane was also dead, along with a mixed-race Delaware named Denny, while one more Delaware was injured. The dead Klamath leader still lay near the fires, with an English ax tied to his wrist. Frémont watched as Kit Carson "seized [the ax] and knocked his head to pieces with it, and one of the Delawares, Sagundai, scalped him." Both Carson and Frémont later described this act of rage, destroying the Klamath's head the way that Basil's had been destroyed, which was the only way either man hinted at the emotions they felt.

The survivors draped their comrades' remains over mules and started north to meet the main force, pausing to bury the bodies in a laurel thicket. "With our knives we dug a shallow grave," John said, "and wrapping their blankets round them, left them among the laurels. There are men above whom the laurels bloom who did not better deserve them than my brave Delaware and Basil. I left Denny's name on the creek where he died." Generations later there is still a Denny Creek on the map near Klamath Lake. When the men reached the main camp, the Delawares there blackened their faces and went into mourning. John sat next to a Delaware man who put his hand on his heart and said, "Very sick here." John replied that they would have vengeance, which white men including Carson wanted too. The work of reprisal began the following morning, when the expedition struck camp and moved out. At Sagundai's suggestion, the surviving Delawares stayed behind in hiding—then ambushed and killed two Klamath men who arrived to inspect the vacant campsite.

Over the next two days the force circled Klamath Lake, hoping to sneak up on a Klamath village. Ten men under Carson went ahead of the main force and discovered Klamaths by a riverside. Carson was outnumbered but chose not to wait for reinforcements. He charged, sending the Klamaths fleeing in canoes across the river. His men fired from the river's edge, then the wildly aggressive Carson led his horsemen plunging into the river to continue the chase. Too impatient to find a shallow ford, he went completely underwater with his men after him, soaking their gunpowder, which would have left them helpless on the far bank but for the timely arrival of the main force, which crossed with greater care. The Klamath people continued retreating, leaving their canoes behind. "In one of them," said expedition member Thomas S. Martin, "we found an old Indian woman who had been shot." The attackers burned the canoes and moved on to set fire to the Klamath village, where the houses were made of reed and willow, built beside racks hung with a bountiful harvest of fish. The huts "being dry," Carson said, "the fire was a beautiful sight."

That was how the attack was described by Carson and Martin, who later gave oral histories. John, with Jessie's assistance, wrote an account that improved certain details. He did not say an old woman was killed in a canoe; he said it was a man: "His hand was still grasping the paddle. On his feet were shoes which I thought Basil wore when he was killed." It would be hard to prove that John's account was the false one—but his vignette of poetic justice was too perfect. It was more honorable to have killed a man than a woman, and better still if his shoes proved him to be guilty of the ambush, rather than a victim of collective punishment. This was one of several occasions on which John recorded vivid details—literary details of which he alone took note—that heightened the emotion of his account and tended to minimize, or at least explain, his men's indiscriminate destruction.

There was a gap between Captain Frémont and his men, which was reflected in the differing stories they told. His men talked with brutal frankness; either they did not know that people outside their world might judge their acts to be wrong, or they did not care. John Frémont knew and cared. The life his men led was not quite his; it was a life he visited, knowing he would go home to his world of books and newspapers, cities and civilization. Writing and editing later, in the presence of his wife and with her influence, he sometimes gave his accounts a layer of Victorian varnish. In fairness, the violence still came through, as did John's continuing flashes of humility: he understood that he was less skilled than his men. He recounted a moment after the torching of the Klamath village: The men were riding back to their camp when John came upon a lone Klamath man about to let loose an arrow at Kit Carson. John fired at the attacker and missed. He was no better at shooting from a horse in 1846 than he had been when failing to shoot buffalo on the plains in 1839. Fortunately for Carson, John's horse leaped forward and trampled the man. Sagundai the Delaware chief then rode up and killed him. Carson generously credited Frémont with saving his life—or rather credited him and his horse. "I owe my life to them two," he said.

Returning to camp, the captain gave the reins to Jacob Dodson, and left the young man to care for his horse while he walked to his tent to lie on a blanket and be alone with his thoughts. He was sharing his tent with Lieutenant Gillespie, the marine messenger. He had been with John five days, every one of them spent hunting other people or being hunted, and this was on Gillespie's mind when he entered the tent: "By Heaven, this is rough work," he said. "I'll take care to let them know in Washington." Frémont replied, "Heaven don't come in for much about here just now," adding that before they made it back to Washington they would have "time enough to forget about this."

Part Three

GOLDEN STATE

✴ ✴ ✴

Rapids captured by early Western photographer Carleton Watkins.

The Delaware leader Sagundai.

Chapter Nine

I AM NOT GOING TO LET YOU WRITE
ANYTHING BUT YOUR NAME

LIEUTENANT COLONEL AND JESSIE B. FRÉMONT,
MAY–JULY 1846

California and Washington, D.C.

Threw the next morning the expedition started for California, fighting off small groups of Klamaths as they went. The men descended into the Sacramento Valley, passing the snowy bulk of Mount Shasta and settling at the same rancho from which John had written Jessie a few weeks earlier. He was well north of Sutter's Fort and the Mexican outpost at Sonoma, so he had time to think before the California authorities learned of his presence. His thoughts were grim. Gillespie's messages had suggested that his help was wanted in California, but it wasn't clear what he should do. He doubted his small force could accomplish much in a country so large. He'd recently written a Californian to say that in case of war, "I shall be outnumbered ten to one and be compelled to make good my retreat." Now he wrote to Senator Benton suggesting he did not plan to stay in California long. "I have but a faint hope that this note will reach you before I do," he said. "I shall now proceed directly homewards [and will] arrive at the frontier . . . late in September." He sent this letter eastward, apparently in the hands of Sagundai. The Delaware leader wanted to return home, and volunteered to carry the letter across two thousand miles of mountains and deserts alone. Yet after the horseman rode out of sight in the direction of the Sierra Nevada, John himself made no move to leave California as he had just said he would. His letter to Benton seemed instead to express his own bafflement. He told a Californian he faced "perplexing complications." He didn't know how to influence California or keep it out of European hands. He began a period of indecision, like the two weeks or so he'd spent wandering the Great Basin in the winter of 1844 before acknowledging he must cross the Sierra Nevada to survive. He shifted camp a bit southward, near a mountain range called Sutter Buttes, and awaited news.

A courier arrived, carrying a parcel from Thomas Larkin, the consul on the coast. The parcel did not contain what John most wanted—any information that would guide his course—though Larkin's cover letter did include a tantalizing reference to the instructions both men had received through Lieutenant Gillespie. "You are aware," Larkin said, "that great changes are about to take place in a country we are both acquainted with. To aid this, I am giving up business, holding myself in readiness for the times to come." To pass the time until the change, Larkin also sent news from home. He was a collector of eastern newspapers; whenever a ship arrived, he worked his way through the crew asking after any papers the crew might have, no matter how out of date. Now he shared with the army captain: "I have been keeping some . . . papers . . . but cannot resist the opportunity of sending them to you," he wrote. One contained a "pretty" article that might be suitable for "your published Books of Travels." This may have been an inspiring biographical sketch of Captain Frémont, written by an anonymous author, which had been spreading from newspaper to newspaper across the country. The story said John was "a native of South Carolina, the son of a widow, and the architect of his own fortunes." He had risen to fame from a hardscrabble youth. He was married to a senator's daughter, but succeeded through his own exertions. He was "light and slender in his person, very youthful in appearance, and wholly different from what would be looked for in the leader of such extended and adventurous expeditions . . . a modest looking youth, almost feminine in the delicacy of his person and features." The writer could have been someone who consulted Jessie for information or even Jessie herself; it had been written in Washington, where Jessie was.

An older article in Larkin's bundle told of Jessie. One of her cousins had married the governor of Maryland and then became involved in a messy divorce; "Mrs. Frémont and two sisters attended the court as witnesses." Then there was an article about Indians visiting Senator Benton—a group of Potawatomi, who had once lived near the Great Lakes but had been pushed across the Mississippi. In Washington they paid their respects to the West's leading senator, who welcomed them into his home. They called him a friend, and he solemnly said that he would "always endeavor to do them justice." Refreshments were served, and the conversation widened to include "the members of Col. Benton's family—among whom, we are tempted to remark, was the accomplished lady of a gallant young officer, who has already, by his distinguished service to the government in the wilds between the Missouri and Pacific, achieved for himself a reputation that will be as lasting as it is enviable." According to the version of the article that Larkin had obtained, the natives also tried to meet three-year-old Lily, but "the little one declined an introduction." All these things John read about while recovering from his recent Indian wars.

✳ ✳ ✳

As John read these papers in the late spring of 1846, Jessie was twenty-eight hundred miles away in Washington, D.C. She was living with Lily amid the polished English furniture in the Benton house on C Street. Larkin's newspapers had given accurate, if outdated, information about her life. The messy divorce had actually taken place in 1844: Jessie's teenage cousin was married to the much older governor, who publicly accused her of infidelity, a charge so destructive to a woman's reputation that her family and friends, including the Bentons, helped her sue for libel and staged a public event testifying to her virtue. The meeting with Indians had taken place more recently, in late 1845. They were part of a stream of visitors who paid homage to her father, who remained an oversize figure after a quarter century in the Senate, his movements followed in the papers, his counsel sought at times by the president. In the spring of 1846 his decades-old dream of taking possession of Oregon was becoming reality. President Polk had held for a time to the expansionist demand for all of Oregon ("Fifty-four forty or fight!"), but renewed diplomatic efforts with Britain produced a treaty that split the territory, mostly along the 49th parallel that served elsewhere as the dividing line between the United States and Canada. The Oregon settlers had strengthened the US claim to the southern areas centering on the Columbia River; the British took the Fraser River to the north. In June 1846, Thomas Hart Benton was one of the senators who went into executive session, clearing the galleries so they could privately debate and approve the treaty.

Washington was about to become the capital of a transcontinental nation with a confirmed Pacific coast. The growing capital was rapidly approaching fifty thousand residents, though it still did not impress visitors, for it was designed to be larger and grander than it yet was. Its broad angled avenues allowed magnificent vistas of the city, but in comparison with European capitals there was not much of a city to see. Still, its leading citizens were members of a globalized community with connections to the wider world. The Bentons had purchased their house from an early member of the global elite, who traveled between Washington, Boston, and London. A short walk east of the house was the railway station, where trains led to cities in the northeast; a short walk west, at the National Hotel, was the new office of the Morse telegraph company, which had now strung its wires all the way to Philadelphia and New York. At least half a dozen newspapers offered stories from home and abroad, and advertised a "magnificent collection of valuable European oil paintings" that was offered at auction in June 1846. Sophisticated buyers could also bid on "a very handsome variety of Chinese articles," recently imported and "beautifully ornamented," including "handsome writing desks," tea caddies, and "bamboo book-cases and couches."

Jessie had little time for shopping; she was absorbed in family difficulties. Her mother's health had grown worse, and often Mrs. Benton seemed disoriented. Once, when Senator Benton was entertaining guests at home, his wife appeared before them less than fully dressed. The family had been told by doctors that it would help Mrs. Benton if they appeared cheerful around her, and they strained to keep up the facade. By the spring, Jessie thought, "the disease seems to have expended itself, and she is quite well again." But Jessie could be forgiven for feeling alone. On her fourth wedding anniversary in October 1845, she could only guess where her spouse was. Lily turned three in November. Then Jessie turned twenty-two on May 31, 1846. Visitors to the Benton home naturally inquired after her famous husband, and newspapers asked for information about him; she could give biographical details, as she may have for that laudatory profile, but she struggled as much as anyone for up-to-date news.

In the spring of 1846 she began receiving the first word since St. Louis. Newspapers were given a report via Mazatlán, Mexico, that Captain Frémont had appeared in California, having "discovered a good wagon road to Oregon, which is much shorter than any heretofore travelled." So intently did the country follow his progress that this brief item was reprinted in at least a dozen papers. A few days later came an update reprinted in more than forty newspapers: "Fremont at Monterey." Now she was living the story of his California exploits, in the order that they happened and several months behind. In May she received a letter from her husband—the one he had written by the vice-consul's fire at San Francisco Bay in January ("I am going now on business to see some gentlemen on the coast"). She arranged for its publication, confidently contacting newspaper offices with a scoop. The letter was reprinted in two Washington papers on May 15 and spread across the country. On May 26 a Washington paper published further news: General Castro's demand in early March that John leave California. "We have not the least apprehension for Captain Frémont," the writer cheerfully concluded. His wife could be forgiven if she did not feel the same. But the very next day a letter arrived from Thomas Larkin, reporting her husband's apparently safe retreat.

In mid-June she thought she found a way to communicate with him. A man appeared at the Benton house: James Wiley Magoffin, a Kentuckian who did business in New Mexico. While visiting Washington he met Senator Benton, and Jessie saw an opportunity. When he next went west toward New Mexico, would he take a letter to John, leaving it at Bent's Fort along the way? Magoffin said he would. If John rode home that summer as expected, he would stop at Bent's Fort and discover the letter.

Washington City June 18 1846.

A Mr. Magoffin says he will be at Bent's Fort a month from tomorrow, and that he will leave [this] letter for you. . . . I hope that as I write, you are rapidly nearing home, and that in early September there will be an end to our anxieties. In your dear letter you tell me that le bon temps viendra [the good time will come], and my faith in you is such that I believe it will come: and it will come to all you love, for during your long absence God has been good to us and kept in health your mother & all you love best.

She offered him the love of a spouse and the shrewdness of a public relations counsel. "I had to publish almost all your letter," she reported, "and like everything you write it has been reprinted all over the country." She did not comment on a peculiar feature of his letter—that so much was suitable for publication, with little private sentiment directed to her alone. It was less a love letter than a report to a trusted partner. To be sure, she was proud to be his trusted partner, and proud of him. She had heard that President Polk was about to approve another promotion for the famous explorer—he had been a second lieutenant, then a first lieutenant, then a captain, and now would skip past the next rank, major, to become a lieutenant colonel. "I am sorry," she said, "that I could not be the first to call you Colonel." She said he was "the most talked of and admired Lieut. Col. in the army," and that "almost all the old officers came to congratulate me on it." She insisted that nepotism had nothing to do with the promotion: "It was certainly a free will offering of the President's, neither father nor I nor anyone for us having asked or said we would like it."

There was in this line a hint that Mrs. Frémont was beginning to see a role for herself as a political operative. By denying that she had lobbied for him, she indicated that she *could* lobby for him. Although she was young and a woman, whose assigned sphere did not include politics, she was an "accomplished lady" with an emerging public profile, who knew the top players throughout Congress, the administration, and the army. Some, like James Buchanan, were family friends who had known her all her life. Others, like Senator John Adams Dix of New York, had arrived in the city in recent years to discover a self-possessed, well-informed, and well-connected young woman who sat in on her father's meetings with them and seemed to be as much a part of Washington's landscape as the green copper Capitol dome.

She told her husband how the public was responding to the combined report of his past two expeditions, the masterpiece they had written together. "Its popularity has astonished even me, your most confirmed & oldest worshiper." People compared it to *Robinson Crusoe*: just as Daniel Defoe's tale of a man shipwrecked on a Caribbean island was "the most natural and interesting fiction of travel, so Frémont's report is the most romantically truthful." A British lord from the Royal Geographical Society wrote to say that he was preparing a paper on the report. It was even providing John with his only connection to his three-and-a-half-year-old daughter:

Lily has it read to her . . . as a reward for good behavior. She asked [the mapmaker Charles] Preuss the other day if it was true that he caught ants on his hands and eat them—he was so much amazed that he could not answer her, & she said, "I read it in papa's lepote [report]; it was when you were lost in California."

Editors were writing Jessie for his "biography and likeness." In spite of the evidence that she may have given them information, she claimed she had not yet done so; "I had no orders from you."

You know it would look odd to leave out your age, & you never told me how old you were yet. How old are you? You might tell me now that I am a Col.'s wife—won't you, old papa? Poor papa, it made tears come to find you had begun to turn gray. You must have suffered much and been very anxious.

She was thinking that when he returned, she would help him rest by taking a larger role in his next report: "I am not going to let you write anything but your name when you get home."

Jessie said John's mother had sent a daguerreotype of her son. Jessie hung it over her bed, where it served as her "guardian angel." Even when she was not gazing upon his likeness, he flashed into her head, as when she started reading a history of the Spanish colonization of North America. "I was by myself, Lily asleep, and reading by our lamp, when I came to De Soto's search for the fountain of youth. I stopped, for it seemed as if pleasant old days had returned; and then I remembered so well what you once wrote to me that I could not help bursting into tears."

Do you remember, darling? It was soon after we were married, & you wrote me, "Fear not for our happiness; if the hope for it be not something wilder than the Spaniards' search for the fountain in Florida, we will find it yet." I remembered it word for word, although it was so long since I read it. Dear, dear husband, you do not know how proud & grateful I am that you love me. We have found the fountain of eternal youth for love, & I believe there are few others who can say so. I try very hard to be worthy of your love.

She kept writing until she could write no more.

Mr. Magoffin has come for the letter & I must stop. I have not had so much pleasure in a very great while as today. . . . Farewell, dear, dear husband. In a few months we shall not know what sorrow means. At least, I humbly hope & pray so. Your own affectionate and devoted wife,

Jessie B. Frémont

She gave the letter, this piece of her heart, to the traveler Magoffin, who packed it away for the long journey to Bent's Fort. Jessie had no way of knowing that by the time she sent the letter her husband had changed his plans, and would not be traveling to Bent's Fort that summer after all.

✳ ✳ ✳

JOHN'S INACTION IN CALIFORNIA could not last. Though still without a strategy, he had already set events in motion. Because he had drifted down to the coast in February with a hazy notion to find real estate, he had prompted General Castro to order his expulsion. Although the Americans slipped away, their temporary defiance made it hard for Castro and other officials to let the matter drop. They had to take additional measures for California's security. On April 11, officials met in Monterey to counter "the imminent risk of invasion founded on the extravagant design of an American Captain of the United States Army, Mr. N. [sic] Frémont." Those in attendance included the prefect of Monterey, as well as General Castro and

General Vallejo, the commander of the northern frontier. They agreed that Castro would command a military response, and moved to cut off John's most obvious potential source of support. On April 30 they issued a declaration targeting American settlers, proclaiming that "a multitude of foreigners" had come to California, "abusing our local circumstances," and had become "owners of real property, this being a right belonging only to citizens." If foreign landowners were "not naturalized" as citizens, their ownership should be declared "null and void," and they were subject to expulsion from the country "whenever the Government may find it convenient."

The threat to expel foreigners was not enforced. The authorities were not likely to "find it convenient," for expulsion was politically hard and the government was weak and divided. Even if the government had been strong, Generals Vallejo and Castro were well disposed toward the Americans. The wording of their proclamation suggested its true purpose was not expelling Americans, merely pressing them to pledge allegiance to the government—but the American settlers missed the nuances. One, a New Englander named William B. Ide, later recalled the proclamation as a death threat, which supposedly said that "all foreigners" who had arrived within the last year must "leave the country, and their property and beasts of burden, without taking arms, on pain of death." Ide seemed baffled that the "naturally humane and generous" General Castro would have issued such a cruel edict—which, of course, he had not.

Ide was a pivotal actor in what happened next. He was a Massachusetts-born carpenter and teacher, a somber man of fifty with a line of whiskers on his chin, and a Mormon. He had arrived in California just two months earlier than John had, crossing the Sierra Nevada with a party of settlers in October 1845. He worked for a few months on the same northern California rancho where John stopped on his way to and from Oregon in early 1846. That was the full extent of his connection to California; he had no claim to it except his long journey to get there. But just as Captain Frémont reached California and instantly began naming landmarks, complaining to the authorities, and shopping for beachfront property, Ide already viewed California as his own. This was not surprising, given the ideas afoot in his country ("This country appears to have been created on a magnificent plan," "Westward the star of empire takes its way," "the manifest purpose of Providence"). When he heard rumors of a Mexican crackdown, he did not think of complying with the authorities' demands and looked for protection to the US Army captain who was camping in the region.

Ide was encouraged to do so: Captain Frémont, also fearing a Mexican attack, had authorized his former employee Neal and other settlers to spread the word that Americans should band together for "their common safety" and that "my camp, wherever it might be, was appointed the place of meeting." These settlers were likely the authors of a letter that a messenger carried through the Sacramento Valley. Ide saw it on June 8, 1846. It falsely claimed that "a large body of Spaniards on horseback" were on their way up the Sacramento, burning crops and houses as they went, and that "Capt. Fremont invites every freeman in the valley to come to his camp" to develop a plan of action.

When Ide visited Captain Frémont at his tent, however, he was disappointed. The army officer still did not think he could hold out against the California authorities and intended to avoid involving himself directly in conflict so that the United States would not be implicated. According to Ide, John proposed a harebrained scheme in which the settlers would rise up to strike some blow against the Mexicans and then flee California, with John escorting them back to the United States. John never recorded making any such proposal, and Ide's memory was not reliable, but the notion fit John's written statements that he intended to retreat to the United States, and it contributed to a mystery: What was the army officer up to? What was his intent? If he believed, as he said later, that he was "required" to do what he could "to promote the object of the President" to "take California," why was he planning to leave? If he believed that he should not involve himself in a war with local authorities, why was he encouraging settlers to join him for their common defense? Was he covertly leading the settlers to rise up or merely stirring the pot? Was he lying about his plans to leave in order to fool Mexican authorities, who might intercept his letters? Or was he lying long afterward, when he forgot that he had ever planned to leave and talked instead of his duty to remain? The simplest explanation is the most likely: the historical record is confusing because John Charles Frémont was confused. He was exhausted after thousands of miles in the saddle. He lacked clear instructions from home. He lacked the information he most needed, whether war had started between Mexico and the United States. He also lacked reliable information about what the Mexicans were doing. He had long ago absorbed Senator Benton's understanding of the strategic power of American settlers to take control of a desired piece of land, but he was not a great strategic thinker. Thus he sent mixed signals, not knowing what to do.

The choice was no longer his, however. Because of his strange wanderings around Monterey, the California authorities had issued their proclamation, and because of the proclamation, settlers were determined to respond. A small group was gathering to strike a blow at the Mexican authorities with or without the army officer. William B. Ide joined the party of gunmen led by a settler named Ezekiel Merritt, who had already conducted a raid to steal Mexican horses. The armed party rode toward the nearest military outpost. Picking up recruits as they went, they eventually totaled more than thirty men. They knew the example of the Texas revolution. With Captain Frémont's implicit support, however contradictory and hesitant it may have been, they meant to take charge of California.

The riders' target was the central square at Sonoma, the location of General Mariano G. Vallejo, who lived with his family in the house with the castle tower and long veranda. Nearby was a barracks in which 250 rifles and a few cannons were stored, although the barracks were otherwise vacant. In past years a small military unit was based at Sonoma, men Vallejo had privately recruited and paid himself, but he had disbanded them. The principal defense of Sonoma was General Vallejo's prestige. And in the early morning hours of June 14, when the riders reached the square after traveling all night, the first thing they did was pound on Vallejo's door.

The riders waited; it was not going to be the kind of revolution that involved breaking down doors. Inside, Vallejo gathered with his six children and his wife, Doña Francisca Vallejo, who urged him to flee through a back entrance. The general refused to do anything so undignified, instead stepping into his uniform and, when he was ready, ordering his servants to open the door so that he could welcome the sleepless gunmen in their torn and dirty clothes. Doña Francisca thought they looked like "banditti." General Vallejo invited a few of the leading rebels to sit in his living room and talk over the terms of surrender, and despite the early hour he called for a bottle of wine. Soon a second bottle was required. By midmorning Ezekiel Merritt was too drunk to command. The men waiting outside held a hasty vote to choose a new commander, who was soon drunk himself. Authority finally devolved on William B. Ide, a teetotaler, who approved an elaborate document for Vallejo's signature: he was to formally surrender and be guaranteed the safety of his family and property. Ide expected that Vallejo would remain at home, but this he proved unable to enforce. Unruly men in his group were spoiling for a fight, and Ide concluded that General Vallejo, his brother, and an aide must be taken prisoner for their own safety.

The gunmen, some drunk and some not, remained in charge of Sonoma, collecting weapons and a hundred pounds of gunpowder from Vallejo's barracks. Soon they raised a homemade flag over the settlement, featuring the image of a bear. "This day we proclaim California a Republic," Ide wrote the day after Vallejo's surrender, adding "our pledge of honor that private property be protected." The independent country would be known as the Bear Flag Republic. Rarely in history had so much land been arrogated by so few; Ide's little force claimed ownership of an empire, displacing several thousand Mexicans who themselves had never wrested more than a portion of it from its several hundred thousand natives.

In a letter a few days later, Ide described a revolution as the settlers' only alternative to being driven away: "We have determined to make this country independent, and to establish a system of government that will be more favorable to us than such a dangerous and long road back." It was not meant to be a long-lasting government, Ide said, expressing his "earnest desire" to unite with the United States in the way that Texas had. Over the next few days, scores of additional gunmen arrived in Sonoma, some bringing their families for their protection. Ide insisted that "the Spaniards are not only satisfied, but pleased" with his movement—and indeed General Vallejo might secretly have approved the desire to join with the United States if he had not been preoccupied with his own capture. By the time of Ide's proclamation, gunmen had escorted Vallejo and the other high-profile prisoners out of town, planning to take the captives to Captain Frémont.

Vallejo did not resist. As a military officer and an admirer of the United States, he found it reassuring that he was being delivered to an American army officer, a trained and educated man who surely would be able to read the terms of the surrender document and release him. The general was so confident and so patient that he even turned down an opportunity to escape on the road to Frémont's camp. Why take such a risk when any honorable American would do as justice required?

✳ ✳ ✳

CAPTAIN FRÉMONT WAS IN HIS TENT when the prisoners and their escorts rode into camp. General Vallejo was not tied or restrained; as he dismounted in his general's uniform, he must have looked more like the commander of his guards than like their captive. He went to find Captain Frémont's tent and introduced himself. Vallejo indicated that he hoped for better treatment now that he was Frémont's prisoner—and that was his first surprise. "No," Frémont replied, "you are the prisoner of these people." He gestured toward the ragged settlers. Frémont was still trying to keep his distance from the uprising.

Yet his thinking quickly evolved. He *was* willing to take the prisoners, just not willing to *say* they were his prisoners. He ordered them to be held at Sutter's Fort in violation of their surrender agreement. He even ordered the arrest of Jacob Leese, an American who had married into Vallejo's family, and who had come with the prisoners to serve as their interpreter. A few of John's men escorted Vallejo and his companions to a dark room inside the fort. They were not allowed to communicate with the outside world, and they waited day after day without being told how they could be freed. As days became weeks, three different men appeared seeking information about General Vallejo that they could deliver to his worried family at Sonoma. Frémont's men locked them up too.

The capture of Sonoma seemed to alter John's calculus for what he could or should achieve. He dropped his pretense that he was not involved in the settlers' uprising and turned his expedition into a revolutionary strike force. First he moved to protect the settlers who held Sonoma: word came that California's General Castro was organizing troops to drive them out—so as Theodore Talbot of Frémont's expedition put it, "we went to the rescue," starting for Sonoma on June 23 and gathering recruits from among the American settlers along the way. They never found the Mexican force, which the Bear Flaggers deflected by themselves, but the move brought John and his men out of the Sacramento Valley and down to the vicinity of San Francisco Bay. The lack of action, yet another anticlimax, proved to be a prelude to Frémont's drastic escalation in his use of force.

A story had spread that the Californians had captured two American settlers. They were messengers, Bear Flaggers sent out of Sonoma to obtain gunpowder, and when they failed to return, rumors spread that their captors had killed them. This put John's growing force in a mood for revenge, and the simplest explanation for what followed was that they targeted the first victims to come within range of their guns. At San Rafael, on San Francisco Bay, they spied several people in a boat approaching shore, and concluded that the distant specks on the water must be spies. One eyewitness, a man named Jasper O'Farrell, said Captain Frémont ordered Kit Carson and two other men to intercept them once they made land. Carson asked, "Shall I take these men prisoners?" According to the witness, Captain Frémont replied, "I have no room for prisoners." Carson's men rode down to meet the men near the water's edge and killed them.

There was reason to doubt the details of the witness's account: very few men could have directly overheard the soft-spoken army captain, and O'Farrell did not write down his damning quotation until a decade later. But there was no doubt that three men were killed. Two were twin brothers about twenty years old, Francisco and Ramon de Haro, sons of a prominent landowner. The third was an elderly rancher, José de los Reyes Berreyesa. One apparently was carrying a message for some of General Castro's troops, which meant there was legitimate reason to detain them. Killing them was another matter. They were alone and posed no apparent threat. John seemed to know that something was wrong about the killings, because when describing them later, he wrote himself out of the event. In a long letter to Senator Benton, he reported the encounter in a single sentence: "Three of Castro's party having landed on the Sonoma side in advance, were killed on the beach; and beyond this there was no loss on either side." In his memoir, he placed himself at even greater distance, blaming the incident not on white men but on Indians who acted in their savage way, overcome by emotion after the deaths of the Americans: "My scouts, mainly Delawares, influenced by these feelings, made sharp retaliation and killed Berreyesa and de Haro, who were the bearers of the . . . messages."

After this atrocity, the men rode south toward the harbor entrance John had labeled the Golden Gate. He stood on the north side of the channel, peering across the waves at the Mexican artillery pieces at the presidio on the south side. He conceived a plan to take them out of action. From an American merchant ship in the bay the men borrowed a small boat, onto which a dozen gunmen crowded for a commando raid. "Pulling across the strait or avenue of water which leads in from the Gate we reached the Fort

Point in the gray dawn of the morning and scrambled up the steep bank just in time to see several horsemen escaping at full speed," he said. The raiders captured six brass cannons (so he reported at the time; in later years he inflated the number to fourteen) and spiked the guns, jamming a long steel file down each cannon's touchhole so it would be impossible to use until repaired. Then the men rowed back across the strait and rode northward to Sonoma, arriving in the central square in front of the home of General Vallejo just in time to mark the Fourth of July. By now his force had grown to 160 men, who mixed with the growing garrison of Sonoma and held a celebration of their independent republic on the American day of independence. And Frémont began to assume command. "It had now become necessary to concentrate the elements of this movement, in order to give it the utmost efficiency [and] the people desired me to take charge of it." He had gone from a reluctant warrior to, in his mind, the keystone of the revolution: "Its existence was due to my presence in the valley, and at any time upon my withdrawal it would have collapsed with absolute ruin to the settlers." No longer did he talk of his own very recent plans to depart. On the morning of July 5, "I called the people together, and spoke to them in relation to the position of the country, advising a course of operations which was unanimously adopted. California was declared independent, the country put under martial law, the force organized and officers elected. A pledge, binding themselves to support these measures, and to obey their officers, was signed by those present. The whole was placed under my direction." What, exactly, was he talking about here? The settlers had already declared independence weeks before. But this declaration included *him*.

✳ ✳ ✳

A few days later, word arrived from the coast: everything had changed. The United States was taking charge. US Navy ships dropped anchor in Monterey Bay, and on the morning of July 8, 1846, men swarmed over the sides of the warships and down into small boats. Under cover from the ships' cannons, about 250 sailors and Marines rowed ashore and took the Monterey custom house with no resistance. The American consul Larkin, whose government had once refused to reimburse him for the cost of a flag, came out of his house to discover that one had been delivered; the Marines organized a flag-raising ceremony, reading aloud a proclamation declaring California to be under the control of the United States. The only shots fired came from the cannons on the warships, which fired a twenty-one-gun salute. In San Francisco Bay, Marines from another warship conducted a similar takeover of Yerba Buena, and soon after that riders arrived at Sonoma with the Stars and Stripes to replace the Bear Flag.

On July 12 Captain Frémont received a letter from the naval officer who had ordered the Marines ashore: Commodore John D. Sloat summoned the army officer to Monterey. "There may be a necessity of one hundred men, well mounted," Sloat said. He wanted a security force to prevent looting. John immediately started for the coast, moving so swiftly that he left behind some unfinished business—he had promised to visit the imprisoned General Vallejo and his companions at Sutter's Fort to discuss their release, but never showed up, leaving them waiting without explanation. Vallejo could do nothing but write Frémont a letter, managing to ask politely when he and his compatriots would be freed. He would remain locked up until August 2, when he was finally paroled on the orders of a navy captain whose ship was in San Francisco Bay.

Leaving men to guard Sonoma and Sutter's Fort, John's main force faced no opposition on the way to Monterey, and heard that General Castro was retreating southward toward Los Angeles. With a single cannon in tow, they trotted through Monterey with its toy-sized Spanish cathedral and Consul Larkin's New England house and United States Marines on the streets. They camped outside town on a hillside, in the shade of fir and pine trees and with a commanding view. "Before us, to the right, was the town of Monterey with its red-tiled roofs and large gardens enclosed by high adobe walls, capped with red tiles; to the left the view was over the ships in the bay and on over the ocean, where the July sun made the sea-breeze and the shade of the pine trees grateful."

One of the ships on the bay was a British man-of-war, which had arrived after the US Marines went ashore. John persuaded himself, without evidence, that the US Navy must have beaten Britain in a race for empire—that the British would have intervened if only they had arrived first. The other four ships in the bay flew the American flag, and were from the US Pacific Squadron. Riding down to the waterfront, John learned that the flagship was a frigate called the *Savannah*—a name he could not help but notice. ("I pleased myself," he said, "with thinking it a good augury that as Savannah was my birthplace, the birth of this new child of our country should have been presided over by this Savannah of the seas.") Accompanied by Lieutenant Gillespie, he found a boat that could take him out to the big sailing ship. They climbed up on deck and greeted Commodore Sloat, who had seized California for the United States.

He did not convey an air of triumph. Even in a formal portrait, John D. Sloat of New York had a worried expression; he was sixty-five, worn down by years at sea, in poor health, and scheduled soon to relinquish his command. He did not want to make a mistake at the very end of his career. A few weeks earlier, when his ship was at anchor at the Mexican port of Mazatlán, Sloat had learned of battles near the Rio Grande between United States and Mexican forces. Knowing that in the event of war his government would want to seize California, Sloat raised anchor and headed north, although he resolved he would not seize California's ports unless he learned of an actual declaration of war. There was still no word of a declaration when he reached Monterey—but he heard of the Bear Flag rebellion and Frémont's operations inland, and seemingly concluded that no United States Army officer would behave as John had unless he knew something. "I have determined to hoist the Flag of the U. States at this place," he informed the captain of another warship on July 6, "as I would prefer being sacrificed for doing too much than too little." Consul Larkin thought Sloat had acted "perhaps fearing some other foreign Officer might do it" if he did not.

Now Sloat met the officer whose activity had provoked him to move. "Commodore Sloat was glad to see me," John said afterward. "He seemed excited over the gravity of the situation in which he was the chief figure; and now, wholly responsible for its consequences." The ailing commodore soon came to the vital question.

"I want to know by what authority you are acting," Sloat said.

"I informed him," John said afterward, "that I had acted solely on my own responsibility, and without any expressed authority from the Government to justify hostilities. He appeared much disturbed by this information," which meant Sloat had no legal cover. "He had expected to find that I had been acting under such *written* authority as would support his action in raising the flag." Sloat "was so discouraged that the interview terminated abruptly." Frémont and Gillespie were soon rowing away from the *Savannah*. They returned to the elevated campsite with its view of Monterey's red tile and the ships on the bay. Miles away, on the north shore of the bay, lay the Santa Cruz Mountains and the Santa Cruz shore—the shoreline he had inspected a few months earlier, when hoping to find a place to live with his mother.

John went for a walk toward Point Pinos, on the Monterey Peninsula, "which juts into the sea. No matter how untoward this interview [with Sloat] had been I felt that the die was cast. . . . Sitting here by the sea and resting and gathering about me these dreams which had become realities, I thought over the long way from Washington to this spot and what little repose of body or mind I had found. . . . But now I was having an ideal rest." His uncertainty resolved into certainty; when he recorded his experiences later, he would forget or omit the moments when he didn't know what to do, didn't receive clear instructions, didn't think he could accomplish anything, kept his distance from the Bear Flag rebellion, and even made plans to leave. What remained was John Charles Frémont, conqueror of California. He deserved credit, just not the way he imagined; his dreamy thrashing about had triggered a chain of events that led Commodore Sloat to stake the American claim by accident. John's work was done.

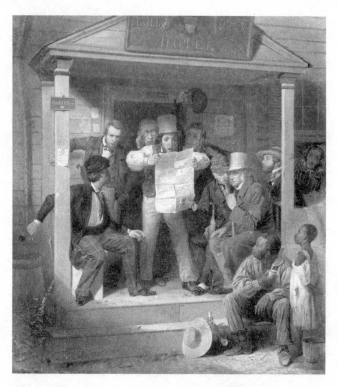

War News from Mexico, by the Frémonts' contemporary Richard Caton Woodville.

Chapter Ten

DO NOT SUPPOSE I LIGHTLY
INTERFERE IN A MATTER
BELONGING TO MEN

JESSIE, 1846–1847

Washington and Westport

Jessie knew nothing of John's acts in California until months after they had occurred. At the Benton house she depended on newspapers and officials who called on her father—and they knew only what they gleaned from months-old dispatches and rumors from the Pacific. When she wrote her heartfelt letter to her husband on June 18, 1846, she had no idea that California settlers loosely associated with John had taken Sonoma four days earlier. Nor did she know a few weeks later when Commodore Sloat sent Marines and sailors ashore. But she did have a vital piece of information that John lacked: during all his weeks of uncertainty, when he was waiting for news that war had begun and agonizing over how far he could go on his own, the war was already under way.

President Polk had provoked war that spring by sending a small army into South Texas. Blue-uniformed soldiers built an earthen-walled fort beside the Rio Grande, at the farthest southern extent of territory that had ever been dubiously claimed by Texas, asserting that it was now the southern border of the United States. American soldiers on patrol near the fort came under fire from Mexican forces who viewed them as invaders. Polk said the United States was under attack and asked Congress for a declaration of war, which Congress granted on May 13, 1846. This made it easier, once the news of the Bear Flag Rebellion reached Washington, to view John's adventures not as unauthorized crimes but as prescient acts of war, justified by events of which he knew nothing. The Washington *Daily Union* of September 2 reported "information, on which we place implicit reliance," that American forces had captured strategic points in California. The conquest began when "a detachment from Col. Frémont's force took possession of a frontier post called Sonoma." John's efforts to keep his distance from the takeover were already being lost in transmission; whoever was the source of this information gave John credit.

News arrived of fresh advances, each event reaching Jessie several months after the fact. Commodore Robert F. Stockton arrived in California, the same Stockton whose warship *Princeton* had steamed to its disastrous demonstration in 1844, and who tried to raise a private army in Texas to attack Mexico before the war. Sent to command the Pacific squadron by the expansionist navy secretary George Bancroft ("Westward the star of empire takes its way"), Stockton arrived with his ambition and self-confidence undiminished. Taking over from the cautious Commodore Sloat, he armed additional sailors and sent them ashore to reinforce his Marines. At Stockton's direction, John mustered his men into the service of the United States, where they would be known as the California Battalion. Many Bear Flag settlers became volunteer soldiers, as did Kit Carson and the other men of the expedition. John allowed Jacob Dodson to enroll as a private; they either did not know or did not care that black men were prohibited by law from US military service.

Stockton sent John's troops down the coast aboard a navy ship to the excellent harbor at San Diego, which they seized without opposition. By December, word reached Washington that Frémont and Stockton had the American flag "flying at every commanding position, and California was in the undisputed military possession of the United States." President Polk's annual message to Congress credited "our squadron in the Pacific, with the co-operation of a gallant officer of the army." Stockton was setting up a government with Jessie's husband at its head—or, as a newspaper said, "Fremont is Governor, pro tem, of California." The war had hardly begun, and its greatest prize was already in hand—John's hands.

Jessie could only welcome this news, though she believed the war was wrong. It was everything her father had warned against for years. It was especially bitter that the fighting began over control of the Rio Grande Valley, the land that Senator Benton described in his 1844 speech as a legitimate part of Mexico, free soil that should never become part of a slave state ("where a slave's face was never seen!"). Now it *was* part of a slave state, and the very ground where the army marched to trigger war. But when Congress considered the declaration of war, Benton and many other senators did not vote their doubts. Polk framed the declaration not as aggression but as recognition that "a state of war exists," and Benton accepted this fait accompli rather than fail to support the troops. Jessie felt more free to scorn the enterprise. "As you may perceive," she said in a letter to one of her husband's colleagues in early 1847, "I have no sympathy for the war, nor has Mr. Frémont. Fighting is not his aim." Jessie said her husband had thrown himself into the conquest "as if revenging a private insult," his treatment by California's General Castro. No evidence suggested that John actually opposed the war—but Jessie was not alone in her distaste for it. Antislavery activists were unsparing in their criticism. The escaped slave turned activist Frederick Douglass attended a meeting of the Western New York Anti-Slavery Society, whose members approved a resolution accusing the president of "a wanton deliberate lie" in claiming that Mexico had invaded the United States; the war's true object was "the extension of slavery." Not for Douglass was Senator Benton's self-imposed restraint.

On New Year's Day 1847, Jessie took part in Washington's annual ritual, standing in line with hundreds of others to shake the hand of the president.

She would not miss the occasion, regardless of her view of Polk's war. A person attending spotted her in the crowd and wrote a description: "Look there in the centre! Who is that young and lovely creature with such intelligence and lovely and agreeable manners, now chatting French with this diplomat, then Spanish with that, anon Italian with another. What a wife she would make for an Ambassador! [But] That lady is married and a mother. She has more discernment than her father, far seeing as he is, and was disobedient enough to think for herself, and to unite her destiny to a young lieutenant, who in the tide of time may, for aught 1 know, become President of a republic on the Western side of this continent." This description was published in a New York newspaper and reprinted by others. Jessie was sharpening her public image. More than an image, she had a narrative. The writer grasped the tale of her elopement and drew from it that Jessie was a woman who decided for herself and was even smarter than her visionary father. While a woman might ordinarily have been seen as a charming appendage of her famous father and husband, they seemed like the ones attached to *her*.

She understood that her fame could translate to influence, and as the new year began, she used it. The ranks of the army were swelling, which created opportunities for advancement for her husband and his friends. Determined to be helpful, the twenty-three-year-old assumed a role as John's political representative in Washington. On February 16, 1847, she wrote a letter to President Polk. "My Dear Sir," she began,

> *There is a very brave young man named Charles Taplin, of education &*
> *respectable family, who was with Mr. Frémont through his second expe-*
> *dition & only returned from the present one when there was nothing left*
> *to be done.*

Taplin was one of the men who had departed California in mid-1846, carrying a letter to Senator Benton in Washington. Now he aspired to join the army and go to Mexico, and Jessie sought an officer's commission for him.

A 2nd Lieutenancy would not only gratify him, but Mr. Frémont and
myself extremely.

She was undertaking the delicate task of seeking Polk's political patronage. To the victors of an election went the spoils, as a supporter of Andrew Jackson once said; dispensing jobs was one of the president's powers,
and it would be smart to confer favors on a friend of Senator Benton's, or a
friend of Benton's daughter. But Polk felt oppressed by job seekers. He complained to his diary about men who flocked to the presidential mansion—"a
herd of loafers who thus annoyed me," he once wrote. Another day's entry
read, "There were many visitors this morning on the patriotic errand of
seeking office for themselves." On still another day of giving time to "lazy-
looking loafers," Polk complained, "I cannot insult or be rude to my fellow
citizens who call, however undeserving or worthless I may believe them to
be." Jessie apparently understood that the president would not appreciate
her taking part in this distasteful work of men, and she offered a playful,
even coy justification:

> [*A Florida senator told me that*] *patronage is only used for bribery but*
> *with me you can be purely disinterested as my good wishes are all I have*
> *to give in return & they are already yours. Unlike other applicants I shall*
> *not entertain much hope of succeeding & disappointments of many kinds*
> *are familiar to me. Still I hope to succeed. Very truly & respectfully yours,*
>
> *Jessie Benton Frémont*

Taplin received his lieutenant's commission.

A few weeks after she wrote the letter, the president publicly affirmed
the Benton family's status by visiting the Benton house. Jessie's older sister,
Elizabeth, was getting married there. Her fiancé was William Carey Jones,
who like Senator Benton was a former newspaper editor and lawyer, and the

wedding attracted the ultimate guest. After the ceremony the president escorted the bride to her seat at the dinner table. Although Polk left shortly after dinner, apparently turning back to work—he was slowly working himself to death—his wife, Sarah Childress Polk, stayed to chat far into the evening with Jessie and other members of the bridal party.

This confirmation of her family's importance did not prevent Jessie's spirits from growing dark. In the spring of 1847 she tried to write a cheerful letter to her dearest friend, Elizabeth Blair Lee, but her thoughts turned to sick friends and relations. Commenting on a woman they knew who had suffered through eight days of labor only to see the baby die, Jessie could not muster much sympathy: "I am sorry for her disappointment, but that is not an irreparable loss & you know children are not necessary to happiness." She confessed, "I have written you a raven's letter in place of the comfort I mean to administer for your loneliness. . . . I will not write any longer now for I feel decidedly that I am not cheerful." Later the two friends met face-to-face. Elizabeth—Lizzie Lee to her friends—was a strikingly beautiful Kentuckian six years older than Jessie, and the daughter of the Democratic newspaper editor Francis Preston Blair. She was among the limited number of women Jessie could relate to and even admire. Lizzie was a keen observer of her friend, noting that Jessie looked "thin and sad," and seemed "tired of her courage & is now really pining for her husband."

✷ ✷ ✷

JESSIE WAS IN WASHINGTON ON MAY 8, 1847, when the city held a celebration of the war. It was the anniversary of the Battle of Palo Alto, the first of many victories as US forces pushed into Mexico. A giant banner stretched across Pennsylvania Avenue, proclaiming patriotic pride while seeming to acknowledge ambivalence about the way the war had begun. "Our country," it read. "May she always be right; but right or wrong, our country." Fireworks burst over the Washington Navy Yard. The presidential mansion was "brilliantly illuminated" in the evening, according to a newspaper, although "it was thought best not to illuminate the offices of the public departments, because they contain the valuable records of the government, and most of them are not fire-proof." The Bentons covered three first-floor windows with transparencies—images and words designed to be lit from behind, naming victories in the war—while the upper windows were decorated with two American flags. It might have been Jessie who told a reporter their history so that they would be mentioned in the paper: one flag was carried by John on his first visit to California in 1844, while the other was "the first and only flag that ever waved from the loftiest peak of the Rocky mountains, and taken there by Col. Frémont, August 15, 1842."

No displays at the Benton house reflected victories in California. There were no large battles to commemorate—and the news from California was turning sour. Word had filtered back east that something was going wrong with John's part of the war. Confirmation came days after the celebration, when a visitor arrived at the Benton home, worn from a journey of some twenty-eight hundred miles: Kit Carson had come all the way from California with dispatches for the government and a letter for Senator Benton. Although Senator Benton was away, the women of the Benton household greeted Carson warmly—so warmly that he grew uncomfortable. He explained that he felt unworthy because his late wife was Indian, and he presumed that his white hosts would disapprove of him once they knew of his interracial marriage.

But he remained welcome, and Jessie became a particular admirer. Carson was already known around Washington as a heroic character from John's reports, and during his visit a long and glowing profile of Carson appeared in the *Daily Union*: "modest as he is brave, with the fire of enterprise in his eye—with the bearing of an Indian, walking even with his toes turned in." He was "one of those bold and enterprising spirits of the west, whom the peculiar influences of the frontier settlements—between the white man and the red man—are so well calculated to produce. Carson, however, is a master spirit." He was like an endangered species whose characteristics ought to be recorded by "the magic pen" of some great writer "before its traits disappear under the advance of civilization." It was a curious article, this promotional profile; the anonymous writer claimed never to have met Carson, but quoted him at length. Jessie's friend Lizzie Lee wrote that she knew the author. "I have my reasons for thinking that 'tis written by Jessie." If Jessie didn't write it, she likely was a source for the writer.

Readable though the article was, it left out the distressing news Kit Carson had brought Jessie, which stretched back to late 1846, when John sent Carson toward Washington with dispatches for the government. Carson and a small group of riders raced eastward from southern California to New Mexico, where they encountered a US Army force, blue-uniformed troops riding in the opposite direction. It was a small army commanded by Brigadier General Stephen Watts Kearny, who had just captured New Mexico on behalf of the United States. Kearny was under orders to continue onward to conquer and govern California. Carson informed Kearny that California had already been conquered by Frémont and Stockton, news that persuaded Kearny to send most of his troops back east for use elsewhere. But he still proceeded toward California with a hundred men, intending to take charge there as ordered, and he insisted that Carson pass his dispatches to another rider while Carson turned around to guide the soldiers to the Pacific.

The small force was approaching San Diego when they learned in the most unpleasant way possible that California was not conquered. Californian forces defeated Kearny's hundred men, forcing them to retreat with heavy casualties. It emerged that Frémont and Stockton, their forces spread too thin, had lost control of Los Angeles in a Mexican uprising. Eventually Stockton's men came to Kearny's rescue, while Frémont advanced on Los Angeles and negotiated its surrender, but John now faced an enemy who was more dangerous to him than the Californians: the rivalry of two commanders. Until that moment, Commodore Stockton had assumed command of all land and sea operations as the senior American officer anywhere near, but

Kearny's orders said *he* should take charge. The navy commodore declined to submit to the army general. In an exchange of frosty letters in January 1847, Kearny told Stockton, "I demand that you cease" giving orders in California, as "I cannot recognize in you any right to perform duties confided to me by the President." Stockton replied, "I cannot do anything, nor desist from doing anything or alter anything on your demand." Both men issued contradictory orders to Frémont. The younger man might have ducked the choice; he could have simply followed the orders of Kearny, his superior in the army, or could have asked both commanders to resolve their dispute and relieve him of his impossible position. Instead he embraced the choice. He made a fateful decision to refuse Kearny and obey the orders of Stockton, who had made him the military governor.

John's shortcuts in life were catching up with him. As an army officer who routinely went beyond his orders, he'd had scant practice with the culture of obedience that was at the heart of military life. As an officer who neither attended West Point nor even served much around other soldiers, he failed to grasp the depth of the military's tribalism. The army and navy served the same country but had separate chains of command, rivaled each other for funding and glory, and viewed each other's cultures as alien. It was not unusual that Stockton and Kearny jostled over who should control an operation that involved both services; what *was* unusual was that John defied his own tribe and sided with the other. It was his own tribe that would ultimately judge him. A refusal to follow orders was mutiny.

John eventually found a second opportunity to send Carson eastward, giving him the letter addressed to Senator Benton, dated February 3, 1847, in which he explained his conduct to his political sponsor—who must now become his political protector. Since Benton was not present upon Carson's arrival in Washington in May, Jessie opened the letter and read:

You are aware that I had contracted relations with Commodore Stockton, and I thought it neither right nor politically honorable to withdraw my support. No reason of interest shall ever compel me to act towards any man in such a way that I should afterwards be ashamed to meet him.

John mixed his high-minded explanation with self-promotion. "I was named Governor," he wrote, "and immediately proclaimed peace and order restored . . . and, like the waters of some small lake over which a sudden storm had passed, it subsided into perfect tranquility. . . . Throughout the Californian population, there is only one feeling of satisfaction and gratitude to myself."

Reading this letter in her father's absence, Jessie felt she understood what must be done. Carson must deliver the letter to President Polk so that he would know John's side of the story. Around midday on June 7, 1847, Jessie in her finest dress and Carson in his cleanest clothes rode a carriage to the presidential mansion and waited in a crowd of job seekers. At last they were ushered in to the president, a quiet and courteous man, his eyes and expression inscrutable. Polk afterward made notes in his diary.

Mrs. Fremont . . . informed me that Mr. Carson had been waiting several days to see me, for the purpose of conversing with me and tendering his services to bear dispatches to California, if any were to be sent.

Of course that was only part of the reason for the visit. Carson handed over John's letter. Jessie did much of the talking, while Polk said little.

Mrs. Fremont seemed anxious to elicit from me some expression of approbation of her husband's conduct, but I evaded. In truth, I consider that Col. Fremont was greatly in the wrong when he refused to obey the orders issued to him by Gen'l Kearney. I think Gen'l Kearney was right also in his controversy with Com. Stockton. It was unnecessary, however, that I should say so to Col. Fremont's wife, and I evaded giving her an answer.

Polk knew that John had finally submitted to Kearny's authority, and "the error being corrected," Polk was hoping the matter would "pass over quietly" without "a Court Martial." Jessie escorted Kit Carson away from the presidential mansion with a feeling of disappointment and foreboding. After nightfall, Polk summoned Carson to talk alone, and without the colonel's wife present, Polk said, they "had a full conversation . . . concerning the State of affairs in California, and especially in relation to the collision between our land & naval commanders in that distant region."

Carson departed Washington June 15, heading toward California. Jessie accompanied him, intending to travel as far as St. Louis in hopes of encountering her husband returning home. When her boat reached the St. Louis waterfront, she stepped ashore in a boomtown; the settlement of barely 5,000 that she remembered as a girl was approaching 75,000 as it supplied wagon trains to Oregon and California and some of the volunteer army forces occupying Mexico. She moved through the crowded streets to her father's house, but it could not contain her. Leaving Lily with a caregiver, she started westward by steamboat up the Missouri River, thinking John must be out there somewhere. The boat let her off at Westport Landing, one of the settlements near the point where the Kansas River meets the Missouri. At a "a cluster of frame and log buildings on the bluff," she found a place to stay in a "log-cabin, hot and stifling in the late summer heat," where she spent several "weary days of suspense." And then one evening, she said, "the rapid trampling of many horses announced the long waiting was over." He was riding with about twenty men, the core of the expedition that had departed from that spot in 1845.

The years and the experiences of those years of great events had made their telling mark on Mr. Frémont and he was still further changed by his dress, the unfamiliar Spanish riding dress of Californians. But the great change was in the stern set look of endurance and self control which the few past months had forced upon him, and with it a silent repressed storm of feeling which entirely dominated his own light hearted courtesy and thought for others.

He appeared stunned to see Jessie there, and "could not recover himself." Something was wrong, but "he could not put it into speech," and though they had been apart so achingly long, he needed to be alone. He went to care for his horses and "escaped from notice into the coming night." Only then did one of the men, Alex Godey, inform Jessie what had happened. Kearny had departed California for home and ordered John to return eastward with him. When they reached Fort Leavenworth, an army post near Missouri's border, Kearny told John to consider himself under arrest for mutiny. The general ordered him to return to Washington and report to the authorities for a court-martial. Jessie understood that his career—their career—was in peril.

✷ ✷ ✷

WHEN PIERRE L'ENFANT LAID OUT A PLAN for Washington, D.C., in the 1790s he included a space for fortifications. At the southern end of the city, about two miles from the Capitol, the Anacostia River flows into the Potomac, and L'Enfant thought that on the point between the two rivers, artillery might command the waterways and defend against invaders. Cannons were placed there but never served their purpose; the only time Washington was attacked, in the War of 1812, British invaders came by land from a different direction, burning the Capitol and the presidential mansion. The military reservation on the southern point of the city continued to be used as an arsenal—long brick buildings in which workmen cast rifles and cannons and arranged them in long rows for the next war. Then, in the fall of 1847, the army assigned a room in the arsenal to be used as a courtroom for the trial of Lieutenant Colonel John Charles Frémont.

Jessie became a full partner in preparing her dispirited husband's defense. He needed her to be; he was distracted. He learned that his mother was ill in South Carolina and hurried southward to be at her side. Anne Pryor died before he could reach her; he buried her in Charleston. It was characteristic of John that he left no record of what he thought as he passed alone through the rituals of farewell, in the city where he once had strolled the Battery and looked out on the water and fallen in love with Cecilia and dreamed; but there could be no doubt that he was out of touch with his court case. Jessie carried his load. Learning that an officer who supported John's version of events had come home from California but expected soon to return to the Pacific, Jessie wrote him. "For a selfish reason I wish your stay a little longer in the country," she told naval officer Edward F. Beale, who at age twenty-five was just two years older than Jessie. "Mr. Frémont... wishes you" to testify. She learned of a newspaper article suggesting that key witnesses against John—possibly even General Kearny himself—were about to be ordered to duty in Mexico, making a court-martial impossible. She appealed to President Polk. "You will see," she declared, "the manifest injustice to Mr. Frémont of letting his accusers escape from the investigation of the charges they have made against him."

> You have the power to do justice & I ask it of you that Mr. Frémont be permitted to make his accusers stand the trial as well as himself. Do not suppose, Sir, that I lightly interfere in a matter properly belonging to men, but in the absence of Mr. Frémont I attend to his affairs at his request. . . . Very respectfully yours,
>
> Jessie Benton Frémont

Jessie got her wish, although it would have been better if she had not. An entirely different scenario had once been within reach—President Polk's desire that a court-martial be avoided. John, like the witnesses, likely would have gone south to the war in Mexico and joined the regiment to which he had already been assigned. Instead the trial was proceeding, and Senator

Benton exulted that improving communications were making it possible to recall witnesses to Washington from across the continent: "Thanks to Morse! The lightning streaked after them. Thanks to Fulton! The invincible steam pursued them."

On November 2 the Benton family rode out of central Washington city and down to the arsenal's improvised court amid the cannons. It was said that the wine-red dress Jessie wore that day had been chosen to show her optimism. She watched as her husband stood to face a dozen officers who would judge him. The gold braid on the shoulders of his uniform hung on a body weathered and toughened by years in the saddle, and his face was maturing: he was thirty-four, in the prime of his life.

Jessie was not alone in the gallery. Reporters attended ("We thank the court and the parties in this case, for the facilities extended to the press thus far," wrote the correspondent for the *New York Herald*) and found that most perfect of political news stories, a clash of personalities seemingly without any larger meaning to complicate the telling. Spectators from the army and navy watched, as did eleven men from John's expedition, including Alex Godey and Richard Owens, two of the men John admired most. "The most interesting group to us," said the *Herald* correspondent, "was a detachment of Col. Fremont's California desert rangers and mountain scalers. . . . These men were with Fremont through all his explorations in California, and know the exact relish of a dish of grasshoppers, or the entrails of a mule, to a hungry man, after two or three days journeying over the desert plains of the Great Basin." The men told stories of their time in California—like when John, with Jacob Dodson and a Californian, rode four hundred miles in four days from Los Angeles to Monterey. They sent spare horses racing in front of them, which Jacob lassoed when it was time to change. Reprinted in many papers, the mind-boggling feat became another element of John's public persona.

The charges against Lieutenant Colonel Frémont were revealing. He was not accused of riding an armed force into the territory of another nation. He was not accused of massacring Indians. He was not accused of provoking conflict against Mexico, or having noncombatants put to death, or imprisoning men without charge. All these acts had been wiped away by victory in California. The charges related only to his disobedience of General Kearny, which had cost neither blood nor treasure but had challenged the order and the culture of the army. It turned out there was a larger meaning to the trial: the army was less concerned with John's record in California than with safeguarding the institution of the army itself. And because the army was defending its own authority, it would be especially hard for the organization to let John off, as the defendant seemed to realize.

He presented a paper stating his view of the case. "It is no part of my intention or desire to make defence on any legal or technical point," he wrote; he simply wanted the facts known and his trial quickly concluded. By a reading of "legal and technical points" there could be little doubt that he was guilty, so he planned a broader and more political defense with the help of his lawyers, one of whom was a leading politician. "I name as the counsel . . . the two friends who accompany me, Thomas H. Benton and William Carey Jones, esquires." The presence of Jones, his brother-in-law, meant that the entire defense was a family enterprise. And the head of the family admitted to no doubt about the outcome. Senator Benton told his son-in-law, "You will be justified, and exalted: your persecutors will be covered with shame & confusion. The process through which you have gone is bitter: but it will have its Sweet." Benton even suggested that being "the subject of an outrage" would, in the long run, enlarge John's reputation and help his public career. It was said that a man who represented himself in a court had a fool for a lawyer; it remained an open question what to call a man whose lawyer was his prideful father-in-law.

General Kearny was in the courtroom, and John had an opportunity to cross-examine his accuser. John thought he was doing well ("we have carried the points which command the issues of the case," he assured a friend on November 5), but his efforts to show Kearny to be deceptive or vindictive fell flat. The army expected John to follow his superior officers and he had not. Commodore Stockton testified but did little good. Senator Benton, too, was of little help, once provoking debate in the court about whether he had violated rules of decorum by staring at General Kearny.

On January 31, 1848, the court found Lieutenant Colonel Frémont guilty and sentenced him "to be dismissed from the service." A majority of officers added, however, that Frémont had been placed in "circumstances... calculated to embarrass the mind, and excite the doubts of officers of greater experience than the accused." Because the defendant had rendered "important professional services" throughout his career, the officers "beg[ged] leave to recommend him to the clemency of the President of the United States." And clemency came. Aside from his relationship to an important senator, John was a national hero who had accomplished a central goal of James K. Polk's presidency. In a letter dated February 16, the president affirmed the sentence against John, but added that "in consideration of the peculiar circumstances of the case" and the "previous meritorious and valuable services of Lieutenant Colonel Frémont," he should "accordingly be released from arrest, will resume his sword, and report for duty." John had escaped all consequences; his career was saved. And then, after brief reflection, he threw it away. Because Polk had not overturned the verdict of the court-martial, instead approving it before granting clemency, John found it intolerable. In the house at C Street, no doubt with Jessie by his side, he wrote the adjutant general of the army.

I... hereby send in my resignation of Lieutenant Colonel in the Army of the United States.

In doing this I take the occasion to say that my reason for resigning is, that I do not feel conscious of having done any thing to merit the finding of the court; and this being the case, I cannot, by accepting the

clemency of the President, admit the justice of the decision against me.
Very respectfully, Sir, your obedt. servt.

J.C. Frémont

His adventures in the military had brought him everything. The navy had taken him out of Charleston and into the Southern Hemisphere. The army had introduced him to Joseph Nicollet and taken him out on the Great Plains. His service had brought him into contact with Senator Benton, and through him to his marriage with Jessie. On the army payroll he had climbed the Rocky Mountains, crossed them to the Great Salt Lake and to Oregon, and continued to the surf of Monterey Bay, achieving fame rivaled by few in his lifetime. Now his military career was over, a self-inflicted wound.

✳ ✳ ✳

SENATOR BENTON WAS RIGHT ABOUT ONE THING: being "the subject of an outrage" did not diminish John's fame. It was after John's guilty verdict and resignation that a town called Lower Sandusky, Ohio, changed its name to Fremont. Citizens signed a petition for the new name, which was presented to local authorities in 1849 by Rutherford B. Hayes, a young lawyer, who said the town was "substantially unanimous" in favor. A newspaper there became the *Fremont Weekly Freeman*. There was soon a Fremont, New Hampshire, and a Fremont, New York.

Benton willingly prolonged the controversy. Seeking compensation for his family's wounded honor, the sixty-six-year-old used his power to try to block a promotion for General Kearny, and spent much of the summer re-litigating the court-martial before the Senate in a massive speech that required portions of thirteen days to deliver. He also blocked the promotion of an army major who had judged John as a member of the court-martial, accusing the man of "malice and envy" until the major requested his own court-martial to clear his name.

Nothing came of Benton's tirades, although the Frémonts enjoyed some benefit from their protector. The Senate commissioned John, at a rate of eight dollars per day, to make a map of California and deliver a report of his most recent adventures, which he wrote in collaboration with Jessie. They decided against a full-blown book, even though it would have been their most newsworthy work—suggesting that John understood his greatest triumph might seem less impressive if examined at length. Instead the Frémonts produced only a "geographical memoir" describing the landscape. While it lacked the narrative drama of previous reports, its designation of the harbor mouth as the Golden Gate made it a historic document, and its brevity meant the Frémonts could quickly finish and clear the way for other work.

Speed was necessary, for Jessie was pregnant. She likely had known since the court-martial—possibly even before she showed up that first day in the red dress. There was no reason to think that she was eager for a second child ("you know children are not necessary to happiness"), but she wanted to give John a son, and undoubtedly faced social pressure to produce a larger family. Her mother, who had borne five children, would have been considered ordinary; Jessie, who had turned twenty-four that spring and still had only one child, was opening herself to questions. She'd had few opportunities because her husband was away more often than he was present. But in the crushing days after his arrest in August 1847, he had needed her.

It was a difficult pregnancy, though she kept working. On May 29, weeks from giving birth, she was sending John's botanist plant samples he had brought from California. In the same letter she reported, "For some months I have been unwell & since the last of April I have not left my room, but have had a battle with a violent bilious fever, which like Bunyan's fight with Apollyon was the dreadfullest fight I ever had." This was a reference to a Christian man's battle with a monster in the popular book *The Pilgrim's Progress.* "However," Jessie added, "I have gained the victory & am more than willing not even to remember it." She gave birth in July 1848—and it was a boy. They called him Benton, and had him christened August 15, at a ceremony attended by Kit Carson, who had just returned with another packet of dispatches from California. Jessie was overjoyed to see the unassuming mountain man, who was as courteous around her as he was ruthless around others; he counted as a dear friend of Jessie's as well as John's, and he was named the baby's godfather. But Benton was a sickly infant, and Carson could not bring himself to sound hopeful about the child's prospects. He told Jessie he doubted Benton would survive. Having seen many deaths, having caused many deaths, having been married and seen the death of his first wife, and having fathered many children, not all of whom lived, he spoke with authority.

The baby's illness did not deter the Frémonts from trying to plan the next stage of their lives. John wanted out of Washington to make a new life in California; Jessie wanted to go with him. But how would they get there and what would they do for a living? A remarkable plan began to take shape, under which John would return to government service: a bill was introduced in the Senate to pay seven hundred thousand dollars in war claims made by Californians—people who had sold horses and supplies to John or to Commodore Stockton on a promise of later payment, or who said their property had been damaged. Senator Benton spoke in favor of the measure, which was no surprise. "It is understood," reported the *New York Herald*, "that on the passage of the bill, Mr. Frémont, (for he has assumed that title since the acceptance of his resignation of his commission as Lieut. Colonel . . .) will proceed at once to San Francisco" to settle with his creditors. Suddenly John faced the prospect of returning to the place he had been forced to leave in disgrace and bringing a fortune that he could distribute to everyone on the Pacific slope who had ever helped him. Nor was that all: defeated Mexico was about to formally cede California to the United States, and the *Herald* reported that John would "go to California with a view to a fixed residence there, under the idea that a new [territorial] Governor may

soon be appointed, in the person of the gallant desert explorer himself."
He would reclaim the very governorship that had been snatched from
him. On his way to California, John would conduct another expedition,
this time finding a route for a transcontinental railroad from St. Louis to
San Francisco.

The plan failed. The Senate approved the $700,000 but the House did
not. Senator Benton arranged a more modest measure to appropriate
$200,000 for payments—which the House also rejected. He blamed "lies
against Col. Frémont" spread by "notorious" partisans of General Kearny.
Still the senator would not give up, writing an open letter to the people of
California vowing that he would somehow have the government repay
them. He next asked the Senate to pass a different appropriation for John's
railroad expedition. He patiently fielded questions from colleagues (once
responding to a skeptical lawmaker with a dad joke: "In speaking of this
railroad, the Senator has run off the track—has run off the track, sir") but
the House killed this measure too. Even then he would not give up. The
railroad, he expected, would begin in St. Louis and confirm it as the capital
of western commerce. He found three St. Louis businessmen who were
willing to put up private money and equipment for an expedition to find the
route.

On this basis John departed for the fourth major expedition he had led
in the West, and the first that he conducted without the support of his
government. Jessie was determined to accompany him as far as she could,
bringing the family along. It may have been for the children's comfort that
the family took a roundabout route, using new rail and steamboat networks
much of the way: up the coast to New York, then up the Hudson River to
Albany, from which railroads led along the Erie Canal to Buffalo, on the
shore of Lake Erie. John was dispirited on the route; maybe the ease of the
journey left him too much time to think. As a steamboat carried them
along the length of Lake Erie toward the far shore in Ohio, they fell into
conversation with a fellow traveler, a New Yorker named T. C. Peters,

who felt that John needed Jessie's "comforting presence. There had been no time in his whole career, when his prospects looked as gloomy as then. . . . He had nearly drained the bitter cup." The Frémonts said they wanted nothing more in life than "to entertain their friends in their own house." After almost seven years of marriage they had yet to call any house their own.

From the Ohio shore the expanding rail network now led nearly to St. Louis, where they reoccupied Senator Benton's house as John filled out his roster of men. It was familiar work for him, though many familiar faces would not surround him. Carson was not available, having returned to a new wife and a growing family at his home in New Mexico, now controlled by the United States. As John interviewed new voyageurs, he surely imagined the face of Basil Lajeunesse, his favorite companion, who had been buried under the laurel in Oregon. By way of compensation, Alex Godey would join him again, Godey who had gone all the way to California and then all the way to Washington for the court-martial. Charles Preuss, the curly-haired German mapmaker who had skipped the conquest of California to stay home with his wife, now returned to work. The artist Edward Kern signed up for another trip and brought his brother Richard. On October 3 the men boarded a steamboat, which shoved off beneath a cloud of smoke and turned westward up the Missouri. Six-year-old Lily stayed behind in St. Louis; baby Benton, not two months old, came along with his mother toward the frontier, where they would see off John's expedition.

They made the newspaper when the boat stopped in Jefferson City, Missouri, a riverside village that contained little more than the state capitol and a prison.

Lieut. Col. Fremont and 35 of his men, passed up the river on board the steamer Martha last Thursday, on their way to California. Col. Fremont's lady accompanies him as far as Westport.

As often happened with the Frémonts, the newspaper missed the news. They had a talent for capturing the public eye without giving any hint of what was really going on in their lives. For it was around Jefferson City that baby Benton grew ill, and on October 6, as the steamboat churned the brown waters, he died. For the first time Jessie was on intimate terms with death. When her friend had lost a baby in childbirth the year before, Jessie had seemed unfeeling ("that is not an irreparable loss"); she knew that infant mortality was commonplace and that a woman must steel herself for it. But nothing could have prepared her for the moment when the loss was her own, the baby dead in her arms. "Grief was new to me," she wrote in a letter, "and I could not bear to give him up."

On October 8, 1848, the steamboat crew tied up at Westport. John's men went down the gangplank with their saddles and rifles, their packages of macaroni, their sacks of coffee. A glance at the foliage confirmed that it was later in the season than for any past expedition. John had intended to start out in the warmer months as he always had in the past, but the delays in financing the expedition and then the birth of the baby had detained him. Now the summer was gone, and his horses and mules would be kicking up snow before the men reached the Rockies. Wisdom suggested waiting to start in the spring; compassion suggested that he spend a season of grief with his wife. But he had always been slow to change course and was in no mood to do so now, while trying to escape the bitterness of his recent past. John began talking of the late start as if he had always planned it, saying that he wanted to prove that the railroad route would be passable through the Rockies in winter. The expedition broke camp to leave, and Jessie, standing by the ashes of his campfire, watched John swing into the saddle and ride off with his men.

While awaiting the next eastbound steamboat, she arranged to stay at Westport with a federal Indian agent who represented the United States to native nations. The older man was sympathetic enough to perceive that Mrs. Frémont was troubled, and generously proposed that they take a ride in the countryside for a "pleasant change of ideas." He had something of interest to show her. He had been on the trail of a she-wolf that was killing his sheep, and he led Jessie to the place where he had found and killed the mother's babies.

That evening they went to the agent's home. It was a dogtrot house, typically two log-cabin rooms separated by a breezeway. He had added to his house until it had many rooms and many dogtrots, creating a compound that was spacious but, in Jessie's state of mind, grotesque. The old man closed the evening complaining of a toothache, while "the creak of his wife's rocking-chair was the only other [sound] to break the silence." Jessie retreated to her room and went to bed. She woke to a noise—"a sound full of pain and grief, and wild rage too—a sound familiar enough to frontier people, but new to me. It was the she-wolf hunting her cubs." Jessie, with "nerves already overstrained," panicked. She felt she was being hunted. She woke Kitty, the maid who had come with her from the East, and made her build a fire, feeling its flames might scare off the animal—but then Jessie changed her mind, deciding the flames might attract the animal to crash through the window. Kitty silently helped Jessie to cover the windowpanes with shawls.

At last Jessie drifted back to sleep, only to be startled awake again. She perceived "a big dark object, rough-coated, and close to me. It was a speaking wolf too." It was John. He had come back. His men had moved only ten miles that day before making camp, so he had ridden through the night to spend one more hour with her. Kitty rose a second time to make them tea. They sat together by the fire and then, finally and for real, he was gone.

The San Juan Mountains in winter.

Chapter Eleven

WE PRESSED ONWARD
WITH FATAL RESOLUTION

Two Travelers, 1848–1849

New York, Panama, and the San Juan Mountains

By the start of 1848, the telegraph network developed by Samuel F. B. Morse was spreading with astonishing speed. Only four years after his first experimental line carried the first message from Washington to Baltimore, lines now shot up the East Coast to New York and Boston, and westward over the Appalachians to Buffalo, Detroit, and Louisville. It was common for newspapers to contain items in a column headlined "By Electric Telegraph," and this was how much of the nation learned of the end of the war. On February 4, the telegraph spread "rumors of peace" from Mexico, based on negotiations over a peace treaty. By February 18 the telegraph spread word that a messenger had reached New Orleans with a copy of the treaty. Its text described the new southern border of the United States, including the new boundary of California: a line starting at the Pacific Ocean near San Diego, the town that John's men had approached by ship and seized in mid-1846. Americans coveted its fine harbor, which was the reason Commodore Stockton had sent John to take it. His action established the farthest southern extent of American possession along the coast, and thus set the terms of the treaty negotiation: Mexicans could be told they might as well surrender that much land since United States troops had occupied it anyway and would never give it up. From San Diego the new border stretched inland, a straight line until it hit the Colorado River some 160 miles away. Land the size of an empire lay north of that line.

California remained isolated for the moment, still thousands of miles from the nearest telegraph line, so Jessie and John were slow to learn what had taken place there as John was leaving the army and the war was nearing its conclusion: gold had been discovered in California. It was found along the American River, the same waterway that John had followed down to safety from the snowy Sierra Nevada in 1844 ("Never did a name sound more sweetly!"). Now it was the setting of a seminal American story, which involved so many people whom the Frémonts knew that they were practically first cousins to the event.

The story started with John Sutter, who approved the construction of a gristmill that would be powered by the waters of the American. It was on land Sutter leased from Indians. In January 1848, the carpenter overseeing the mill construction discovered something glittering in a water channel. Sutter asked the mill workers to keep the news secret, but bragged about it himself. One of the first people he told was Mariano G. Vallejo, John's one-time prisoner at Sutter's Fort who was now refashioning his life under United States rule. In February, Sutter decided to inform the military governor of California, hoping to obtain official protection of his claim; his messenger brought a gold sample to show the governor and an aide, both of whom had met John during the war. The aide, Lieutenant William Tecumseh Sherman, bit the gold and pounded it flat with an ax to test its properties. Gold fever spread quickly; by the time Sherman escorted the governor to inspect the area of the discovery in July, about four thousand men were spread over the land surrounding Sutter's claim, digging holes and using water to sift the earth. They might find several thousand dollars' worth of gold in a day; they might find nothing. "For a time it seemed as though somebody would reach solid gold," Sherman said. The governor purchased an oyster can filled with gold at ten dollars per ounce and sent small vials of it to Washington. Thomas Larkin, the US consul, added a letter describing the find.

Two messengers, by two different routes, raced for the East, and the one who moved faster was Edward F. Beale, a friend of the Frémonts. He was in his midtwenties, with eager, observant eyes and a fringe of beard along his chin. Beale was the young naval officer who had served with John during the war. He returned to Washington by late 1847, which was when Jessie asked him to linger long enough to testify on John's behalf at the court-martial. Afterward her loyal friend reported to the navy's Pacific Squadron, but had hardly arrived on station when he volunteered for the task of racing eastward again to bring the container of gold to the capital. President Polk seemed unimpressed when young Beale first showed him the gold in September 1848 (Polk, exhausted and a lame duck after declining to run for a second term, told his diary that "nothing of importance occurred" on the day of Beale's visit), but the family of Jessie Benton Frémont knew better.

William Carey Jones, Jessie's brother-in-law and John's onetime defense counsel, learned that Beale had smuggled the gold vial past bandits in a journey across war-torn Mexico, and Jones wrote it up as an adventure story for a newspaper. Other papers picked up the story, and Jessie's friend Beale grew famous. The tale further spread news of the gold, which was capturing the country's imagination. Even Jessie was intrigued when she returned to Washington late that fall. "Are there any flowers or plants peculiar to a gold region?" she wrote John's botanist, apparently curious if underground riches might be located through study of the flora.

The same letter made it clear that she was still grieving her losses. She confessed, "I have had neither the quiet nor the strength" to copy out a list of plants for the botanist. Home was not relaxing, with her mother's condition worse, her father's mood increasingly bitter, and her husband gone. But at least Jessie could say she would not be apart from John for long, for she planned to travel westward with Lily by her side in early 1849. "I shall go by the isthmus after the steamers commence running," she explained. The lure of California was inspiring the creation of a new steamship line to carry passengers in comfort from New York southward to Panama, where they would cross the narrow country to catch a California-bound ship on its Pacific coast. The overland portion of Jessie's journey would be fifty miles, compared with John's roughly two thousand from St. Louis to San Francisco—"a much less interesting, but shorter & safer way for women & children."

Safety, of course, was relative. A newspaper article in early 1849 reported that of eight ships that had recently attempted to anchor on Panama's Caribbean coast, six had run aground. Once people reached the isthmus they risked tropical diseases, and some were turned away from overcrowded ships departing from the Pacific side. But the newspapers also contained enticing tales. One ship was said to have brought twelve thousand dollars' worth of gold to Charleston, South Carolina, and the captain of another returning ship declared that "the gold stories are not at all exaggerated, but are rather below the truth."

Steamers to Panama departed from New York, which Jessie reached in early 1849, days before her ship sailed. She checked into the finest of the city's hotels, which was a fitting place to launch a journey west. Many years before, John Jacob Astor had run his western fur empire from his home on that property; now Astor's house was replaced by the Astor House, a six-story building of white stone. Shops lined the facade, including a bookstore called Bedford and Co., which was selling a twenty-five-cent edition of *Fremont's Exploring Expedition*. Steps led up to the lobby, where Jessie stood on marble floors between piles of luggage that awaited the attention of porters. Hallways to either side led to sitting areas segregated by gender and family status: parlors to one side were "devoted to the single male guests," while the opposite corridor led to "a suite of public apartments used by ladies and married people," decorated with "velvet, lace, satin, gilding, rich carpets and mirrors." Jessie went for a walk in the Astor's upscale neighborhood. She found a jeweler's shop and showed the proprietor three emeralds that she wanted to have set in gold. John had given her the emeralds, which he had brought from the conquest of California, mysterious prizes of war. As was the case with John, anything she did now made the papers: the *New York Sun* wrote a story about the emeralds that was picked up by other papers across the country. The article speculated without evidence that Colonel Frémont had either obtained precious stones once owned by "Mexican and Peruvian Emperors" or discovered a secret emerald mine.

Returning to the hotel, Jessie had experiences sure to play on her mind. She discovered relatives who were staying at the Astor, but her delight at familiar faces became dismay as they questioned her plans. "I was much in the position of a nun carried into the world for the last time before taking the veil. All the arguments, all the reasons, all the fors and againsts, had to be gone over with this set of friends; all the griefs opened up again, and the starting made harder than ever." Hardly had she completed this inquisition when she faced a crisis involving one of her companions. Jessie was planning to travel with a maid, a young woman named Harriot, who was following her to California, less out of eagerness than a sense of duty. Harriot was engaged to a man who did not want her to go, and as Jessie later told the story, the fiancé appeared in New York and took desperate measures. "He went off," she said, "and raised the whole force of people who were allied for rescuing colored people being carried off to the South against their will." A crowd of African Americans began gathering at the hotel.

New York's black community knew that free black residents had been kidnapped and sold into slavery—people such as Solomon Northup, a musician lured away from Rochester, New York, in 1841 who had not been seen since. So many people had disappeared that state law provided assistance for efforts to recover them, and Jessie realized that "the cry of 'carrying off a free colored girl against her will' had the same effect . . . as an alarm of fire." Protesters, or a "colored mob," as Jessie called them, "poured into the Astor House, filling the lower halls, and raising such a commotion that Mr. Stetson," the hotel manager, "came for us to see what could be done." The crowd refused to trust the intentions of Jessie or her family. "It was true that we were Southerners . . . [but] not true that [Harriot] was being carried off against her will. The trouble was that she had no will; she had only affections, and these pulled her in contrary directions." Another possibility didn't occur to Jessie—that Harriot was pulled less by affection than by society's expectations. She was trapped between the competing demands of two people whom she likely felt she could not refuse: her assertive white employer and a man. The protest at last decided the issue. Jessie released the maid from her obligation and sent her into her fiancé's arms.

Stetson, the hotel manager, found a substitute servant, a white woman, who joined the traveling party when the steamship *Crescent City* glided out of New York Harbor on March 15, 1849. A cheering crowd bid the ship good-bye, and many newspapers took note of the famous explorer's wife on board. Jessie was on deck with three companions: her daughter, Lily; the new maid; and one of her brothers-in-law, Richard T. Jacob, who had been told to travel for his health and who could serve as Jessie's escort. Three hundred and thirty-eight passengers crowded the vessel, which a newspaper said was "a larger number . . . than has heretofore gone in any steamer" for Panama. Only 5 of the 338 were female, including Jessie, Lily, and the servant. The men and boys included would-be prospectors and others who hoped to profit by them. One burly passenger, twenty-seven-year-old Collis P. Huntington, was the co-owner of a hardware store in Oneonta, New York, and hoped to set up a branch store in California, obtaining his gold by selling goods that were needed in the goldfields. He was traveling with an initial stock that included rifles, woolen socks, and medicine.

Jessie avoided all such people and retreated to her cabin: "I was too worn down and silenced to care to know strangers." Once the ship cleared New York Harbor and emerged on the ocean, her brother-in-law also retired to his berth, "thoroughly seasick." And then Jessie woke in the night to discover the servant stealing items from her trunk. She reported the crime to the captain, who had the servant placed in another part of the ship. Only Lily remained with her. Jessie was more alone than she had ever been.

On the choppy sea off Cape Hatteras, she received a visit from a stewardess, who "made me go into the air." The sympathetic stewardess arranged a seat for her on the rocking wooden deck beneath the masts and the smoking funnel. "I had never seen the sea," she said, and "no one had ever told me of the wonderful new life it could bring . . . that grand solitude, that wide look from horizon to horizon, the sense of space, of freshness." She began to feel of the sea as her husband did. She found some relief from "the numbness of grief" and "morbid dwelling on what was now ended." In short order she had lost her son, said good-bye to her husband, let go of her mother and father, and separated from nearly everything of the life she had known. Now she plunged forward in a way she never had before. She became aware of the buzz of excitement on the ship and remembered the gold strikes. Above all she remembered her chance to reunite with John, and to do so in the West, which he loved. He might already be in California by now. She felt her optimism return. "Perhaps the sharpest lesson of life," she said, "is that we outlast so much—even ourselves—so that one, looking back, might say, 'When I died the first time . . . '"

✸ ✸ ✸

THE LAST LETTER JESSIE HAD RECEIVED from John placed him at Bent's Fort, the adobe-walled trading post just east of the Rockies. It was the place to which Jessie had addressed her passionate letter to John in 1846, hoping in vain that he would soon find it there. In November 1848 John did stop there to buy extra mules and supplies. The expedition had encountered snow on the prairie and ice when fording the Arkansas River, and men at Bent's Fort affirmed that winter was arriving early. John didn't stay long. He pushed westward up the Arkansas to Pueblo, in the future state of Colorado, facing the snowcapped Rockies. He was near the 38th parallel, almost directly west of St. Louis and directly east of San Francisco Bay; and here he asked around for a guide. He needed one because he was not aiming for well-known passes. He meant to move directly westward, through territory much less familiar.

Many lives depended on who gave directions, and the man who took up the challenge was William Williams, known as Old Bill Williams. John knew him; he had worked for the previous expedition when it passed through this region in 1845. Williams was "a man about six feet one inch in height," according to one description, "gaunt, red-headed, with a hard, weather-beaten face, marked deeply with the small pox." He was said to be "all muscle and sinew," worn from his travels but more comfortable outdoors than in. He was an eccentric horseman, who rode with the stirrups so short that his knees nearly touched his chest. But he said he knew passes in the direction John wanted to go, and agreed to try for them even though he expressed doubt about the wisdom of a winter crossing.

Williams, it seemed, had been everywhere and seen everything. As a young man he had lived in western Missouri as a missionary to Indians, but lost interest in converting them and went to live among them. He married an Osage woman, learned the language, and worked for federal Indian authorities as an interpreter and messenger. Sometimes he delivered documents to William Clark, the explorer turned Indian superintendent, and he assisted when Clark persuaded the Osage to sell their land and leave Missouri. Later Williams worked as a fur trapper, ranging as far as California and Canada. Although the perilous and exhausting trade was a young man's game, he kept on for decades, spending months or years at a time in the mountains before descending into Taos, New Mexico, to cash in his pelts and spend his profits on a drunken spree. He was sixty-two when he proposed to apply his rich experience to guide John's men, starting by crossing the Sangre de Cristo ("Blood of Christ") Mountains, which they reached on

November 26, 1848. The party numbered thirty-three, after a few had dropped out and Williams joined. They had more than a hundred mules, though the men started out on foot to spare the animals, which were loaded with shelled corn so they could be fed when the grass was covered with snow.

At the end of the first day of climbing, the group made camp near an overlook, where several men had a last glimpse of safety in the east. "The sight was beautiful," said one of the men, Micajah McGehee, "the snow-covered plain far beneath us stretching eastward as far as the eye could reach, while on the opposite side frowned the almost perpendicular wall of high mountains." Each day afterward the journey grew more difficult and the snow deeper, and they had not gone far before John began to lose faith in Bill Williams. "We occupied more than half a month in making the journey of a few days," John complained, "blundering a tortuous way through deep snow, which already began to choke up the passes, for which we were obliged to waste time in searching." The loss of time was dangerous, damaging the men's morale and using the mules' rapidly dwindling supply of corn. John thought Williams must have "entirely forgotten" the mountains they were crossing, while the mapmaker Charles Preuss wrote a summary judgment in his diary: "It was obvious that Bill had never been here." Williams did make one remark that suggested he knew the ground, though it was not reassuring: Micajah McGehee heard him say that "two trappers . . . had been frozen to death here the year previous."

Some expedition members blamed their trouble on John, who was giving the orders. Richard H. Kern, brother of the artist Edward Kern, wrote in his journal that exceptionally deep snow on December 9 should have persuaded John to turn back, but "with the willfully blind eyes of rashness and self-conceit and confidence he pushed on." At last they descended to the broad valley of the Rio Grande, which led in a westerly direction. John was expecting to follow it upstream to the next mountain chain. ("Usually the snow forms no obstacle to winter traveling" in the valley, he said.) But they found the valley covered in powder too deep for the mules to get at grass, and the animals had eaten nearly all their corn supply. As the men camped in a treeless region of snow-covered sand dunes, the hungry mules tried to flee, setting off eastward en masse. "We had to rise from our beds," said McGehee, "lifting half a foot of snow with our top blankets, and strike out in pursuit of them."

The Rio Grande Valley presented the men with an opportunity to show that they were as wise as the mules, because it gave them a chance to escape. Although John was aiming upriver to the west, he knew that if he changed directions and marched downriver, the valley would bend southward toward small settlements not many miles downstream. Beyond those settlements, about a hundred miles away, was Taos, New Mexico, where Kit Carson lived. A detour of several days could bring the men to safety, supplies, a better pass, and possibly a different guide. John did not detour. He was not ready to admit defeat, just as he had delayed almost two weeks before giving up his effort to cross the Great Basin in 1844.

They climbed westward into the San Juan Mountains. Richard H. Kern, who, like his brother Edward, was an artist, sketched bare trees and vertical rock walls, beneath which the men seemed like dots on the snow. John considered this terrain to be "the most rugged, and impracticable of all the Rocky Mountain ranges, inaccessible to trappers and hunters even in the summertime." If this was so, why was he attempting to cross these mountains in winter, and why would he imagine that railroad tracks could run through them? A railroad required a pass with a slope gradual enough for locomotives pulling heavy loads; John seemed to have lost sight of his purpose. "We pressed onward with fatal resolution," he confessed. "Even along the river-bottoms the snow was already belly-deep for the mules . . . The cold was extraordinary; at the warmest hours of the day (between one and two) the thermometer (Fahrenheit) standing in the shade of only a tree trunk at zero." The men in the lead beat down the snow with mauls so that it might hold the weight of those who followed. "Nothing was visible at times through the thick driving snow," said McGehee. "For days in succession we would labor to beat a trail a few hundred yards in length, but the next day the storm would leave no trace of the previous day's work." Men suffered frostbite in their "noses, ears, faces, fingers, and feet." In the evenings their fires sank down as the snow melted beneath them, creating holes where the men ate from their dwindling food stores; the only item of which they seemed to have brought an inexhaustible supply was coffee. At night, after the men had gone to sleep, starving mules ate the blankets off the backs of other mules, or wandered into camp and tried to eat the blankets off the men.

Having forgotten about finding a pass that was gradual enough for a railroad, John seemed even to forget about finding a pass suitable for men. He led the movement toward a final, bare summit ridge high above the tree line. If they could cross this ridge, he believed, they would leave the watershed of the Rio Grande and enter the watershed of the Colorado River, which would lead them on a mostly downhill path to the west and south. On their first try they were beaten back by a snowstorm. "Old Bill Williams," said McGehee, "was nearly frozen; he dropped down upon his mule in a stupor and was nearly senseless when we got into camp." The men lit their fires that night at the same place as the night before. On a second try they crested the ridge, descended the far slope to the first stand of timber, and gathered wood for their fires at an altitude of about twelve thousand feet. John looked back up their trail, which resembled the path of a defeated army: "pack saddles and packs, scattered articles of clothing, and dead mules strewed along." When he studied the vista westward he saw nothing but snow and more mountains. There was no green grass visible down below, no temperate lower valley as there had been when they emerged from the Sierra Nevada in 1844. There was almost nothing to feed the animals, and no sign of game to feed the men. At last John acknowledged his situation: "It was impossible to advance, and to turn back was equally impracticable. We were overtaken by sudden and inevitable ruin."

San Francisco Bay lay roughly a thousand miles to the west.

✳ ✳ ✳

JESSIE'S SHIP, THE CRESCENT CITY, was carrying her into a world she had known only through books. The ship was bound through Caribbean waters to the coastline of Panama, which she had first learned about in 1842, when she translated the memoir of the Spanish conquistador Bernal Díaz. His story had begun at the Spanish gold port of Nombre de Dios, on the Panamanian coast, as she recalled when that coast came into view. The pilot of Jessie's ship maneuvered toward the port of Chagres, where it must have been possible by now to find the harbor entrance by watching out for the wrecks of other ships that had run aground. When the Crescent City safely dropped anchor, the passengers looked out over woodlands. A fort from Spanish times spread across a hilltop to the left, its stone walls gray and mossy in the heat. Nearby lay a town, which a passenger on the ship described as "two or three hundred huts made of bamboo poles and covered with the leaves of the palm."

Smoke rose over the water, and a little steamboat came into focus beneath it. The boat pulled up alongside the Crescent City, taking on the first of several loads of passengers and mailbags. The boat, Jessie thought when her turn came to transfer over the side, was "as small as a craft could well be to hold an engine . . . It seemed like stepping down upon a toy." With Jessie's party and a few others on board it chugged up the tree-lined Chagres River, which led inland and partway across the isthmus. Soon the river became too shallow and rocky for the steamboat, forcing the passengers to transfer to smaller boats, mostly dugout canoes paddled by local crews. Swarms of Americans were making their way up the river that spring, a journey inland of only thirty miles or so that nevertheless took several days against the current. Sleeping in barns or on the bamboo floors of houses, crowds of men woke each morning and spread through the river valley like locusts, paying high prices for coffee and eggs, which they supplemented by hunting in the woods. "The scenery is delightful—the most beautiful I ever saw," one traveler wrote home, describing how he and his companions shot birds that resembled wild turkeys, lizards on the riverbanks, and even a monkey, which "cried like a child" when hit. "The woods are alive with parrots, chattering away like so many demons."

Jessie enjoyed a more comfortable journey, because people in Panama had instructions to care for her. They were American engineers, conducting surveys for a railroad across the isthmus to speed the way to California. An investor in the railroad, William Aspinwall, intended it to connect with his new steamship line, the Pacific Mail Steamship Company, which was starting service from Panama up the coast to California. Aspinwall had spent time in Washington obtaining a $199,000 contract to carry the US Mail to the west coast, and had become a friend of Senator Benton. Naturally the man with the federal contract was pleased to look after the influential senator's daughter, "with all the sympathies of his kind nature," as Jessie put it, and he made arrangements for "my comfort and security." Rather than a dugout canoe, Jessie's party boarded a whaleboat, larger and steadier on the water. Coming ashore each evening, she slept in an oversize tent prepared by the surveyors. US Army officers were part of the survey, and at each campsite she would find one or two waiting "to see that everything was right, and to have the pleasure of home talk with a lady."

The Chagres was nevertheless a miserable river for travel. The whaleboat was repeatedly stuck on sandbars. On the last of these Jessie's brother-in-law Richard Jacob, "being young and strong and a Kentuckian," impatiently leaped out and helped to drag the boat into deeper water. "He was very triumphant," Jessie said, until a short time afterward, "when suddenly his eyes rolled back in his head and he fell prostrate from sunstroke." Jacob was treated by a doctor at Gorgona, the next town, who insisted he must flee this climate and recover in New York. Soon Jessie was even more alone.

While lingering at Gorgona—another collection of bamboo huts, surrounding a handful of stone houses—she began to notice something wrong. The town was supposed to be a way station for travelers, where they left the boats and climbed on mules for the next part of the journey, but people seemed to be stuck. "There were hundreds of people camped out on the hill-slopes," said Jessie. They had yet to make it to Panama City on the Pacific coast—and there was no rush, because Panama City was crowded with travelers awaiting boats to California. The hillsides around Gorgona were, in effect, the back of a line that stretched more than twenty miles to the ocean. "There were many women, some with babies, among these; they were in a hot, unhealthy climate, and the uncertainty of everything was making them ill: loss of hope brings loss of strength: they were living on salt provisions brought from home with them, which were not fit for such a climate, and already many had died."

Eventually the engineers arranged mules for Jessie's party, and the ladies joined the line of other travelers that wound through a tropical forest and over a low chain of mountains. They followed a trail that, Jessie was told, had been used since Spanish times. Generations of travelers had worn a groove into the ground ("It was more trough than trail"), yet the path was still barely the width of one mule. They passed through a rock cut so narrow that men had to ride sidesaddle as Jessie did. Jessie was praised for her fortitude by one of the men from the railroad survey, though she felt that she was deceiving him: "The whole thing was so like a nightmare that one took it as a bad dream—in helpless silence."

At the old walled city of Panama, cannons jutted out of slots in the tops of the walls, and the ocean glittered beyond. Centuries ago the Spanish authorities had built the city on a peninsula jutting into the Pacific; now, for the American travelers, that peninsula was a magnificent dead end. Pacific Mail steamers were supposed to depart regularly between Panama City and San Francisco Bay, but there was a gap in service. A steamship that had departed for California weeks ago had not returned on schedule; another ship that was expected to begin plying the route had yet to make an appearance at all. Any ships in the harbor that could be chartered had long since sailed away filled with would-be gold prospectors. Stranded Americans were crowding into hotels or camping.

Jessie went to the city square, which was dominated by an old Spanish cathedral, its two white bell towers separated by the ornate and curving stone facade. She located a particular house facing the square, knocked, and presented a letter of introduction that she had wisely obtained back in Washington; a Latin American diplomat had written it to his aunt in Panama City, and she took in Jessie and Lily, assigning them to a room with a balcony overlooking the square. Jessie was so charmed by the view that she wrote a poetic description—although, as with her husband's reports, she submerged her own voice beneath that of someone else. Six-year-old Lily wanted to write her grandfather Senator Benton, so on April 27 Jessie took dictation of what Lily said, performing a tiny masterpiece of ghostwriting that preserved the cadence and imperfect grammar of a six-year-old while doubtless improving a few words.

> From here I see the jail and the government house and the water carts
> and the little Indians flocking about. . . . I see horses coming along with
> water. I saw a plenty processions [Catholic funeral processions] and one
> the man that led it was dressed all in gold cloth that shined like the sun;
> we saw the prisoners marching with dirt on their shoulders and chains
> around their waists and one of the guard masters with a gun on his
> shoulder to make them march about.

The stranded Americans formed a temporary community, organizing a vigilance committee to guard against crime, as well as Protestant church services to burnish their souls, while also doing what they could to make money. Panama City "is apparently completely in possession of our countrymen," said one. "There are American water-carriers, porters, boatmen, builders of canoes; there are auctions held hourly, when trunks, tents, camp stools, watches, preserved meats and even gold washers, are knocked down by the inevitable hammer." Mailbags were arriving from New York, sealed and marked for delivery to San Francisco; realizing that many of the letters must be intended for them, the Americans elected another committee to open the bags and look. Newcomers from the East brought newspapers, which passed from hand to hand.

It is likely that in some of these newspapers, Jessie spied her own name. Papers across the nation had picked up the story of the bold travels of "Mrs. Fremont," as she was called (Jessie was virtually never referred to by her given name), and all through that spring and summer, brief updates on the progress of the explorer's wife were making the papers in New York and Washington, then spreading to places as distant as Worcester, Massachusetts; Charleston, South Carolina; and even Tahlequah, the new capital of the relocated Cherokee Nation, in Indian Territory west of the Mississippi. But any pleasure she may have felt at her growing fame was destroyed when she began to learn the fate of her husband. A headline in the *New York Herald* read:

DREADFUL INTELLIGENCE FROM THE ROCKY MOUNTAINS—
Horrible Sufferings of Colonel Fremont's Party.

She clutched the paper and sat on the sofa and read. The paper, of course, took her back in time, because information traveled so slowly. She was reading of events from December and January—long before she had even departed New York.

✳ ✳ ✳

WHEN JOHN REACHED the western side of the mountain in December 1848, he instructed his men to remain a few days in camp. They ate their macaroni and cooked the meat of dead mules. John drank coffee and developed a plan of retreat. First the men would lug their baggage and equipment back over the windy summit they had just crossed, returning to the eastern side of the mountain so they could descend to one of the streams that fed the Rio Grande. That river would be their highway to safety, although once the men began to move they found the labor brutal and demoralizing. "A few days were sufficient to destroy our fine band of mules," John said. "They generally kept huddled together, and as they froze, one would be seen to tumble down, and the snow would cover him.... The courage of the men failed fast: In fact, I have never seen men so discouraged by misfortune." A handful refused to quit, above all Alex Godey, who had gone with John to California and then to the court-martial and was with him still. By Christmas Day they were on a tributary of the Rio Grande, and John sent four volunteers ahead in search of aid. He assigned Old Bill Williams to guide the group, a bizarre choice given his work so far, but these were desperate times. The remaining twenty-nine men, including John, would slowly shift their baggage down to the main channel of the Rio Grande and wait there, tending fires to stay alive and rationing the food that remained. John had a simpler option available: abandoning most of the equipment and marching everyone to safety while they still had some food left. But leaving the equipment would mean ending the expedition; he thought he could resume on a new route once the fresh supplies came up.

At quiet moments in a tent or wrapped in a blanket near a fire, John reached into a bag and fished out a set of books: William Blackstone's *Commentaries on the Laws of England*. He had borrowed them from Senator Benton's library in Washington, dense and demanding volumes commonly read by aspiring lawyers. The Illinois lawmaker Abraham Lincoln had read them twice and later kept them in his cluttered law office; now John was reading them in his shelter in the ever-deepening snow. He was thinking of a career mixing law and politics, still focused on his California future amid the increasing pain of hunger and cold.

One day a man named Proue vanished from camp. "In a sunshiny day," John said, "and having with him the means to make a fire, he threw his blankets down in the trail and lay there till he froze to death." Now they were twenty-eight by the riverside in the snow, and some were increasingly bitter toward their commander. The artist Richard H. Kern entered in his journal that Proue had really died "by Frémont's harsh treatment," though he didn't specify what the treatment was. Given the way that John occasionally humiliated men who did not share his single-minded focus on his mission, it is plausible that he treated Proue poorly, although that was not the true cause of death. The cause of death was John's ordering his men into the San Juan Mountains in winter.

Around January 8 John concluded that they could wait no longer for relief. He formed a second party to go for help and led it himself, bringing along four others: the mapmaker Preuss, his best man Godey, Godey's nephew, and Jackson Saunders, a black man who had been a servant in the Benton household and now served as John's orderly. The men he left behind could be forgiven for thinking, as the small party walked out of camp, that John was taking only the men he knew best and cared for the most, but John surely thought that these were the men he could rely upon the most. Their journey was bleak. For the first four days walking downriver in the snow, the little party did not spy another person. They built a fire each evening and ate the last of their meat and macaroni. After that they had nothing but strong coffee, heavily sugared, and this alone sustained them. On the fifth day they surprised an Indian man, a member of the Utah Nation who was walking on the ice of the river. The man agreed to lead them to his house some miles away, and when they reached it the following morning they sat down to eat what Charles Preuss called "a magnificent breakfast of corn mush and venison, together with our coffee."

It was the latest of many times that John could say he owed his life to a native; however, the man's help was not yet enough. They needed animals and food to rescue the men left behind. In exchange for a rifle and John's own two blankets, the Utah man agreed to guide them onward, bringing four "wretchedly poor" horses that were too weak to carry the men but that could at least carry their few supplies. They had not walked far before they discovered three men huddled around a fire. They seemed like strangers at first. "We had to open our eyes to recognize them," said Preuss, "so skinny and hollow-eyed did they look." They were the remnants of the party John had sent for relief. Exhausted and starving, they seemed to have "entirely lost sight of the purpose of their expedition," as Preuss put it, and they focused only on finding food while walking short distances each day. They had boiled and eaten straps, gun cases, and anything else made of leather. One had died. When discovered, the survivors were gnawing the meat of a deer they had killed, having spent twenty-two days walking the distance that John's party had just covered in six. Gathering up the three men, John's group staggered into a little town. When they learned that the settlement could not offer enough animals to relieve the men still stranded upriver, heroic Alex Godey rode downriver to the next town and returned with a string of mules.

Some of his men would later view John as their savior. Others took a darker view. He had led them on an absurdly dangerous mission, persisted long after its hopelessness was apparent, and at the end walked away from the bulk of his men. That John had led them all on a delusional expedition was undeniable; that he had disregarded their welfare in the interest of his goals was obvious. That he had abandoned them was somewhat unfair. John had at last moved to find help, succeeding where a previous party of experienced men had failed, and after he was safe he traded away his own gun and blankets to find help for the others. But it was accurate that John did not personally return to relieve his men, as a commander might have been expected to do. Eager to continue to California—he seemed never to consider turning back east—he focused on reorganizing his expedition and left the rescue to Godey, who enlisted a handful of generous Mexican residents and soldiers from a nearby army post and worked upriver to discover the remaining men of the expedition in small groups—walking, huddled by fires, or dead.

From these men Godey learned what had happened. After waiting a few days in camp, the twenty-three men had started for help on foot. They had walked only two miles when an Indian called Manuel returned to camp to die. After ten miles another man, named Wise, threw away his gun and blankets, staggered forward, and died; his comrades buried him in the snow. Two days later another man raved all night about things he imagined eating, and in the morning wandered off and disappeared. Later that day two more men said they could walk no farther, and their comrades built them a fire before leaving them. That evening, one of the remaining eighteen men killed a deer, which sustained the ravenous group for another day. A day or two afterward, Vincent Haler, the man in charge, said the party should break into smaller groups. Haler said he was determined to keep walking until he was rescued or died, while another group was willing to build a fire, wait for help, and if necessary eat those who perished first. The men who were left in the trailing group described the separation differently—that the stronger men were abandoning the weaker. The last days of the flight would be clouded by conflicting accounts, rumors, and shame, but some of the men said their comrades ate the bodies of the dead.

Haler staggered onward at the head of a party of eight, though two of his men gave up in the days that followed and had to be left beside fires. At last two Indian youths in Haler's party walked ahead of the others, and it was these Indians who made it possible to save all who remained alive. Haler heard gunshots in the distance—a signal that the two youths had found the approaching relief party—and came forward to find Godey. Upon seeing each other, the men cried. After a meal, Haler's men and the relief party turned upstream together, gathering the wreckage of men huddled by firesides. In all, eleven had died, one-third of those who had ridden into the mountains at the end of November. One of the survivors, Andrew Cathcart, described himself as "a perfect skeleton, snowblind, frostbitten and hardly able to stand."

John decided that the survivors should continue down the Rio Grande to recover at Taos, New Mexico. He led the way there, riding by the end of

January into the old Spanish colonial settlement overlooked by snowcapped mountains. Until recently the town had been part of Mexico; now there was a United States Army post, where the commander ordered rations distributed to John's men. Near the army post John found the home of his friend Kit Carson: a low adobe structure where Carson lived with his third wife, who was Mexican, as well as several children. It was here, with a family, that John rested and began to compose a letter to his wife.

Taos, New Mexico, January 27, 1849

I write you from the house of our good friend Carson. This morning a cup of chocolate was brought to me while yet in bed. To an overworn, overworked, much-fatigued and starving traveller these little luxuries of the world offer an interest which in your comfortable home it is not possible for you to conceive.

He told her all that had gone wrong, though he blamed it all on Old Bill Williams. He said he still expected to proceed west, regrouping the men who were willing and able to continue, and starting for California by a southerly route, along old Spanish trails.

. . . How rapid are the changes of life! A few days ago, and I was struggling through the snow. . . . Now I am seated by a comfortable fire, alone— pursuing my own thoughts—writing to you in the certainty of reaching you—a French volume of Balzac on the table—a colored print of the landing of Columbus on the wall before me—listening in safety to the raging storm without!

He insisted the mental stress of his experience had no effect on him. "You will wish to know what effect the scenes I have passed through have had upon me. In person, none." He then said the same thing a second time.

"The destruction of my party, and the loss of friends, are causes of grief; but I have not been injured in body or mind. Both have been strained, and severely taxed, but neither hurt." As if trying to persuade himself, he then phrased it a third time: he had seen "strong frames, strong minds, and stout hearts" give way in others, "but, as heretofore, I have come out unhurt." He added that "the remembrance of friends" had sustained him.

Over the next few days he reorganized as quickly as possible to continue westward, preparing to leave town so swiftly that some of the men who dropped out of the expedition, such as Richard H. Kern, felt abandoned. They complained that they were left to buy their own meals while John hoarded all the rations he'd been given by the army. That John was determined to reach the Pacific there could be no doubt; his search for a rail route had failed, but he meant to meet Jessie at their new home.

He had marked his thirty-sixth birthday on January 21, soon after escaping the snow.

✴ ✴ ✴

JESSIE READ HIS LETTER three months later, in May, thirty-six hundred miles away in Panama City. Near the end she saw this sentence: "It will not be necessary to tell you anything further. It has been sufficient pain for you to read what I have already written." That was wrong. Jessie wanted to know one more thing that she had no chance of knowing: What had become of her husband in the months since his letter? What were his odds of survival when he set out across the southwestern mountains and deserts? As the news of John's predicament spread among the other travelers stranded in Panama City, "friends and strangers both rose to protest against my going any farther." Even if Jessie and Lily made it safely to California, it was reasonable to fear that John would not be there to meet them. Jessie spent an entire day sitting on a sofa in her host's house by the square, "my forehead purple from congestion of the brain, and entirely unable to understand anything said to me." To combat her "brain-fever," Jessie's hosts summoned a physician, who proposed that she raise blisters on her skin. She rubbed a substance called croton oil on her chest, believing that the blisters it caused would pull impurities from her body.

After a few days she felt well enough to walk out to the ramparts of the old walled city. Stranded Americans strolled atop the walls during the cool hour before sunset. "They were an eager, animated set of people when first there, but the failure of the steamers to arrive had told upon every one. They felt, like shipwrecked people, that there was no escape." While many, like Jessie, were living in hotels or houses in town, others were living in tents just outside the city walls; Jessie would have seen their camps from her perch on the ramparts. One of the men in the tents was Collis P. Huntington, the New York hardware store owner, who had decided against a hotel so he could save money and camp near his supply of guns, socks, and other goods. Huntington, at least, was thriving: he was already starting his career as a gold rush trader, ranging into the Panamanian countryside for goods to sell to his fellow emigrants. But others ran short of money, caught tropical fevers, or buried members of their parties who fell ill and died. It was the frustrated, sick, and idle who caught Jessie's eye as she sat on the barrel of an old brass cannon. "The sight of this discouraged set of people almost decided me to go home," she said, but she persisted until the evening the travelers heard a cannon shot in the harbor. It was the signal of a ship arriving. A second cannon blast announced that another steamer had arrived almost simultaneously. One ship, called the *Oregon*, had returned from San Francisco Bay, and the other had arrived to work the San Francisco route for the Pacific Mail Steamship Company, having come from New York all the way around Cape Horn at the southern tip of South America. The moonlit square in front of Jessie's house filled with disembarking passengers. "Of course I was up, dressed, and looking at all this busy throng," Jessie said, when she heard a man call out her name: "Mrs. Frémont here! Heavens, what a crib for a lady!"

The man in the crowd was Jessie's friend Edward F. Beale, the naval officer who had brought the news of California gold to Washington. She drew the bearded man away from the raucous mass so they could talk; these two young people, both in their midtwenties, were equally astonished to discover each other. After delivering the news of the gold strike, Beale had accepted an assignment to return to California with dispatches in the fall of 1848; Jessie knew this much, and might reasonably have expected to encounter him after her arrival at San Francisco Bay. But now, after less than two weeks in California, he was rushing back eastward, completing his third round trip from one coast to the other in three years. He had reached Panama City on the *Oregon*. Only in an excited whisper would he have said what he was carrying: a gold nugget that weighed eight pounds, which he expected to show off to investors in New York. He had grown from a mere messenger to an active promoter of California's riches. He was carrying a watch newly encased in gold. Several gold nuggets dangled from the watch chain. Many men were mining for gold, Beale said, and this was the reason that the steamship *Oregon* had been delayed in returning from California to Panama; its crew had abandoned it for the goldfields, and the steamer rode eerily at anchor in San Francisco for weeks until the captain could round up another crew. Almost every ship that reached San Francisco suffered the same fate.

Beale was in an enormous hurry—he was determined to cross the isthmus in hours, rather than weeks, to catch the next ship on the Caribbean side—but he lingered long enough to hear Jessie's story. When he learned of John's misfortunes, Jessie recounted, "I was not advised but ordered to go home." Beale insisted that she gather up Lily and her baggage; he would escort her. Just as firmly, Jessie refused. She bade Beale good-bye, then made sure she had tickets for herself and for Lily on one of the steamers bound for California. After Beale departed, she paid an emotional price for her decision, suffering the pangs of rethinking a choice made in haste. The book about the Spanish conquistador returned to her mind. "In the chronicle of the conquest of Mexico there is one night of disaster and massacres which Bernal Díaz records under the head tristissima noche [the saddest night]; I had had many sad nights since leaving home, but after my old friend left I think I could name this my saddest."

The Pacific Mail steamship *Panama* raised anchor carrying more than three hundred passengers on a vessel built with berths for something closer to two hundred. Extra passengers spread blankets on deck around the funnel, beneath the ship's three masts, and between the two huge side paddle wheels that propelled the ship. A newspaper correspondent who was among the passengers wrote that the "throng" of people with their "motley" manners and appearances were "full of picturesque interest . . . but to the comfort loving traveller, who had to hob nob with and elbow this strange crowd of varied hue, within the contracted limits of a steamboat . . . it was any thing but agreeable." Pacific Mail ships had a design flaw that caused them to roll side to side so sharply that the paddle wheel on the high side might rise six feet out of the water, spinning uselessly in the air. Yet for all the rocking of the deck, the "equatorial heat," and the "bilge water," the newspaper correspondent said "it ill became us to grow querulous, when the ladies bore their part of suffering and discomfort so heroically. Mrs. Fremont, who was on her way to join her husband, showed a power of endurance that was a fit counterpart to the heroism of that adventurer." The *New York Evening Post* eventually printed this description.

The few women were allowed some separation from the mass of men; Jessie received one of the staterooms belowdecks. But within a few days at sea, she developed a cough so severe that a man in the next cabin heard her through the wall. Blaming the dank air inside the coal-fired ship, he led her up on deck and helped arrange for her to spend most of her time on the quarterdeck, the raised area toward the back of the ship that was typically occupied by its officers. The crew draped an oversize flag over a boom to form a tent, which soon became a refuge for all the females on board. Jessie, Lily, and the others had a view of other passengers as they kept up the patterns of the temporary society they had created during their delay on land.

A pastor stood on the rocking deck and continued the Protestant Sunday services that had begun in Panama City; Jessie would have caught his voice when it carried over the sound of the steam engine and the creaking of the masts in the wind.

By now she had run through all of her reading material and all that she could borrow ("Everybody had a Shakespeare and not much besides"), so she had time to study the faces of the men on the main deck below. Some were familiar. There was a sitting congressman from Georgia on board, a man she might have spied around Washington and whose presence was somewhat mysterious. ("No one knows what business has brought him here," the *New York Post* correspondent said.) A former congressman from Mississippi was also on board, along with several other politicians, their business equally undefined. There were at least two military officers in the crowd, one from the army and one from the navy. The navy lieutenant proved to be useful. Late one night Jessie woke to a commotion of voices and realized in the darkness that some crisis was unfolding. Beyond the voices she heard "a low, busy, grating, whispering sound of waters—and [on the otherwise dark sea] I could see long broken lines of foamy white, which even my inexperience told me were unusual." These were breakers—waves crashing over a shoal, on which the steamer was about to run aground. The captain did not wake when men pounded on his door, so the navy man, Cadwalader Ringgold, took charge and directed the steamer away from danger.

Jessie rose the next morning and stood in the pure ocean air. She passed her birthday on the Pacific on May 31, 1849, with the mountains of California somewhere off to her right as the ship worked its way up the coast. She was twenty-five years old, starting a new life, shielded from the sun and rain by the colors of the flag.

California gold miners, 1851–52.

Chapter Twelve

JESSIE BENTON FRÉMONT WAS
THE BETTER MAN OF THE TWO

Two Californians, 1849

San Francisco, San Jose, and Monterey

J essie was on deck beneath her flag when the *Panama* turned eastward toward the early morning light on June 4. It steamed between rugged mountain slopes through the passage that her husband had named the Golden Gate. Ahead lay the rocky knob of Alcatraz Island and the open water of the bay. On the shoreline to the right was the presidio that John had raided by boat in 1846, and just beyond it the little town of Yerba Buena, which many were calling by a new name, San Francisco. From the deck of the *Panama*, she found the town to be "a bleak and meagre frontispiece to our Book of Fate. A few low houses, and many tents, such as they were, covered the base of some of the wind-swept treeless hills, over which the June fog rolled its chilling mist." The tents held the sudden increase in population. People "swarmed" around "the mud shore of the bay," but the waters of the harbor were eerily quiet: "Deserted ships of all sorts were swinging with the tide." Something about the sight of the place caused many passengers to hesitate before going ashore. They lingered, ate another meal or two from the ship's stores, and spent a last few hours in the floating society they had built. A man rowed out to the ship and offered sobering information: many men in the goldfields were working for ten dollars per day, excellent wages but hardly the fortune that was inspiring so many to make the passage, and "so hard was the work" that some discouraged men had already given up to find jobs in the shantytown that was San Francisco.

It was too late to turn back. The passengers hoisted their "salt pork, tin kettles, tools, and India rubber contrivances," and started finding ways ashore, and the moment they went over the side of the ship many abandoned their orderly and generous society. "The mere landing of the passengers was a problem," Jessie said, because "the crews who took boats to shore were pretty sure not to come back." Fortunately a San Francisco merchant sent his own boat to help pick up passengers. Once ashore, the three hundred people from the *Panama* had to find places to stay in a town that had no room for those already present; one of the men who arrived that summer said it was typical to sleep on a plank while fending off "the attacks of innumerable fleas," and to be awakened before sunrise "by the sounds of building, with which the hills are all alive." But passengers from the *Panama* promptly established the patterns of new lives, as the correspondent for the *New York Evening Post* observed: "The parson, who had each Sunday during the voyage, read to us the service, and preached against this world with its lusts, was off to the mines, with tin pan and shovel. A sober, staid, and smooth-faced man, that had conducted himself like a saint on board ship, was to be seen, much to the surprise of all, dealing cards at a faro table, at the Parker Hotel." Amid the "wooden sheds, mud huts and streets, scattered pell mell along the gorge," some men set up as "speculators and financiers," even if they did not have offices and had to do business on a "tin plate."

Jessie was able to launch her own new life with a feeling of triumph and relief. On the way up the coast she had received glorious news: when a boat put ashore during a stop at San Diego, its crew brought back word that John was alive, and had been seen in Los Angeles, heading north. Jessie's decision to complete her journey was vindicated, and the rest of the way up the coast she was able to imagine him riding a parallel course in the interior. But he was not yet in San Francisco when she arrived. She managed to find a place to stay in one of the best houses in town, which was unexpectedly available: the home of William Leidesdorff, the merchant and former vice-consul. The black diplomat, who had hosted John in his house at the start of 1846, had recently died short of his fortieth birthday, and the location of his "girl-like" Russian wife was unclear. Their house was now occupied by a "club of wealthy merchants," who shared it and hired Chinese immigrants as servants. Standing on the veranda, Jessie admired the "beautiful garden kept in old-world order by a Scotch gardener." She walked inside, studied the carpets, and noticed the English brand name Broadwood on the piano. The merchants offered her, as the only woman among them, "the one room with a fire-place," a luxury in a town where, it was said, "there daily blows a hurricane."

The merchants' house would have contained the latest issues of the San Francisco newspaper, the *Alta California*, which described a region near anarchy. A military governor was in charge down the coast at Monterey, but there was no fully developed civil government, and the institutions that existed were overwhelmed by the flood of population and wealth. "Every man carried his code of laws on his hip and administered it according to his own pleasure," said one of the new arrivals. "There was no safety of life or property. . . . We were absolutely in a state of chaos." Congress had failed to organize a territorial or state government, and an improvised California legislature was clashing with the military governor over its authority. The governor, General Bennet Riley, had proposed a solution the day before Jessie arrived: his proclamation called on Californians to elect representatives to a constitutional convention to organize a state government, which would appeal to Congress for recognition. Soon San Franciscans were announcing a mass meeting to discuss proposals for statehood. Jessie might well have attended the meeting, and was surely nearby when it was called to order at Portsmouth Square, barely a thousand feet from the house where she was staying, at three o'clock in the afternoon on June 12. The speakers included current and former lawmakers who had just arrived on the same steamer as Jessie, yet now addressed the crowd as if they were longtime California leaders. Word was spreading that the Georgia congressman Thomas Butler King was in California as a confidential agent of Zachary Taylor, the newly inaugurated president of the United States. King's job was to bring California into the Union as a state; the two military officers who had traveled on the *Panama* were his aides. A witness to the mass meeting said King spoke "with his accustomed eloquence and ability." The speakers also included the former Mississippi congressman from Jessie's ship, William M. Gwin, a man with a chiseled face and high cheekbones and burning ambition. Each of the eastern lawmakers dreamed of returning to Congress as one of California's first United States senators. The *Post* correspondent sarcastically marveled that the men could "understand the wants and necessities of California after only a few weeks' residence in the Territory! . . . It is to be regretted, however, that they could not have found some Territory nearer home worthy of their patriotism and sacrifices."

If Jessie heard or read such remarks, she had to make an effort not to take them personally. Her husband had an ambition similar to that of the other new arrivals; John would have been delighted to become governor once military rule had ended. He would have an advantage over other new-comers in seeking such a post: he, at least, had a past connection to California. Jessie could see that John's family name—*their* name—was visible all over. The *Alta California* carried advertisements that summer for tradesmen and services at a new town called Fremont, established by the Sacramento River and serving the nearby goldfields. It was in this period or soon after that San Francisco named Fremont Street. One of the new businesses in San Francisco was called the Frémont Family Hotel, which became, among other things, the location for regular drawings in "The Grand Californian Lottery." Shortly after Jessie's arrival, a ship arrived in San Francisco Bay from Baltimore; it was called the *Colonel Fremont*. (The newspaper advertised the goods it brought for sale: "whiskey, 4th proof brandy, apple brandy, cordials, champagne, wine, gin, rum, gunpowder, shot," along with dried beef, pork, shovels, boots, and "Penn[sylvania] cheese.") Not all of John's publicity was favorable: the *Alta California* that was current when Jessie arrived included a long article on its front page detailing an old controversy over the payment for horses that John had purchased during his disputed tenure as the military governor of California. Yet even this awkward news underlined his ties to the place. He was as well positioned as anyone to rise to power, whenever he finally turned up.

✳ ✳ ✳

As Jessie was arriving in San Francisco, John was approximately two hundred miles southeast, at Tulare Lake in the Central Valley, swatting away insects. On the first of June, he sat down to write a greeting to a friend elsewhere in California. He kept it short: "The mosquitoes torment me here so much that I absolutely cannot write. You have passed them here yourself and know them by experience." He signed the letter and handed it to Alex Godey, who was to deliver the note and ask if the friend had any horses to sell. John was short of cash, and hoped his friend would sell horses cheap and put them "on my account," meaning on credit. Godey had already made a long ride to Monterey on the coast and had been unable to find animals that they could afford.

John was at the head of the remnant of his expedition. Just short of twenty men had spent two months, from mid-February to mid-April, crossing the mountains and deserts to southern California. They passed near desert hot springs known as Agua Caliente, later the site of a town called Palm Springs. They reached a rancho controlled by an American outside Los Angeles. Some then broke off to seek their fortunes, while John gathered supplies from Los Angeles and continued north. Jackson Saunders, the black servant, was still with him, as was Preuss the mapmaker, although Preuss would soon find work in California. John was also traveling with a large group of people he had recently met: men, women, and children who were migrating from the Mexican state of Sonora. The Mexicans had experience working in Sonora's gold mines, and wanted to put their skills to use in California. It may have been when John met them in the southwestern desert that he first heard of California's gold—and he quickly understood what it could mean for him. The two groups traveled together for a time for mutual protection against Indians, and John recorded in his notes: "Some of the Sonorians decide[d] to go . . . with me to look for gold which I told them would be found [on my land]."

His land: he was a significant landowner in California. He had been for more than two years, after obtaining property during the war. Given the central role that his interest in California real estate had played in his past actions, it should have been no surprise that while collaborating with Commodore Stockton, clashing with General Kearny, fending off the Mexican uprising in Los Angeles, assuming the governorship, and losing it, he had also found time to purchase real estate. Conducting land deals while commanding troops in a war zone created considerable risk that he could abuse his power—indeed, it seemed the definition of an abuse of power—but he did not hide his transactions: "I had always intended to make my home in the country if possible," he explained, "and for this purpose desired a foothold in it." He bought properties on the peninsula near the Golden Gate, anticipating the city that would grow there. In early 1847 he asked the consul Thomas O. Larkin to help him buy more land, and Larkin found an opportunity that seemed too good to refuse: an enormous land grant in the Central Valley, extending into the foothills of the Sierra Nevada, near Yosemite Valley.

The grant belonged to Juan B. Alvarado, a former governor of Alta California, although his claim might have surprised the Miwok Indians who lived there. The land was not settled by outsiders or even surveyed. It was believed to extend over ten square leagues, or 44,280 acres, more than

sixty-nine square miles—an area more than three times the size of the island of Manhattan, and slightly larger than the District of Columbia. The
grant centered on Mariposa Creek, and would be known as Las Mariposas.
Alvarado had received it from the Mexican government on condition that
he would never sell, but with Mexican authority crumbling, he disregarded
this and sold to John for three thousand dollars, less than seven cents per
acre. It was pure speculation. "I had never seen the place," John said, and he
knew "nothing of its character or value." Weeks later he was ordered eastward by General Kearny for his eventual arrest and court-martial, and
he never inspected the land; later he contemplated suing Larkin to undo
the sale.

He also made plans to set up as a land baron in the manner of John
Sutter. He arranged for sawmill machinery to be shipped to California by
sea, along with items suitable for a country squire. William Aspinwall, the
Pacific Mail Steamship Company executive who had eased Jessie's passage
across Panama, performed another favor by making arrangements to build
a special traveling coach for the Frémonts. This had been sent by sea and,
John hoped, was awaiting pickup at a warehouse in San Francisco.

When he met the Sonorans in the desert, he proposed a deal. They
had mining skills; he had land. If some wanted to prospect on his property, John would split the proceeds. Twenty-eight accepted. Once enough
fresh horses were in hand, John escorted them to Las Mariposas and left
them to their work.

Next he went in search of Jessie, reaching San Francisco in mid-June.
They spent only a few days together there; she felt the climate was damaging her health, so they tried the air in Monterey. It was a half-empty town,
where almost the only men who had not left for the gold region were
those such as the consul and businessman Thomas Larkin, who was already rich, or US troops whose enlistments prevented them from seeking
their fortune—and even many soldiers deserted. One of the few men who

remained for Jessie to meet was "long thin young" William Tecumseh Sherman, the officer who had been among the first to be told of the gold strike. There were also Californian women, among them the wife of General José Castro, the former Mexican official whose troops had once confronted John's force. General Castro was away but his spouse shared their house, renting the Frémonts one wing of it, with a window overlooking the bay. Jessie sensed that she was not the most welcome visitor; to the Californians "my name represented only invasion and defeat," but they helped her scrounge milk and food for Lily: "every eatable thing had been eaten off the face of the country, and nothing raised."

For some days the Frémonts explored the country in their carriage, taking a kind of holiday and sleeping on the cushions. Then, while keeping their rooms in Monterey, they moved to San Jose, just south of San Francisco Bay, where John was setting up the sawmill machinery he'd had shipped from the East. He saw an opportunity. The shrewder characters in California grasped that while it was a gamble to seek one's fortune by mining, they could make a more certain income selling supplies to miners. That was the plan of Collis P. Huntington, the New York hardware store owner who, along with Jessie, had been on the *Crescent City* out of New York; arriving on a different ship in late August, he peddled goods in the goldfields and then opened a store in Sacramento, his first step toward becoming one of the richest men in California. A similar possibility was open to John when he started his sawmill and a steam engine to turn it. Timber was wanted everywhere—for every building, for underground mines, even for the creation of wood-plank streets in San Francisco—and John soon had men hacking down enormous redwood trees to feed them into the whining saw.

In the overcrowded town they were able to rent only a single dusty room ("Fleas swarmed there," Jessie said unfairly, "as they do wherever the Spanish language is spoken"), and she cast about to find a servant. John had intended for Jackson Saunders to work as a cook, but the African American man made a request the Frémonts could not refuse: his wife back east was enslaved, which meant that by law his children were enslaved, and upon reaching California he realized that he could dig for the gold to buy their freedom. John helped him obtain equipment and sent him off to Las Mariposas among the Sonorans. Next Jessie learned of a "cook, washer, and ironer for sale." A white migrant to California had brought along a black slave and was now willing to part with her. Residents informed Jessie of the opportunity, "as I was thought to be the most helpless woman in town," but she held to the principles she had learned from her mother and refused to become a slave owner. Another person in San Jose later bought the woman for the extravagant price of four thousand dollars.

✳ ✳ ✳

IN AUGUST, JOHN WAS ON A PORCH IN SAN JOSE when he looked up to see his friend Edward F. Beale approaching. Incredibly, the naval officer turned gold promoter had completed the ordeal of returning to California yet again, having become one of the first Americans to lead a bicoastal life. Since spotting Jessie in Panama in May as he traveled to the East, Beale had reached New York and held up his eight-pound lump of gold in front of a crowd of men on Wall Street before turning back toward the Pacific. Now he was moving about California with a journalist, who wanted the opportunity to introduce himself to John. The journalist took a careful look at Colonel Frémont, who was "wearing a sombrero and a Californian jacket, and showing no trace of the terrible hardships he had lately undergone." John was so reserved and unassuming that the journalist, Bayard Taylor, would not have guessed that he was looking at "the Columbus of our central wildernesses"; perhaps this was another way of saying that John's celebrity made him so much larger than life that John, when encountered in person, seemed a bit smaller than expected. Still the reporter was impressed that John was "compactly knit—in fact, I have seen in no other man the qualities of lightness, activity, strength and physical endurance in so perfect an equilibrium." His thin, tanned face featured a "bold aquiline" nose and deep-set eyes that were "keen as a hawk's."

Edward F. Beale had come carrying a letter for John from the East, which John opened and read. It said President Zachary Taylor had appointed him to a commission assigned to draw the new boundary between the United States and Mexico. John sent an immediate letter of acceptance, thanking the president for "the mark of confidence bestowed upon me"; he viewed the appointment as vindication, presuming the government's call to service implied an acknowledgment that the judgment of his court-martial had been wrong after all.

The Frémonts were still in San Jose when they received even more up-lifting news. A convoy of animals arrived, driven by some of the Sonorans who had been digging for gold at Las Mariposas. One animal bore a buckskin bag holding the first diggings, which Jessie believed to be one hundred pounds of gold, or at least of quartz shot through with gold. Either way it was a fortune, and more bags soon arrived. Jessie said they "were put for safety under the straw mattress. There were no banks nor places of deposit of any kind. You had to trust some man that you knew, or keep guard yourself." Whenever possible, the Frémonts shipped the bags to Monterey, "and it accumulated in trunks in our rooms there." They were rich—so absurdly rich they hardly knew what to do, so rich they stopped trying even to keep track of their wealth. When, after a few months, the Sonorans reported to John that they were ready to take their share of the gold and go home, John did not take the time to travel with them to open the trunks of gold in Monterey. He simply gave them the keys to the trunks, trusting them to divide the fortune and leave the proper share behind. The lure of gold had driven much of the settlement of the New World, had enticed men to the greatest heights of bravery, ingenuity, cruelty, and madness—yet Jessie said afterward that the Sonorans divided the gold "with scrupulous honor, not taking an ounce more than their stipulated portion."

John Charles Frémont.

Jessie Benton Frémont.

There may be circumstances, however, which will induce you to refuse my request. Should it be so, let me, Dear Sir, take advantage of this occasion to express to you my thanks for your former kindness, and my pride at having been once distinguished by your notice —

I have the honor to be With much respect, Your Obt. Servt. J. Charles Fremont.

Honble. Joel R. Poinsett.

Greenville —

John's 1835 appeal to his mentor, Joel R. Poinsett, to "aid me with your influence" and help him get a job.

The mountains of California's Yosemite Valley.

Kit Carson, western trapper, guide,
and—when provoked—ruthless killer.

Thomas Hart Benton, Jessie's father
and a US Senator from 1821–51.

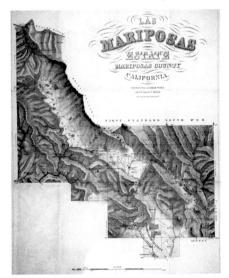

A map meant to promote the riches
of the Las Mariposas estate.

A contemporary drawing showing part
of the explorer's 1842 return from the
Rocky Mountains.

An artist's depiction of the moment when Indians
warned Frémont's 1842 expedition not to continue.

Francis Preston Blair, counselor to presidents from Jackson to Lincoln, who became one of John's campaign managers in 1856.

Horace Greeley, of the *New York Tribune*, who was inspired by John Frémont's western explorations and later promoted him for president.

Astor House in Manhattan, the luxury hotel where Jessie faced black protesters in 1849.

The office where Frederick Douglass published the *North Star,* later *Frederick Douglass's Paper.*

The Rochester, New York, building where Douglass published his newspaper in the 1840s and 1850s.

Douglass predicted a "powerful Northern party" would rise up to keep slavery out of western territories.

A campaign cartoon that was published before the 1856 election.

James Buchanan, whose life constantly intersected with that of the Frémonts, from Jessie's teenage days through the 1856 campaign.

John Bigelow of the *New York Post*, who authored a Frémont campaign biography while allowing Jessie to ghostwrite the most sensitive chapter.

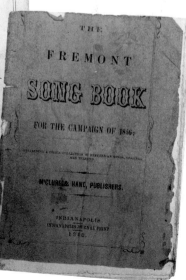

BLACK REPUBLICAN

IMPOSTURE EXPOSED!

FRAUD UPON THE PEOPLE!

THE ACCOUNTS OF FREMONT EXAMINED;

SHOWING

AN ASTOUNDING DISREGARD OF THE PUBLIC INTEREST, ONLY TO BE AC-
COUNTED FOR BY EXTRAVAGANCE, RECKLESSNESS, OR
AN UTTER WANT OF JUDGMENT!

To pry away Frémont's nativist supporters, Democrats accused him of being both Catholic and a foreigner—and a "Black Republican," who not only opposed slavery but favored racial equality.

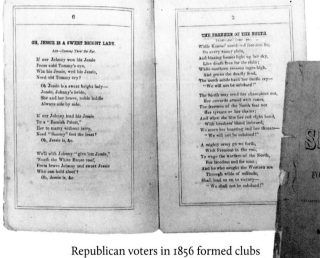

Republican voters in 1856 formed clubs to sing campaign ads, whose lyrics were found in songbooks like this.

Fremont Papers
Bancroft Library

1.

Page 1.

Precedes everything.

Preface.

When I had the misfortune, *more than also* two years since, to break my

leg, the agony of the first four months fully engrossed me. About the end of

that time I tried to read and occupy myself, but the nerves of the spine had

had too serious a wrench and I could not see . Therefore, for months longer,

I sat in darkness. A green shade was needed over my eyes, and no attempt was

made to use them.

In this enforced seclusion I thought, naturally, of the

most pleasant things in my long life, and always two figures came out and

"Stood by me like my glorious youth".

Then came to me the wish to tell of them as I knew them. So pressing was this

wish that I thought out whole chapters which I have since written out as under

dictation. Fragmentory, often broken and incomplete, this record follows no

received lines but to me the large life they enfold though given in outline

and no more is full of my lifes history. I beg it may be so read by those

who can bring to it the spirit in which I wrote it, imprisoned by pain in a

rolling chair, but hoping always I will live to see it, in book form. I dedicate

it to my youngest grandson who reproduces in a singular way the governing

Jessie Benton Frémont, a behind-the-scenes political player who moved increasingly to the front of the stage.

The first page of the typescript of Jessie's final memoir, written in 1902, the year of her death.

The Frémonts.

Other prospectors were more troublesome. Many raced to Las Mariposas without making any arrangements with John. He declared in a letter that "hundreds—soon becoming thousands—crowded to the same place." He could do little except hope that some would give him a share of their bounty in tribute for access to his property: his title had not included mineral rights, and his claim to the land itself was uncertain, since he had bought it from a man who had committed not to sell it and its boundaries were undefined. Even if his title was unquestioned, the lure of gold would have overwhelmed his defenses—John Sutter's far better-established empire to the north was being trampled. John faced years of litigation over his ownership, and in the meantime watched as a town called Mariposa grew up to become the seat of a new county. By 1850, when California participated in its first United States census, Mariposa County had gone from a non-Indian population of virtually no one to 1,512, including a scattering of merchants, hotelkeepers, carpenters, stonecutters, and a justice of the peace; 43 women, who mostly seemed to be the wives and daughters of miners or other recent emigrants; and 1,105 miners, no more than a few of whom worked for John Frémont.

* * *

THE DELEGATES TO CALIFORNIA'S constitutional convention gathered in Monterey at the start of September. They had come from all over the territory; delegates from San Francisco had taken passage down the coast in the ship called *Colonel Fremont*. They met in Monterey's new town hall, two stories high with a sloping roof and walls of solid yellow stone. It was called Colton Hall, after Walter Colton, a Monterey resident who had overseen its construction as the city's alcalde, or mayor. He had paid for the building by collecting fines from criminals, which was why he called it "the culprit hall," and said his name would "go down to posterity with the odor of gamblers, convicts, and tipplers."

The upper floor of Colton Hall formed a single room for public meetings. A railing separated the forty-eight delegates from spectators including William T. Sherman, the red-haired army officer, who had been sent as an observer by the military governor. It was a gathering of many big names in California's recent history: delegates included John Sutter, though he was said to be "a sort of ornamental appendage," rapidly losing influence; businessman Thomas O. Larkin, who was no longer consul, since California was no longer Mexican soil, but remained influential, daily hosting other delegates for dinner at his New England–style home; and Lansford Hastings, an ambitious self-promoter whose place in history had been established with the Hastings Cutoff, his problematic shortcut on the trail to California that was tried, to their sorrow, by the Donner Party on the way to their doom in 1846. Leaders of the Bear Flag Rebellion were in the room with former enemies among the old Californians. "The Spaniards," said one delegate, "served in the convention because they saw the necessity. . . . American occupation was inevitable, and they submitted with what grace they could." Mariano G. Vallejo, the Mexican general who had been imprisoned by John Frémont, was also a delegate. A journalist who met Vallejo at the convention described him as "tall and of commanding presence," his "eyes dark with a grave, dignified expression." He maintained his dignity amid the very sorts of foreign interlopers who had once invaded his house: one delegate was a Florida man who, it was said, "carried an enormous bowie knife & was half drunk most of the time."

William Gwin had been elected. The former Mississippi congressman who had arrived on Jessie's boat was well prepared, carrying copies of the state constitutions of Iowa and Ohio, which he believed could be used as templates for the California constitution to save time. Delegates with a longer history in California pushed back against Gwin's efforts to dominate the proceeding, but eventually did crib from the constitutions he had brought, and leaned on his experience as a legislator. Gwin's influence was significant because he had a definite position on an especially sensitive issue: slavery. The proposed state constitution must declare California to be a free state or a slave state. Of Gwin's personal view there could be no doubt: he was the owner of a Mississippi plantation worked by slaves, and called slavery "the foundation of civilization." He was in a position to urge that view—yet did not. He knew that if he and other delegates from the South demanded the right to bring slaves to California, they might create a deadlock with delegates from the North, reproducing the chaos then prevailing in Washington. Congress had failed to organize a territorial or state government in California because lawmakers could not agree on whether to allow slavery there. If California also failed to act, Gwin would lose: he wanted to be a senator, which required California to become a state. "Gwin, with good grace adopted the clause prohibiting slavery," said his follow delegate and friend, Elisha Crosby of New York. Section 18 of the state constitution read: "Neither slavery, nor involuntary servitude, unless for the punishment of crimes, shall ever be tolerated in this State."

"The admission of California to the Union was paramount to every other consideration," said delegate Crosby. Thus the clause was adopted almost unanimously, thanks in part to the ambition of a man who so strongly favored slavery that in future years he would side with the Confederacy. Thomas Butler King, the presidential emissary, was also a Southerner but favored the clause too; he had been told that President Taylor preferred a free state as part of his larger strategy for resolving the dispute over slavery in the conquered territory. The constitution certainly was not driven by an overwhelming desire for social equality: having approved the antislavery clause, the convention nearly approved a clause that prohibited the entry of any black people at all. That was eventually removed, but what remained was a clause similar to that in Iowa's constitution, explicitly granting the vote only to "every white male citizen of the United States." Free white Mexicans could also vote if they assumed American citizenship. People of African descent, Indians, Chinese, and others were defined out of the electorate.

The constitution was made less unfair through the intervention of the Californian delegates, who on issue after issue offered a different perspective than the newcomers from the United States. The Americans may have come from the land of liberty, but the Mexicans had a broader conception of it. Mexico had always outlawed slavery, which made it easy for the Californian delegates to endorse the antislavery clause. When it became clear that Indians would be denied the vote, the Californians objected: some of the delegates themselves had Indian ancestry, and a nephew of General Vallejo informed the assembly that landowning Indians had previously enjoyed the franchise. The American delegates grudgingly added a clause that the legislature could, by a two-thirds vote, allow voting to select Indians. The Californians scored a clearer victory in upholding the rights of women. A delegate from Virginia urged that wives should be denied the right to own property because their husbands could better provide for them; a committee that included General Vallejo and other Californians rejected this. They prevailed on the delegates to agree that "all property" that a woman brought into marriage, including real estate, "shall be her separate property."

In a further gesture, General Vallejo tried to have a Mexican vaquero added to the various images that crowded the new state seal. The seal featured grapes, mountains, ships in harbor, the Roman goddess Minerva, and a bear. Vallejo thought the vaquero should be lassoing the bear, but by a single vote he was defeated.

※ ※ ※

WHERE WERE THE FRÉMONTS during the convention? John, at least, made no impression. He had not chosen to stand for election to the convention and was taking a short break from public service. Having accepted his appointment to the boundary commission, he resigned; he wanted the vindication that the appointment represented to him but had no time for the work. Moving about in his sombrero and Californian jacket, he focused on business and his sudden fortune. He did appear in Monterey, where William T. Sherman saw him; he also appeared in San Francisco, lingering at the United States Hotel and showing off samples of gold from Las Mariposas. He encountered the newspaperman Bayard Taylor there, and told him that the Mariposa land had a vein of gold that seemed to be a mile long; he was trying to drum up investments that would allow him to more fully exploit it.

Jessie, by her own account, had more time for the convention. She said she was staying in Monterey, in the rooms the Frémonts had been granted within Madam Castro's house, and she began to play a political role. Convention delegates visited. Men in an overcrowded town, which apparently had just one restaurant, welcomed refreshments, a comfortable chair, and an opportunity to talk with that rarity in California, a lady from the States. Having drawn them in, Jessie took the opportunity to assure them "that I really did not want slaves"—in other words, that upscale women could make homes in California without them. (She had hired two Indian men as domestic help.) "Our decision," she said of herself and her husband, "was made on the side of free labor. It was not only the question of injustice to the blacks, but justice to the white men crowding into the country." Prospectors should be allowed to seek their fortune without facing unfair competition from other prospectors who had gangs of enslaved men at their command. This was, she suggested later, the beginning of her life as an antislavery activist.

One delegate cast doubt on Jessie's story—Elisha Crosby, the New Yorker, a critic of John Frémont. ("Frémont was a very nice little gentleman," Crosby said, "but I thought as many others did, that Jessie Benton Frémont was the better man of the two, far more intelligent and comprehensive.") Years later, Crosby denied that Jessie had influenced the convention and even that she was in Monterey at the time. To be fair to Jessie, she may have been in Monterey, even if Crosby did not remember her. She may have hosted delegates in her home, and it would have been natural, given her confidence in speaking to men about politics, that she would express her long-standing antislavery views. But in a larger sense, Crosby was right:

Jessie could not have significantly influenced the convention. The antislavery provision passed for pragmatic reasons, with the votes even of proslavery men like Gwin, and for some delegates Jessie's reasoned arguments against slavery were irrelevant.

Gwin, the Mississippi plantation owner, was like a sailor who placed his hand on the tiller to steer away from breakers and mistakenly thought it was a momentary change in course. The ship would never sail exactly the same heading again. For thirty years the nation's leaders had consciously maintained a balance between free and slave states. When Thomas Hart Benton's Missouri agitated for admission as a slave state in 1820, the free state of Maine had to be admitted in compensation. In the 1830s, the slave state of Arkansas was soon followed by the free state of Michigan. In the 1840s, the admission of both Texas and Florida made it urgent to follow with the free states of Iowa and Wisconsin. Now the free and slave states numbered fifteen against fifteen, which made them evenly balanced in the Senate. The admission of California as a free state would make it sixteen against fifteen, with other free states coming soon and no clear prospect of another slave state in view. Some Southerners talked of dividing California in two, forming a northern free and a southern slave state, with a border along the same Missouri Compromise line that had divided the Louisiana Purchase; but the Californians were preempting this talk by drawing their own borders and presenting their constitution as a fait accompli. If their act was upheld, Southerners would begin to lose their grip on the Senate. The North's growing population had already given it a majority of the House, and with California's rise, more and more of the electoral votes used to choose the president would be coming from free states. The balance of power was permanently shifting. Someday it might be possible to imagine the election of a president based on northern votes alone.

For Gwin, at the moment, all was working as planned. In mid-October 1849, the delegates signed the new constitution and sent it to Washington in hopes that Congress would approve it. In November, Californians elected a state legislature, and in December the lawmakers met in San Jose—in an adobe building that local leaders had purchased as an improvised state capital—to choose two prospective United States senators. Both would hurry to Washington, lobby for statehood, and then take their seats in the Senate if successful. One of the chosen was William M. Gwin. The New Yorker Elisha Crosby thought his presence might help the case for statehood, offering Southerners in Congress a reliable proslavery vote: "I was induced to vote for him as a U.S. Senator because he was known as an extreme Southern man." Failure to send such a man to the Senate would have been "so palpable a cut or insult to the South that the State never would have had a chance of admission."

For the other seat one name loomed above all others: John Charles Frémont. The conqueror of California had made it known that his brief hiatus from public life was over. In Jessie's view, his ambition grew out of their antislavery activism—which was to say her activism. "What we had done in Monterey when the State Constitution was being framed there had enrolled us on the antislavery side," she said. "It would have been deserting not to continue the work." He might have sought California's governorship instead, but a post in the Senate would allow them to return to Washington and "our old home life to be restored."

When asked to state his positions just before the vote, John spoke of slavery much more cautiously than Jessie did. Jacob R. Snyder, a California settler and frontiersman, wrote him a letter asking several questions, and John replied with a letter that was published in the *Alta California* on the day the legislature began its session. He declared his adherence to the Democratic Party ("By association, feeling, principle and education, I am thoroughly a democrat") and then ducked any discussion of slavery, saying he was not "entering into any discussion of the question at issue between the two great parties." He favored "a central, national railroad from the Mississippi River to the Pacific Ocean." Its "stupendous magnitude," he said, working up to a Thomas Hart Benton level of enthusiasm about global trade, made the railroad "the greatest enterprise of the age," which would bring changes "throughout the Pacific Ocean and eastern Asia— commingling together the European, American, and Asiatic races." It probably was not politically shrewd to speak of "commingling" the races before the all-white legislature, but he was too excited to contain himself. Even the catastrophe of his recent expedition became a success. "The result was entirely satisfactory," he wrote. "It convinced me that neither the snow of winter nor the mountain ranges were obstacles in the way of the road." He acknowledged that he had not actually located the necessary pass, but believed it existed. He fielded a few pointed questions about his ownership of Las Mariposas, but nothing prevented his easy election.

When John learned the news, he promptly departed San Jose. It was a rainy day, but that did not stop him from riding seventy miles southwest to Monterey, where Jessie had gone in another effort to improve her health. She was spending her days in their wing of the Castro house, which featured a bearskin rug and a fire. "The rains set in furiously," she said, "and I was completely house-bound; but I could see the bay, and even through the closed windows I could hear the delightful boom of the long rollers falling regularly and heavily on the beach." She sewed new clothes. She read old magazines to Lily. She spent time with an Australian woman who had signed on as a cook. Jessie and Lily were sitting with the cook during an evening of "tremendous rain" when "Mr. Frémont came in upon us, dripping wet, as well he might be, for he had come through from San Jose. . . . He was so wet that we could hardly make him cross the pretty room," but she urged him not to worry about the floor. He informed her that he had been elected senator, and added that he wanted to start for Washington within a few days.

Jessie was overjoyed. She wanted back her father and mother and siblings. She was lonely—she had only her husband, who was living with her yet not truly beside her, because he could not stop moving around

California. When he was done delivering the news about the Senate, he spent but a single night in Monterey and then departed, riding the same horse seventy miles back again through the rain to San Jose. To judge by the time spent, he was happier in motion than with her. Was there something off about him? Something she truly didn't know? He was, as ever, so respectful and reserved, so reluctant to drip water on the bear rug on his own floor. Yet that very reserve made him seem distant, even to her.

Jessie's final evening in California was the final evening of the year. "When we heard the steamer's gun, New-year's night, the rain was pouring in torrents, and every street crossing was a living brook. Mr. Frémont carried me down, warmly wrapped up, to the wharf, where we got into a little boat and rowed out. I have found that it changes the climate and removes illness to have the ship's head turned the way you wish to go." Surely John Charles Frémont had his own emotions as the ship raised anchor and the year 1850 arrived. One year ago he had been reading Blackstone's commentaries on the English law while sitting in a snowbound tent, his men near death all around him as he dreamed of building a career in California as a lawyer and a landowner. He had been thinking it might take seven years to establish himself. The gold rush had accelerated everything.

A newspaper reported that on his way out of California, Colonel Frémont had made "a timely and excellent donation for this state." He had given away books to help in creating a new state library, one hundred volumes in all, according to the journal of the state senate. The volumes revealed something about his life and interests, as did his decision to part with them. He gave away books associated with his former life as a soldier and explorer: one on astronomy, one on drawing with shades and shadows, and a "treatise on field fortification." He gave away books with which he had been preparing for a future as a lawyer: volumes on evidence and writing wills, and commentaries by the Supreme Court justice Joseph Story. He gave away the volumes of Blackstone that he had lifted from Senator

Benton's library and carried over the plains, the Rockies, and the south-western deserts, holding on to them even when he was walking for help in the snow and starving. Now he didn't need them anymore. He also let go a single work of fiction. It was a Spanish copy of *Don Quixote*, Cervantes's novel about the travels of an overly romantic man who had lost touch with the world.

Part Four

BLACK
REPUBLICANS

❋ ❋ ❋

Antebellum political heroes: Henry Clay sits beside John C. Calhoun, who holds a feather pen. Thomas Hart Benton is the fourth figure from the left, behind General Winfield Scott. Gray-haired James Buchanan is tucked behind the Romanesque statue. Bearded John Charles Frémont stands in the upper right.

San Francisco in 1850.

Chapter Thirteen

WE THOUGHT MONEY
MIGHT COME IN HANDY

Senator and Mrs. Frémont, 1850–1851

Washington and San Francisco

I f a single moment could illustrate the congressional debate over California statehood, it came on April 17, 1850, when Senator Henry Foote
of Mississippi prepared to walk into the Senate chamber by tucking a
pistol into his suit. It was a Colt revolver, available to him thanks to a revolution that was subtly changing American society. Samuel Colt, a Connecticut man, had begun making his patented revolvers in the 1830s, although
they were slow to catch on; the revolver that John Frémont fired at a Klamath man in Oregon in 1846 would have been one of the relatively few in
existence. But in the late 1840s Colt perfected his assembly-line production,
first selling revolvers to the Texas Rangers and then mass-producing a
small, five-shot weapon for civilian use, the 1849 Colt Pocket. With a barrel
as short as three inches, it could be dropped into a man's coat. Colt eventually sold more than 325,000 copies of the pistol as the United States, already
an armed society, took a giant leap forward in the power and convenience
of its concealed weapons. Foote carried his five-shooter into the Senate

because he was debating California statehood and feared a confrontation with an opponent, Senator Thomas Hart Benton.

Foote took his seat on the outermost semicircle of desks, from which he had a view of his Senate colleagues. The bitterness was palpable. Ever since news of California's constitution had reached Washington in late 1849, a faction of Southern men had labeled it a conspiracy to deprive them of their national power. Their leader was Senator John C. Calhoun of South Carolina, the man who had quietly orchestrated the nullification movement in the 1830s and advocated taking Texas in the 1840s. In March 1850 Calhoun requested time for a speech against California statehood. Emaciated and ill, the white-haired, stern-faced senator did not have the strength to deliver what he had written, so he huddled in his cloak at his Senate desk while a colleague from Virginia stood behind him reading it aloud. His speech said the "great and primary cause" of the South's discontent was that "the equilibrium between the two sections . . . has been destroyed." The North had become more populous and more powerful, and now that new territory had been won from Mexico, "the North is making the most strenuous efforts to appropriate the whole to herself." It would soon be impossible for the South to protect itself from an unrestrained federal government. "Seceding from the Union" would be justified if the Union was "oppressing instead of protecting us."

Benton considered Calhoun a traitor, trying to "pick a quarrel for a wicked purpose" of encouraging the South to secede. He forgave Calhoun nothing when the South Carolinian died a few weeks after his speech, and this helped to provoke his quarrel with Henry Foote of Mississippi, who was publicly defending Calhoun's memory. A balding, prickly man in his midforties, Foote recently had compared Benton to "a degenerate Roman senator." Now, on April 17, he rose to speak again. He declared that Benton, "the oldest member of the Senate," was one of the "calumniators" who spoke malicious falsehoods against the fallen hero Calhoun. Calling Benton a liar crossed a line. The Mississippi senator was mid-sentence when the massive sixty-eight-year-old Benton rose from his desk and began walking toward him. Foote retreated down the aisle and drew his five-shot Colt revolver. "In a moment," said a reporter afterward, "almost every Senator was on his feet." Some shouted for order. Some shouted for the sergeant at arms. Colleagues of Benton restrained him, while senators near Foote tried to take away his gun. Benton shook off his colleagues and advanced a second time, shouting, "I have no pistols! Let him fire! Stand out of the way, and let the assassin fire!" Instead another senator took charge of Foote's gun and "locked it in his desk." As the presiding officer tried to quiet the spectators in the gallery overhead, Benton declared that Foote wanted to "assassinate" him and demanded an investigation. The next day he wrote the United States attorney for Washington, requesting that Foote be charged with a crime.

The bitter feelings masked a reality: the gun remained unfired. The Union was not yet torn in two. Benton and Foote had different visions of the country, but on the immediate issue disagreed less than it seemed. Both knew California statehood had enough votes to pass, and differed only on how it should be done; Foote wanted the South to be compensated for its loss. There was a compromise available, which Senator Henry Clay of Kentucky already had proposed in an emotional speech, interrupted by shouts from spectators who crowded the gallery and the hall outside. Clay said Congress should organize California and New Mexico without regard to whether they were slave or free. The same would be done for Utah, a new territory surrounding the Great Salt Lake, settled by Mormons in 1846 after John Frémont's explorations promoted the area. White Southerners could be assured that they were not banned from introducing slavery somewhere in the conquered land; Northerners that slavery was unlikely to spread anyway, since the climate in the new lands was not thought to favor slave-grown crops. Clay offered further benefits for each side. For the North, Congress would ban the slave trade in the District of Columbia, though not slavery itself. For the South, Congress would pass a fugitive-slave law compelling Northern states to return escaped human property to the South.

The Mississippian Henry Foote supported Clay's compromise. Benton did not. He thought California statehood should simply be accepted on its own, not attached to proslavery measures as a "surrender" to a hostile minority; the compromise was a "monster." Lawmakers were at an impasse until a leading Democrat, Stephen A. Douglas of Illinois, orchestrated a compromise of the compromise. Clay's legislation had so many provisions that were noxious to so many senators that it could never pass, but Douglas calculated that each could pass separately. All were approved in a series of votes over the summer, and each bill was carried up Pennsylvania Avenue by messenger and laid upon the desk of the president—a new president, Millard Fillmore. Zachary Taylor had died of an acute intestinal disease, apparently poisoned by a contaminated supply of milk or water, the second president within a decade to be killed by Washington, D.C.

Some lawmakers decried the whole process. One was a newly elected Whig lawmaker from the state of New York, who took the occasion to deliver his first-ever speech in the Senate. William Henry Seward rose to tell his colleagues that he would not compromise, would not risk leaving the new land even slightly open to the South's institution. Thin and red-haired, with bushy eyebrows and a confident expression, the Whig said he must follow "a higher law than the Constitution," for God frowned on slavery even if the Constitution allowed it. Whigs and Democrats alike criticized Seward for what they construed as opposition to the founding document, and the Senate otherwise dismissed him.

✳ ✳ ✳

OUTSIDE THE SENATE CHAMBER was a different matter. Seward's speech was reprinted and shared in antislavery circles, where it inspired a prophecy from Frederick Douglass. The former slave wrote that Seward's "higher law" concept would resonate in a God-fearing nation. Although most Americans, even in free states, were "dark and depraved on this subject" of slavery, they would finally choose the justice that was demanded by their faith. If both Whigs and Democrats continued resisting this truth, "they will have, for their pains, a new and powerful Northern party," which would righteously rise to crush them both.

Douglass had been busy since the National Convention of Colored Citizens in 1843, when he pressed for nonviolent change only to be attacked by a mob weeks later. Funded by antislavery groups, he traveled to Britain to lecture. He published a popular autobiography detailing his enslavement and escape. Then he moved with his wife, Anna, and their children to a brick house in Rochester, New York, where he established a newspaper called the *North Star*. Naturally it was an abolitionist sheet, although its content was broader than that phrase would imply. Articles about slavery shared space with whatever else awakened the editor's curiosity; it was a view of the world through the eyes of Frederick Douglass. The paper on April 20, 1849, included an item about Louis-Napoléon, the leader of France, who "rambles much about the Parisian streets, unattended," and also an update on the progress of the famed explorer John Charles Frémont. It was a story of the disastrous expedition in which men "were compelled to eat the dead bodies of their comrades, before they became cold." Later that year the paper noted the gold on John's land ("Col. Fremont is said to have fallen upon untold riches") and then his election to the Senate.

The two-story brick house where Douglass lived with his family was selected for its location between the homes of white abolitionists, minimizing friction with the neighbors. It was about a one-mile walk to his newspaper office, leading through the busy mill town and across the Genesee River on the Main Street Bridge, which had mills and a market built along its sides, propped directly over the river so that businesses could use it to turn waterwheels and dump waste. Reaching the west bank, Douglass entered a four-story stone office building, where a single room contained an iron printing press, a desk in the corner, and wooden type cases along the walls. Aided by an assistant and sometimes by his young daughter and son, he set articles into type. He expressed himself without apology as a black man. "Colored newspapers," he wrote, "are sometimes objected to on the ground that they serve to keep up an odious and wicked distinction between white and colored persons, and are a barrier to that very equality which we are wont to advocate. We have, sometimes, heard persons regret the very mention of color. . . . We confess to no such feelings." Black people would achieve equality by doing all that white people could do, working as "doctors, lawyers, merchants, teachers, professors and editors." He was the change he wanted to see.

Douglass felt free to say things that mainstream white leaders would not dare. Few in power would have spoken as he did about the Christian church, when he said American churches had "volunteered in aid of the inhuman man-stealer." The Western New York Anti-Slavery Society, whose meetings Douglass attended, endorsed a view held by the most uncompromising abolitionists: "the doctrine of NO UNION WITH SLAVE-HOLDERS," which meant they wanted to seek, "by all rightful means, the rejection of the Constitution of the United States, on account of its slaveholding character." This was heresy to those who revered both the Constitution and the Union, but the meeting ended as "three cheers for liberty were proposed and heartily given. . . . We trust each member resolved to do what in him lay for the downfall of tyranny in this otherwise happy republic."

The minutes of the antislavery meeting were printed in the *North Star* and revealed something notable. A list of participants showed that many were women. Women were considered to have no place in politics, but by tradition could speak up for a benevolent cause, as some had on slavery for years. Douglass engaged with such women and was intrigued to learn that some were plotting their own movement against oppression. At least four women at the Western New York Anti-Slavery Society meeting in 1848—Mary Hallowell, Maria E. Wilbur, Mary M'Clintock, and Amy Post— were among those who, a few months later, helped to organize a meeting in Seneca Falls outside Rochester. Douglass attended their "convention to discuss the social, civil, and religious condition of woman." They criticized marriage laws and religious conservatism. They demanded the right to vote. They even adopted a Declaration of Sentiments that revised the Declaration of Independence ("We hold these truths to be self-evident; that all men and women are created equal"). Douglass placed his signature on a list of "gentlemen present in favor of the movement," and then he joined many of the same women for a follow-up meeting at a Unitarian church in Rochester. His newspaper described a poignant moment shortly after Amy Post called the Rochester meeting to order: "Anxiety was manifest" from the people in the more distant pews "concerning the low voices of the women, and when reading or speaking was attempted, cries of louder, louder, nearly drowned them." Abigail Bush, the president of the meeting, made symbolic use of the disruption, saying women stood before the gathering as "an oppressed class, with trembling frames and faltering tongues," but they would proceed nevertheless, trusting in "the omnipotency of right."

So he had allies, who supported his cause as he supported theirs, and he published his newspaper in a way that was calculated to draw in more allies. He began printing proslavery declarations—the fiercest arguments he could find *in favor* of slavery in California or New Mexico. He knew these arguments from the South would be badly received in the North. He published a statement by Southern members of Congress, who talked of seceding from the Union and said "the faith of each State is pledged to protect her interests in said territories at the point of the bayonet." A gathering of Virginians said "it is the imperative duty of the Southern States to resist any further interference on the subject of slavery, either in the States or Territories . . . at all hazards and to the last extremity." On February 9, 1849, John C. Calhoun was quoted at enormous length in Douglass's paper; his characteristically abrasive words defending slavery and the rights of the white South filled almost five whole columns of the oversize page. Douglass felt sure that such demands and threats would provoke even racist Northern audiences: "Those who cared nothing for the slave, and were willing to tolerate slavery inside the slave States, were nevertheless not quite prepared to find themselves and their children excluded from [the territories,] the common inheritance of the nation." Where slavery existed, it was presumed that free settlers would not thrive. The Compromise of 1850 was meant to ease the very tensions that Douglass perceived and encouraged, but the legislation "was hardly dry on the page of the statute book before the whole land was rocked with rumoured agitation, and for one, I did my best, by pen and voice, and by ceaseless activity, to keep it alive and vigorous."

✳ ✳ ✳

SOME PARTS OF THE COMPROMISE were still being maneuvered through Congress when, on September 10, 1850, William M. Gwin presented his credentials as a senator from California. So, too, did John Charles Frémont, who, having traded in his military uniform for a Californian jacket, now traded in the jacket for the dark suit favored on the floor of the Senate. Jessie Benton Frémont held the distinction of being both the daughter and the wife of senators. There remained only the question of how long John could serve. Senators served six-year terms, but their elections were staggered—meaning that one of California's first two senators must accept a much shorter term. They drew lots, and John lost. His term was to end on March 3, 1851, leaving him just a few months to prove himself before reelection.

His fame, at least, seemed secure. A Philadelphia literary magazine that autumn ranked John among the most important men to walk the earth since Jesus: "Since the mission of Him who came into the world to suffer that mankind might find redemption, the three greatest events that have occurred, are connected with the rise and progress of our own happy country;—the discovery of America; the American Revolution, and the establishment of the American empire on the coast of the Pacific ocean." Each great event was associated with a great man: Columbus, then Washington, then Frémont, who "lifted the veil which, since time first began, had hidden from view the real El Dorado."

Unlike the other two, John was still on earth and was therefore compelled to face the consequences of his achievements. His Senate term was like a trial in which he was constantly confronted with his past. One day the Senate received a petition from "F. Hultmann, of San Francisco, California," who said he had loaned "Lieutenant Colonel J.C. Frémont" some $19,500 during the war. This was a small portion of the debts John had built up to supply his troops, which Senator Benton had tried to have Congress assume in 1848. Congress still had not acted, and Hultmann (his name was actually spelled Huttmann) wanted his money back.

Slavery demanded John's attention when senators considered a part of the great compromise, Henry Clay's bill to ban the slave trade in the District of Columbia. It contained a few stirring phrases: "Any slave" brought into Washington "for the purpose of being sold" would "thereupon become liberated and free." It also contained disturbing clauses revealing that this element of the compromise was itself deeply compromised. It strengthened the shackles on slaves already within the district, mandating prison for anyone who helped a slave "to run away from his, her, or their owner or lawful possessor." It even allowed local authorities, if they chose, "to prohibit the coming of free negroes to reside" in Washington. The free African Americans who could be banned from Washington were the kind of people whom the Bentons hired, and they included Jacob Dodson, who had traveled twice with John to the Pacific and served alongside him in the war. (When veterans were paid after the war, Dodson was unable to collect for years, because federal law did not provide for "the mustering of colored men into the service of the country.") To say such a man could be banned from entering the capital was sickening. Yet this bill was part of the compromise that gained California statehood, and few wanted to revisit it. William Seward of New York was almost alone when he proposed to amend the bill by stripping the racist provisions and adding a public referendum to *abolish* slavery in Washington. Senators North and South voted to block Seward and protect the compromise, and John voted along with them, sacrificing the likes of Dodson for what was seen as the greater good; maybe he assumed that the local government would never really ban free black residents anyway. John then joined the majority who passed the overall legislation, which by the standards of the moment counted as an antislavery measure.

John tripped over more of his past when the senators from California proposed laws for the special problems of the new state. Frémont and Gwin agreed that because John faced reelection first, he would introduce the necessary legislation so that he would have a record to run on. This seemingly collegial move by Gwin handed John a dangerous honor, since anything John proposed would be controversial. Who really owned California, its land, and its mineral wealth? Under what rules would they operate? Who had a place in the new American West—the Indians, the Spanish and Mexicans who had come after them, the American settlers who had come after *them*, or the prospectors who were flooding in now? John was being asked to resolve the contradictions of manifest destiny, which he had done so much to make reality.

He tried. He introduced a bill offering a system to confirm the land titles of California property owners who had bought their real estate under Mexican law. This would be deeply reassuring to the Mexicans who had remained in California since the conquest, as well as the American settlers John knew from Bear Flag days. But critics observed that a major landowner who might benefit was John C. Frémont, the master of Las Mariposas and other properties with shaky titles from Mexican times. He was instantly open to the charge of corruption. Pistol-toting Senator Foote declared on the Senate floor that the bill could bring disgrace to the republic. Afterward, in the stone-walled hallway outside the chamber, John confronted the Mississippian and said he was no gentleman. Foote struck him in the face. It was only through the negotiations of their friends that the senators from California and Mississippi avoided a duel.

Boldly, if perilously, Senator Frémont pushed on. He offered a bill "to preserve peace with the Indian tribes in California by extinguishing their territorial claims in the gold-mine districts." Senator Frémont's constituents wanted protection from the natives, which was another way of saying that Indians must be shoved off their own land. John doubtless considered his solution to be pro-Indian—he asserted that natives had legal rights to their property. "In California," he told his Senate colleagues in a speech, "we are at this moment invading those rights. We lived there by the strong hand alone," and Indians naturally felt justified in killing invaders when they could. To keep the peace, he said, Indians should be paid for their land and encouraged to move. But he received little credit among white Californians for affirming Indian rights, and his experience should have told him that his plan was unlikely to succeed. In 1837 he had played his small role in the operation to pry Cherokees away from their homeland in the East, and he understood that Indians were forced to give up far more than they gained (as he later said, "there has been no continuous effective policy" toward Indians except their removal "out of the way of the white man"). The only argument for repeating this terrible operation in California in 1850 was that the alternative was worse—white rampages that risked killing the entire native populace.

Senator Frémont also tried to regulate gold mining, introducing a bill that he cast as favoring small prospectors. While underground minerals would belong to the United States, John proposed that anyone could stake a claim and keep the wealth, as long as they turned in gold to the United States Mint in exchange for gold coins. Each prospector simply had to buy a mining permit and could work only one small square of land at a time. A mountainside might become a vast grid split among thousands of small prospectors, and "moneyed capital" would be prevented from "driving out or overpowering the population who have no capital but their courage and industry." It was a measure against the concentration of wealth and inequality. But a single phrase of the bill provoked intense debate. Who was allowed to prospect? The agents "shall have the authority to grant permits to American citizens." William Henry Seward of New York read this phrase and objected: Why should immigrants be blocked from the goldfields? The citizenship clause would exclude many of them, ranging from Mexicans to many of Seward's own New York constituents who had come from Ireland and Germany. He proposed that permits should also be sold to anyone who "declared their intention to become" citizens, saying that immigrants, alongside citizens, would bring up more of the national wealth than citizens alone.

Senator Frémont of California rose to disagree. "All our American population are entirely opposed to the working of the mines by foreigners," he said. Word of the gold strike had hardly begun to spread in April 1849 when some Californians made the first proposals to ban foreigners from the mines. White Californians attacked Chinese miners, approved a punishing mining tax that applied only to foreigners, and drove away Mexicans by the thousands. But in challenging Seward in the Senate chamber, John did more than pass on his white constituents' concerns—he endorsed them. He said that California's gold rush was drawing "civilized Indians and inferior castes" out of the Mexican state of Sonora, where they had gained experience in gold mining. "This brought into California a class of population of very doubtful character, operating in some cases to the exclusion of Americans."

This was a betrayal. He *knew* Sonorans; he had encountered them on his way to California in 1849. Rather than operating "to the exclusion of Americans," they had accepted the leadership of the American they had just met and even agreed to work on his land, where he welcomed their labor. With little effort on his part they had made him rich beyond his dreams. Jessie described them not as people "of very doubtful character" but as people who acted honorably when dividing the gold ("not taking an ounce more than their stipulated portion"). Having profited from the labor of immigrants in a way that changed his life, Senator Frémont opposed granting opportunities to others exactly like them. What changed? As a private individual in 1849, he saw his interests clearly, acted sensibly, and employed people with the skills he needed. As a legislator in 1850, he was part of a system, joining a group of men who were thinking in the abstract about categories of people who were not like them.

Several lawmakers joined the debate over the citizenship clause on the floor of the Senate, each man rising in turn at his desk. One said it would be unfair for foreigners to benefit because Americans had fought and died to conquer California. Seward of New York replied that he was happy to focus on the more than seventeen hundred American lives lost in the war, because it was customary for immigrants to join the army with its hazards and low pay: "More than half of those lives were the lives of men born aliens," outside the United States. Henry Foote of Mississippi, the next to speak, replied with a personal attack: Seward was a "presidential aspirant" who was cynically appealing to voters "of foreign birth," but secretly thought his German and Irish constituents were worse than black people.

Senators from the recently formed states of Iowa and Wisconsin rose to defend the foreign born; many of the settlers now filling the prairies had come from Europe and were not yet citizens. Isaac Walker of Wisconsin said "they were voters in Wisconsin," which was true; numerous states in the nineteenth century allowed noncitizen residents to vote. Walker added that "they worked on our roads; they paid taxes; they performed all the duties of citizens." He could not "blast all their hopes" by blocking those who were moving to California intent on prospecting. Augustus Dodge of Iowa hit on a compromise: perhaps the bill should be amended to allow *European* immigrants to mine for California's gold. Those were the kinds of immigrants who voted in Iowa. Dodge cared less about Mexicans: "I think Mexicans are a miserable people, who should be excluded from the mines."

John's fellow Californian William M. Gwin rose to agree about "miserable" Mexicans: the crowds of them who came out of Mexico were "peons," who would take over multiple mining claims and work them in the service of a single aristocratic master. "We know nothing of their institutions," he confessed, "but we know that one man gets all the gold." It sounded very much like slavery, and Gwin, the slave owner from Mississippi, found it unacceptable.

Walker of Wisconsin replied, "Make them all free when they get there."

"But we do not want them at all," Gwin exclaimed, confessing that the true defect of Mexicans as he saw them was that they were Mexican. The bill was amended to allow mining by United States citizens and "persons from Europe who produce testimonials of good character."

* * *

SENATOR FRÉMONT'S TERM WAS SO BRIEF that he ran out of time to guide his proposals into law. Late in September he left the work to Senator Gwin while he returned to California to campaign for reelection. He knew the state legislature would meet sometime before March 3 to pick a senator for a full six-year term. Jessie did not relish the trip; she was pregnant. But she would not remain in Washington without him, and in October 1850 the family caught a steamer to Panama and crossed over to a ship on the Pacific side. On November 21 they were gliding through the Golden Gate and glimpsing San Francisco growing up its hillsides beside the bay. The city looked different than it had the year before. A long wharf extended into the water now, constantly under construction and stretching into deep water to reach oceangoing ships, like the Pacific Mail steamer that deposited Jessie and John. It took "over seven hundred paces" from the end of the wharf to the shoreline, according to a journalist who walked it, "good, long paces at that." Jessie, with John beside her, would have taken the walk slowly. She was avoiding exertion as expectant mothers were urged to do, while he had grown ill on the voyage and still felt weak. Gradually they approached the city that spread out before them.

A census taker and his assistants had been moving about San Francisco that fall, introducing themselves to people and scrawling information on paper forms. They identified at least 12,625 residents in San Francisco

County, which three years before had been a handful of residents in a village. The census takers marked down where all residents were born, creating a sample of California migration. Of the 12,625, about five thousand were born in eastern states, mainly Massachusetts and New York. More than thirty were babies born during the arduous ocean journey from the East, including one born "on the Equator" and two born "off Cape Horn." A few were born in wagon trains while crossing the Great Plains or Rocky Mountains. A solid majority of San Franciscans—7,423 people—were listed as "born in foreign countries," a sweeping category that included European immigrants, Australians, Chinese who had ventured across the Pacific, and Hawaiians who had come to California as laborers. The "foreign" majority apparently also included *native Californians*, those born in California when it was part of Mexico, who were now regarded as immigrants in their own land. The only people the census takers listed as California-born were one hundred babies born during the previous year of United States rule.

The Frémonts came ashore, walking streets paved with wooden planks. Several streets were named after men John had known during the war, such as Vallejo Street for the Mexican general John had imprisoned at Sutter's Fort. Kearny Street was named for the general who had arrested John and put him on trial. It was understandable that when finding a place to live, the Frémonts crossed Kearny and continued uphill, through an immigrant neighborhood soon to be known as Chinatown, to take a house on Stockton Street, named after the commodore who briefly made John governor. Jessie and Lilly took up residence in this house while John slowly recovered from his illness—and then, as soon as he was able, he left town.

Maybe it was his restlessness that had prompted him to leave Washington so soon. He would spend the year of 1851 in near-constant motion from place to place. To be sure, he had obligations. He had business at Las Mariposas, where associates had organized a corporation, to be capitalized at one million dollars, to exploit a mining site there called Agua Fria. He also had to face reelection. By mid-January, a newspaper said, "Col. Frémont is now sojourning at San Jose," still the state capital, and was "mingling freely with the members" of the legislature who would decide his fate. He was shocked to discover that he was the target of fierce criticism. California, which did not have a single newspaper a few years earlier—the only way to get the news was the way Thomas O. Larkin got it, collecting months-old papers from passing ships—now had multiple papers in San Francisco, Sacramento, San Jose, and elsewhere. They carried on a ferocious public debate, and much of it was critical of his work in the Senate. About half a dozen California politicos, sensing his vulnerability, were maneuvering for his job.

In later years the Frémonts would suggest that his opposition to slavery had caused his political trouble in California. There was little evidence to support this. It was true that proslavery forces in California would have been happy to see him replaced with someone like his fellow senator Gwin, vocally in favor of slavery and tied to Southern interests. But this was a subterranean factor. John's more immediate problem was his record: the bills he had proposed to address the great questions of manifest destiny were met with resentment and scorn. The land bill, critics shouted, allotted more acreage on better terms to the old settlers of California than to new ones. "If this bill passes," declared a Whig newspaper that identified with the newcomers, the lawmakers who wrote it should "keep out of the country—California will be no pleasant residence for them." The old settlers who stood to benefit were "runaways from justice, negroes, Indians, Kanakas [Hawaiians], and the scum of Christendom." California's lawmakers were "senseless. And yet some persons are talking of re-electing Fremont to the Senate."

Worse was the reception for his mining bill; even a newspaper that supported him said that "we are not at all sorry" that it had not yet become law. The citizenship provision was profoundly divisive, yet it somehow united the state against its author—everyone hated it. California's foreign-born residents and the old Californians understood that they were targeted.

John felt forced to write a public defense of his record, acknowledging that the mining bill "has been condemned in general terms for excluding foreigners." He tried to save himself by ducking responsibility, saying that "your delegation" in Washington had "every reason to believe" that they were simply following California public opinion, and now "your returning representative finds himself unexpectedly censured for a proposed measure which he did not originate, and for which he is only accidentally in a situation to be held responsible." Racists didn't like the bill either. The modification to allow Europeans was far too liberal for some: Why were "sallow emigrants" from Spain or Italy any better than Mexicans? Other critics creatively misread the citizenship provision. They noted that prospectors had to pay a modest fee for permits, and that because of the citizenship restriction, the fees would be paid mainly by United States citizens. It was therefore, declared a Sacramento newspaper, "a tax upon American citizens to work in the mines"—bias against citizens! "Our people are already taxed enough," the paper declared, blaming the scheme on lawmakers in faraway Washington. Having given in to the impulse to cynically play for the nativist American vote, John discovered he was not cynical enough; nativists outdid him and recast him as an out-of-touch elitist.

What remained to support him was his immense reputation (one paper called him "the talented, urbane, and unsullied Fremont"), his connections ("I hope you will be at San Jose in time for the election," he wrote a prominent landowner whose influence he could rely on), and his money. Just before the voting began on February 20, he threw open rooms in San Jose to entertain state lawmakers, offering what one observer called "the good things, which nourish and make glad the physical nature of man"—certainly food and drink, if not other things of a "physical nature." Across the street, lawmakers and voters attended a banquet thrown by one of John's Senate rivals—T. Butler King, the Georgia congressman who had arrived in 1849 on the boat with Jessie, and had remained to seek his fortune.

Lavish spending did neither of the contenders any good. When the state legislators met in convention starting on February 20, they were hopelessly deadlocked between multiple candidates. Lawmakers cast ballots twenty times without anyone nearing a majority. Ordinarily deals would be struck and some candidates would withdraw in favor of others, but neither John nor anyone else seemed to have the political strength to end the fight. One lawmaker wryly "suggested as a mode of getting along faster that the next ballot should be regarded as the 31st ballot instead of the 21st ballot." The suggestion was not taken, but soon they were on the thirty-first ballot anyway, and then beyond it. After voting 142 times over the course of two weeks, the legislators gave up on electing any senator at all. California would have to do with just one, Gwin, until January 1852, when the legislators agreed they would meet and try again.

* * *

JESSIE, NOW HEAVILY PREGNANT IN SAN FRANCISCO, was able to follow the Senate fight through the newspapers. In truth she had two races to follow; her father was facing reelection before the Missouri legislature that winter. In late February, even as the Californians were balloting, the Missouri news began to reach the Pacific. The California papers reported that Benton Democrats in his state's legislature gathered to plot strategy. They declared that Benton was their candidate, and in dramatic Bentonian fashion resolved "to sustain the nominee until the present Legislature ceases to exist." They would never surrender. But another faction of Democrats joined the Whigs in supporting a Whig who was willing to be more flexible than Benton on slavery. On March 6, just one day after the papers carried news of John's defeat, a Sacramento newspaper carried a single sentence from afar: "In Missouri, Mr. Geyer has been elected in place of Mr. Benton." Jessie had been the daughter and the wife of a senator; now she was neither. She had never *not* been a senator's daughter—she was nearing her twenty-seventh birthday, and Benton had been in office thirty years.

Her two senators responded differently to defeat. Benton's instinct was to fight. His beloved Democratic Party was fatally split over slavery's expansion; Missouri's other Democratic senator, David Atchison, was a radical supporter of slavery whose allies led the way in defeating Senator Benton. But Benton still enjoyed the support of his faction, and though he was about to turn sixty-nine he began considering which office he could seek next. John Charles Frémont, too, still had supporters, but took his defeat as a cue to step away from politics. He left the capital at San Jose, riding home to San Francisco to spend a day or two with his wife. Then he rode away again, 160 miles out to Las Mariposas in the company of the Frémonts' friend Edward F. Beale. Although he would have known from a glance at his wife that she was due within weeks, business and the mountains called him. Besides the Mariposa gold mines, he was making an offer to buy an immense rancho outside Los Angeles. The Frémonts envisioned large-scale farming—"olives figs & grapes, as well as peaches & apricots," Jessie said. She wrote her father's friend Francis P. Blair in Washington, asking him to ship them seeds.

Yet it was not quite accurate to say that John was focused on business. He kept undertaking projects and losing his way. He kept undermining himself. What compelled him was the mountains, the land, the adventure, the separation from other people. He saw the possibilities of the West and dreamed up schemes for his place within it, yet lacked the sustained focus on details that were essential to success. He did not manage to buy the Los Angeles ranch. His San Jose sawmill vanished from the record, apparently abandoned or sold. While he was military governor he had purchased several plots of real estate in San Francisco, including an orchard in what would become the city's Mission District, but as with so much real estate in California his title was cloudy. He had assigned seventeen leases to various companies and prospectors authorizing them to prospect on his Mariposa land, but not all struck gold, and his title remained uncertain enough that other prospectors continued to work his land without permission. "Mr. Frémont has had heavy losses in his gold experiments," Jessie reported in a letter. He had an agent in London, David Hoffman, working to organize British capitalists into companies that would invest in large-scale mining—but John stopped answering Hoffman's increasingly urgent letters seeking decisions and information. (Jessie finally intervened, asking a mutual friend, "Will you please write to Mr. Hoffman who will I fear think Mr. Frémont a myth.") Because John engaged multiple agents who sold leases for various Mariposa claims, the agents made competing bids for capital and cast suspicion on one another.

Worse, John's finances were growing confused, as men who had lent him money over the years continued demanding payment. The habits he had developed over the years were catching up with him. From his earliest days as an expedition leader, when he purchased instruments in New York by writing vouchers against the government that had not been authorized in advance, he had shown his talent for living on credit. He had traveled back and forth across the continent, sometimes with cash on hand but just as often without, buying horses and food and supplies, offering nothing in return but little pieces of paper—bank drafts and promises of payment that a remote seller in the West could only hope to cash at some later place and time. This kind of paper juggling was an essential skill on the cash-poor frontier. He could never have completed his great expeditions without it. But it was a dangerous game when enlarged to the scale on which he now operated.

His critics saw in his chaotic business dealings signs of dishonesty and greed, but John was likely also revealing his mental state. In the previous decade he had led four great expeditions that in terms of exertion, isolation, danger, and death were much like going to war. One had ended in an actual war. Many of his men had been killed, and others had come apart under stress. Surely their commander was also affected, despite his own insistence to the contrary ("I have not been injured in body or mind"). He was unsettled, racing from place to place, seeking some venture that was enthralling enough to hold his attention. He was exceptionally lucky that the Sonoran immigrants had made him a fortune almost without his participation in 1849; the trunks of gold from those times left him room for many mistakes.

❋ ❋ ❋

IN THE MONTHS THAT JESSIE LIVED IN SAN FRANCISCO, the city was developing many classes of people. There were elites like the Frémonts and their friends, who rapidly filled their houses with all the comforts of the East. There were powerful merchants like Sam Brannan, a Mormon businessman who had come from New York before the gold rush. There were Mexican elites, marginalized but still present, while many Chinese, commonly pushed away from gold mining, were forming a laboring underclass. European immigrants were better off than the Chinese, but not fully accepted: Jessie learned that anyone with a British accent was suspected of being a convict from a British penal colony in Australia. The Australians were blamed for a crime wave and dealt with ruthlessly. One day, a newspaper reported, a person "said to be a Sydney man" was caught stealing a safe. Local men gave him a "pretty severe drubbing" and dragged him to the police station. Members of a private "Committee of Vigilance," unwilling to wait for punishment through the justice system, then seized the foreigner, conducted their own trial, and marched him to Portsmouth Square, where "a dozen willing hands" put a rope around his neck. Ignoring his protests of innocence, as well as his appeal to be shot instead, they "immediately ran him up" on a beam that extended from a building. They left the body up for hours, "swinging in the night air." At a coroner's inquest afterward, leading citizens were called to the stand but gave unhelpful testimony. "I was present when a man was hung," said the merchant Sam Brannan. "I don't know who had hold of the rope."

For the sake of her baby and herself, Jessie cloistered herself from such scenes. Keeping to the house on Stockton, she wrote letters to the East—to Lizzie Lee and to her father; and to Francis P. Blair, the ex-editor, who wrote back to her with political news. On March 14 Jessie wrote to console a Delaware woman on the death of her young daughter: "I know that the sympathy of friends can do very little in such an affliction but I cannot refrain from expressing mine." She mentioned her own loss of little Benton in 1848. "Before this reaches you I shall have another, and my health has been so good that I have all reason to believe it will not have the fate of my dear little boy." On April 19 her baby was born, another boy. He was named John Charles Frémont, and she called him Charlie. He was healthy. For a few weeks the elder John Charles came home, and Jessie was surrounded by friends and family.

Their house was on the high side of Stockton Street. Its windows offered a view downhill, past Chinatown to the open plaza at Portsmouth Square, which gave them a perfect vantage on the night of May 3, 1851, when San Francisco caught fire. Flames shot out of the windows of Baker and Messerve, a business facing the plaza. It did not take much to destroy a wooden city lit by fire. The flames spread from building to building. "Who could see the end?" Jessie asked. "The planked streets were conductors of fire, the sea winds carried it overhead, and on and on through the long night it raged and roared." Flames approached the US Custom House, where the authorities saved one million dollars' worth of gold by throwing it down a well. A journalist on the street watched the Union Hotel, which "burned like a furnace until the woodwork was nearly destroyed, when the huge walls, five stories high, pitched headlong into the street." Eighteen city blocks, and parts of others, were destroyed. John and Edward Beale, who was staying with them, prepared to carry off Jessie and the two-week-old infant, but their house was spared.

In June, fire struck again, approaching the house from a new direction. This time John and Beale were out at Las Mariposas, so it was Jessie who made the decision to abandon the house. She ordered a servant to carry boxes of papers up the hill to a friend's house and out of danger, telling Lily to go along with him ("I could not trust the man, but I did trust the child").

Jessie followed with the six-week-old baby. In their friend's house, crowded with refugees, one woman sat at the window and watched her own house burn down. When it was gone she yielded the chair to Jessie, and "I in my turn watched from that window the burning of my home."

Only later did she learn that her belongings had been saved. The credit belonged to a group of English immigrants, who knew the Frémonts as landlords; John had leased property to them, allowing them to build houses and a brewery on it. Early in the fire some of these immigrants perceived that the flames were approaching the Frémont house and went to see if Mrs. Frémont needed help. Discovering that she had already evacuated, they rescued objects instead. They picked up "mirrors, china and glass, several hundred books, furniture, even kitchen utensils, and all our clothing." Working with "cool method," the immigrants carried it all away from the approaching flames. Afterward, one of the women laundered the Frémont family's clothes and brought them to Jessie in her refuge. A man came along with her and placed a parcel in front of Jessie, tied in a red silk handkerchief. "We thought money might come in handy," he said, "so we brought a quarter's rent in advance." He untied the bundle to show "silver and some gold" within. Jessie cried. "It was all so kind, so unexpected, and from people who were kept chilled by public ill-will."

When John returned to San Francisco days later, he walked through blocks of ashes and found nothing remaining of the house on Stockton except a chimney. He had to search up and down the streets before he found his family. When Jessie informed him what the English immigrants had done, he sent for them, and as a gesture of gratitude he said he would sell them the land on which they had built their homes. The tenants, said Jessie, were deeply moved. Land was the best possible gift he could have offered as they built their new lives in America, although of course the continued questions about land titles meant there was no telling if John had any right to sell it to them.

Jessie Benton Frémont in California in the 1860s.

Chapter Fourteen

ALL THE STUPID LAURELS
THAT EVER GREW

CELEBRITIES, 1851–1854

San Francisco, London, Paris, New York, and Washington

I n the summer of 1851 Jessie recorded that rarest of events: both Frémonts together, at home and at rest. They were in their new lodgings
in San Francisco, and she was composing one of her letters to Francis
P. Blair in Washington. She was sitting with her husband by the fireside, she
told Blair, "even in this month of August, for as our season of fogs is not over
we need bright fires morning & night." John, just returned from a journey
to Los Angeles, "sits nearest the fire being the thinnest & most cold blooded
of the two." They were drinking "some real China tea." They were watching
"little Charley in his basket." Jessie called across to John: Did he have anything he would like to say to Francis P. Blair? John answered and she wrote:
"I have asked Mr. Frémont for a message and he says I must tell you to prepare yourself for a Whig Senator in his place, politics being too costly an
amusement in this country just now."

California was Whig now, Jessie said. The elections within a few
months would produce not only a Whig senator but also a Whig governor.
But the Frémonts didn't mind—the likely Whig governor was, like the

Frémonts, a big landowner with property on the edge of Indian country, which meant that he would do something to remove the threat of Indians. "You will see how fortunate it is for our interests that he should be in power." This was a striking political forecast, both because of its calculated self-interest and because it was wrong. Democrats were not about to lose power. Within a few months they captured both the governorship and the Senate seat, and neither went to John, who had withdrawn from the arena. He continued riding across the state in pursuit of business schemes, and by late 1851, not even California's vastness gave him room enough to move. He presented steamer tickets to Jessie, who was delighted to be told it was time for their first real vacation: an extended visit to Paris, taking time away at last from duty and ambition.

On closer examination, there was more to the journey than a vacation. John was still seeking British investors to expand his operations on Las Mariposas. He decided to visit London on the way to Paris, because the competing stories told by his agents were beginning to undermine his credibility there. His relations remained strained with the agent Hoffman, such an obsessive letter-writer that neither of the Frémonts had the patience to read all that he wrote them. (Hoffman himself was running out of patience while waiting for John's tardy responses, and finished one note with the line, "The mail has this moment arrived—not a line from you—the world here is astounded.") Then came a further complication, which involved Thomas Hart Benton. John's father-in-law had never seen Las Mariposas, but believed the land grant was becoming a danger and distraction to his son-in-law. Benton arranged for the Mariposas to be sold for one million dollars, conditional on John's approval. The move revealed the arrogance, and the foresight, for which the former senator was famous: in a letter to Hoffman, the London agent, Benton explained that John was "not adapted to such business and it interferes with his attention to other business to which he is adapted." John wavered, first seeming to accept the sale, then revoking it. This angered Benton, opening a breach with his sponsor. Worse,

Benton had been right. John was not "adapted" to business, didn't know what he was doing, and would have better served himself to sell. Allegations of scandal were beginning to surround the land grant: a newspaper in the new settlement of Stockton, California, alleged that "extensive frauds were about to be perpetrated in Europe" by John's agents. John filed a libel suit against the paper, but the claim still reached newspapers in New York within weeks, which guaranteed that it would also be read in London.

On February 1, 1852, the Frémonts boarded a steamer for Panama. The railroad across the isthmus was not finished, so it remained a rough passage; nine-month-old Charlie was wrapped in a tablecloth and slung onto the back of a porter. A second ship took them to New York; then, for the first time in their lives, they started across the Atlantic, on a ship called the *Africa*, with the family taking over the whole ladies' salon since Jessie was the only woman traveling. The transatlantic crossing that had taken their ancestors months to complete now took ten days or less, and in late March they arrived in the capital of the British empire, 2.5 million people spread along the Thames, the closest thing to a capital of the world. As always, the papers took note of the Frémonts; a correspondent in London, writing for a newly established American sheet called the *New York Times*, said John had arrived just in time to rescue his prospects. It was "a great relief" to London investors that "the Colonel was coming in person to clear up all doubts, and remove the ugly suspicions." The couple checked into a suite at the Clarendon Hotel, with "chintz and flowers and wood fire," an address that "becomes a millionaire fresh from California."

It was uncertain how rich John really was, but he surely had fame—even in London, where he recently had been the star of a smash-hit documentary. From April 1850 to late 1851, a lecturer in London had shown an art display on the explorations of John Charles Frémont. His lecture featured eighty scenes of John's adventures that were painted on a single enormous canvas, scrolled with hand cranks as awestruck audiences sat for two hours watching the procession of pictures. During nineteen months of performances in a packed lecture hall, some 350,000 people saw the story of the dashing explorer, which was advertised both in general newspapers and in women's publications. John's agent in London was bothered to discover that the lecturer had obtained his information from Senator Benton and from John himself; the self-promotion seemed gauche. But fame could be like gold. "The leaders of fashion are ever on the watch for every fresh celebrity," said the *Times* correspondent. Mrs. Frémont was welcomed at the regular reception of the Duchess of Derby, the wife of the prime minister, and shook the hand of the aged Duke of Wellington. Both Frémonts were taken to dinner with the leader of the Barings banking house, and welcomed at the home of the head of the Royal Geographical Society. Jessie, dressed in a gown of pink satin with blond lace, attended a reception where she kissed the hand of Queen Victoria.

Fame also attracted less flattering forms of attention. On April 7, the Frémonts were stepping out of the Clarendon on their way to another elegant dinner when four policemen appeared. As Jessie watched, the policemen arrested John and led him into custody. He had been seized, the policemen said, for nonpayment of a debt. It was the $19,500 he had borrowed from a California merchant during the war, now alleged to have grown to $50,000 with interest—the money that the merchant had demanded from the Senate the year before. When Congress did not act, the merchant sold the debt to British investors, who saw their chance to collect when the newspapers announced John's presence in London.

The policemen took John to a "sponging house," a holding facility for debtors, which he described as the "ante-room to the jail." He spent the night there. Jessie spent the night racing through London in search of bail money, no doubt still wearing the clothes in which she had planned to go out that evening. One of her visits was to David Hoffman, John's long-suffering agent, with whom John had grown so disappointed that he had suspended their business. She found his home and demanded to see him after nine o'clock at night. Hoffman—an American from Maryland, a onetime law professor turned land promoter—was in his late sixties and suffering from a cold. Summoned from his bed by a servant, he stumbled out of his bedroom to meet Jessie in the parlor of his home. She was accompanied by one of John's business associates, but she did all the talking.

"My husband is arrested," Jessie said.

"I am grieved to hear it," Hoffman replied.

She held up one of Hoffman's letters. "You say [here that] you are still loyal to Colonel Frémont."

"I certainly am," Hoffman said, and then asked if Jessie had read the remainder of the letter, which warned John that his contradictory acts were endangering his hold on the Mariposas.

"Oh no!" Jessie said. "It's too long."

Moving on, Hoffman gestured toward a chair. "Do be seated."

"No. I want no words. I have no time for that. I want four thousand pounds and I must have it."

Hoffman said he didn't keep that kind of money at his house. "I have but six hundred pounds."

"Oh don't tell me that," Jessie said. "I know all about it. I know you have money there. I was told so. I must have it."

Jessie believed that Hoffman had collected funds from Mariposa investors. Hoffman answered that it would be improper to turn over investors' money if he had any, and John owed *him* money for expenses. "Colonel Frémont is my debtor—not my creditor."

"Do you know who I am?" Jessie took out a pen and wrote her name at full length, so that Hoffman would see both Benton and Frémont. The agent replied that he did not doubt who she was, but that he did not have bail money.

"You are a great rascal," Jessie said as she left. "My father says so."

Hoffman, the obsessive letter-writer, afterward set down all the dialogue he could remember, preserving a picture of Mrs. Frémont in furious defense of her husband. He sent the dialogue in a letter to Mr. Frémont, apparently to show his own innocence as well as to inform John of Jessie's imperious behavior. It was a long letter, and it was not clear if John ever read it.

Jessie reached out to other associates of her husband, and John spent only one night in custody before an American merchant in London arranged his bail. The great explorer finished his business meetings as though nothing was wrong, and when news reached the United States the press took his side. "The arrest, from all accounts, was outrageous," a New York paper said.

The Frémonts moved on to Paris as planned. But from Paris, John wrote Thomas Hart Benton to say, "I have reason to believe that many others of these liabilities will be urged upon me." He thought the various notes he had signed during the war could total more than one million dollars with interest, and none had been reimbursed by Congress. "If I was [as] great a patriot as you," John said, "I would go to jail and stay there until Congress paid these demands . . . but my patriotism has been oozing out for the last five years." He asked if Benton could help find him a job with an American embassy while in Europe, so that he would be protected from arrest by diplomatic immunity. The job would also "help pay expenses." He was apparently spending enough of his fortune to worry about the cost of travel.

✳ ✳ ✳

WHILE THE FRÉMONTS WERE AWAY, first on the Pacific coast and then in Europe, a literary sensation was sweeping the country. It began on June 5, 1851, when a story took up more than half the front page of a Washington, D.C., newspaper called the *National Era*. It was the beginning of a novel. The opening chapter featured a slave trader, "a short, thick-set man," with "a gaudy vest of many colors" and a "swaggering air of pretension," bargaining with a Kentucky plantation owner to purchase a four-year-old slave. The headline of the story read:

UNCLE TOM'S CABIN:

OR,

LIFE AMONG THE LOWLY.

By Mrs. H.B. Stowe.

The story was serialized in the paper throughout the remainder of the year. Readers followed, week after week, as the slave child escaped with her mother, while the title character, Uncle Tom, was sold down the river to New Orleans, sold again to a sadistic master in the Red River Valley, and beaten to death.

Harriet Beecher Stowe was a member of a prominent New England family. Her father, Lyman Beecher, had been a Calvinist minister who in the 1830s moved from Boston to Cincinnati hoping to win the West for Christ. Harriet's older sister Catharine Beecher was a girls' educator who once had secretly coordinated a women's campaign in defense of Cherokee Indians. Her brother Henry Ward Beecher was an enormously popular Brooklyn preacher who had grown fiercely critical of slavery. Now Harriet made her own contribution to public affairs. Her newspaper serial was not unique; so many slave narratives, both factual and fictional, had been published over the previous two decades that Harriet Beecher Stowe's story seemed to have been loosely based on earlier works. But coming as it did after the Compromise of 1850, her novel reached a public that was ready for the subject. The serialized "Uncle Tom's Cabin" was published in book form on March 20, 1852. The first edition sold out in four days, and the publisher had such trouble keeping up with demand that the reviewer for Frederick Douglass's newspaper in Rochester was compelled to write an article based on the earlier newspaper version. "The [book] has not yet reached us," the reviewer confessed, but given its power, "we are not surprised at the delay." The reviewer predicted that Uncle Tom's Cabin would "rise up a host of enemies against the fearful system of slavery." It was the first of many articles Douglass would publish about the book.

He had changed his paper's name from the *North Star* to *Frederick Douglass' Paper*, a shift that reflected his increasing prominence. He saw in *Uncle Tom's Cabin* another opportunity to engage Northern public opinion, and when he received a letter from the author saying she would like to meet him, he traveled from Rochester to Andover, Massachusetts, for the conversation. Stowe asked his advice "as to what can be done for the free colored people of the country," and he suggested a focus on education ("I am for no fancied or artificial elevation, but only ask fair play"). Nothing concrete came of their meeting, but it reflected Douglass's strategic goal: engaging white Northern allies in the fight against slavery. Not every antislavery activist felt the same way; in 1852, one of Douglass's former colleagues on his newspaper, the black activist Martin Delany, published his own book that called on African Americans to rely on themselves and ultimately to leave the United States—an emigration like the "Exodus of the Jews from Egypt," to colonize some corner of the Americas. But Douglass saw the answer within the United States, as he wrote Harriet Beecher Stowe: "The truth is, dear madam, we are here, and we are likely to remain." This meant they must gain relief through the democratic process.

When the Democrats and Whigs nominated their presidential candidates in the election year of 1852, Douglass was unimpressed. He viewed the Democrat, Franklin Pierce of New Hampshire, as a hopeless captive of Southern interests. The Whig, General Winfield Scott, a hero of the recent war, kept some distance from the party's Southern wing, which was "an encouraging sign of the times." But Scott was still no abolitionist. Douglass believed the Whig Party's "destruction is necessary to the abolition of slavery." If the Whigs fell apart, it would free more genuine antislavery Whigs such as William Henry Seward to form the "new and powerful Northern party" that Douglass had spoken of for some time.

That summer Douglass attended the national convention of an antislavery party. They were known as the Free Democracy, and their three hundred delegates met in the Pittsburgh Masonic Hall, where Douglass, among other speakers, held the floor while a committee offstage drafted a platform. Their slogan was "Free soil, free speech, free labor, and free men!" They supported the free distribution of public lands to "landless settlers." They promised immigrants a "cordial welcome" and an easy path to citizenship. They demanded the abolition of slavery, "a sin against God, and a crime against man, which no human enactment or usage can make right." They nominated a presidential candidate, John P. Hale, who had been elected to the Senate from New Hampshire by the very sort of Northern coalition that Douglass was hoping for—a coalition of antislavery Whigs and Democrats combined with hard-core abolitionists. Nobody thought Hale could win the presidency, but it was possible for Douglass to look out over the Pittsburgh convention and imagine what could someday be.

❊ ❊ ❊

IN THIS POLITICAL AND INTELLECTUAL FERMENT, the Frémonts played no part. Despite their antislavery views, neither was deeply engaged in the antislavery movement. Both seemed unready to return to politics. (Shortly before leaving for Europe, Jessie had written her friend Lizzie Lee, "I should dissolve the Union sooner than let Mr. Frémont go away a year to Congress.") By the time of the 1852 conventions, they were settled in Paris at number 61 Champs-Élysées, the grandest boulevard in the city. The Arc de Triomphe was visible a few blocks down the boulevard in one direction; in the other lay the Tuileries Garden. They were renting one of the homes of an English nobleman, Thomas Cochrane, the Earl of Dundonald. Now their journey became more like the promised vacation; French-speaking Jessie was introduced to high society and observed the changing urban landscape. The local prefect, Baron Haussmann, was cutting new boulevards through crowded ancient quarters, and she disapproved of the "frenzy for building and speculating in city property." The closest the Frémonts came to trouble was when Lord Dundonald wrote to ask that they be better about keeping the gate closed against burglars. ("Give instructions to the porter and his wife to attend to the only duty they have to perform.")

In Paris they received news of the 1852 elections, which were largely good for them. Pierce, the Democrat, won in a landslide, and Thomas Hart Benton won too. After losing his Senate seat in 1851, Jessie's father had run for the House from St. Louis, and the voters returned him to Washington, back to his home on C Street and the green-domed Capitol, where he remained a man to reckon with, still with unmatched knowledge of the government and the leader of a faction of Missouri Democrats called "the Benton Democracy." News also arrived that Congress would pay the creditors who'd had John arrested in London, thanks to the intervention of his former Senate colleague William M. Gwin. John wrote Gwin a letter of thanks, and added a complaint: a federal land commission had not confirmed his title to Las Mariposas, which still frustrated his drive for European investment. His anxiety was evident: "My counsel promised me the ratification by several mails back, but we have been disappointed & have not heard a word by the last several mails." European money was increasingly drawn away from chaotic California and toward a gold strike in Australia. At the end of 1852 the land commission confirmed John's title, but he still faced an appeal of the decision as well as European investors' well-earned distrust of the whole project.

John's feet grew twitchy again. In early 1853, the new president appointed as secretary of war his fellow Democrat Jefferson Davis, who organized three expeditions to explore the best possible routes for a transcontinental railroad to California. Davis gave the command of each expedition to a serving military officer, bypassing John C. Frémont, but John would not be deterred, resolving to finance his own expedition for what he said was the public good. He intended to find a route along the same line of travel that had led to his disaster in the expedition of 1848 to 1849. "Above every other consideration," he explained to a scientific journal that took an interest in his journey, "I have a natural desire to do something in the finishing up of a great work in which I had been so long engaged." He intended to depart from Missouri in the fall of 1853, traveling due west once again near the 38th parallel, venturing into the same mountains in the same season as before.

The family returned to New York on a steamer called the *Asia*, arriving just after midnight on June 16 in a country that was celebrating its prosperity. Workers in Manhattan were completing an enormous building of glass and iron, New York's Crystal Palace—a vast octagon, topped by a dome, with walls and roof entirely of glass plates on an iron frame. Built at Sixth Avenue and Forty-second Street at the northern edge of the city, the see-through building was finished just in time to hold the Exhibition of the Industry of All Nations. Thousands paid the fifty-cent admission or purchased ten-dollar season tickets to study sculpture, agricultural products, and industrial machinery from Europe, the Ottoman empire, and Mexico. A writer for the *New York Herald* said the hundreds of products from the United States were "impossible to mistake" for those from any other country because of their "utilitarian characteristics," and this was true; some of the most significant American items were familiar from their increasing use in everyday life. There were steam engines. There was railroad track. Railway cars and wheels made of steel. Advanced rifles and pistols. Daguerreotype cameras. Gas meters, gas lights, and gas burners. There was an exhibit of "Morse's patent electric telegraph apparatus in operation," which was now such a common feature that the telegraph set in the Crystal Palace was connected to the network of wires stretching as far west as New Orleans and St. Louis; the Crystal Palace was just another telegraph office. There was a "printing telegraph," which spat out characters on paper tape. Americans saw the display as further evidence of the miracle of their country, and a writer for the *New York Times* observed that several European powers were at war, "while we, thanks be to the Providence that has so favored us, [are dedicating the Crystal Palace as] the divinest temple to Peace that ever shadowed American soil."

There were nonetheless hints of history moving in a less placid direction. When John woke in New York on August 22, that day's *Herald* offered reactions from Latin America to a proposal that the United States should purchase Cuba from Spain. Southerners wanted the island for slavery. An inside page of the same paper contained the headline IS THE WHIG PARTY DEAD? There was also a revealing item in the column called "Theatrical Intelligence": a stage production of *Uncle Tom's Cabin* was "still attractive at the National. How much longer it will run we could not say, as the houses now are as full as ever."

If John picked up the *Herald* that day in 1853, he left no record of it. He was absorbed with preparations for what he viewed as his own contribution to history. Preparing for his expedition, he went through the crowded streets in search of a photographer. For his 1842 journey he had bought a camera in New York, but his images never came out; now he wanted a professional. At a photo studio on Broadway he met Solomon Nunes Carvalho, who at thirty-eight was two years younger than John, with carefully coiffed hair and a fringe of beard along the bottom of his jaw. He was a son of immigrants, a Portuguese-American Jew. Like John, Carvalho had grown up in Charleston, where his father played a role in founding the first Reform Jewish synagogue in the United States. Their lives had since diverged, as Carvalho became a denizen of eastern cities with no wilderness experience. But John was unlikely to find an experienced outdoor photographer and offered Carvalho a job. "A half hour previously," Carvalho said, "if anybody had suggested to me, the probability of my undertaking an overland journey to California . . . I should have replied there were no inducements sufficiently powerful to have tempted me." Yet Carvalho was unable to refuse the famed explorer. "I impulsively, without even a consultation with my family, passed my word to join [the] expedition . . . with the full expectation of being exposed to the inclemencies of arctic winter. I know of no other man to whom I would have entrusted my life, under similar circumstances." He consulted other photographers about how to make his daguerreotype camera function; the chemical processes worked best around 70 degrees Fahrenheit, and Carvalho had been warned to expect temperatures ranging "from freezing point to thirty degrees below zero." He started for the West still uncertain if the experiment would work.

✳ ✳ ✳

John's men gathered that fall at the regular point of departure on the western border of Missouri. The familiar plain was changing. The region west of Missouri was becoming known as Nebraska, although Congress had not formally recognized it as a territory. The Indians of the Wyandot Nation, forced to relocate from Ohio some years earlier, were building towns by the mouth of the Kansas River; they commonly dressed like white people, attended a Methodist church, had joined a Masonic lodge, and governed themselves with written laws. They were leading the movement to organize Nebraska Territory, electing one of their own as a provisional governor. In the fall of 1853 they were preparing to send a delegate to Congress to make their case for recognition, and politicians from neighboring Missouri had taken an interest. One visiting politico was a representative of Thomas Hart Benton, who favored a Nebraska free of slavery; all the Nebraska land lay north of the historic Missouri Compromise line dividing free and slave territory. Benton's representative was opposed by men linked with Senator David Atchison, his proslavery archrival, who claimed that Benton was plotting to create a new state that would make him a senator. They were like rival colonial powers, the proslavery and antislavery Missourians, making their first moves to capture the land beyond the state's border.

Refusing to be distracted by this political tension, John's expedition made its final preparations. Now that John was financing the expedition, he planned to travel with a smaller party than in the past. That party would also be easier to feed when supplies grew scarce in the snow. Twelve men—nine white Americans, one American of mixed race, and two Mexicans—formed the bulk of the group. He made arrangements for ten Delaware hunters to meet them well out on the prairie, where he would pay the Indians two dollars per day. The roster was mainly notable for who was absent: there was no Carson, no Godey, no Owens. No Preuss, no Kern, nor the voyageurs he knew best, nor the Delaware leader Sagundai, nor Jacob Dodson. Although at least one of the men had traveled previously with John, the heroes and stalwarts of his past expeditions were gone. Some were dead, some worn out. At least three had signed up with a government-sponsored railroad expedition that was, in effect, competing with his own. Others had passed into new phases of their lives, leaving John as the one who had not let go. The photographer Carvalho formed a low opinion of the men who signed up this time. When hungry they pilfered food from one another, and when thirsty they stole alcohol he had brought to use in his daguerreotype process. John himself did not seem to trust them. He told them that no one except he should talk with reporters about their work, and asked that no one keep a journal of the expedition. He was determined this time to control the public relations.

The men were just starting west when their leader fell ill with rheumatism, an inflammation of the joints, causing pain so intense that it spread to his chest, throat, and head. It was, at age forty, the strongest sign his body had yet sent him that it would not forever endure the demands he made on it. He decided to return to St. Louis for treatment, and told his team to proceed to their prairie rendezvous with the Delawares; he would catch up.

At Westport he was able to send a telegram to Jessie in Washington, and she received his message in time to meet him in St. Louis. On a relay of trains and boats, she spent the time in "undefined dread," unsure of his true condition as she watched the scenery pass. Reaching the waterfront at St. Louis, she plunged into the city, embracing her husband and consulting doctors. The first physician could do no good. A second doctor, a homeopath, "soothed the pain, uprooted the inflammation," and though her husband was "greatly shaken," the doctor helped him get "literally 'on his legs.'" Jessie had been hoping he would call off the expedition; before leaving

Washington, she was likely the source of a newspaper report suggesting he had already abandoned it. Instead, as he started west once again, Jessie wrote her friend Lizzie Lee, "I can't say I am satisfied." Although it felt "mean-spirited" to put it into words, "I would rather have Mr. Frémont at the fireside taking care of himself, writing out what he has done & enjoying the repose and happiness of our quiet home, than getting all the stupid laurels that ever grew. I think he has done enough—but he does not. If this ends well, I shall be glad for his sake that it was done for he would have always regretted it—but nothing it can ever bring can reward either of us for its cost in suffering to him & anxieties to me."

Two of his men were waiting at Westport to escort him back to the main party. The prairie had caught fire in his absence, filling the days with hazy smoke, and lighting the nights with "a horrid, lurid glare, all along the horizon." The flames didn't stop him. He had been seeing prairie fires for fifteen years now, ever since the voyageurs under Joseph Nicollet had taught him to survive by staying in burned areas. He rode onward with his escorts, evading the flames along the Kansas River until they caught up with the main party at the start of November.

There would have been only a limited record of the expedition except that the photographer Solomon Carvalho skirted the prohibition against keeping a journal. He composed notes in the form of a series of letters to his wife, and in this way kept track of his experiences. (He occasionally slipped up while writing, and referred to his letters as "my journal.") As an amateur in the wilderness, he noticed essential chores of daily life that were new to him—like the hour he might spend chasing down a mule that had been turned out to graze and did not care to be caught. When the men began climbing into snowy mountains, where temperatures sometimes fell to 30 degrees below zero, they faced the nightly labor of gathering enough firewood to last until dawn. One man might return to camp "with a decayed trunk on his shoulder," while others teamed up to drag in an entire fallen tree. Conditions often made it impossible to pitch tents. Each man had two

India-rubber blankets, and would lay one rubber sheet atop the snow and then wrap himself in cloth blankets on top of it, finally pulling another rubber blanket over everything. "We generally slept double [and] communicated warmth to each other. . . . During the whole journey, exposed to the most furious snow-storms, I never slept cold, although when I have been called for guard duty I often found some difficulty in rising from the weight of the snow resting on me."

John veered slightly north of the route that had brought him grief in 1848 and 1849. At high altitude one bitterly cold day, he pointed Carvalho toward mountains some forty miles distant and, "in a voice tremulous with emotion," said that those were the mountains on which so many of his men had died. The photographer solemnly set up his camera and took a daguerreotype of the distant snowy range. A few days later, on December 14, they reached their objective, the Continental Divide, crossing through Cochetopa Pass, which led between snowbound peaks at an altitude of 10,160 feet. John was triumphant—on the day they crossed, he noted only four inches of snow on the ground. Nearby the men observed the stumps of recently felled trees, and a wooden cross. The pass had been used, at least in warmer months, by travelers for many years. Unbeknownst to John, it had also just been used by the United States Army; one of the three government-sponsored railroad studies had crossed this way two months earlier.

The pass was the beginning of their trouble, as they descended into deeper wilderness with dwindling food supplies. Wild game vanished as the snow grew deeper. Men sank to their waists or even higher. The animals began to die. A butchered horse or mule produced enough meat for about six meals per man; each man was given his share and told he must make it last until the next horse died. Each dead animal also meant a man had to walk, until all were on foot and the surviving animals carried only baggage. Carvalho, suffering from a frostbitten foot that made it excruciating to move, began to fall behind the rest of the men each day. After sunset one evening, he was so far behind the others that he was left guessing which way to walk in the dark. No one came to look for him. In terror of death, he staggered forward alone until he spied the campfires around ten o'clock. John came to stand by the haggard photographer as he warmed himself by a fire, and said he had been certain that Carvalho would make it; left unsaid was the reality that so few strong men or animals remained that it would not have been easy to mount a search party. "Col. Frémont put out his hand and touched my breast, giving me a slight push; I immediately threw back my foot to keep myself from falling. Col. Frémont laughed at me and remarked that I had not 'half given out,' any man who could act as I did on the occasion, was good for many more miles of travel."

One man died in the mountains. He fell behind the others, his feet blackened with frostbite. This time John did send a search party, which brought back the man, Oliver Fuller, barely alive, but he never recovered. Given one of the dwindling supply of mules to ride, he had to be helped onto the animal and was finally found dead in his saddle. The slowly starving survivors abandoned all excess supplies, freeing enough pack animals that all the men could ride, at least until more animals died; Carvalho had to bury his daguerreotype equipment, although he escaped with the metal plates holding the images he had captured. John also preserved his instruments for celestial navigation, as well as his curiosity; one evening he announced that he expected an "occultation" that night, meaning that the moon would pass in front of a star. He wanted to see it. He engaged the photographer as his assistant, and the two men walked by lantern light to a patch of open ground, "almost up to our middle in snow," as John made observations "for hours" until the occultation took place.

In the morning he told Carvalho that he was certain there was a small Mormon settlement on the far side of the next snow-covered mountain range. They were in Utah Territory now, and the settlement, well south of Salt Lake City, was called Parowan. John had already sent one of the Delawares, known as Wolf, to scout the way ahead; Wolf returned with news that there was no way to ride their animals over the mountains, so steep was the slope and so deep was the snow. "That is not the point," John replied; "we must cross, the question is . . . how we can do it." They did it on foot, leading their animals by the reins. Though many of the men no longer had proper shoes, they wrapped their feet in rawhide and climbed over rocks and snow. Within a few days they staggered down the far side of the range and into the Utah settlement, which was exactly where John had promised them it would be. It was February 8, 1854. Since crossing the Continental Divide they had spent eight weeks traveling some five hundred miles over country so snowy, harsh, and remote that, except for a few Ute Indians near the end, they never saw another human being.

The men rested in Parowan, a town of about four hundred. It was only three years old, a product of the Mormon migration to the region in the late 1840s. Had the expedition failed to locate it, there probably was no other town near enough for them to reach. Writing a letter to Benton, John said that "the Delawares all came in sound, but the whites of my party were all exhausted and broken up, and more or less frost-bitten." John released two men who did not want to continue, including the photographer Carvalho— lame, exhausted, suffering from diarrhea, and without his daguerreotype equipment. Upon reaching the town, Carvalho was sent to the house of a Mormon family, and saw their "three beautiful children. I covered my eyes and wept for joy to think I might yet be restored to embrace my own." He caught a wagon bound for Salt Lake City, planning to return home by the emigrant route when his health and the weather improved.

John planned to resume his survey as soon as he could resupply his men, which proved to be difficult. He had failed to bring enough cash to buy fresh animals. He offered to pay with drafts against Palmer, Cook and Company, his financial agents in San Francisco, but his checks were of little value to people living so far from a bank. He was lucky to discover almost the only person in the territory who was in a position to help: Almon Babbitt, a senior figure in the Mormon church, who was also the secretary and treasurer of Utah Territory, an aide to the territorial governor Brigham

Young. Babbitt was about to travel on territorial business to San Francisco and Washington, D.C. He arranged for a Mormon bishop to buy horses for the expedition using money from church tithes; in exchange, Babbitt would accept John's notes and cash them in San Francisco in the name of Brigham Young. Without Babbitt, John said he would have faced "the alternative of continuing on foot."

Reaching the Pacific coast by mid-April, John publicized the route he had traveled, writing letters to newspapers in San Francisco and Washington, but his case for the railroad line was not persuasive. When at last it was built, more than a decade later, the line would follow a different route several hundred miles farther north. The most concrete achievement of this, John's final expedition, was Carvalho's daguerreotypes. No one had photographed such wilderness scenes before, though the images were scant compensation for the suffering. Maybe the true purpose of the expedition *was* the suffering. John could say, in the words of the oration he had memorized and recited as a youth, that he and his men were achieving "mental and moral greatness" by overcoming the western landscape, whose "awful grandeur" proclaimed "the residence of freemen." At the beginning of his ordeal he had been so ill he could barely get started; by the time he reached San Francisco he said he felt restored and energized, writing in a letter that he was "well and so hearty that [I am] actually some 14 pounds heavier than ever before."

An 1850s political stump speech, by St. Louis artist George Caleb Bingham.

Chapter Fifteen

DECIDEDLY, THIS OUGHT
TO BE STRUCK OUT

PRESIDENTIAL ASPIRANTS, 1854–1856

Washington, Nantucket, and New York

Jessie spent those months in Washington, preoccupied with her absent spouse. "In midwinter, without any reason, I became possessed by the conviction that he was starving," she said. The feeling "made a physical effect on me. Sleep and appetite were broken up, and in spite of my father's and my own efforts to dissipate it by reasoning . . . nothing dulled my sense of increasing suffering from hunger to Mr. Frémont and his party." She became convinced that she shared a telepathic link with her husband that caused her to feel his suffering. No telepathy was necessary; it was reasonable to assume that her husband was starving, knowing what she did of his previous expedition. "When I have no more anxious thoughts pressing on my heart it will not ache," she wrote Lizzie Lee. In the same letter she spoke of parenting twelve-year-old Lily, which, needless to say, she was doing alone.

She faced the added stress of a political controversy, which she could not help but take personally; it involved the land John had been crossing and the railroad he was risking his life to advance. At the Capitol a few blocks from the Frémont house, Democratic senator Stephen A. Douglas sponsored a bill to organize a government for the Nebraska lands, which his Committee on Territories reported to the Senate on January 4, 1854. Douglas was a frontier lawmaker from Illinois, equally adept at roaring speeches to rural audiences and maneuvering legislation through Congress. He had managed the Compromise of 1850 to completion and brought California into the Union. Now he believed proper government for Nebraska would improve the prospects of building the Pacific railroad across it. But as in 1850, proslavery lawmakers did not want another free state without compensation. Douglas obliged. His bill divided the land into two territories, to be known as Kansas and Nebraska, and although both lay north of the Missouri Compromise line dividing slave territory from free, Douglas agreed to have that compromise repealed. He would leave all questions of slavery to the people who settled there. It was not hard to imagine Kansas, which was farther south, becoming a slave state while Nebraska became a free one.

The *Washington Union*, the leading organ of the Democratic Party, described it as a "measure of peace and compromise," but the reaction was anything but peaceful. Horace Greeley's antislavery *New York Tribune* assailed the Kansas-Nebraska Act and its Northern author, saying Douglas was not "manly, noble or independent," and behaved as if "subjection to the slaveholding interest is now the only sure path to political honors and distinction." Frederick Douglass had been right: many Northerners who were "willing to tolerate slavery inside the slave States" were not willing to be "excluded" by slavery from any new land, not even the remote plains of Kansas. Kansas was known to the public through the travel writing of John C. Frémont, and it sounded attractive: In his first report he described looking down from a bluff at the Kansas River, 230 yards wide. The river was lined by "a broad belt of heavy timber," and beyond the river valley stretched prairies of "the richest verdure."

Although the Kansas-Nebraska Act became an official Democratic Party measure that was backed by the president and was soon on its way to passage, it began to crack the party. Frustrated Democrats joined equally frustrated Whigs to discuss forming a new antislavery political party, who would call themselves Republicans. Congressman Thomas Hart Benton was unwilling to go that far, but delivered a speech in the House, thundering far past the hour he had been allotted that the bill would destroy "the peace of the country." The old lawmaker was so estranged from President Pierce that when the president appointed a new postmaster in St. Louis, Benton stopped using the post office, hiring a private express company instead. He drew closer to antislavery lawmakers, and one evening invited Senator Seward of New York to walk home with him. "I am heart-sick being here," Seward said. "I look around me in the Senate and find all demoralized," with many Northern states represented by men who upheld Southern interests. Seward was cheered by his conversation with Benton, the first of a number they would have as they strategized against the Nebraska bill. In a letter to his wife, Seward said he was further cheered when he left Benton's house and went "over to Mrs. Frémont's," which required a separate call, since the Frémonts at last had their own home in Washington, close to the Benton house on C Street. "She is a noble-spirited woman. Has much character. I am sure you would like her. She is very outspoken." It was notable that Seward had gone to hear the views of Mrs. Frémont, not her husband, who he knew was away in the West.

In April a visitor brought news of John. Almon Babbitt, the Utah territorial secretary who had rescued John's finances in Parowan, arrived in Washington. He carried a letter from John to Benton, and also visited Jessie, who marveled at Babbitt's story. Because the Church of Jesus Christ of Latter-day Saints had relocated its people to Utah after careful study of John's maps and reports, it was partly because of John that the Mormons founded a town in the place where he eventually needed to find one. "Safety had come to him," she said, "and to those who had entrusted him with their lives, through the results of his previous work." John had saved himself.

Jessie invited Babbitt to return for dinner, and invited Francis Preston

Blair to join them. (She dryly asked Blair to "forget he has lots of wives," which was assuming too much; the Mormon appeared to have one wife.) She instructed Blair to bring Lizzie and her husband. It was a perfect Washington dinner, so gracefully arranged that Jessie's various purposes might not be noticed. The Saturday meal would reward Babbitt, a Democrat, with an introduction to Blair, who was a living link to Jackson, the party founder. Blair would make a political connection in Utah. And Jessie could gratify her friends with firsthand news of her husband.

✳ ✳ ✳

JOHN REACHED HOME IN LATE SPRING, which allowed him to support Jessie in her mother's final months. Elizabeth Benton, who had taught Jessie to despise slavery and likely influenced her husband's growing opposition to it, died on September 10, 1854. Because of her long illness, the family had been "deprived of her companionship" for years, as Jessie put it; the end may have come as a relief, although that was not something Jessie wanted to express. "How great a loss this was . . . can only be known to those who knew her."

Her father understandably remained in Washington during Elizabeth's final months, though he faced reelection in Missouri. Benton's organization handled the campaign for him and added a special new feature. He had long wanted political party nominees to be chosen by voters, not by party conventions or caucuses, and that year St. Louis Democrats held what was called a "primary election," arguably the first of its kind in the nation. Benton was nominated without opposition. But the general election was different. As the political parties fractured, a new political movement had been gaining strength, formed of groups opposed to immigration. Benton's challenger, a former mayor of St. Louis, collected both Whig and anti-immigrant support. In the election on August 7, Benton was defeated. The telegraph sped the news to Washington, adding that as the votes were counted, "a riot was then taking place." The riot had started on election day, when an election judge slowed down voting by scrutinizing the naturalization papers of voters in an Irish neighborhood. Conflict between Irishmen and natives escalated into full-scale gunfights, in which ten people were killed.

Benton pressed on, changing nothing that he stood for, still a national figure and the leader of many Democrats in Missouri. He served out his House term, which was to last until March 3, 1855. On one of his final days, February 27, he woke in his home on C Street and prepared himself for work. It was a bitterly cold day of the sort he had always found to be good for his lungs, and though the streets were icy, he no doubt had slept with his windows open as he always did. This would explain why he did not detect the faint smell of smoke in the house; when one of his daughters mentioned it, he dismissed it. He left the house at eleven o'clock in the morning, making the short walk he had taken thousands of times up the hill to the Capitol.

In the afternoon he was at work beneath the arched ceiling of the House of Representatives when a messenger told him his house was on fire. The news so startled lawmakers that the House halted most of its business, and many of them followed the seventy-two-year-old as he hurried back along frozen Pennsylvania Avenue toward C Street. They could do nothing when they arrived. A reporter watched Benton "standing in the crowd, looking, with others, on the blazing roof of his dwelling." Jessie stood with him. Thinking back to the smoky smell his daughter had noticed, he decided that the woodwork near a defective chimney must have smoldered for days before spreading. The fire centered on his third-floor study, the location of all his books and the half-finished manuscript of a book he was writing. A fire company arrived, but water ran short and later froze in a hose. Nothing of value was saved from the house except, by chance, a portrait of Thomas Hart Benton as a young man. Once firefighters were able to enter, they went from room to room tossing furniture out the windows to reduce the fuel for the fire; a looking glass sailed out of a third-floor window and shattered on the street.

After a night of watching his house burn, Benton came with Jessie to her nearby house. "Neither of us had slept," Jessie said, "but he made me lie down." She was about six months pregnant, and he was more solicitous of her welfare than his own. Father and daughter "talked together as only those who love one another can talk after a calamity." Of his lost possessions he said, "It is well, there is less to leave now—this has made death more easy." After Congress adjourned a few days later, he returned to St. Louis, where the remains of his late wife had been sent for burial, and watched the gravediggers cover her coffin in Bellefontaine Cemetery. But in no other way did he act like he was ready for death. He began rewriting his lost manuscript and making plans to run again for elective office.

His son-in-law was considering his own future. John received promising news in early 1855. After years of litigation, the Supreme Court upheld his title to the Mariposa grant. Roger Taney, the chief justice, wrote the majority opinion in *Frémont v. United States*, which was considered a landmark case affirming the titles of many California landholders; it was said to cause "considerable rejoicing among the land claimants." The news seemed to vindicate John's refusal to sell the property, and brightened his prospects for enlarging his fortune. But he was being lured in another direction, toward what seemed like an even bigger opportunity, which soon became so appealing that John put off a planned trip to California.

A visitor was making regular appearances at the Frémont house in those days. Jessie identified him as Edward Carrington, a man related to the Bentons and to Jessie's extended family—probably Edward Codrington Carrington Jr., from an old Virginia family in Botetourt County, just south of Jessie's ancestral home. The elder Edward Codrington Carrington had served in the War of 1812, while Mrs. Edward Carrington of Botecourt County was raising funds to maintain George Washington's estate at Mount Vernon. The younger Mr. Carrington was a onetime student at

Virginia Military Institute who volunteered for the war against Mexico, then in 1853 moved to Washington to practice law. He was twenty-nine, one of a number of men drawn into the Frémont orbit who were much closer in age to Jessie than to John; yet the visitor seemed to influence the older man. Do you not think, Carrington asked, that the time has come to restrict immigration? John agreed. Not that immigrants should be banned—but "indiscriminate immigration" would bring the problems of the crowded old world, because newcomers arrived "without a comprehension of American history and of their duties." John endorsed the old nativist idea of limiting immigrants' ability to vote, believing the foreign-born should be denied the franchise until they had been in the country twenty-one years. Young Carrington was delighted because, Jessie said, "he was a member of the Native American party."

The view John had picked up was impossible to reconcile with his experience. His writings were streaked with tributes to men of different nationalities and cultures who not only knew the history of the country but had made history with him. ("It was a serious enterprise . . . to undertake a traverse of such a region, and with a party . . . of many nations—American, French, German, Canadian, Indian, and colored—and most of them young, several being under twenty-one years of age.") It was, however, possible to reconcile skepticism of immigration with the moment in history and with his ambition. As the defeat of Benton suggested, anti-immigrant sentiment was the next big thing. Carrington was connected with other men in the nativist movement, who were thinking of "making an offer" to John, "looking towards his nomination as a Democratic candidate for the Presidency."

✳ ✳ ✳

THE POLITICAL POWER OF NATIVISM had grown since the Catholic church burnings in Philadelphia in 1844. The resistance to immigrants in the California goldfields, which Senator Frémont had tried to exploit in

1850 only to be damaged by it, was representative of the era. Some nativists founded secret societies with names such as the Order of the Star-Spangled Banner. They had secret handshakes and passwords. Entry-level members of the Order of the Star-Spangled Banner were not even told the name of the organization at first. (Newspapers nicknamed them the Order of Know-Nothings, because they claimed to know nothing when questioned about the order; junior members apparently were telling the truth.) More senior members of the order took an oath to use all legal means to "remove all foreigners, aliens or Roman Catholics from office." The old nativist talking point that John repeated—that adult immigrants should wait twenty-one years to vote because newborn native children did—was a more polished form of such thinking, processed for mass consumption. By comparing immigrants to native children rather than other adults, the idea offered a memorable combination of illogic and grievance, making an arbitrary rule sound like it was based on reason, and positioning the equal treatment of immigrants as unfair to natives.

New waves of Irish Catholic immigration since the late 1840s had triggered fresh nativist grievances and energized the secret societies to reach for power. Professional politicians were unsure how to contain them, and quickly found that ignoring them didn't work. When supporting Winfield Scott in 1852, the Whigs tried to compete with Democrats for the immigrant vote, but seemed to push away nativist Whig voters, losing more than they gained. Soon the nativists, temporarily abandoned by both parties, rose as a power all their own. The leader of a Know-Nothing order began giving public speeches in New York, while a nativist youth movement called themselves the Wide-Awakes and walked the streets wearing their own distinctive white felt hats. The Know-Nothings generated drama by engineering protests that seemed designed to provoke violence: five thousand of them escorted an anti-Catholic preacher through Brooklyn until they were battling with crowds of Irishmen—and a week later they repeated the process. A church was blown up in Dorchester, Massachusetts, while another was burned in Maine. In Washington, men broke into the construction site for the Washington Monument and stole a block of marble that had been donated by the pope for incorporation in the structure. They threw it in the Potomac River.

Thomas Hart Benton's defeat in August 1854 by a Whig who was also a nativist set the pattern for other elections that fall. Some candidates ran openly under a Native American banner, while in other races nativists used their influence to nominate friendly candidates on both Whig and Democratic tickets. In Massachusetts, the Know-Nothings elected their candidate for governor—one of several governorships they eventually would control—and virtually the entire state legislature, as well as much of the congressional delegation. The order attracted ambitious political professionals, such as Nathaniel P. Banks of Massachusetts, a Democrat, who survived the political hurricane and won reelection to his congressional seat in 1854 by welcoming nativist support.

Lawmakers who would not bend to the nativists were left politically homeless. One of them was Abraham Lincoln, a former Whig representative. In the summer of 1855 the Illinois lawyer received a letter from a friend asking where he stood. "That is a disputed point," Lincoln replied.

I think I am a whig, but others say there are no whigs . . . I am not a Know-Nothing. This is certain. How could I be? How can any one who abhors the oppression of negroes, be in favor of degrading classes of white people? Our progress in degeneracy appears to me to be pretty rapid. As a nation, we began by declaring that "all men are created equal." We now practically read it "all men are created equal, except negroes." When the Know-Nothings get control, it will read "all men are created equal, except negroes, and foreigners, and catholics." When it comes to this I should prefer emigrating to some country where they made no pretence of loving

liberty—to Russia, for instance, where despotism can be taken pure, and
without the base alloy of hypocrisy.

Lincoln knew what he stood for—he spent much of 1855 organizing opposition to the Kansas-Nebraska Act in Illinois—but did not know where his efforts would lead.

Some Southern Democrats saw nativism as an issue that could bring them new Northern allies. Of course Democrats themselves were courting immigrants, but consistency was not the point. By raising the illusory dangers of immigrants, they could unite native-born voters from the North and South, distracting from the divisive question of what to do about black people.

A Democratic/Know-Nothing combination was what John's friend Carrington proposed, and John seriously considered tying his fortune to this collection of misled patriots, bigots, and cynics. Carrington revealed himself as an emissary from a group of politicos who thought Frémont could be their presidential candidate. John B. Floyd, a former governor of Virginia, was said to be among the Frémont enthusiasts; so, too, was William Preston, another of Jessie's politically active relations. In the summer of 1855, Floyd and other Democrats met John in New York at the St. Nicholas, a new luxury hotel on Broadway. Amid its "profusion of mirrors, gilding, tapestry, and crystal," which reminded one visitor of "the palace of some Eastern prince," John and his political suitors walked velvet-pile carpets and conferred across marble tables. The men suggested they could support John at the following year's Democratic convention. Floyd and others also made clear that any Democrat must support the South, upholding the repeal of the Missouri Compromise. These were terms that John found "impossible . . . to accept." The meeting broke up without agreement; John walked away doubting that he could work with the Southern men, who themselves walked away with a lower opinion of the great explorer. The Democrat

Floyd later insisted that he was the one who had rejected John: "I . . . considered him very light metal (notwithstanding Mariposa,) and extremely ill-formed on all political subjects. . . . The influences which governed him were Abolition."

John was indeed being influenced by antislavery forces, as was apparent by a friend he brought to the meeting: Nathaniel P. Banks, the Massachusetts Democratic congressman turned nativist. Banks was taken with the idea that John's heroic reputation made him an ideal presidential candidate. But he was also an antislavery man, and triggered arguments by stating his views during the meeting; he may not have minded that the conference failed. Professional politicians such as Banks were puzzling over the problem of assembling a majority in a fragmented electorate. There was a very large proslavery vote. There was a very large nativist vote. It was hard to imagine winning a national election without pandering to one constituency or both. Yet there was also a very large antislavery vote, and some states had a substantial immigrant vote. How could a candidate attract any of these groups without fatally alienating others? Solving this problem would take the perfect blend of issues, words, and men. Clearly John's friend Banks did not think the politicos at the St. Nicholas had the winning combination, though there might be other combinations available.

✳ ✳ ✳

AFTER THE DEMOCRATIC CONFERENCE John visited his most important political adviser. He caught the relay of trains and boats northeastward toward Cape Cod and took a ferry to Nantucket Island. He passed through the wealthy old whaling town by the harbor, with its brick-and-glass storefronts and horses clattering on cobblestone streets, and crossed the sandy hills of the island toward the lighthouse at its far end. Jessie had taken the children there for the summer.

She was hoping the ocean air would help her recover from childbirth. A son had been born to the Frémonts on May 17, the third of their children to survive: Francis Preston Frémont, named in honor of Lizzie Lee's father, Francis Preston Blair. Jessie and the children were staying at Siasconset, on the seaward point of the island; she wrote a letter to Lizzie saying it was a village of "old sailors and whaling captains" and their families, where four-year-old Charlie played with "a little crowd of boys who will inevitably go whaling in their turn." The air was invigorating, the ocean beyond the lighthouse was awe-inspiring, and Jessie hated it. "I shall not begin to tell you how forlornly lonesome this island is," she wrote Lizzie. For days they shared the house with a Quaker family, including grandchildren of the famed abolitionist Lucretia Mott. Jessie agreed with Mott about slavery but took offense at her self-righteous style: "Badly as she thinks of southern people I always thought worse of a 'strong-minded' speech making woman," she said, and she was disappointed to find Mott's relations to be as irritating as Mott.

John arrived a few days after Jessie mailed this letter. They went for a walk out to the Siasconset lighthouse, and he told her of the Democratic conference in New York. Despite its failure, John's prospects seemed bright; Banks still favored him, and Jessie was able to report that John also had support from key politicos who had met in Philadelphia in the summer of 1855. One of the people at the meeting had gone on to stay on Nantucket near Jessie, and kept her posted on the Pennsylvanians' efforts. Jessie concluded that John needed more advice, and when he departed Siasconset she sent a letter ahead to her newborn baby's namesake, Francis Preston Blair.

My dear Mr. Blair,

Mr. Frémont has under consideration so important a step, that before taking it he wishes for the advice and friendly counsel which have

*heretofore proved so full of sagacity and led to such success. In talking of
it together I offered to ask it from you again, and my own little judgment
being favorable I almost ventured to promise your assistance.*

Within days, Blair not only met with John but began drafting a platform of ideas on which he might run. The central plank was restoring the
Missouri Compromise. From that moment, with characteristic energy, he
became John's principal political manager, guiding him toward an antislavery candidacy.

An observer in the 1850s described Blair as "a little old gentleman, thin,
slender, and feeble in appearance," who was "given a top-heavy appearance
by the fact that his head is too big for his body, and his hat too big for his
head." When he doffed the hat, it revealed a nearly bald head. His eyes blazed
with enthusiasm; he was a gregarious man, talented at making and keeping
friends. He was also brilliant with words. In the 1820s he was a Kentucky
court clerk, political partisan, and newspaper writer who worked to elect
Andrew Jackson; in 1830 Jackson brought him to Washington. The Democratic Party founder installed him as the editor of the new Democratic
newspaper, the *Washington Globe*, which Blair ran for fifteen years. He was
Jackson's voice and shameless promoter, recasting the stubborn, furious,
half-dead old duelist as a colossus who shrugged off all attacks. ("The
storms of faction beat around him unheeded," Blair wrote early on. "The
cloud rests upon him but a moment and leaves him more bright than before, towering in the sunshine of spotless honor and eternal truth.") He
became one of the newsmen in Jackson's informal kitchen cabinet, then a
permanent counselor to presidents, with a house across Pennsylvania Avenue from the executive mansion and an estate outside town called Silver
Spring. He worked closely with Jackson's successor, Van Buren, although
more recent Democratic presidents had discarded him. He was still angry
that Polk had removed him from the *Globe* (and, to Blair's further fury, had
changed the newspaper's name to the *Union*, thus ending the *Globe* and

erasing Blair's legacy). Blair blamed slave interests for his political exile because, although he was a slave owner himself, he shared Benton's dim view of slavery expansion. If he could find the right candidate in 1856 he could strike back and recover his influence.

At first Blair thought of running John as an independent Democrat, but he was drawn toward the Republicans. The new party was attracting converts, such as Seward, the once-discouraged Whig from New York, and Salmon P. Chase, an antislavery Democrat elected governor of Ohio in late 1855. Both had statewide political organizations behind them. Nathaniel Banks—once a Democrat, then a Know-Nothing—was drifting toward the new party, and Blair prepared for his own party switch while Jessie traded conspiratorial notes with him. She reported on the movements of "Mr. B," which was how she referred to Banks, fearing that Democratic postmasters appointed by President Pierce were reading Blair's mail. Banks was maneuvering to become Speaker of the House. In another letter she relayed a message from John: "I am told to tell you that satisfactory intelligence has been brought in from the east & west—the details are to be given you in your own library."

In December, Blair wrote a letter to the Republican Association of Washington effectively pledging his support to the party. His shift made news, denounced in Democratic papers and embraced by Republicans. "I thank you from the bottom of my heart," an Albany man wrote Blair, saying his link to the old Unionist Andrew Jackson "carries with it a prestige that you yourself may not be fully aware of." Blair had been writing articles for John Bigelow, the editor of the New York Evening Post, and when Bigelow asked for a series of articles about prospective Republican candidates, Blair delivered a single article about John Charles Frémont. He drew Bigelow into the circle of Frémont advisers, and the circle gradually gained members such as Thurlow Weed, Seward's political manager. He invited major party figures to a Christmas dinner at his home. Having been present at the creation of the Democratic Party in the early 1830s, Blair was present as the Republicans took shape.

The presidential campaign that now loomed would be a vast, boisterous, roaring affair of rallies, speeches, bonfires, songs, pamphlets, parades, articles, and insults—but that was for the candidate's supporters, not the candidate. A presidential contender was supposed to rise above it all. No matter how desperately he was scheming for election, he was to pretend he wasn't trying, but was merely answering the call of the people. A presidential candidate avoided giving speeches, and if compelled to speak tried not to say anything important; if forced to say something important, he would express it in a private letter to a friend that would be deliberately leaked to the newspapers. The Frémonts followed this template in the winter of 1855 to 1856. The closest they came to a public statement was when they changed their address, moving north to New York City, in a state that any Northern candidate must win. Jessie marveled at the New York amenities of their rented house on the Bowery ("water, fire, and gas all over," she gushed), but they soon moved to a still more elegant address, a marble-fronted house at 56 West Ninth Street, near Washington Square.

John acted as though he was focused on exploration, not politics. After the move he unpacked containers holding carefully preserved metal plates, which were daguerreotypes—the images that Solomon Carvalho had captured during the 1853 to 1854 expedition across the Rockies. He carried the chemically treated metal plates to the studio of a New York photographer named Mathew Brady, and spent part of the winter having the images developed. Jessie set up a room in their house as an artist's studio, where, by the light of a bay window, an oil painter and a woodcutter used the photos as the basis for images that could be reproduced in John's next book.

Brady, the photographer, was in his early thirties, clean-shaven, with tiny spectacles and a stylish mass of dark hair. He was the son of Irish immigrants. As a youth, coming from upstate New York to study art in the city, he was introduced to the New York University professor Samuel F. B. Morse, who had just recently passed through his short career of railing against Catholics and foreign influence and was experimenting with daguerreotypes. Morse was generous in sharing his knowledge, and the young Irish-American gave him some credit for the direction of his later career. By the mid-1850s Brady had two studios on Broadway with multiple employees, and while developing John's images he also arranged to take a portrait of his famous customer. John arrived wearing a light-colored suit. Brady posed him sitting sideways, with his left shoulder to the camera, and had John turn his head for a three-quarter view of the face. John was bearded, hair combed but curling around his ears. His face looked weathered and strong, though his expression hinted at a man who was vulnerable, hidden.

✳ ✳ ✳

REPUBLICANS PLANNED A PRELIMINARY CONVENTION in February to better organize the party, followed by a presidential nominating convention in June. They had several potential candidates, though most had disadvantages. John McLean, a Supreme Court justice, wanted the nomination but had no real antislavery record. Chase of Ohio believed he had earned the nomination, but had *too much* of an antislavery record; managers of the antislavery party wanted a man who had not taken such strong positions that he could be painted as extremist. Seward wanted the nomination, but his political adviser, Thurlow Weed, counseled him to hold back: Seward had been supportive of Catholics and immigrants, so he must wait until 1860 in hopes that the nativist wave would recede. John's short Senate career and long absences in the West during many political controversies made him a nearly ideal choice. Horace Greeley, who had brought his *New York Tribune* into the new party, said that "a candidate must have a slim record in these times."

The Democrats nominated their candidate first, meeting in Cincinnati in May. Casting aside the unpopular President Pierce, they chose James

Buchanan—the Bentons' longtime neighbor, who escorted teenage Jessie at an 1840 wedding, and sent his frustratingly vague letter to John on the Pacific coast in 1846. Buchanan, the political survivor. He could win votes North and South—he had powerful Southern friends (he had been so close to William R. King, an Alabama senator, that one lawmaker referred to them as "Buchanan and his wife") and could use his strong political organization to capture his home state of Pennsylvania. He had such vast government experience that few men had been so qualified on paper. Best of all, from the Democrats' point of view, he was serving as ambassador to Britain, which meant that he had been absent for the Kansas-Nebraska Act. His positions could be trimmed as necessity required; the Democrats, too, wanted a man with "a slim record" on the issues that mattered most.

The Democrats and Republicans would be joined by a third party: the remnants of the Whigs were absorbed by a faction of Know-Nothings and rebranded the American Party. Meeting in Philadelphia, they nominated former Whig president Millard Fillmore. Their vice presidential choice reflected the fracturing political world: delegates selected Andrew Jackson Donelson, the former president's nephew and adopted son. While the Democrats were the party of Jackson, and the Republicans had won over Blair and other acolytes of Jackson, the nativists nominated a Jackson; the dominant political movement of the past generation was split in three.

If John were nominated, then, he would be facing a deeply experienced presidential candidate and a former president. He needed to polish his own credentials. His principal qualification was his inspiring life story, and so Jessie began the critical work of gathering information for two writers who produced book-length campaign biographies. The most ambitious effort was by John Bigelow, the editor of the *Evening Post*, who in the spring and summer of 1856 was "obliged to apply to Mrs. Frémont for information about her husband's parentage." This created a problem: John's illegitimate birth was deeply embarrassing, and Jessie did not want this fact printed. She traveled to Virginia to talk with John's mother's relations and find a presentable story, but only so much could be done. So Jessie became an uncredited coauthor, writing the first chapter of Bigelow's book herself, offering a sympathetic version of Anne Pryor's separation from her spouse (the much older husband was "repulsive," Jessie reported), and adding the false claim that Anne divorced and remarried before John's birth. Nowhere in the book was Jessie credited with this act of ghostwriting, although Bigelow acknowledged it more than half a century later in his memoirs. (He also seemed to confess to the falsehood at the heart of the chapter: "Her account of the colonel's origin and early life was not as full as I desired, but it answered our purpose very well.")

Another biography was to be written by Charles Upham, a former congressman. Jessie proofread Upham's manuscript and saw a passage she disliked—a description of the young couple's elopement in 1841. With playful formality she wrote a letter to the biographer, appealing to him in the third person:

> Will Mr. Upham let my alterations stand? There was no "dash" [to get married]—it was done in sober sadness on my part and as sober judgment on Mr. Frémont's.

An act of "sober judgment" would play better with the voting public, who might make judgments of their own about John rashly "dashing" off with Jessie when she was hardly more than a girl. The biographer apparently cut the section she disapproved; his published volume described the marriage in a few sentences and did not directly mention that it was an elopement.

More revisions were to come. Isaac Sherman, a politico attached to the campaign, wrote Upham to say he was troubled that the manuscript described the California gold-mining bill that Senator Frémont had proposed in 1850. Some of "our friends," wrote Sherman, "doubt the propriety of making any observation on the Bill which legitimated Americans only to procure gold from the public lands. Could you forward that chapter by express to the Col. [on] 9th Street?" Republicans were aiming to co-opt nativists, but did not want their candidate to *be* one of the nativists, with their bigoted ideas and affection for violence. Upham forwarded the manuscript and soon received a note from Jessie Benton Frémont—it was in her hand, signed "J.B."—regarding "the second section of the bill," which limited gold-mining permits to citizens. Jessie liked not a word of the four pages Upham had devoted to it: "Decidedly, this ought to be struck out." Upham complied. The published version of the biography mentioned other parts of the mining bill while ignoring the ban on noncitizens.

Jessie was becoming a campaign adviser despite a personal cost. Virtually all members of her family by blood or marriage were Southern, and if a few agreed with her views of slavery, virtually none approved of the new Northern party. According to Jessie, John understood that his candidacy would disrupt her personal relationships, and he said he would not proceed unless she consented. She did. "This ended my old life," she said. "Except for my Father, and the one cousin, now and always our loving sister-friend, I was dropped by every relative." Even some of her siblings cooled toward her. Her father agreed with her antislavery stance—yet her relationship with him had become the most fraught of all. In late 1855, as John began moving toward the presidency, it became clear that Thomas Hart Benton would not support him. Jessie could not persuade him. His old friend Francis P. Blair could not persuade him either. Benton would neither give political advice to his son-in-law nor endorse him. He said a sectional party would destroy the Union.

He had also come to doubt John's ability. Jessie traced the break between them to the winter of 1851 to 1852, when Senator Benton had attempted to sell Las Mariposas (saying John was "not adapted to such business") and John had revoked the sale. Benton also seemed unimpressed with John's expedition in 1853 to 1854, even after John flattered him by saying it had borne out Benton's vision for where the rail route should be found. By April 1856, relations were so strained that Jessie could not bear to see her father. Writing a letter from New York to her best friend, Lizzie Lee, she said, "I do not think I can go to Washington," because her father would be there. "I have made one thing a fixed resolve—not to be hurt at heart any oftener than it is forced upon me—to go deliberately into agitation and pain is almost suicide."

> I know both my people too well ever to look for concession from either side. And with Father this is only the expression of years distrust of Mr. Frémont's judgment. . . . I think Mr. Frémont could not have done other-wise than revoke [the Mariposas] sale. I know more facts than father did. Indeed Mr. Frémont would have had small respect for himself to allow of such an administration of his estate during his life. . . . I have written constantly to Father. I always tell him whatever I think may interest him—never saying politics—but for four months I have not had a line from him.

If Jessie thought her father had at last had found "a fair occasion" to express his old resentments, there was another possible explanation: Benton had worked with the most consequential presidents of his time, and did not see John among them. Benton, the old newspaperman, knew how much of his son-in-law's reputation had been manufactured.

Jessie finally received a warm letter from her father, inviting her to Washington with the grandchildren. John and Blair encouraged her to go, still hoping she could recruit him. But she dreaded the meeting and allowed herself to be delayed several weeks before traveling. When at last she reached Washington she found her father was absent, having just caught a train toward Missouri.

✳ ✳ ✳

BEFORE THE REPUBLICAN CONVENTION, violent events gave new force to the party and to John's efforts to lead it. First, the Kansas-Nebraska Act intensified the conflict between proslavery and antislavery forces. Missourians swept across the state border, seizing land and brushing aside Indians who had made their homes in Kansas. Some Missourians wanted profit from real estate, while others, led by the proslavery senator David Atchison, meant to make Kansas a slave state. Northern settlers arrived, some assisted by the New England Emigrant Aid Company. It had been founded by Eli Thayer, a Massachusetts politician and educator, who dreamed of colonizing Kansas as a free state. Pro- and antislavery settlers established separate towns along the Kansas River and traded gunshots. Proslavery territorial governors appointed by President Pierce failed to keep order, and Charles Robinson, an agent of the Emigrant Aid Company, claimed that *he* was governor.

John knew Robinson. He had been in during California the gold rush, becoming a leader in sometimes-violent battles over land ownership and supporting John's failed Senate reelection in 1851. John's managers sensed an opportunity to make John a part of the Kansas story by writing a supportive letter to his friend, designed to fall into the hands of news editors. The letter to Robinson in April recounted John's Senate defeat in a way that artfully suggested, without evidence, that he had lost because of his antislavery beliefs.

> We were defeated then, but that contest was only an incident in the great struggle—the victory was deferred, not lost. You have carried to another field [Kansas] the same principle, with courage and ability. . . . I can only say that I sympathize cordially with you, and that as you stood by me firmly and generously when we were defeated by the nullifiers in California, I have every disposition to stand by you in your battle with them in Kansas.

In a few sentences John recast himself as an antislavery fighter and connected himself to a radical voice in Kansas. Newspapers across the country reprinted the letter. The *Washington Star*, critical of the Republicans, added a sneering commentary: the letter would have been more "complete if it had given the world the Colonel's opinion upon 'the equality of the races.'" Democrats claimed "black Republicans" favored social equality for African Americans. But Republicans praised the letter, which fixed attention on Robinson just before his story took a dark turn. Weeks later, federal authorities arrested the would-be governor and accused him of treason, a charge that made national headlines and marked him as an antislavery martyr.

Kansas received even more attention when a proslavery sheriff linked with David Atchison led a party of gunmen into the settlement of Lawrence, which had been founded by free-soil settlers. The gunmen sacked the offices of an antislavery newspaper called the *Herald of Freedom* and threw its printing press in the Kansas River. They burned a building called the Free State Hotel and torched the houses of residents. It took a few days for fleeing residents to carry the story to the nearest telegraph office, from which it almost instantly reached Horace Greeley's *New York Tribune*, more than a thousand miles away. Greeley spared no ink: Lawrence had been "devastated and burned to ashes by the Border Ruffians," the label given to proslavery gunmen from Missouri. "A few bare and tottering chimneys, a charred and blackened waste, now mark the site [attacked by the] myrmidons of Border-Ruffianism, intent on the transformation of Kansas into a breeding ground and fortress of Human Slavery." Antislavery activists in Kansas struck back. John Brown, a New Englander whose messianic opposition to slavery had led him to join a free-state militia in Kansas, slipped away from the militia to conduct a retaliatory raid on his own authority. Moving at night, at the head of a small group of loyalists that included four of his sons, they rounded up five proslavery settlers and executed them.

By then the dispute over Kansas had triggered political violence in Washington itself. Republican senator Charles Sumner of Massachusetts delivered a lengthy talk in May on what he called the crime of Kansas. In an especially withering passage, he mocked a South Carolina senator named Andrew Butler for his "incoherent phrases" and "the loose expectoration of his speech" while opposing Kansas as a free state. "There was," Sumner said, no "possible deviation from truth which he did not make." Senator Butler was not present for this tirade, but Butler's nephew learned of the speech afterward and considered it an insult to his family. The nephew, Preston Brooks, was a member of the House of Representatives. He walked across the Capitol to the Senate chamber, found Sumner writing at his desk, and beat him again and again with a heavy cane until he was unconscious. Brooks kept thrashing him even after the cane broke into pieces over Sumner's head.

Now that the conflict had reached one of the principal media centers, the country learned of every detail. The telegraph and daily newspapers allowed people across vast distances to read about the caning almost simultaneously, and to read daily updates as further facts became known. Nothing like this would have been possible a decade earlier. Of course the news was filtered through Northern and Southern editors, which meant Northerners and Southerners were simultaneously reading different versions of the same event. A witness quoted in a Chicago newspaper said Sumner was ambushed, "hemmed in" at his desk and beaten mercilessly until he "had by a great effort torn [his] desk from its fastenings, and then he pitched forward insensible on the floor." A correspondent for South Carolina's *Charleston Courier* all but rolled his eyes. "The telegraph has already spread a thousand and one stories about this transaction," he wrote, many of them "incorrect." Sumner "was beaten, it is true, but not so badly . . . he is not seriously hurt. His whole speech was of a character very irritating to Southern men."

The partisan reporting played to, and likely reinforced, partisan attitudes. A paper in Columbia, South Carolina, declared that Brooks had "the hearty congratulations of the people of South Carolina for his summary chastisement of the Abolitionist Sumner." South Carolinians held public meetings to vote Brooks resolutions of thanks and a "handsome gold headed cane," while a woman from his congressional district promised to send "hickory sticks, with which to chastise Abolitionists." It was even alleged that "the slaves of Columbia" had taken up a "subscription" to buy Brooks a gift for his "protection in their rights and enjoyments as the happiest laborers on the face of the globe."

As quickly as the telegraph had spread the news of the caning everywhere, it spread the Southern reaction across the North. Readers of the *New York Herald* unfolded their papers to discover extended excerpts of the Southern press praising "chivalrous" Brooks for beating "the poltroon Senator of Massachusetts." And this was a new phenomenon in itself. Masses of Americans learned not only of a disturbing event more rapidly than ever before but also that other Americans celebrated the very event that horrified them. While editors had always reprinted opposing views to demonstrate how wrong they were, the telegraph allowed them to do so with unprecedented speed and force. Northern Democrats immediately began reporting declines in support for their party, while more Northern voters began turning to Republicans. Even those who did not feel strongly about the freedom of slaves cared about the freedom of speech, and Sumner's caning in response to his words was seen as the latest evidence that the South would never tolerate that freedom. "Has it come to this," asked John Bigelow's *Evening Post*, "that we must speak with bated breath in the presence of our Southern masters? . . . Are we too, slaves, slaves for life, a target for their brutal blows, when we do not comport ourselves to please them?" The Constitution and the country seemed in danger. As the Republican convention neared, the party's 1856 campaign began to take on the character of a righteous cause.

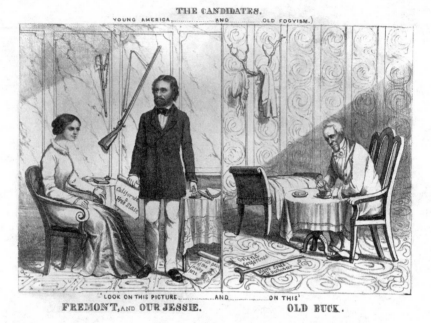

Campaign art contrasting married John Frémont with his bachelor opponent.

Chapter Sixteen

HE THROWS AWAY HIS HEART

THE FRÉMONTS, 1856

New York

On December 11, 1854, Jacob Dodson filed a petition in Congress. Eight years after serving in the California Battalion during the war against Mexico, he was still unpaid. Because John had violated the law by allowing his black former servant to enlist, the government had never recognized his service. Now Dodson wanted compensation. John B. Weller, one of the senators from California, took up the cause and introduced a bill to allow "Jacob Dodson, a colored man," to receive "all the pay and allowances to which he would be entitled . . . if he had been legally enlisted." It took more than a year for the measure to pass both houses of Congress; Dodson himself may have been able to lobby for its passage, since he worked as a Senate messenger and also was "in charge of the retiring rooms" of the Senate for many years, making him known and useful to many lawmakers. President Pierce signed the bill into law in April 1856, acknowledging Dodson's place among the African Americans who had served, despite the law, in every war. It was an act of justice to pay the thirty-year-old the same as any white man, although it underlined the inequity of the system. Congress compensated Dodson without making the slightest move toward repealing the law that barred Negroes from military service.

Dodson's story reflected the wider political landscape Republican managers surveyed in 1856. It was true that the new party gave voice to the widening Northern unrest against the slave power—but also true that white society still broadly accepted racism and prejudice. There were only so many white men who opposed slavery strongly enough to let it determine their votes, and Republicans needed virtually all of them. This included a group of Northern voters whom Republican leaders found distasteful: Northern nativists. Some anti-immigrant voters were also antislavery—immigrants, like slaves, could be seen as competition against native white labor—and they could not be discarded. James Gordon Bennett's *Herald*, in a shockingly worded column that John or Jessie would surely have seen at home, described the emerging Republican coalition as a combination of "anti-slavery Know Nothings and nigger worshipers." It was a measure of the times that Bennett published this racist language in an article *approving* the coalition, which he considered better than the "corrupt, imbecile and most wretched" Democrats.

Before the Republican convention, the problem of seeking the Know-Nothing vote became a crisis. The nativist American Party divided over slavery, as every institution in the country was doing: hostility toward Catholics and immigrants, the force that was supposed to transcend slavery, was not strong enough to bind the anti-immigrant party. Northern delegates, objecting to their party's position on slavery in the territories, bolted the American Party convention that nominated Millard Fillmore and planned their own convention in New York. These antislavery Know-Nothings, casting about for a celebrity candidate, talked of drafting John Charles Frémont—and presented him with a perilous choice. If the Know-Nothings nominated John they would brand him with their tainted label and drive away many voters. But if they did *not* nominate him, they would pick some other antislavery candidate, who would divide the antislavery vote. The *Tribune's* Greeley saw the entire operation as a cynical plot inspired by proslavery Democrats, who by highlighting nativist issues on the antislavery side would "frighten Adopted Citizens into their net." John privately drafted a letter refusing the nativists' nomination, ready to send if needed.

The antislavery nativist convention's 250 delegates met on June 12 at the Apollo Rooms, a music hall better known as the birthplace of the New York Philharmonic. The meeting was public, as a reporter noted: "The dark lanterns, sentinels, pass-words, grips, winks, and locks and keys upon which the Order was founded, having been abolished, this Convention is held with open doors—wide open to Broadway." The same correspondent noticed "a large proportion of sharp, hungry, and calculating politicians" among the delegates, adding that "Thurlow Weed and his set have a pretty long finger in the pie." Seward's political manager had undertaken to solve John's problem. Weed's team of political "wire workers" strategized beforehand in the ornate rooms of the Astor House, then walked the few blocks up Broadway to the Apollo Rooms and swept through its open doors. Using persuasion and an alleged thirty thousand dollars in cash payments, they convinced the delegates to support Nathanial Banks for president. The delegates also agreed to delay the final choice of their convention for a few days, until after the Republican convention; once the Republicans had safely nominated John, Banks would refuse the Know-Nothings, who would then give their endorsement to John. By then their label would carry less stigma, because John would be established in the public mind as the Republican nominee—and the nativists would be subsumed in the Republican Party. This, the *Herald* correspondent said, was Weed's "amiable" plan for "snuffing out this independent Northern Know Nothing movement like a farthing candle." It worked as intended. The Know-Nothings were persuaded that they were driving the train when they were being driven.

Next the Republicans gathered June 17 in Philadelphia. In keeping with custom, John and Jessie stayed away. Messages snapped back and forth on Morse's lines between the Frémonts in New York, Banks in Washington, and managers such as Francis Blair in Philadelphia. The delegates gathered behind the brick-and-stone facade of Philadelphia's Musical Fund Hall; Jenny Lind had once sung from its stage, Charles Dickens had spoken from it, and now Republicans swarmed it. "Long before the hour for the assembling of the Convention," said the *Herald*, "the passages leading to the hall were crowded with people, and it was with a good deal of trouble that the delegates were able to gain admission." Blair moved through the crowds, where an observer said "the old fellow's big head glistens with intelligence" and "mention of his name is invariably followed by uproarious applause." In the packed music hall the righteous cause reasserted itself. Robert Emmett, a former Democrat, was elected chairman of the convention and addressed the crowd:

> *The delegates to this Convention occupy a higher position than any body on earth (Applause.) They may call us what they please—black republicans, nigger worshippers, or anything else—and they may say that we intend to drag in all the isms of the day. So we do. We invite them to come with us, and we will unite them in the one great ism—patriotism. (Loud cheers.) . . . Honest abolitionism looks forward to the day when there shall be no such thing as human bondage on the face of the earth. (Loud applause.)*

The Republicans had decided to welcome a delegation from Kansas Territory, and its members were "received with loud cheering, and all the Eastern patriots jumped on the seats to have a good look at the frontier heroes."

Delegates were also circulating copies of a letter John had written weeks earlier. He had declined an invitation to give a speech before a mass meeting of Republicans, but had written the organizers a letter stating his views: "Gentlemen . . . I am opposed to Slavery in the abstract and upon principle, sustained and made habitual by long settled convictions. While I feel inflexible in the belief that it ought not to be interfered with where it exists under the shield of State Sovereignty, I am as inflexibly opposed to its extension on this Continent beyond its present limits." This expressed the essence of the platform that Republicans soon approved: slavery could not be touched where it was, but must never be allowed to spread where it was not. David Wilmot of Pennsylvania, who had given his name to the Wilmot Proviso demanding a ban on slavery in new territories, read the platform aloud: the party vowed to uphold the Constitution, which made room for slavery, but also vowed to uphold "the principles promulgated in the Declaration of Independence," which declared all men created equal. They supported the Missouri Compromise and insisted that Kansas become a free state. They said that under President Pierce and his administration, Kansans "have been deprived of life, liberty and property without due process of law," and that for this "high crime against the Constitution . . . it is our fixed purpose to bring the actual perpetrators of these atrocious outrages and their accomplices to a sure and condign punishment." The Republicans favored a transcontinental railroad. They addressed the problem of nativism—or to be precise, they addressed the *political* problem of nativism, not the moral problem. Needing to attract nativists without being nativist themselves, Republicans endorsed a vaguely worded plank favoring "liberty of conscience and equality of rights among citizens." Depending on the needs of the moment, this could be read as supporting Catholics ("liberty of conscience"), supporting immigrants ("equality of rights"), or supporting nativists ("among citizens").

When the time came to cast ballots for a presidential nominee, it seemed obvious to everyone that John would prevail, though some had misgivings. Seward and Chase regarded him as less committed to the antislavery cause than they were. His political experience was obviously thin. Charles J. Upham's otherwise carefully massaged biography contained this sentence about John's Senate career: "His three weeks' parliamentary service is very interesting, as an example well worthy of imitation." Three weeks—all the time that passed between the day he was sworn in and the day he departed for California to campaign for reelection.

Some were mystified by John's popularity. Charles Francis Adams, son of John Quincy Adams, was a delegate from Massachusetts and saw no evidence that John was a longtime opponent of slavery. Other delegates reassured him, although Adams still felt John's "reputation has been marvelously made within six months for this emergency." What overcame the lack of a record was John's personal narrative of exploration and conquest, which resonated with the larger narrative of the country. The *Herald*, in giving his qualifications, said the nation was "indebted to Fremont for the acquisition of the California gold fields, the treasures of which have revolutionized the financial and commercial relations of the world." The *Herald* did not say how his role in that achievement prepared him to lead a divided nation, but people assumed he was courageous and decisive. Murat Halstead, a Cincinnati journalist at the convention, found "a deep and solemn conviction in a large majority of the delegates" that John was "not only a good man but THE MAN," which Halstead found "unaccountable." He credited "a popular instinct, such as sometimes, on great occasions, leaps chasms in logic." Why, Halstead mused, did colonists divine that George Washington must command their army during the Revolution? It was hard to say, but they did.

So it was with John, nominated on the first ballot and paired with a vice-presidential running mate, former senator William L. Dayton of New Jersey. Cheering Frémont supporters raised a giant American flag bearing the explorer's name. As the news spread, Horace Greeley took an unusual step: though it was rare for newspapers to print illustrations, his *Tribune* published a woodcut portrait of the nominee. His image resembled popular depictions of Jesus Christ—young but wise, impassive, bearded, with tumbling locks of hair. He was admired, he was famous, and it seemed he could win. He gave the papers a letter accepting the nomination, pledging "a desperate struggle" for free labor in Kansas, and warning that slave labor would "reduce emigrants to labor on the same terms as slaves."

Aside from his other qualities, he had the perfect name. The Republican slogan became "Free Soil, Free Speech, Free Men and Frémont."

✳ ✳ ✳

Shortly after the telegraph flashed the convention results to New York, Republicans organized a torchlight procession to the Frémont house. Several thousand boisterous men marched up Broadway to Ninth Street, then elbowed for space as they shouted for their candidate to emerge on the iron balcony. Several unidentified men came out instead. A piece of the iron railing broke off and crashed down, miraculously harming no one below. Then John C. Frémont stepped out to what remained of the railing and gave a short speech, or tried. "He is cheered so much and so long," noted a young man in the crowd, "you can only catch little pieces of what he is saying." The candidate withdrew, but the crowd wanted more. "Mrs. Frémont!" someone cried, then others took up the refrain. "Madam Frémont! Jessie! Jessie! Give us Jessie!"

Nothing quite like this moment had happened before. "For a lady to make her appearance before a political crowd like this is an innovation," observed the young man. Disapproving, a man beside him tried to hush the calls for Jessie, but his was a lonely voice as many shouted louder. A man appeared on the balcony and tried to explain why Jessie should not come out: "Such occasions as this are apt to disconcert ladies," he called down, but the crowd refused to leave. At last, to "a universal shout," Mrs. Frémont appeared on the balcony. "The crowd are crazy with enthusiasm," noted the young man below. "They sway to and fro. They are bareheaded almost to a man, cheering with hats in hand in the air." As Jessie acknowledged the men in the torchlight, the Republicans beneath her roared so loudly that it seemed all their previous cheers for John had been "a mere practice to train their voices" for her.

It was apparent to Republican managers and editors what an asset Jessie was. Buchanan, the unmarried Democrat, had no one comparable.

While Republican papers did not question Buchanan's sexuality—same-sex relationships were so deeply buried that there was hardly the language to discuss them in public—Republicans portrayed the unmarried politico as lonely and dull. An editorial cartoon presented two pictures side by side: one, labeled "Young America," showed John standing beside his shapely wife with a rifle hanging on the wall; the other, labeled "Old Fogyism," showed Buchanan eating soup in his bedroom alone. In late June the *New York Evening Mirror* described the latest Republican gathering:

> *"GIVE 'EM JESSIE."–At an impromptu gathering of Fremonters up town, the other evening, an enthusiastic advocate of the Rocky Mountain candidate put it to the crowd whether it would not be better to send a man to the White House who had completed his humanities by marrying an accomplished woman, than to send there such a rusty old bachelor as Buchanan . . . A gentleman present, who remembered the maiden name of Mrs. Fremont (Jessie Benton), shouted "WE'LL GIVE 'EM JESSIE!"*

"Give 'em Jesse" was an old-fashioned way to say something like "Give 'em hell."

> *The felicitous double entendre only needs to be published to become the watchword of the campaign, and the Mirror takes the liberty of adding, that if the gallantry of the country demanded a Queen at the head of the nation, the lovely lady of the Republican nominee would command the universal suffrages of the people. She is a woman as eminently fitted to adorn the White House as she has proved herself worthy to be a hero's bride. . . . Beautiful, graceful, intellectual and enthusiastic, she will make more proselytes to the Rocky Mountain platform in fifteen minutes than fifty stump orators can win over in a month.*

It was true, the paper added, that John had eloped with Jessie when she was so very young that he could be accused of "taking away an old man's daughter," but this was understandable, and "the sympathies of the world always run with runaway lovers." The article was reprinted in northern New York, Massachusetts, Maine, New Jersey, Pennsylvania, and Washington, D.C.

Republicans distributed multiple songbooks, offering new lyrics to popular melodies, which Frémont fans could sing at home or at campaign rallies.

> *Freemen of the North awake!*
> *Grasp your arms, your all's at stake!*
> *Vows once more to Freedom make—*
>   *On to Victory!*
> *Spirits of our sainted sires!*
> *Kindle Freedom's hallowed fires!*
> *Fremont's name our zeal inspires,*
>   *Down with Slavery!*

The same songbook featured a tune about the candidate's spouse: "Oh Jessie is a sweet bright lady," the lyric said. And if the quality of the lyrics fell short of Stephen Foster, they were sung with enthusiasm. Women in some cities formed "Jessie Circles," who would gather to sing. "Give 'Em Jessie" was to be sung to the refrain of "Yankee Doodle," using Buchanan's nickname, Old Buck:

> *Fire away, my gallant lads*
> *And Freedom's sons will bless ye,*
> *And if old Buck don't clear the track*
> *Fremont will "give him Jessie."*

People read that Jessie herself "gave them Jessie." Newspapers circulated a story of Mrs. Frémont, months before the presidential nomination, falling into an argument with a prominent Boston man she encountered on a train. As the cars rattled between Washington and Baltimore, the Bostonian expressed surprise that a "Southern lady" would support "demagogues" opposed to the South's "institutions." Jessie replied that she was surprised that a Northern man was so deferential to those institutions.

A newspaper dispatch from Buffalo, New York, in July reported "a new feature in political gatherings." A rally for Frémont and Dayton included "the presence of some 400 ladies, seats having been reserved. The ladies here 'go in' for Fremont and 'our Jessie.'" The women did not have a single vote among them, but their presence linked the party to the women who had powered the antislavery movement. In Indiana, the newspapers said, a young woman identified as Miss Carrie Filkins addressed crowds at Republican events; she "attended all the great mass meetings held in that State," raised her voice to "thousands assembled on the Tippecanoe battle ground," and then delivered another speech at a Frémont meeting in Dayton, Ohio. In Fremont, Ohio, organizers of a Frémont singing club declared, "We must enlist music and ladies in our cause." Women's participation grew out of the times, reflecting the related energies of the women's movement and the antislavery movement, but one woman was made the symbol of their cause. It was said many babies born that year were named Jessie.

Although Jessie had played no significant role in the abolitionist movement, she made contact with it, exchanging letters with the writer Lydia Maria Child. Child was famed for books including *The Frugal Housewife*, which gave advice on housekeeping and parenting, and her poem "Over the River and Through the Wood," about a Thanksgiving sleigh ride. She was also a women's rights advocate who had once edited an antislavery newspaper. Child asked if it was true that Jessie had refused an offer to buy a slave in California. Jessie wrote back that she had, crediting her mother for her beliefs. In her letter to the parenting expert, Jessie emphasized that slavery corrupted "the temper of children," meaning the white children of slave owners. "I would as soon place my children in the midst of small pox, as rear them under the influences of slavery."

Articles about both Frémonts began appearing in *Frederick Douglass' Paper* in Rochester, New York. It was not automatic that this would be so. Abolitionist leaders such as William Lloyd Garrsion denounced the entire slavery-tainted political process, while others supported third-party candidates instead of the compromised major parties. Douglass was no exception: he was promoting the little-noticed candidacy of Gerrit Smith, a New York abolitionist and reformer. But Douglass acknowledged debate on the issue. On July 4 he said in his paper, "The enquiry has repeatedly reached us—why can you not give to Fremont and Dayton . . . your undivided support?" He acknowledged that Frémont was a better choice than Buchanan, but "we are Abolitionists; Fremont and Dayton are not, and votes are sought for them on that very ground." (It was true; one pro-Frémont pamphlet proclaimed that not even 1 percent of his supporters were abolitionists, "much less can Frémont himself be suspected by any honest man of abolitionism.") Although Douglass understood why Republicans must refrain from pushing abolition in order to build a political majority, "a black man in this country" could not abide it: "If white men were enslaved in South Carolina, no pretense of State's rights would shield it from the [thunder] bolts of the Republican party." Yet the same issue of Douglass's paper included articles about John, and two articles about Jessie, including the one about her arguing with a man on a train. Douglass was clearly intrigued by both Frémonts.

Six weeks later, on August 15, Douglass changed his stance. The name of the abolitionist candidate disappeared from its place atop his paper's masthead. "We would rather see this just man made President," he wrote, but an idealistic third-party campaign did not rise to the moment. Douglass's paper would support Frémont "with whatever influence we possess." He made no apology for inconsistency: "Right Anti-slavery action is that which deals the severest deadliest blow upon Slavery that can be given at that particular time." Douglass would not "abandon a single Anti-Slavery Truth or Principle," but would change his strategy. Weeks earlier, in justifying his support for the abolitionist campaign, he had written that he was thinking long term: "The present . . . is not an isolated speck of time . . . These are the harvest hours of history. The good or evil of the present, the wisdom or folly of present actions, [will] reproduce themselves a thousand fold in the future." The rise of the Republicans had prompted him to rethink what the long term required of him. The "new and powerful Northern party" of which he had written had arrived, and his endorsement of it was the moral highlight of the 1856 campaign. A leader who knew slavery from experience—and understood the Republicans' compromises and half measures—determined that the party would shift national life in a better direction.

✸ ✸ ✸

Douglass's decision caused a stir in abolition circles—he had to write a letter of explanation to the radical candidate he had abandoned—and set him on a course toward becoming a man of influence within the Republican Party. Yet it was hard to find major Republican papers that amplified his message or even mentioned it. When Douglass made news in mainstream papers that summer, it was in a different way. The papers carried the story of a man who had walked into a bookstore in Mobile, Alabama, and searched the shelves until he found a half-hidden copy of *The Life and Writings of Frederick Douglass*. The man bought the story of the slave's escape for the premium price of $2.50, and brought his discovery to a local Committee of Vigilance, which an Alabama resident described as "twenty-five of our leading men." The committee seized the store's records and discovered the two owners of the shop had ordered fifty copies of the banned book. Some had been sold to slaves. The vigilantes instructed the booksellers—both foreigners, one from England and one from Scotland—to leave town within five days or face prosecution for inciting a slave insurrection, which carried a punishment of ten years in prison or hanging.

When a *New York Herald* correspondent revealed this story, numerous papers North and South reprinted it. The *Richmond Dispatch* commented bitterly that the immigrants had made a fortune selling books, and had returned the "kindness" of their adopted community by "sowing . . . the seeds of a St. Domingo revolution." Even the *Herald* sympathized with the banishment of the booksellers, saying that it had been "incendiary" for Douglass to write down the facts of his life, and that his book had a "fiendish aim." The usual Northern concern for freedom of speech was absent.

Given the way news editors viewed Douglass, it was no surprise that Republicans made no effort to promote his endorsement. But Democrats did. A Pennsylvania newspaper, reporting his action, said, "Let all who follow negro dictation and morals under the leadership of a negro editor mark well his reasons for this course." The *Daily Iowa State Democrat* listed former presidents and war heroes who supported the Democrat Buchanan, then contrasted it with the radical voices who favored the Republican ticket: Seward, Greeley, and the abolitionist preacher Henry Ward Beecher. "Frederick Douglass supports Fremont," the paper said. "And all the Abolitionist and Disunion crew supports Fremont."

That was the essence of the Democrats' case for Buchanan, which they made both North and South: Republicans were extremists. No matter what they said, they were out to abolish slavery, despite white citizens' fears about what black people would do with their freedom. Above all, they would destroy the Union; Southerners said so. The *Richmond Dispatch* declared, "There was never half the reason . . . for shaking off British allegiance than there will be for dissolving the Union, if the Free Soilers elect Frémont and Dayton." If defeated by the new party, Southerners would secede—and this would not be the fault of Southerners for failing to accept an election result, but of Northerners for threatening the South and blocking it from power. A pamphlet said the Democrats were the last national party and the Union's last hope.

THE FEARFUL ISSUE
TO BE DECIDED IN NOVEMBER NEXT!

SHALL THE

CONSTITUTION

AND

THE UNION

STAND OR FALL?

FREMONT,

THE SECTIONAL CANDIDATE

OF THE

ADVOCATES OF DISSOLUTION!

BUCHANAN,

THE CANDIDATE OF THOSE WHO ADVOCATE

ONE COUNTRY! ONE UNION!

ONE CONSTITUTION!

AND

ONE DESTINY!

The pamphlet quoted the abolitionist William Lloyd Garrison, one of those who vowed "no Union with slaveholders," and claimed Garrison's view was the Republican view.

This line of attack was mixed with attacks on John's character. The campaign was like a national grand jury investigation, in which anyone interested in the outcome had motive to examine every part of his life. Many focused on California. BLACK REPUBLICAN IMPOSTURE EXPOSED! proclaimed one pamphlet, adding, FRAUD UPON THE PEOPLE! Tables inside showed that while supplying his troops during the war, John had incurred debts on the United States totaling $960,614. Mariano G. Vallejo, the Californian whom John had needlessly imprisoned at the start of the conflict, apparently had been rewarded at last for his patience, and sold John $107,875 worth of horses and supplies. By 1856 the government had settled such debts for a fraction of the wartime prices, but the pamphlet laid out the numbers to suggest that John was extravagant or corrupt. In the Senate, a Democratic lawmaker made news by formally requesting an investigation of John's travel accounts. Voters in California read additional allegations: one newspaper printed the story of a man who claimed to have witnessed John ordering the killings of three messengers on the shore of San Francisco Bay ("I have no room for prisoners"). And there were all the dealings that surrounded Las Mariposas. The accusations were too murky to easily refute, especially since many were plausibly true.

With Jessie's help, John avoided some of this vitriol. She filtered his newspapers and mail. "Quite at the beginning," she said, "I asked that all mail should pass through me and the few friends qualified to decide what part of it needed to reach Mr. Frémont. We agreed that in this way only, could he be left quite himself, to meet the more or less friendly crowds, who came daily to see him—there must be no effort to maintain his usual courteous dignity." Each day John rose early and, to keep in shape, practiced fencing with another man in the hallway of the house on Ninth Street. Next he met visitors. One day a national publishers' and booksellers' convention in New York voted to support Frémont, signaling the literary establishment's approval of him—and after the vote the convention adjourned so its nearly three hundred members could walk to the Frémont house, where the candidate invited as many as possible to cram inside. "As booksellers, we have all known you by your writings," an Iowan declared to applause, praising John's "energy of character." John replied with gratitude that "the men who are most immediately engaged in elevating and directing our social progress" would be supporting "this great movement of the people to regenerate the Government." When such visits were through for the day, the candidate went on "tremendous walks" through the city.

Jessie had a daily pattern of her own. She sat at the dining room table with a pot of coffee and fruit, and welcomed John Bigelow of the *Evening Post* and two other men who formed a correspondence committee.

Eventually Francis P. Blair relocated to New York to join them. Each day the men brought "market baskets of mail matter." They answered what they could, handed John what they had to, and let Jessie cull the newspapers before showing them to the candidate. Lily Frémont, who would turn fourteen around election time, said her father's "nature was such that he could not have withstood" the "bitterness" of the campaign; "he was used to life in the open and wanted a square fight." So the committee worked each morning "while the hearty laughs and broken words and stamping feet of the two skillful fencers in the hall rang up to the roof."

Jessie, of course, did read the assaults on John, which "gave me all the pain intended." Some of the attacks were against her, as Democratic and Southern papers seized on her prominence to paint her as radical. The *Pittsburgh Evening Chronicle* printed, and the *Charleston Mercury* reprinted, a slyly suggestive article about a "Jessie Circle" in New York City, which was alleged to consist of "the female friends and admirers of Mrs. Jessie Fremont." It was said to be a "progressive" group abandoning traditional female roles: "It is now admitted that the 'home circle' is not a proper place for our American ladies . . . domestic duties are unworthy of their attention; and teething children, and invalid husbands, are permitted to nurse themselves, while wives and daughters are fired with an ardent love of country, don their bonnets and calico, and meet in 'Jessie Circles' to regulate the affairs of the nation."

Jessie had played no larger role in the movement for women's rights than she had for abolition. She had not openly questioned gender roles since her teenage years, when she had cut off her hair, and as an adult she managed an adventurous and unusual life without throwing off her assigned roles as wife and mother. (This was true of many women's activists; Elizabeth Cady Stanton was a mother of seven.) But the early women's movement apparently troubled enough of the public that it seemed profitable to smear Jessie with it. She learned of such attacks while filtering her husband's mail, and then, at the end of each day, she left the house. One-year-old Francis Preston had grown sick while teething, and Jessie had sent him with a nursemaid across New York Harbor to Staten Island, believing the ocean air at a hilltop farmhouse would help. In the evening Jessie walked to the Manhattan shoreline and caught the last ferryboat to the island, "taking my watch with the baby from midnight to six," then returning on a morning boat for another day's work in town.

✳ ✳ ✳

FOR ALL HER EFFORTS, she failed to keep the secret of John's illegitimate birth. The *Richmond Enquirer* had its own sources of information. John's father, Charles Fremon, was described suggestively as "a small, swarthy individual" who had "French peculiarities, strongly developed," while his mother "was never divorced" before running off with him. Jessie's only consolation was delaying John from seeing the articles about his mother—"which by the way I have still managed to keep him ignorant of," as she wrote Francis Blair.

If he was the illegitimate son of a "swarthy" foreigner, it was only a short leap to allege that John himself was a foreigner. An article reprinted in Democratic papers suggested that Charles Fremon and Anne Pryor had left the country when they departed Richmond together in 1811: "If, as alleged, and as believed by many, the French father of Colonel Fremont took the mother of Colonel Fremont out of the United States, with the intent to live abroad, the son born abroad is Constitutionally disqualified from being President." This conspiracy theory was doubly false: contemporary newspaper advertisements traced Charles Fremon's presence in Savannah and then Nashville at the time of John's birth and infancy—and even if it were true that he had been born abroad, the son of a United States citizen was still a "natural-born citizen," as the Constitution said, eligible for the presidency. But it was a damaging accusation when Republicans were hoping to passively capture much of the nativist vote. Millard Fillmore, the Know-Nothing candidate, was still in the race along with Frémont and Buchanan.

Even worse than the claims of John's foreign birth were the claims about his religion.

FREMONT'S ROMANISM ESTABLISHED.

ACKNOWLEDGED BY ARCHBISHOP HUGHES...

Hughes, Seward, Fremont and the Foreigners—a most foul coalition.

So began one of the pamphlets that spread across the country. John was Catholic, it said. Fragments of evidence supported this conspiracy theory. His French father was presumably Catholic, and John and Jessie had been married by a Catholic priest. Before his nomination, a Republican paper in Boston had mistakenly referred to him as Catholic. The *Daily American Organ*, a nativist newspaper in Washington, printed the alleged story of one of John's men during the conquest of California, a man who "might say he had slept under the same blanket as [Frémont] for eight months." The former comrade—or rather, a friend of the former comrade who alleged he had told the story—asserted that John was Catholic and "made no secret of it." Scouring his famous reports, nativists found the detail that he had carved a cross into the stone of Independence Rock: Could this be a Catholic rather than a Protestant symbol?

Thurlow Weed, one of the Republicans' sharpest operators, reported that the claims of John's Catholicism were "doing much damage." John Bigelow received a note from an Indiana congressman who said the failure to answer the Catholic charge made it seem true; the same congressman wrote Blair to say if the story was not put to rest, "we shall lose Pa., N.J., Inda., Conn., & the Lord knows how many other states." John was Episcopalian like his mother, and his children had been baptized in that Protestant denomination, but Republicans across the country reported an alarming loss of support. What had happened to John when he lost his California Senate seat was happening again: for the sake of ambition he had dabbled in nativism, only to be outdone by far more committed nativists. There was no way to win over bigots by being just a little biased, just a little ruthless; others would be more ruthless. They did not merely make him out to be soft on the enemy, they turned him into the enemy.

Republicans tried to counter the charge. Protestant clergymen visited the house on Ninth Street, privately questioned the candidate, and came away offering public testimonials to his faith. Several Republican papers tried satire. One article, much reprinted, was headlined MORE EVIDENCE; FREMONT A MOHAMEDAN! The article told an extended joke purporting to prove that John was Muslim, adding, "We bring this charge at a time when he is unquestionably proved to be a Catholic and a Protestant." Nothing worked. At last some of his advisers felt John himself must issue a public statement about his faith. Francis Blair began drafting a statement, for which his daughter Lizzie Lee wrote Jessie with a list of questions about the Frémonts' association with Catholics. Jessie, while looking after little Francis on Staten Island, replied that John had spent time with Catholics, particularly at St. Mary's College in Baltimore while visiting his mentor Nicollet, "but he never was at any time or in any way more closely connected with that Church."

His advisers disagreed about whether the statement would help: How would a man prove his innermost beliefs? And if he answered this charge, what would he be accused of next? The decision had to be left to John himself. According to his daughter, Lily, John was told, in essence, "The charge is losing votes for you."

And John replied, in essence, "Then I must lose them. My religion is a matter between myself and my Maker, and I will not make it a matter of politics."

He would not approve the statement. To declare that he was Protestant in such circumstances would be to deny the freedom of worship. It would admit, even if only by implication, that a Catholic was not fit to be president. It would refute the equality of men who had brought him fortune and fame. He would have to turn his back on Joseph Nicollet, who had taught him the art of exploration, and on the Chouteau family, who had outfitted his early expeditions, and the Frenchman Basil Lajeunesse, his favorite companion, who had been killed by Klamath men and buried in Oregon ("With our knives we dug a shallow grave, and . . . left them among the laurels"). To proclaim his Protestantism was to deny the truth of what the country really was and always had been, accepting the nativists' narrow vision of what it should be. He would not do it. John's refusal was not quite the final word— he did want to win, and the attacks so alarmed his managers that they arranged a conference of leading Republican figures at the Astor House to consider what to do. But after much debate they agreed that John should remain silent.

It was arguably the bravest decision of his life. He had often shown physical courage, choosing a hazardous vocation and pursuing his work in ways that made it more dangerous than duty required. This was an act of moral courage: maintaining his silence in the face of abuse that he could hardly bear, and doing so for a cause larger than himself. In purely political terms, one of the most thorough analysts of the 1856 election later concluded that the decision was "a mistake." The story had to be countered more effectively. Still, John remained silent on this and all the charges that built up through the summer and fall—charges that, despite Jessie's efforts, he mostly knew by August. Once John talked of leaving New York to find and confront James Buchanan, who had returned from his ambassadorial post to spend the summer at a Pennsylvania resort. "I would go with him," Jessie said in a letter to Lizzie Lee, but "I don't know what mischief might come of temptation." A face-to-face encounter could never happen. "Mr. Frémont will keep silence until November. I suppose they wish to force him into some act of resentment. I wish they could understand how useless that is. He considers himself as belonging to the greatest cause ever at stake since the Revolution & his whole life shows that he 'throws away his body' for his duty. In this case he 'throws away his heart' & lets them slander & attack, in silence—knowing . . . how inadequate anything but death would be as punishment to such slanderers."

The hours spent fencing, the long walks in the evening, were the only ways that remained for him to burn off the rage.

＊ ＊ ＊

THE PAIN MIGHT HAVE BEEN MORE BEARABLE to Jessie had it not also been for her father. Though they exchanged polite letters, he still declined to become a Republican or endorse his son-in-law. He did not defend John when his former colleagues in the Senate began investigating John's California finances. Jessie wrote that John was outraged: "Mr. Frémont says if Father takes no notice of that & continues to work with them he will never speak to him nor shall any of his children." So she said in a letter to Lizzie Lee: "That I only tell you—you are my confessional." She did not convey the threat to her father.

Still hoping to bring Benton around, or at least keep him busy, Francis P. Blair had used his influence to help him mount a campaign for governor of Missouri. Blair's son Frank had been building a political career in St. Louis and was running for Congress; Benton could run alongside him. Benton accepted the help but would not desert his party. The seventy-four-year-old attended the Democratic national convention in May, and said that Buchanan was the safest choice for the Union. In June he returned to Missouri for a three-way contest: the Benton Democrats, the proslavery Democrats, and the Know-Nothings each had a candidate. Riflemen fired a hundred-gun salute when Benton arrived at the St. Louis waterfront, and when he walked to Washington Square, in the center of the city, a crowd estimated at ten thousand roared for him. He told them he supported the Missouri Compromise. He said he wanted to restore "family harmony"—by which he meant the harmony of the Union, not necessarily of his family. He said the country needed national "parties founded on principle," and then dismissed a sectional party "with which the name of a member of my family is connected." He did not attack John but made it clear that he would never follow his son-in-law's course. He stood for "order, law, and justice."

He swept across the state, the gray-haired old lawmaker, traveling by train and by buggy to a round of mass meetings. One of the last was in St. Joseph, near the western edge of the state, which was a starting point for some emigrants on the Oregon Trail. It was as near as he ever got to Oregon. In his decades of work to win the Pacific coast for the United States, he never had seen it. He had thought of going to California with Jessie in 1849, but so certain was he of his vision that he had never really needed to go. On this summer day he addressed the St. Joseph crowd from a grassy hillside, where he could look out across the Missouri River to the plains of Kansas beyond. He told the crowd he wanted Kansas as a free state. He said he wanted the Union, and peace. And then he returned to St. Louis to await the election. On August 4, 1856, Missouri voters went to the polls and defeated him. The proslavery Democrat won the governorship; the Know-Nothing candidate finished second. Benton was third.

Benton returned to Washington, and in September Jessie came down the coast to see him, bringing along her two older children. "Father is very much changed I think," she wrote Lizzie Lee. "Very much thinner and so still—it seems as if sadness and silence were so fixed upon him that he could not shake them off. I will keep with him all the time I can." She persuaded herself that if John won the presidency it would "enliven" her father, for "he could not help taking interest too in public affairs." After a week Jessie returned to New York and the campaign. She asked him to visit New York but he declined, remaining in Washington alone to complete a long-running project that allowed him to retreat into the past. It was a multivolume selection of the debates of Congress, every significant issue discussed from 1789 to 1850, a period of sixty-one years, thirty of them featuring appearances by Senator Thomas Hart Benton. Shortly before the presidential election day, he would return to Missouri for one final political speech in favor of James Buchanan.

All that summer and fall, Republicans organized enormous events across the North. It was to attend one such event that Abraham Lincoln, the

Illinois lawyer, boarded a train in Chicago in August. Since his frustrated letter to a friend in 1855 ("Our progress in degeneracy appears to me to be pretty rapid") he had found a political home, helping to organize the Republican party in Illinois. He received several invitations to speak outside his state, and agreed to attend a rally in Kalamazoo, Michigan, that also featured the state's governor. His train arrived on the morning of the event and he went from the station to his lodgings, where he was shaving when the organizing committee arrived to pick him up. Lincoln cleaned his face, shook on his black coat, and accompanied the committee to the park, where thousands had gathered. There were several speakers' stands, making a kind of political festival, and the lanky visitor mounted one. "Fellow countrymen," he called out, in his tenor voice that had a way of carrying through a crowd. "The question of slavery, at the present day, should not only be the greatest question, but very nearly the sole question. Our opponents, however, prefer that this should not be the case."

Lincoln took no notice of the personal invective in the campaign. He focused only on slavery in the territories. "You who hate slavery and love freedom, why not . . . vote for Frémont? Why not vote for the man who takes your side of the question?" The people in the park listened. "We are a great empire. We are eighty years old. We stand at once the wonder and admiration of the whole world, and we must enquire what it is that has given us so much prosperity. . . . To give up that one thing, would be to give up all future prosperity." The one thing that made America the wonder of the world was that "every man can make himself. . . . The man who labored for another last year, this year labors for himself, and next year he will hire others to labor for him." But slavery would smother that system. "Tell me not that we have no interest in keeping the territories free for the settlement of free laborers. . . . Come to the rescue of the great principle of equality."

In October the electoral map came into focus. Republicans had known all along they would lose every slave state, while it seemed likely they would carry New England and New York. The election would be decided in James

Buchanan's Pennsylvania and a handful of western states. Pennsylvania held state elections in mid-October, weeks before the presidential contest, and they were seen as an early test of party strength. The Frémonts could do nothing but gather information from party operatives and the New York papers:

THE LATEST NEWS.

RECEIVED BY

MAGNETIC TELEGRAPH.

PHILADELPHIA, OCT. 16–2 ½ P.M.

The returns are so utterly confused and unreliable that it is impossible to decide how the election has resulted. The city is full of forged returns from different counties [which] are being extensively circulated for gambling purposes.

It took a few days to grasp that Democrats had won the state elections, though Republicans alleged without evidence that the Democrats had stuffed ballot boxes. It seemed that there was time to recover—three weeks remained before the presidential vote, and Greeley's *New York Tribune* refused to give up: "Republican reader! is your township or ward organized? Have you a working Fremont Committee? . . . If untiring and incessant husbandry be expended on the soil of Pennsylvania, and of every other doubtful State, *and not otherwise*, a harvest of living men may be made to spring up sufficient to save this nation." But as the presidential election day neared, journalists less attached to the Republican cause were doubtful. The *New York Mirror* declared, and the *Washington Star* agreed: "If [Frémont] is defeated in the great contest . . . it will be entirely owing to this 'damnable iteration' that he is a Roman Catholic . . . the Protestant American masses . . . have set their faces like flints against the elevation to higher offices of the

Government, of a man whose allegiance to the Pope is stronger than his allegiance to the State. And we have no doubt that tens of thousands of the more bigoted Protestants persist in the belief . . . that Col. Fremont is a little fishy on the Catholic question."

A Fillmore paper in Ohio posted a mock advertisement for the sailing of the passenger ship "*Disunion*," captained by "John C. Fremont," with a crew that included Sumner and Horace Greeley as the second and third mates, along with "Clerk, Fred Douglas," and some of the cabins reserved for "Jessie . . . the Jessie Clubs, and the *Fremont Clergy*. No ticket will be delivered to any clergyman who does not acknowledge an 'anti-slavery God.'"

On Friday night, October 31, Republicans planned a mass gathering in New York City for mechanics and workmen. A Republican club rented the performance hall at the Academy of Music; Greeley's *Tribune* called it "one of the largest and most enthusiastic gatherings" ever seen there, "and a large number of ladies graced the meeting by their presence." A group that called itself the Rocky Mountain Glee Club sang a rallying song for Frémont, and when the cheering crowd looked up at one of the private boxes in the theater, they spied their candidate, who, in a deviation from ordinary practice, had chosen to attend the event with his wife. John Charles Frémont—the illegitimate son of an immigrant, inventor of his own name, young man on the make, survivor of snowstorms and hunger, famed beyond measure, wounded by experience and often lost inside his own head—was granted this one evening to take in the applause; and it could have been that on this evening, as the speakers railed against the evils of slavery, he thought of Cecilia, the brown-skinned girl he'd known as a youth, whom he had loved with a passion that "extended its refining influence over my whole life." Beside John in the theater box sat Jessie Benton Frémont, who had chosen her husband, borne his absences and his children, then exalted him and protected him from that which he could not bear—Jessie, who had wanted nothing more as a girl than to be her father's son, who had made her mark on the world even when that wish was denied, and who had lost her father when she stood up for what she believed was right.

One of the speakers at the Academy of Music that evening was Henry B. Stanton, a man with mutton-chop whiskers and deep-set eyes—a writer, reformer, and abolitionist. He was married to Elizabeth Cady Stanton, one of the women's rights activists who had attended the convention at Seneca Falls. On this night, Mr. Stanton offered his vision of the stakes of the election—whether or not the territories would be ruined by "the curse of human Slavery." Stanton said he was certain the Republican presidential candidate was Protestant, but he also said that it did not matter: "I had rather be ruled over for the next four years by a liberty-loving Catholic who is true to the Union than by a Slavery loving Protestant, who is false to Freedom, Free Soil and humanity." The crowd applauded. When election day arrived, Stanton said, "we will touch those cords which will vibrate down the vista of the future, and which will not cease to reverberate until, for good or evil, the Republic shall cease to exist."

That weekend—it was Sunday, November 2—Jessie wrote a letter to Lizzie Lee. She remained so certain Democratic postmasters were reading her mail that she facetiously wrote on the inside of the letter, "Post Master please send as soon as read, to Mrs. Lee." To Lizzie she said, "I don't dare say anything more than to tell you we may be successful. Telegraphs will do the rest." In 1845 Congress had passed a law creating a single presidential election day, sweeping away the old practice of staggered elections that unfolded across weeks. It was the first Tuesday after the first Monday of November, which in 1856 would be November 4. The telegraph wires would bring results from across the country as quickly as each state's ballots could be collected and counted.

✳ ✳ ✳

WHEN THE NEWS SPREAD that Buchanan had won New Jersey, college students at Princeton celebrated in the streets. The school was favored by elite families from the South, which may have affected the tone of the demonstrations. Students "marched around the town in procession" while "bearing a black coffin," which was said to hold the body of John C. Frémont. One of the students, presumably a man, donned "black bonnets and dress, riding on a little Canadian stallion, representing Fremont's widow, the now disconsolate Jessie. After a general round of the town, a funeral oration was delivered, and the coffin burned."

When the Democrats won Pennsylvania, the election was all but decided. Word came that Buchanan also carried Indiana and Illinois. It took a few weeks to hear from the Pacific coast, which was still beyond the telegraph lines, but eventually it became clear that John had lost his own state of California. Every other free state had gone to the Republicans—New York and all the states of New England, along with Ohio, Iowa, Michigan, and Wisconsin—but it was not enough to overcome the Democratic dominance of the South. Fillmore carried a single state, Maryland, with eight electoral votes. Buchanan won the electoral vote, 174 to John's 114. The count was near enough that a flip of Pennsylvania and just one other free state would have changed the outcome. Still it was a Democratic victory. Democrats, and the South, declared that the Constitution and the Union had prevailed. The threat of Southern secession receded. Lily Frémont said afterward that when the results were known, old Francis P. Blair wept openly over breakfast at the Frémont house, though John and Jessie, at least in front of others, took the news in silence.

Horace Greeley, in the pages of the *Tribune*, portrayed the result as one lost battle in a war; under the headline HOW LIBERTY BEARS DEFEAT, he reprinted editorials from Republican newspapers across the country that called for John to run again in 1860. It was true that Republicans, in their first national election, had made a strong showing. Far more Americans had voted in 1856 than in any other election in history—roughly four million in all, a million more than in 1852. Democrats had carried the popular vote with a plurality of 1.8 million; Republicans tallied 1.3 million, despite failing to make the ballot in Southern states. The Know-Nothings finished a distant third with some 800,000, a sign that their power was waning and that Republicans had become the main opposition party. There was no telling what Republicans might do as they grew more organized. Clearly the South did not consider the crisis to be over: when Northern papers began speculating about a new Republican campaign in 1860, an ominous reaction bounced back from the South. A Charleston newspaper said that Buchanan's election was merely an armistice between the sections, and the next election could ignite greater conflict. A Richmond paper warned that merely *talking* about 1860 was already igniting it.

Weeks after the election, a Woman's Rights Convention came to order at the Tabernacle on Broadway in New York City. The *Herald* gave it sneering coverage: "The audience included more *outre* specimens of the human race than could be found in any other place . . . all shades and grades of insanity, [including] a lady who thought that she ought to be President in place of Mr. Buchanan . . . persons supposed to be women, with all the surroundings of masculinity, [and] their husbands, mild, broken in spirit, and with all the effeminacy generally supposed to be the most effective panoply of the opposite sex." Inside the hall, however, the participants were buoyant. Lucy Stone, the convention president, declared that it could not be much longer before women received the right to vote, now that "women were urged to attend political meetings, and a woman's name was made one of the rallying cries of the party of progress."

The house on Ninth Street was quiet. On November 18, Jessie wrote a letter to Lizzie Lee: "We are subsiding into former habits, not without some of the giddy feeling one has after having been a long while on ship board. Things hardly have their natural value and attraction after the engrossing excitement of the one idea we have had in our heads for so many months." She asked Lizzie to have some of her papers and a rug sent up from Washington. "I am gathering up my household belongings from California and elsewhere. Mr. Frémont says I may live where I like & I like here." She could not bear to return to Washington after the bitterness of the campaign; her father was there, but so were other relations who had turned against her. She focused on domestic matters as the New York winter set in. One day tiny Francis Preston tumbled down a flight of stairs. He managed to roll sideways on the steps and landed in the dining room unhurt. Another day, inside the warm house, Jessie had time to look out the window and study "a fierce sleeting rain that makes man and beast go on their way with bowed heads."

On the day of the sleeting rain, a Saturday, her husband bowed his head and went outdoors by himself, saying he had business downtown. Their relations had changed; John had grown more distant. After the election the Frémonts' friend and political ally John Bigelow stopped communicating with them, although Jessie did not seem to know the reason. Bigelow told others that he could no longer be around the couple because he suspected that John had "debauched" one of the family's French maids. If Jessie had the slightest suspicion she left no sign of it. But her interests and those of her husband were diverging. Jessie was ready to settle down and focus on her children. John was growing restless again. He made plans to return to California, where he could try again to expand the gold-mining operations at Las Mariposas. Jessie, given a choice to travel with him, decided that for now she would renounce the Pacific coast and remain in New York. She said she would only be in the way.

In the spring of 1857 John bought a ticket on a steamer for Panama. The railroad was finished across the isthmus now, connecting the Atlantic to the Pacific and bringing California ever closer, though the journey to San Francisco would still take weeks. It was hard to say how long he would be gone—several months at least, maybe half a year. He packed his bags at the house on Ninth Street and said farewell to his children, aged fourteen, six, and two. And then John and Jessie bid each other good-bye, having agreed that they would endure, for a time, a separation.

John and Jessie, late in life, with daughter, Lily, before a California redwood tree.

Epilogue

On March 4, 1857, a parade of floats and soldiers marched through Washington to the sounds of a military band. The marchers were militia units from many states. They halted in front of the National Hotel on Pennsylvania Avenue, waiting until white-haired James Buchanan emerged to join the march toward the Capitol for his inauguration. Near him rolled a wooden sailing ship, fully rigged, which had been built for the occasion, placed on wheels, and pulled down the street by horses as "an emblem of national unity and power." On the steps of the Capitol the new president declared, "I owe my election to the inherent love for the Constitution and the Union which still animates the hearts of the American people." He said the nation's differences over slavery were not as great as they seemed, and he predicted the question would be "speedily and finally settled" by the Supreme Court.

The chief justice of the court was on hand for the inauguration, where seventy-nine-year-old Roger Taney administered Buchanan's oath of office. Two days after Buchanan's inauguration, Taney released his opinion in the case of *Dred Scott v. Sandford*. Writing for the majority, Taney delivered a ruling that Buchanan, as president-elect, had been privately lobbying for. It found that Dred Scott, an enslaved man who had been taken into free states, had no standing to sue for his freedom because black people were not and never had been citizens of the United States: "History shows they have, for more than a century, been regarded as beings of an inferior order, and unfit associates for the white race, either socially or politically." Slavery was justified because it had existed in the past. The chief justice acknowledged that the Declaration of Independence said "all men are created equal," words that "would seem to embrace the whole human family; and if used in a similar instrument at this day, would be so understood." But it was "too clear for dispute" that the founders could not have meant what they said in 1776, because they practiced slavery, which would put them "flagrantly against the principles which they asserted." So began the administration of James Buchanan, the man who had defeated the Frémonts; having engineered one of the worst rulings in Supreme Court history, he launched his term as one of the worst presidents in history. The ruling failed to quiet abolitionist fervor, as the enraged Northern reaction intensified it. Southerners renewed threats of secession as the president drifted helplessly.

Republicans began framing change as inevitable. "A house divided against itself cannot stand," the Republican lawyer Abraham Lincoln said as he campaigned for Senate against Democrat Stephen Douglas in 1858. The Union could not endure "permanently half slave and half free"; slavery would either become lawful everywhere, or else "the public mind shall rest in the belief that it is in the course of ultimate extinction." It was the new party, not beholden to slave interests, that made "ultimate extinction" possible.

Stephen Douglas saw something destabilizing in the new party. "Why can we not have peace?" he roared to an Illinois crowd during the last of his seven debates against Lincoln. "Why should we allow a sectional party to agitate this country?" Northerners once had opposed sectionalism, "but the moment the North obtained the majority in the House and Senate by the admission of California, and could elect a President without the aid of Southern votes, that moment ambitious Northern men formed a scheme to . . . make the people be governed in their votes by geographical lines." Douglas was not entirely wrong. The work of John Charles Frémont and others had disrupted both society and the power structure. They set in motion events that must end with the fall of slavery.

Horace Greeley wanted John to seek the Republican nomination again, and in 1858 visited him in California to discuss it. John wasn't interested. It was a missed opportunity: when 1860 arrived, the Democrats divided over slavery, splitting their votes between Northern and Southern candidates and dramatically increasing the Republican chance of victory. Nominating Abraham Lincoln at their convention in Chicago, Republicans swept all the Northern states along with California and the new state of Oregon, which was participating in its first presidential election. Lincoln won the electoral vote "without the aid of Southern votes," precisely as Stephen Douglas had predicted; he defeated three rivals, including Stephen Douglas. Lincoln named William H. Seward secretary of state, and Salmon P. Chase secretary of the treasury. Francis P. Blair became an adviser to the president—still a connection to the Unionist Jackson, whose portrait hung on Lincoln's wall.

Modern-day Americans are not entirely unfamiliar with the emotions that underlay the Southern reaction. In the twenty-first century, the increasing diversity of the country has triggered fear among some white voters that they will be permanently outnumbered. Nineteenth-century white Southerners found proof in Lincoln's election that they were outnumbered, and resolved to leave the Union rather than risk the threat to slavery. Seven Southern states seceded before Lincoln's inauguration. John Frémont's South Carolina led the way on December 20, 1860. Soldiers of the newly declared Confederacy placed gun batteries on the Charleston Harbor islands where John had once played with Cecilia and her brothers, and opened fire on the still-incomplete Fort Sumter in April 1861. Lincoln's call for troops to suppress the rebellion prompted four more states to secede, including Jessie Frémont's Virginia. Virginians were forced to choose sides, and Robert E. Lee, the officer who mapped St. Louis around the time John first arrived there, chose his native state. So did John B. Floyd, the former Virginia governor who had once talked with John of a pro-Southern presidential campaign. In the last days of the Buchanan administration Floyd was secretary of war, covertly trying to ship weapons to the South. Then he became a Confederate general. In 1862, surrounded at Fort Donelson in Tennessee by Union forces, Floyd slipped away and escaped in the night, leaving a more junior officer to surrender most of his troops.

Floyd's superior officer in the Confederate army was Albert Sidney Johnston, Jessie's kindly relative who reassured her when she was terrified by Indians as a girl. General Johnston, commanding Confederate troops at the Battle of Shiloh, sent away his personal physician to care for wounded soldiers on one of the bloodiest days of the war. Then Johnston himself was shot, and bled to death surrounded by men who did not know how to help him.

Jacob Dodson, John's former servant and a veteran of the war against Mexico, wanted to fight against the rebellion. Now thirty-five years old, he was still working as a Senate messenger and keeper of the Senate "retiring rooms." Early in the conflict, when the Union Army was still forming and the capital was defended by only a few hundred soldiers, Dodson wrote Lincoln's secretary of war proposing that "three hundred reliable colored free citizens" should be allowed to "enter the service for the defence of the City." He reminded Cameron that he had already served his country, but Cameron wrote back that the administration had no plans to use black soldiers.

Frederick Douglass pressed for that policy to change, insisting that black troops should be welcomed in the Union Army. Congress and Lincoln gradually altered course; advancing Union armies were desperate for manpower and were flocked by escaping slaves. A law passed in 1862 allowed black men to work as laborers for the military, and then to enlist in the newly formed United States Colored Troops. Douglass and his fellow black activist Martin Delany became prominent recruiters, and 179,000 black men served. So many died for their country that Douglass asserted, and Lincoln agreed, that no one could deny their right to citizenship after the war.

William M. Gwin, John's Senate colleague from California who was instrumental in making it a free state, attempted to avoid war in 1861. He assisted last-minute efforts by Seward to negotiate with Southern leaders, but later chose his former home in a slave state over the free state he had represented, personally seceding from the Union and returning to Mississippi. Late in the war he tried to lay the groundwork for slave owners to resettle with their slaves in northern Mexico. After the war, when all was lost, the man who had called slavery "the foundation of civilization" wrote a memoir claiming he had privately opposed slavery all along.

David Farragut of Tennessee, the naval officer John met while serving as a mathematician on the navy ship *Natchez*, remained loyal to the Union and commanded US forces as they captured Mobile Bay and New Orleans. William T. Sherman, who bit the gold found at John Sutter's mill, eventually commanded a destructive march across Georgia, ending at John's birthplace of Savannah. John Ericsson, the immigrant from Sweden who designed the innovative if ill-fated warship *Princeton*, in 1862 designed the Union's first ironclad warship, known as the *Monitor*, which fought the first Confederate ironclad to a standstill and became a model for generations of warships to follow. Mathew Brady, who developed the daguerreotypes John brought from the West, became the Civil War's most famous photographer. He organized teams who crossed the country to capture images of soldiers on the march, beside their cannons, wounded in hospitals, and dead in their trenches.

Kit Carson, famed from John's expeditions, joined the Union Army and led a unit that helped to drive Confederates out of New Mexico. He went on to lead army forces in Indian wars, ruthlessly defeating Apaches and Navajos. William Chinook, the young Indian from the Columbia River who traveled east with John in 1844 and grew homesick in Philadelphia, returned to his people in 1845 and later joined the Union Army. In the 1860s, he fought in the Snake War, against rebellious Indians in the Snake River valley, an especially bloody conflict overshadowed by the Civil War and little noticed by the country at large, though the Pacific Northwest remembered it. A reservoir, Lake Billy Chinook, was later named for him.

Thomas Hart Benton did not live to see the Union fractured and restored. He died in 1858, at age seventy-six, confident that his own legacy was secure. In an autobiographical sketch written late in life, he said there was no need to list his important legislation, for it was "known throughout the length and breadth of the land," and was even recited by schoolchildren. In truth his name largely faded from public notice; to later generations, his great-nephew Thomas Hart Benton, the painter, was probably more famous. But the larger themes of Senator Benton's career captured the interest of future leaders. Young Theodore Roosevelt, fascinated by the West, felt a connection to Benton, and wrote a biography of him between roundups on the ranch where he lived in Dakota Territory in 1886. (Roosevelt confessed to a friend that in such a remote location he was short of research material on Benton, and was "mainly evolving him from my inner consciousness.") In 1955, Senator John F. Kennedy was taken by Benton's stubborn defense of the Union, and devoted a chapter to him in his book *Profiles in Courage*.

✳ ✳ ✳

JOHN CHARLES FRÉMONT WAS WITH JESSIE in Europe during the outbreak of the American Civil War in 1861. Volunteering to serve the Union, he raced home in time for President Lincoln to appoint him as the general in command of the West, with headquarters at St. Louis. (He was one of

several prominent Republicans appointed to senior commands; his friend
Nathaniel Banks was another.) Although Missouri remained in the Union,
it was boiling with proslavery sentiment and was soon attacked from the
south by Confederate forces. John, who never had commanded a military
unit larger than a few hundred men, struggled to turn thousands of raw
recruits into a coherent force. Rather than command his army in the field,
General Frémont set up headquarters in a St. Louis mansion and quickly
became isolated: a soldier with saber drawn guarded the door, and it was
rumored that officers on urgent business might wait for hours to see him.
Jessie kept up his political connections, writing to members of Congress
and even to President Lincoln. In mid-1861, John startled the country by
declaring martial law and issuing a decree freeing the slaves of Missouri
rebels. Lincoln had not yet freed any slave; John's act was the first demonstration that the ruthless logic of the war would lead to freedom. But his
move came too soon. The president, unwilling to alienate slave states that
were still loyal to the Union, instructed General Frémont to reverse his
order—and John declined, creating one of the early political crises of the
war. Just as he once had ignored the orders of Colonel Abert and then defied
the orders of General Kearny, he could not bring himself to obey the president. Lincoln did not immediately fire him, but was also hearing disturbing
rumors of disorganization and corruption.

In September 1861 John allowed Jessie to do what she had been urging
for months: she traveled to Washington to set Lincoln straight. Riding the
trains—it now took only two nights to travel the eight hundred miles—she
arrived in the capital and sent a note by messenger asking the president
when would be a convenient time to meet. He wrote a single word in reply:
"Now." When she entered his office, the president did not speak. He bowed
slightly. She handed him a letter from General Frémont, which he read silently. At last he said, "I have written to the General and he knows what I
want done." Jessie tried to argue that John's emancipation order was helpful

in Missouri and would play well in Europe, too. "You are quite a female politician," Lincoln replied. Jessie said afterward, "I felt the sneering tone and saw there was a foregone decision against all listening."

The president soon relieved John of his command, and the Frémonts returned to Washington. They were living there in early 1862 when Ralph Waldo Emerson visited the capital and called upon Mrs. Frémont. She was "excellent company," he said, showing "good sense and good humour," but also expressing "musical indignation" as she was "incessantly accusing the Government of the vast wrong that had been done to the General." Though John was soon assigned to command an army in western Virginia, he was outmaneuvered in battle and relieved again. He played no role in the later part of the war, although he made news by mounting a short-lived challenge to Lincoln's reelection in 1864. General Frémont's principal contribution to the war effort had come at the beginning, when he was organizing his army and gave several assignments to a formerly washed-up army officer named Ulysses S. Grant, who rose to command all Union forces by the end of the war and accepted Lee's surrender at Appomattox.

After the war's end in 1865, John tried again to enlarge his fortune, this time by investing in railroads. In his mind, of course, these were more than mere investments. He sought a role in transcontinental railroads, of the sort he had advocated since the conquest of California. They would complete Senator Benton's vision of a road to Asia, linking the eastern United States with the Golden Gate. Although John was not involved in the first transcontinental railroad, its construction began soon after the war. It was finished in 1869, and was celebrated soon after by Walt Whitman in a poem that John and Senator Benton would have appreciated. Whitman wrote that the tracks unified not merely two coasts but the world:

> *Passage to India!*
> *Lo, soul, seest thou not God's purpose from the first?*
> *The earth to be spann'd, connected by network,*

The races, neighbors, to marry and be given in marriage . . .
I see continual trains of cars winding along the Platte . . .
Tying the Eastern to the Western sea,
The road between Europe and Asia.

John was trying for his own transcontinental project. He served as the de facto president of a railroad called the Memphis, El Paso, and Pacific, with a name that spoke of its ambitions to become a transcontinental line reaching Los Angeles. But the company struggled to raise money in the United States for construction, and when its agents sold millions of dollars' worth of bonds in Paris, they were accused of fraud. More than a few railroad builders multiplied their fortunes through self-dealing and misrepresentation, but John was not among those artful enough to get away with it. He was tried in absentia and convicted by a French court in 1871, and though he never served prison time, he lost control of the railroad and, soon, his fortune. He had spent twenty years since the gold rush as an absurdly rich man, or at least seeming to be one; now it was during the Gilded Age that the Frémonts lost their gilding. They were eventually forced to surrender an estate they had bought on the Hudson River above New York City, exchanging it for an apartment in Manhattan.

They remained famous. Thousands of newspaper articles mentioned them between 1875 and 1889. Some chronicled their past exploits, including a retelling of John's four-hundred-mile horse ride through California during the conquest. Others covered their more recent humiliations: because they were celebrities, they lived their growing financial nightmare in public. One headline in 1878 read, GENERAL FRÉMONT: ALTHOUGH NOT STARVING, HE IS IN VERY REDUCED CIRCUMSTANCES. The article included the detail that "since the sale of General Frémont's library some months ago by the Sheriff, it is true that he has been without income." Some articles spoke far better of Mrs. Frémont than of her husband. "It was no great disappointment that Gen. Fremont was never President," said one newspaper writer, "but I think that we all regret that his wife should never have been Mrs. President." The writer, who seemed to have met Mrs. Frémont, added that "she is in a high sense a masculine woman. Her powers are those we call masculine, as representing greater strength . . . If she had the fortune to be born a man, she would beyond doubt have achieved a place among the controlling spirits of this country from which the limitations of her sex have debarred her."

John was rescued in 1878 by Rutherford B. Hayes, the lawyer who once had arranged for his hometown to be renamed Fremont, Ohio. Hayes was now president, and appointed the great explorer as the governor of Arizona Territory. Traveling westward by train, then by coach through the region he had helped to open, John was greeted as a hero, to the relief of Jessie, who rode along with him and tried to keep up his spirits. (She wrote that the region "deserves its name of the Great West—great-hearted we have found it.") John completed three years of undistinguished service but still struggled to pay bills, and afterward Jessie's letters reflected the bitter decline of their fortunes. In 1883, regarding a friend whose newborn girl had died, fifty-nine-year-old Jessie wrote that "for the death of a baby girl there should be no sorrow," because "life is hard on women."

The Frémonts began to rely on Jessie's income. She was writing under her own name now—books and magazine articles, commonly reflecting on their earlier lives; *A Year of American Travel*, for example, recounted her voyage to California in 1849. As a memoir, it was observant and entertaining, although it was as notable for what it left out as for what it said. She included references to her depression and despair, but never mentioned that her baby Benton had died just days before the beginning of the story. The same was true of John's autobiography, which she helped him to complete in 1887. The 655-page volume contained brief references to John's mother, but no mention of his father at all, and it left out decades of his life. It ended with the events of early 1847, just after he accepted the surrender of Los Angeles, and just before his arrest and court-martial—omitting the forty years the followed, including his later expeditions, the presidential campaign, the Civil War, and his business career. "I close the page," he wrote at the end of the narrative, "because my path of life led out from among the grand and lovely features of nature, and its pure and wholesome air, into the poisoned atmosphere and jarring circumstances of conflict among men."

Living with John in Washington and then, as money ran even lower, in an inexpensive house on the New Jersey shore, Jessie grew concerned about her husband's health, and decided in 1887 that California's drier climate would better suit him. Unable to afford train tickets to cross the continent, she went into New York City to see Collis P. Huntington. Since arriving in California to start his Sacramento hardware store serving gold prospectors in 1849, Huntington had become an investor in the first transcontinental railroad, then the dominant figure on other railroads, one of the wealthiest and most powerful men in the country—the magnate that John had never managed to be. Huntington had always admired John C. Frémont. He had voted for him in 1856 and felt he owed his fortune in part to John's explorations. To honor the conqueror of California, Huntington provided Jessie with tickets, letters of introduction along the route, and expense money.

Shepherding John and Lily westward, Jessie would live the rest of her life in Los Angeles, in the state her husband had helped to bring into the Union. The Frémonts were surrounded by admirers, who asked John to speak on special occasions and honored him for his service. For a short time, it even seemed that he could make a living. He involved himself in Los Angeles real estate, but in the fall of 1888, at age seventy-five, he felt the urge to move again. Having so often left her in order to travel the West, he told Jessie he must return to the East, lobbying for a military pension in Washington and pursuing business opportunities in New York. He remained in the East, with only a short visit back to Los Angeles, for most of the final two years of his life. He died a continent away from Jessie, in a New York boardinghouse, on July 13, 1890.

✳ ✳ ✳

DID THE FRÉMONTS, for all their manifest flaws, help to build a more just and equal nation? Eventually they did. The sharpest judgment of how they advanced the cause of equality came from John Bigelow, the *New York Post* editor and John's early biographer, who lived long enough to look back upon them from a different century. Having distanced himself from the Frémonts after 1856, Bigelow supported Lincoln for president in 1860 and was rewarded with a position at the US embassy in Paris, the start of a lengthy diplomatic career. Later he returned to New York, and in 1895, in his late seventies, was appointed the first president of the New York Public Library. He oversaw the construction of its main building, which opened in 1902 and still stands on Fifth Avenue, fronted by its famous stone lions. Shortly before his death in 1911 at the age of ninety-four, Bigelow wrote a memoir that included an assessment of John's presidential campaign. It was a cutting judgment, colored by Bigelow's later distaste for John, but fair. Bigelow insisted that it would have been "impossible" for Republicans to select a better nominee in 1856 than John C. Frémont, who "rendered his country as a candidate all the service he was capable of rendering it." Only the hero of western exploration had the celebrity and reputation to unify the new antislavery coalition, which held together after his defeat, eventually saving the Union and ending slavery. But Bigelow confessed that John might have been a terrible president. "He owed such success as he had at this election— and it was very flattering—largely to his wife, a remarkably capable and accomplished woman . . . and to his utterly neuter gender in politics." He wasn't a statesman, Bigelow said, shuddering at the idea that it could have been Frémont, rather than Lincoln, who faced the crisis of secession. "Much as the country was to be congratulated for his nomination, it was equally to be congratulated upon his defeat."

For all the disappointments of the Frémonts' later lives, their contemporaries reflected upon the 1840s and '50s and sensed that the pair had done something special, and some offered a token of thanks to John's widow after his death. In 1891, Jessie's friend Caroline Severance, a women's rights activist, learned that Mrs. Frémont was destitute and borrowing money to pay expenses. Severance formed a committee of California women who raised money to build Mrs. Frémont a house in recognition of her past services. Living in the house with her unmarried daughter, Lily, Jessie continued writing about her life, sometimes telling the same story again and again in different ways. Collaborating with her son Frank, she composed a memoir of John's later life—the ultimate act of ghostwriting, although it was never published. She began drafting a memoir of her own, and in recounting episodes of her life she included details that she had never written down before—details that might have seemed too personal to put down earlier. She had previously published an acerbic account of the 1840 wedding of her school classmate to the Russian ambassador, but only now did she reveal that the experience so troubled her that afterward she cut her hair and briefly proposed to live as if she were a man.

Sometimes her memoir clashed with known facts, and did so in revealing ways. This was the case when she wrote a story of Charles Preuss, the German mapmaker. She said Preuss was forced to miss one of John's expeditions because "his wife—there are many such—resented his leaving his family often." Preuss obeyed her selfish desire and stayed home, but was so depressed to have lost his "free manly life" that he wrote a farewell letter, went outside Washington, and "going to the Bladensburg woods near by, hanged himself." This story, with all its shocking and specific details, was incorrect. It was true that Preuss took a break from travel at the request of his wife in 1845 and missed the conquest of California, but he suffered no known ill effects and rejoined John for the disastrous expedition of 1848 to 1849. He later left John's service but worked on one of the government's Pacific railroad surveys, continuing in the field until the strain of the work ruined his physical and, apparently, mental health. It was only in 1854, when he was in his early fifties, that Preuss became "deranged," according to friends, and did hang himself. Rather than dying from any lack of travel, he seemed more likely to have died as a *result* of traveling so much, repeatedly going through horrifying scenes and near-death experiences of the kind that today are understood to be a factor in post-traumatic stress. Jessie's reinterpretation of his death suggested what *she* needed to believe: it gave meaning to the lonely months and years that she had endured at home. She could tell herself that John's work in the West had been so important and fulfilling that if she had ever asked him to spend more time with his family it would have killed him. And Jessie made clear in her memoir that she had never asked. Unpolished, meandering, at once unreliable and informative, her book was unfinished when Jessie, age seventy-eight, died on December 27, 1902.

Her estate included two paintings, which had hung over her writing desk in her final years. One was a portrait of Jessie as a young woman. The other was of John as an old man. She had loved this painting of him, weathered, bearded, and white haired. It had been made by a young artist to whom Jessie had become something of a patron: John Gutzon Borglum. The artist, a son of immigrants, had been born in 1867 at Bear Lake, Idaho, on land near the Oregon Trail that John had helped to open for settlement. Later his family moved eastward to Fremont, Nebraska. The artist was in his early twenties when he had the opportunity to paint the great explorer, and in Borglum's hands the old man seemed gentle, vulnerable, his face translucent against a background of darkness. Afterward Jessie supported Borglum's career—not with money, since she had so little, but by making use of her name to write him letters of introduction to the wealthy and famous. Borglum went on to live in Paris and New York and became known as a sculptor, who once created a six-foot bust of Abraham Lincoln. In 1927, invited to expand upon this theme, John Frémont's former portrait painter accepted a commission to carve the faces of Lincoln, Washington, Jefferson, and Theodore Roosevelt on the side of Mount Rushmore, a project that occupied the remainder of his life.

Today John Charles Frémont's name is on two mountain peaks, one in Wyoming and one in California. If Borglum had ever considered carving Frémont into a mountainside, any sculpture true to life would need to show many faces. The faces would represent those who had buoyed him—men and women, white and black and brown, who together changed the country. The sculpture would show the men and women who roared his name in 1856, and laid the foundation for progress in defeat. It would show Basil Lajeunesse the French voyageur, the Delaware Sagundai, and the white runaway Kit Carson. Near them would be Nicollet the immigrant, broke and seeking a new life, Preuss the immigrant mapmaker, and the Sonorans who made John's fortune. There would be Jacob Dodson, the son of black servants, holding steady while other men went mad in the snow. Above all there would be Jessie Benton Frémont, who worked to build John up until he seemed as large as those figures on Mount Rushmore—Jessie, who made the man she loved and then, little by little, lost him.

Sources and Acknowledgments

Considering the Frémonts' fame, not many writers have deeply explored them. For decades after the campaign biographies of 1856, no full-length biographies were published, and much of what was written about them during their later lives was brief, unflattering, or both. Civil War heroes such as Sherman made dismissive mentions of John in their memoirs. In the 1880s the philosopher Josiah Royce thoroughly examined the conquest of California, and even interviewed both Frémonts before writing that the conquest was a moral failure. John's name came up in the popular press—newspaper features, dime novels, and half-true histories through which nineteenth-century young people absorbed the mythology of the Wild West. But he was not always a leading character. Kit Carson, with his longer and much bloodier frontier career, loomed larger and was the protagonist of works with titles such as "Kit Carson, King of Guides."

Upon the Frémonts' deaths, their personal papers gradually became accessible thanks to a few scholars who conducted a kind of relay across generations. The first to pick up the baton was Allan Nevins, a young New York newspaperman, who met the Frémonts' son Frank in 1926. When Frank offered him access to some family papers—the few that hadn't been burned by his sister, Lily, while housecleaning—Nevins used them and other sources to produce a 1928 biography of John called *Frémont: The World's Greatest Adventurer.* The book was so admiring that it provoked a rebuttal in 1930: historian Cardinal Goodwin accused Nevins of buying the Frémont myth, and wrote his own biography damning John as a drifter, "a vagrant by instinct—one might almost say a vagabond," a man with no moral compass who took up one adventure after another and wandered by mistake into fame. Nevins later revised his *Greatest Adventurer* to make it more measured, describing its 1939 and 1955 editions as "chastened in style and much enlarged in content," and retitled the work *Fremont: Pathmarker of the West.* He arranged for the papers he had collected to be placed at the Bancroft Library at the University of California, Berkeley, and later became chairman of a committee that oversaw publication in book form of the papers from John's expeditions. Nevins did not live to see the project's completion, but handed the baton to editors Donald Jackson and Mary Lee Spence, who between 1970 and 1984 completed a multivolume set of letters and writings called *The Expeditions of John Charles Frémont.* Spence edited the last of these volumes alone, then passed the baton to one more scholar, collaborating with Pamela Herr to edit a volume called *The Letters of Jessie Benton Frémont* in 1993. Although *Expeditions* and *Letters* do not include all known documents, they are extensive and richly footnoted, and the efforts to complete them over nearly seven decades are priceless for anyone studying the Frémonts.

Those who have undertaken that study include Catherine Coffin Phillips, who produced a biography of Jessie in 1935 by consulting the papers Nevins had gathered (as well as her own memory, having grown up next door to Jessie in Los Angeles). Pamela Herr, the coeditor of Jessie's letters, published a thorough biography of Jessie in 1988. In 1991, Andrew Rolle said he "used psychiatric techniques" to compose a psychological portrait of John's erratic decision-making, while Tom Chaffin completed a deeply researched biography of John in 2002. In 2007 Sally Denton wrote an exuberant biography of both Frémonts. My own explorations gained immensely from those who walked the trails before me, even when my emphasis or conclusions are different.

Beyond the biographies, the Frémonts' sprawling lives make them characters in many books about California, westward expansion, transcontinental railroads, the war with Mexico, the American Civil War, and the creation of the Republican Party. It was through such works that I first learned of them, reading Time-Life books about the Old West that my parents, Roland and Judy Inskeep, bought for me growing up. These books were filled with illustrations and tales of adventure that made them descendants of those old Western dime novels. In later years I remembered the Frémonts, and realized that they could help me think more broadly about who is included in the American story.

The search for primary source material led me first to the Library of Congress in Washington, D.C. Its manuscript collections include numerous papers of the Frémonts, Thomas Hart Benton, and others including Joseph Nicollet, Horace Greeley, Nathaniel Banks, and members of the Blair family. Librarians wheeled out cartons that held, among other items, Thomas Hart Benton's 1813 letter describing his gunfight with Andrew Jackson; John's letter to Joel Poinsett appealing for help with a job in 1835; journals Nicollet kept of his journeys with John in 1838 and 1839; and Jessie's 1847 letter to President Polk seeking an army appointment for a friend. Studying 1856 campaign paraphernalia in the Frémont files brought the election to life. The library staff also guided me to digital newspaper databases that were not available to earlier generations of researchers; these made it possible to follow the Frémonts in the media with a degree of breadth and detail that, to my knowledge, had never been attempted. The result was new information about the mechanics of fame—how the Frémonts generated stories about themselves, what was said about them, and how those stories spread across the country. The databases also made it practical to seek out information about less famous characters such as Jacob Dodson.

The Bancroft Library at the University of California, Berkeley, contains essential papers including drafts of Jessie's unpublished writings. The California State Library still has a list of books that John contributed to start the library at the end of 1849. Charleston College dug into its archives to produce John's academic and attendance records. Christine Ridarsky and Emily Morrow, of the Rochester Public Library, shared research on the life of Frederick Douglass there; Gabrielle Foreman, of the University of Delaware, provided guidance regarding Colored Citizens conventions. The Hathi Trust has curated digital versions of numerous nineteenth-century texts, turning any coffee shop or train into my research library; and the paper copies of many old volumes reached my home shelves from various sources. It was a delight to learn that someone had made a book-length study of accelerating travel times between various places in the United States prior to 1840, while another scholar had studied county-by-county results from the 1856 presidential election.

Some of the most satisfying research was conducted on the road, where I traced a few of John's routes by car. One began at Klamath Lake in Oregon, where John was attacked and retaliated, and continued southward past Mount Shasta to the Central Valley and the San Francisco Bay. The landscape around the California-Oregon border is so sparsely populated and epic in scale that a modern traveler feels some of the wonder and dread that travelers of past generations must have felt. On another journey I started at Lake Tahoe, on the California-Nevada border, and crossed westward over the Sierra Nevada by the approximate route that John's party used in the winter of 1844. The high mountain pass they found is called Carson Pass now, and a two-lane road runs through it, with signs to alert drivers when it is closed in times of high snow. The log cabin visitor's center in the pass cannot be far from the spot where John paused to boil water and estimate the altitude. From there I followed the road westward and downslope toward Sutter's Fort. The fort is in a little state park—two city blocks of tranquil green in the center of Sacramento, which has grown all around it. Its white brick walls contrast with the glassy facades of the Sutter Medical Center across the street.

Fires, earthquakes, and new construction have long since swept away the San Francisco that the Frémonts knew, yet one may still walk the street grid they walked—including Stockton, Kearny, Fremont, and Vallejo streets. The streets of central Washington, D.C., are also the same. A federal courthouse occupies the block of C Street Northwest where the Benton house stood. The White House has been expanded and renovated, but its ceremonial rooms are not so different from those the Frémonts saw as they called upon presidents. As a journalist, it has been my fortune over the years to have visited those rooms and many other scenes of the Frémont story. The Battery in Charleston, South Carolina looks not so different than it did when John knew it. The site of New York's Astor House, where Jessie confronted antislavery protesters, is now the location of the Woolworth Building. In St. Louis, much of the town the Frémonts knew was destroyed in the 1930s for a waterfront park where the Gateway Arch was eventually built. William Clark's farm, where the explorer was served by slaves, is now covered by the racially diverse suburban neighborhoods of St. Louis County, and the site of his farmhouse is not far from Barack Obama Elementary School in Pine Lawn. Westport, Missouri, has been absorbed into Kansas City, while the landscape of Kansas is now dotted with spinning wind turbines. In Portland, near the end point of John's first journey to Oregon, commuters cross the Fremont Bridge. Nantucket is more developed than when the Frémonts discussed their presidential prospects there, but is still an escape for the national elite, surrounded by the ocean that is at once unchanging and in motion. The Rocky Mountains, too, maintain their eternal grandeur, dwarfing the old mining towns, highways, and ski resorts that form the most visible signs of human habitation.

During the years that I lived with this story, friends and loved ones were compelled to live with it, too. Many politely asked how the book was coming and had to put up with the answers. Some became part of the work;

Ava, Ana, and Molly went along on one of my rambling drives through California and Oregon—as did Carolee, whose strategic advice and critiques were priceless throughout this work, and whose forbearance during weekends and evenings of writing were beyond what any spouse and partner should have to bear. The strain on those close to me was at least reduced thanks to three NPR managers: Sarah Gilbert, Kenya Young, and Chris Turpin, who graciously helped to arrange two brief leaves from my day job. My NPR cohosts David Greene, Rachel Martin, and Noel King performed extra work in my absence and never said a word about it. The tireless agent Gail Ross, her insightful colleague Dara Kaye, and my friend and colleague Nishant Dahiya read some or all chapters in their early versions and gave immensely useful commentary. The historian Jon Meacham also read the manuscript, while historian Candice Millard offered encouragement and an example to follow. My friends and former colleagues Madhulika Sikka and Michele Norris have been constant sources of inspiration and support.

Ann Godoff, my wise and patient publisher, worked with me to shape this book in 2016, and hardly had I signed a contract to complete it when I wondered if the project was a mistake. The destructive politics of the time made it hard to focus on history, especially as I was covering the news as a journalist. Occasionally I asked myself how I could find time to finish and even why I should bother. "Hell," a Pennsylvania voter told me in 2017, "if we're still alive next year at this time, I'd be surprised." But the next year we were still alive, and I had time to recall that the history I was writing and the news I was covering were part of the same story. The debates that perplex us build on our shared and living past; human patterns of thought and action persist, though we change the names of our obsessions. Modern leaders copy the political techniques of our forebears and justify their actions by citing bits of American history, real or imagined. If it is vital for journalists to paint a true picture of the country as it is, then it is equally vital for historians to paint a true picture of the country as it was.

Notes

JCF = John Charles Frémont; JBF = Jessie Benton Frémont; LOC = Library of Congress

Some documents that were reviewed in archives for this book are more easily accessible in *The Expeditions of John C. Frémont* or *The Letters of Jessie Benton Frémont*. In such cases the *Expeditions* or the *Letters* are cited.

EPIGRAPH

xi **It would hardly do to tell the whole truth about everything:** JBF, *A Year of American Travel*, 44.

INTRODUCTION

xix **Arriving on a steamboat from the east on May 30:** Theodore Talbot to Adelaide Talbot, May 30, 1845, Hine and Lotttinville, eds., *Soldier in the West*, 10.

xx **"He was assailed":** Ibid.

xx **"hid himself in some French house down the City":** Theodore Talbot to Adelaide Talbot, June 1, 1845, ibid., 11.

xx **"Captain Frémont Did Not Stay Here":** Ibid.

xx–xxi **"You ought to have witnessed . . . strength and vigilance":** Theodore Talbot to Adelaide Talbot, June 4, 1845, ibid. 11–2.

xxi **"This is the strongest manifestation . . . yet witnessed":** *St. Louis Daily New Era*, June 3, 1845, reprinted in *Washington Union*, June 12, 1845.

xxi **"the Columbus of our central wildernesses":** Taylor, *Prose Writings of Bayard Taylor,* 69.

xxi **three most important historical figures since Jesus Christ:** James Rhoads, "Colonel Frémont," *Sartain's Union Magazine of Literature and Art 7* (October 1850): 241.

xxi **350,000 people attended a long-running stage show:** Spence, "David Hoffman."

xxii **"our manifest destiny . . . multiplying millions":** John L. O'Sullivan, "Statue to Jackson," *United States Magazine and Democratic Review* (July–August 1845): 5.

xxii **"famed as Yankee Hill":** Maura L. Jortner, "Playing 'America' on Nineteenth-Century Stages; or, Jonathan in England and Jonathan at Home" (PhD diss., University of Pittsburgh, 2005).

xxii **worked the phrase into his popular stand-up routine:** Newspapers in late 1845 and early 1846 showed him in New York; Washington; Wilmington, North Carolina; and back to multiple theaters in New York.

xxii–xxiii **"a clean fight . . . It is our 'manifest destiny' . . . whar's the enemy?":** "Yankee Hill for Oregon," *American Republican,* January 16, 1846.

xxiii **"I thought . . . the better man of the two":** Crosby, *Memoirs of Elisha Oscar Crosby,* 35.

xxiv **"Madam Frémont! . . . Give us Jessie!":** Abbott, *Reminiscences,* 108–9.

xxiv **she could have been elected queen:** *New York Evening Mirror,* reprinted in *Frederick Douglass' Paper,* January 18, 1856.

xxiv **"You are quite a female politician":** JBF and F. P. Frémont, *Great Events in the Life of Major General John C. Frémont,* 271.

xxiv **The cultural elites of Europe celebrated writers and artists:** Inglis, *A Short History of Celebrity,* 37–73.

xxv **"a transcontinental railroad . . . Asiatic races":** JCF to Snyder, December 15, 1849. Spence, *Expeditions,* vol. 3.

xxvi–xxvii **eight thousand workers, mostly women . . . fifty-eight million yards of cloth:** "Lowell," *New York Tribune,* January 1, 1842.

xxvii **ginseng . . . and lead . . . shipped to China in exchange for porcelain and tea:** In 1842 about $1 million in ginseng was shipped to China, and $250,000 in Missouri lead: "China—Western Products," *New York Tribune,* January 9, 1843. The ginseng-for-tea trade dated back at least to 1784, just after U.S. independence from Britain made it possible: Swift, Hodgkinson, and Woodhouse, "The Voyage of the Empress of China," 25.

xxvii **a revolution in communications:** Daniel Walker Howe, in *What Hath God Wrought,* argues that this was the single most important development of the era.

xxvii **"a new species of consciousness . . . distant city":** "Correspondence of the Herald," *New York Herald,* May 30, 1844.

xxvii **1.95 million pounds of cotton:** "Lowell," *New York Tribune,* January 1, 1842.

CHAPTER ONE: AID ME WITH YOUR INFLUENCE

3 **"French and Dancing Academy":** Fremon advertised in *The Republican, and Savannah Evening Ledger,* November 28, 1811.

3 Hannah . . . "redish complexion": "Fifteen Dollars Reward," *Republican, and Savannah Evening Ledger,* April 23, 1812.

4 the maid tried to follow her own heart, and escaped: Fremon placed an ad offering a $15 reward for her return. Ibid.

4 returned . . . and was on hand: Jackson and Spence, *Expeditions,* vol. 1, xxiv.

4 Virginia refused to grant a divorce: Nevins, *Fremont: Pathmarker of the West,* 8.

4 another French and dancing school: "French and Dancing Academy," *Nashville Examiner,* October 20, 1813, p. 6. Family legend holds that the little family was actually in a Nashville hotel when Thomas Hart Benton and Andrew Jackson fought a gun battle there on September 4, but this is improbable. It seems unlikely that the family would have reached Nashville by September 4, given that the cash-strapped Fremon made no known arrangements to resume his dance and language instruction until six weeks later.

4 Charles Fremon died around 1818: Bigelow, *Memoir of the Life and Public Services of John Charles Fremont,* 22.

4 He did not speak of his father: His 655-page autobiography, which included brief references to his mother, contained no mention of his father at all.

4 J. Charles Fremont: Jackson and Spence, *Expeditions,* vol. 1, xxiv.

4 Charles Fremont or . . . C.J. Fremont: Attendance records, College of Charleston Archives, 1785–1970, Special Collections, College of Charleston.

4 Not until his twenties did he add an accent mark: Jackson and Spence, *Expeditions,* vol. 1, xxxviii.

4 his mother moved the family to Charleston: They arrived around the time John was ten, according to a chronology of Frémont's life, "Chronological Table of Frémont's Life," *New York Times,* July 21, 1856.

4 "go and feel the freedom . . . face of the ocean": JCF, *Memoirs of My Life,* 30.

4 Liverpool or Boston: Advertised in *City Gazette and Commercial Advertiser,* April 5, 1832.

5 steamer coming up the coast from Savannah: Ibid.

5 he interrupted his education: Nevins, *Fremont: Pathmarker of the West,* 12.

5 for a lawyer, serving subpoenas: A sworn statement signed by "J. Charles Frémont" relating to one batch of subpoenas is reprinted in Jackson and Spence, *Expeditions,* vol. 1, xxiv.

5 "middle size, graceful in manners, rather slender . . . forehead": Nevins, *Fremont: Pathmarker of the West,* 13.

5 cornerstone having been laid just three years earlier: Easterby, *History of the College of Charleston,* 78.

5 its roof leaked: Chaddock and Matalene, *College of Charleston Voices,* 26.

5 three thousand books . . . record high of sixty-two: Easterby, *History of the College of Charleston,* 81.

5 Adams . . . from Brown University: Ibid., 74.

5 "Extract from Mr. Crafts' Oration, 4th July 1812": "Order of Exercises, at the Exhibition of the Charleston College, This Day," *Charleston Courier,* April 10, 1829.

5–6 "This country appears to have been created . . . residence of freemen": Crafts, *An Oration, Delivered in St. Michael's Church,* 5–6.

6 **"teaching in the country by permission":** Attendance records, College of Charleston Archives.

6 **sometimes vanishing for a week:** Ibid. Also Frémont obituary, including remarks of a classmate, reprinted in Chaddock and Matalene, *College of Charleston Voices*, 28.

6 **"The whole course . . . frequent absences!":** Attendance records, College of Charleston Archives.

6 **gave him "frequent reprimands":** JCF, *Memoirs of My Life*, 19.

6 **his friends were mystified:** "None of us knew how he spent his time," said a classmate in an obituary, reprinted in Chaddock and Matalene, *College of Charleston Voices*, 28. The same classmate passed on a rumor that John "belonged to a Thespian club" that performed in a park; here it seems likely the classmate confused quiet and reserved John for John's brother, who became an actor.

6 **knew his students well and sometimes visited their parents:** So Adams said in an unpublished memoir, quoted in Chaddock and Matalene, *College of Charleston Voices*, 25.

6 **"C.J. Fremont . . . incorrigible negligence":** Attendance records, College of Charleston Archives.

6 **"I knew that I was a transgressor . . . the broken career":** JCF, *Memoirs of My Life*, 19.

6 **"passionately in love":** Ibid.

7 **house on a Charleston street corner:** Ibid., 20.

7 **"little circle of sworn friends":** Ibid.

7 **Drunken Dick, a hazardous shoal on which ships sometimes foundered:** JCF describes the incident in his *Memoirs of My Life*, p. 20. One shipwreck on Drunken Dick Shoal in 1848 is recorded in Dawson and DeSaussure, *Census of the City of Charleston*, 89.

7 **allowing them to flee when the grandmother approached:** JCF, *Memoirs of My Life*, 20.

7 **"This is an autobiography . . . my whole life":** Ibid., 20–21.

7 **"clear brunette . . . large dark eyes and abundant blue-black hair":** Ibid., 20.

7 **the same "brunette complexions":** Ibid.

8 **"clear ruddy skin":** The biographer is Allan Nevins, who cites no source for Cecilia's altered skin tone (*Fremont: Pathmarker of the West*, 16).

8 **people of all racial identities had to flee:** Gillikin, in *Saint Dominguan Refugees in Charleston*, details many years of events that produced refugees, and reports, "Saint Domingue's refugees, unlike many other immigrant groups, were diverse in terms of race, economics, and even political ideology" (13).

8 **minor teaching jobs:** He'd been elected a teacher of the "Charleston Apprentices' Library Society" (*Charleston Courier*, November 3, 1830); and in 1832, "Messrs. Wotton and Fremont" were teaching at a "Male and Female Seminary" in subjects including French (*Charleston Courier*, November 5, 1832).

8 **"beautifully clear maps . . . of astronomical calculations":** JCF, *Memoirs of My Life*, 21.

8 **"men who had made themselves famous . . . base acts":** Ibid.

9 **Poinsett attended the same church:** Nevins, *Fremont: Pathmarker of the West*, 19.

9 **served as a trustee:** Easterby, *History of the College of Charleston*, 88.

9 **Poinsett was a Unionist:** JCF, *Memoirs of My Life*, 63–64.

9 **"states-rights ball" . . . "Disunion Drama":** Hunt, "South Carolina During the Nullification Struggle."

9 **"beyond patient endurance . . . mad-houses":** Ibid., 242.

10 **Northern and western states were gaining far more rapidly . . . losing power:** Crouthamel, "Tocqueville's South," 390.

10 **"saw the dark spot on the sun":** JCF, *Memoirs of My Life*, 63.

10 **a waste of Fremont's talent:** JCF said he got the job "by [Poinsett's] aid, but not with his approval." Ibid., 22.

10 **Lieutenant David G. Farragut:** JCF, *Memoirs of My Life*, 22; also Mahan, *Admiral Farragut*, 73.

10–11 **"Professor of Mathematics in the Navy":** JCF, *Memoirs of My Life*, 23.

11 **"Your kindness . . . Your Ob't Servt J. Charles Fremont":** Fremont to Poinsett, November 5, 1835, Frémont papers, Box 1, LOC.

11 **Joel Poinsett of Charleston was among the investors:** Jackson and Spence, *Expeditions*, vol. 1, xxix.

11 **"The Rail Road will be built . . . five years":** Letter dated July 8, 1836, to *Charleston Courier*, reprinted in *Cheraw Gazette*, August 2, 1836.

12 **Fremont was hired to go along:** JCF, *Memoirs of My Life*, 23.

12 **the army officer who led:** JCF identified him as W. G. Williams. JCF, *Memoirs of My Life*, 23.

12 **and moving "hurriedly":** Ibid., 24.

12 **"so stiff next morning I moved like a foundered horse":** Ibid., 25.

12 **"many of their farms . . . remote frontier":** Ibid.

13 **"wise and humane":** Ibid., 24.

13 **"There has been no continuous effective policy . . . white man":** Ibid., 27.

13 **"this accident of employment . . . way for myself":** Ibid.

13 **Elizabeth, had died in her teens:** Chaffin, *Pathfinder*, 28.

13 **his brother, Frank, had left Charleston:** JCF, *Memoirs of My Life*, 21.

13 **a career in the theater:** Chaffin, *Pathfinder*, 28.

13 **appointed second lieutenant:** "Army Order," *National Intelligencer*, February 19, 1839. The formal date of his appointment was July 7, although he had gone west to take up his duties earlier.

14 **Captain Robert E. Lee:** JCF, *Memoirs of My Life*, 31.

15 **"delightful . . . sole object of his existence":** Fremont to Joel R. Poinsett, June 8, 1838, Jackson and Spence, *Expeditions*, vol. 1, 12.

15 **a new start after going bankrupt:** Bray, *Joseph Nicollet and His Map*, 41–43.

15 **five by seven inches or smaller:** The notebooks can be found in the Joseph Nicollet papers, Boxes 3 and 4, LOC.

15 **"Departed Traverse . . . heat is overwhelming":** Ibid., Box 3.

15 **"the beautiful lawns we are crossing":** Ibid.

15 **river resembled a little snake on his page:** Several such drawings are in the Nicollet notebooks, ibid.

16 **stepped into the blackened area:** JCF, *Memoirs of My Life*, 38.

16 "was an event on which . . . such a proof": Ibid., 41.
17 the map projection, which was blank: Ibid., 64.
17 "She was just then in the bloom . . . I was attracted": Ibid., 66.

CHAPTER TWO: THE EQUAL MERITS OF DIFFERING PEOPLES

20 May 27, when Congress adjourned: 42 Annals of Cong. 790 (1824).
20 he was hoping this time for a son: Herr, *Jessie Benton Frémont*, 9.
20 purple, with chinchilla trim: JBF, *Memoir*, 1.
20 "It's a little girl who cries, 'Hurrah for Jackson!'": Ibid., 3.
21 "Catching me up . . . made us one?": Ibid.
21 "My father gave me early the place a son would have had": JBF, *A Year of American Travel*, 44.
21 "Especially he liked autumn shooting": Ibid., 41.
21 "I stuck to him . . . limp warm thing": JBF, *Memoir*, 25–26.
21 Foreign Book Store . . . "very little worn": Bookstore and chariot were advertised in the *National Intelligencer*, May 27, 1824.
22 he would deposit her at the Library of Congress: JBF, *Memoir*, 31–32.
22 "where the tall south windows . . . large wood-fire": Ibid., 88–89.
22 "sadness and loneliness": Ibid., 89.
22 "I was to keep still . . . unconscious grip": Ibid., 88.
22–23 slept with the windows open: JBF, *Memoir*, 35.
23 he left behind a trail of notes: Two examples, undated, to the editor of the *Missouri Gazette* are in the Thomas Hart Benton Papers, LOC.
23 "almost as a reproach . . . friends and relations": JBF, *Souvenirs of My Time*, 131.
23 In 1832 . . . the family made one of its journeys . . . to St. Louis: Jessie's account of this journey does not name the year, but it says that in St. Louis she saw Washington Irving, who visited in 1832. JBF, *Souvenirs of My Time*, 135.
23 In 1800 . . . six weeks . . . under three: Pred, *Urban Growth and the Circulation of Information*, 176–77.
23 a "reserved" stagecoach: JBF, *Souvenirs of My Time*, 132.
23 there were five now: One more sister would later arrive to make six, but James, the infant, lived only to the age of four. Jessie later wrote of herself as one of five siblings. Herr, *Jessie Benton Frémont*, 10.
24 "the four eager horses dash away . . . cheered them off": JBF, *Souvenirs of My Time*, 133.
24 The rising facade of a cathedral under construction: The cornerstone had been laid around 1831; Moore notes it was completed by 1834. Robert Moore, "Lewis and Clark Post-expedition," National Park Service, undated paper, 3.
24 lined by locust trees . . . city block amid more locusts: JBF, *A Year of American Travel*, 35; *Souvenirs of My Time*, 143.
24 liked to sit on an upholstered sofa: JBF, *Souvenirs of My Time*, 143–4.
24 "kaleidoscopic variety of figures . . . each could be right": Ibid., 32–3.
24 only 4,977 inhabitants: "Population of the 90 Urban Places: 1830," US Bureau of the Census, June 15, 1998.

24 **less than a square mile:** Robert E. Lee's map of St. Louis showed about a mile of waterfront, and a street grid extending, at most, eight blocks inland, considerably less than a mile. Robert E. Lee, Montgomery C. Meigs, H. Kayser, J. S. Morehead, Maskell C. Ewing, and William James Stone, "Map of the Harbor of St. Louis, Mississippi River, Oct. 1837," US Army Corps of Engineers, 1837.

25 **borrowed money . . . Pierre Chouteau Jr.:** Chambers, *Old Bullion Benton*, 263.

25 **"St. Louis . . . accosting each other in the street":** William P. Trent and George S. Hellman, eds., *The Journals of Washington Irving*, 112.

25 **he had freed several slaves, including York:** Ibid.

25 **known as his "Indian museum":** Moore, "Lewis and Clark Post-expedition," 10.

25 **"profuse and almost gorgeous display . . . horns, and bird skins":** Ibid., 11.

25–26 **"a war dance . . . threw me into a panic. . . . A tall strong kind-faced young officer . . . comforted me":** JBF, *Souvenirs of My Time*, 135–6.

26 **just back from an Indian war:** His journals of the Black Hawk War are reprinted in a biography by his son. William Preston Johnston, *The Life of Albert Sidney Johnston* (New York, NY: Appleton, 1879), 33–42.

26 **clutching the tail feathers of a black hawk:** Trent and Hellman, *The Journals of Washington Irving*, 113.

26 **"the most outrageous affray ever witnessed in a civilized country":** Thomas Hart Benton, "Senator Benton and Gen. Jackson," September 10, 1813. Benton papers, LOC.

26 **transferred away from combat assignments:** Chambers, *Old Bullion Benton*, 54–56.

26–27 **"any part of the Territory of Missouri":** "The Undersigned," *St. Louis Enquirer*, November 10, 1819.

27 **He also ran for political office and lost:** Chambers, *Old Bullion Benton*, 81.

27 **"Newspapers . . . what the Forum was in Greece and Rome":** Ibid., 82.

27 **"I looked across the Pacific Ocean . . . better and safer route":** Benton, in an 1844 speech in St. Louis, was summarizing his reasons for objecting to the joint occupancy a quarter-century earlier. "Substance of Mr. Benton's Speech," *Washington Globe*, November 6, 1844.

28 **sending a ship called *Empress of China*:** The story is well told in Swift, Hodgkinson, and Woodhouse, "The Voyage of the Empress of China."

28 **"success will attend . . . Pacific":** "Texas," *St. Louis Enquirer*, August 18, 1819.

29 **he learned to read Spanish:** JBF, *Memoir*, 9.

29 **translated Mexican newspapers aloud:** For example, his Senate speech on June 1, 1844. Appendix to *Congressional Globe*, 28th Congress, 1st Session, 498.

29 **Senate business . . . documents himself:** Benton, *Thirty Years' View*, vol. 1, iv.

29 **more than twenty African slaves:** Ibid., ii.

29 **"never been without":** Meigs, *Life of Thomas Hart Benton*, 324.

29 **questioning whether he had paid property taxes:** Bay, *Reminiscences of the Bench and Bar of Missouri*, 11.

29 **Bloody Island, that dueling ground:** The duel and follow-up duel are reconstructed in Meigs, *Life of Thomas Hart Benton*, 105–13.

29 **"deplorable . . . consent on both sides":** Benton, *Thirty Years' View*, vol. 2, 148.

29 **"Many remained at the doors and windows":** "St. Louis County Meeting," *St. Louis Enquirer,* May 19, 1819.

29 **Benton spoke against proposals that Missouri should be forced to abolish slavery:** Ibid.

29 **"dishonorable to the United States":** "Missouri Question," *St. Louis Enquirer,* March 4, 1820.

29–30 **"free negroes . . . intermarry with the whites":** Ibid.

30 **He argued that the state could justly interfere:** Brophy and Thie, "Land, Slaves, and Bonds."

30 **"When the South grew stormy . . . Northern aggression":** JBF to Lydia Maria Child, July–August 1856, Herr and Spence, *Letters,* 122.

30–31 **"courage in the cause . . . of a more enduring nature":** Ibid.

31 **"the grim Scotch Puritan atmosphere that dominated her own home":** JBF, *Memoir,* 21.

31 **"a generous spirit . . . the oppressed":** Ibid.

31 **she kept her word:** Herr, *Jessie Benton Frémont,* 35.

31 **"to think it good fortune to be free from owning slaves":** JBF to Lydia Maria Child, July–August 1856, Herr and Spence, *Letters,* 122.

31 **"making them domineering, passionate, and arbitrary":** Ibid.

31 **"were all freed, or born free":** JBF, *Souvenirs of My Time,* 97.

31 **"T. H. Benton" of St. Louis with four slaves:** Sixth Census of the United States, St. Louis Ward 4, St. Louis, Missouri, Roll 231, Page 144, Family History Library Film 0014858, accessed via ancestry.com.

31 **"a great misfortune":** JBF, *Memoir,* 39.

31 **"no end to the conceit, the assumption, the class distinction":** Ibid.

31 **felt "miserably lost":** Ibid.

32 **for April 9, 1840:** The date is given in the *New York Herald,* April 13, 1840.

32 **"very long . . . neck and sleeves":** JBF, *Souvenirs of My Time,* 21.

32 **and fortysomething groom:** He was so described in the *New York Herald,* April 4, 1840.

32 **"Contrasted by my father's superb physique . . . restless little eyes":** JBF, *Souvenirs of My Time,* 19–20.

32 **"horrified . . . I meant to study . . . short-haired variety":** JBF, *Memoir,* 31.

33 **clean-shaven . . . long in a fashionable style:** An undated painting of a younger Frémont by George Peter Alexander Healy shows him with shoulder-length hair and no beard.

33 **He did not . . . mention his age:** This is clear because he *still* had not told his age to Jessie by 1846, when they had been married almost five years, and she asked him in a letter if he would disclose it. JBF to JCF, June 18, 1846, Herr and Spence, *Letters,* 24–7.

CHAPTER THREE: THE CURRENT OF IMPORTANT EVENTS

35 **"clear, strong and harmonious . . . erect and manly form":** "The Inauguration," *Daily Madisonian,* March 6, 1841.

35 **researchers later identified more likely causes:** Jane McHugh and Philip A. Mackowiack, "What Really Killed William Henry Harrison?" *New York Times*, March 31, 2014.

36 **4½ Street near the Capitol:** The address is given in a letter from Fremont to J. J. Abert, November 10, 1840. Jackson and Spence, *Expeditions*, vol. 1, 84.

36 **black velvet . . . swords . . . scroll:** Details of the procession are from the *Daily Madisonian*, April 9, 1841.

36 **"was something to see and remember":** JCF, *Memoirs of My Life*, 68.

36 **"The funeral . . . my red-letter day":** Ibid.

36 **beginning "without delay":** Abert to Frémont, June 4, 1841, Jackson and Spence, *Expeditions*, vol. 1, 96.

36 **"old uniforms and gowns":** JBF, *Memoir*, 46.

36 **"Go to your room and dress properly":** Ibid.

36 **"The survey was a health-giving excursion . . . special complaint":** JCF, *Memoirs of My Life*, 68.

37 **"was in a drawing room . . . any such thing":** JBF to Elizabeth Blair Lee, July 23, 1856, Herr and Spence, *Letters*, 118.

37 **"Any delay of an open declaration . . . more difficult":** Gerdes to Fremont, November 7, 1841, Jackson and Spence, *Expeditions*, vol. 1, 102.

37 **"would not let her remain in his house":** Spence and Herr, *Letters*, fn p. 120.

38 **"Fear not for our happiness . . . we will find it yet":** JCF's letter does not survive, but JBF quoted it to him in a letter on June 18, 1846. Herr and Spence, *Letters*, 24–7.

38 **"The President . . . 12 and 3 o'clock.":** "The President of the United States," *Daily Madisonian*, January 1, 1842.

38 **"the dashing dweller . . . homespun costume":** "New Year's Day," *Daily Madisonian*, January 3, 1842.

38 **blue velvet gown . . . ostrich feathers:** Phillips, *Jessie Benton Fremont*, 61.

38 **decorated with the image of an eagle, topped by a plume:** The Corps of Topographical Engineers uniform is illustrated in Bray, *Joseph Nicollet and His Map*, 59.

39 **"I felt . . . important political events":** JCF, *Memoirs of My Life*, 70.

40 **"An Act to Authorize the Occupation of the Oregon River":** *Senate Journal*, January 11, 1825, 81, American State Papers.

40 **hardy and well-armed settlers could be turned into a military force:** This idea of "50,000 settlers with their 50,000 rifles" found expression in 1843 legislation, never passed. JBF, writing in an introduction to JCF, *Memoirs of My Life*, 13.

41 **"undried copy . . . directly into the hands of the compositor":** Chambers, *Old Bullion Benton*, 293.

41 **"Daily intercourse . . . unstinted devotion":** JCF, *Memoirs of My Life*, 72.

41 **"I think it would be well . . . the end of time":** Chaffin, *Pathfinder*, 99.

41–42 **"Upon its outside view . . . the design was unknown":** Benton, *Thirty Years' View*, vol. 2, 178.

42 **Colonel Abert, who said Frémont was not following procedure:** Abert to Frémont, May 26, 1842, Jackson and Spence, *Expeditions*, vol. 1, 123.

42 **"Fickle, changeable, cold, and uncomfortable":** "The Weather," *New York Herald*, May 4, 1842.

42 **more than six thousand people:** "Great Cold-Water Mass Anniversary," *New York Herald,* May 5, 1842.

42 **he passed near the Broadway meeting hall:** It was the Tabernacle, at Broadway and Worth Street, a few blocks north of the district where John did some of his shopping. Ibid.

42 **"hundreds . . . the four broad aisles":** Ibid.

42 **"young, lovely, and most beautiful women":** Ibid.

42 **"first-class" chronometer:** Voucher no. 20, 4 May 1842, Jackson and Spence, *Expeditions,* vol. 1, 140. Also J. J. Abert to Frémont, May 9, 1842, ibid., 123.

43 **barometer in a leather case, and thermometers:** Voucher no. 22, ibid., 141.

43 **a district of camera sellers:** In addition to the doctor who sold Frémont a camera at 263 Broadway, newspaper advertisements showed camera sellers in the early 1840s at Broadway and Chambers Street (*New York Herald,* April 25, 1842), 247 Broadway (*New York Herald,* November 20, 1844), and 72 Nassau Street (*New York Herald,* September 9, 1842).

43 **"It is sun-painting":** "Miraculous Miniature Paintings," *New York Herald,* April 25, 1842.

43 **and paid $78.50:** "Important Expedition," *Louisville Messenger,* July 16, 1842. Also Subvoucher, New York, May 6, 1842, Jackson and Spence, *Expeditions,* vol. 1, 144.

43 **sent an angry letter down the road:** J. J. Abert to Frémont, May 9, 1842, Jackson and Spence, *Expeditions,* vol. 1, 123.

43 **"It would have needed only a request . . . being of use to my father":** JBF, "The Origin of the Frémont Explorations," *Century Magazine,* vol. 41, March 1891, 768.

43 **"Mr. Frémont was gone . . . to make clear":** JBF, *Memoir,* 50.

44 **"Young women . . . own destruction":** Leavitt, "Under the Shadow of Maternity."

44 **"translations . . . occupied my mornings":** JBF, *Memoir,* 38.

44 **"an intolerable headache":** JBF, *Memoir,* second draft, 39.

44–45 **lay for days "looking dead":** Ibid., 38–39.

CHAPTER FOUR: MISERIES THAT ATTEND A SEPARATION

47 **assigned him to wind the chronometers:** JCF, *Report on an Exploration,* 41.

47 **"a shock of light curly hair standing up thick about his head":** JCF, *Memoirs of My Life,* 70.

47 **John again disregarded army procedure:** J. J. Abert to Frémont, July 8, 1842, Abert to P. Chouteau Jr. and Company, July 28, 1842, Jackson and Spence, *Expeditions,* vol. 1, 126–7.

48 **run away from his youthful apprenticeship:** Quaife, *Kit Carson's Autobiography,* x.

48 **"satisfaction for the trouble":** Ibid., 26.

49 **IMPORTANT EXPEDITION . . . Columbia River":** The article, which appeared in number of papers, is attributed to the *Missouri Reporter.* "Important Expedition," *Louisville Messenger,* July 16, 1842.

49 **"though young . . . surveys of this kind":** Ibid.

49 **June 26, in the *New York Herald*:** Ibid.

50 **of "Dresden chocolate":** Voucher no. 23, Jackson and Spence, *Expeditions,* vol. 1, 141.

50 **148 pounds of tobacco:** Voucher no. 31, ibid., 154.

50 **"Our friends . . . smoking supper on the grass":** JCF, *Report on an Exploration,* reprinted in Jackson and Spence, *Expeditions,* vol. 1, 192.

50 **150 pounds of coffee:** Ibid., 174.

50 **"a loss that none but a traveller in a strange and inhospitable land can appreciate":** Ibid.

50 **Kit Carson made out his will:** Ibid., 224.

50 **"I asked . . . let him go":** Ibid., 226.

51 **"The observations of the savage appeared reasonable":** Ibid., 229.

51 **"a bloody pair of trousers . . . still in the pocket":** Charles Preuss, diary entry, August 1, 1842, in Gudde and Gudde, eds., *Exploring with Frémont,* 32.

51 **"numerous strange instruments . . . the sun and stars":** JCF, *Report on an Exploration,* in Jackson and Spence, *Expeditions,* vol. 1, 225.

51 **a fresh supply of coffee:** Ibid., 174.

51 **"we were obliged to watch . . . culminating point":** Ibid, 253.

52 **"A great part . . . and contradictory":** JCF, *Report on an Exploration,* in Jackson and Spence, *Expeditions,* vol. 1, 256.

52 **"The air at sunrise . . . reached us":** Ibid, 255.

52 **a group of fifteen:** Ibid., 259.

52 **"a gigantic disorder . . . naked rock":** Ibid., 262.

53 **headaches and to vomit:** Ibid., 266.

53 **He continued some two hundred feet:** Preuss diary entry, August 17, 1842, Gudde and Gudde, *Exploring with Frémont,* 41.

53 **"Well, Mr. Preuss . . . of the mountain":** Ibid., 43.

53 **His men were exhausted:** Ibid., 258.

53 **two pairs of pants:** Preuss, diary entry, August 31, 1842, Gudde and Gudde, *Exploring with Fremont,* 59.

54 **"That's the way it is with these Americans . . . fail miserably":** Preuss, diary entry, August 2, 1842, ibid., 32.

54 **prairie chicken, turtles, buffalo, and polecat:** Preuss, diary entries, June 20, August 21, August 30, 1842, ibid., 9, 49–50, 59.

54 **"foolish," short-tempered, "childishly passionate," and far too prone to headaches:** Preuss, diary entries, ibid., 3, 46, 50.

54 **who was lugging the fragile wood-and-glass barometer:** Preuss diary entry for August 17, 1842, in Gudde and Gudde, *Exploring with Fremont,* 43.

54 **"mulatto . . . had no privilege to choose":** Ibid., 44.

54 **the summer air was above freezing:** The temperature at the summit was 44 degrees Fahrenheit. JCF, *Report on an Exploration,* Jackson and Spence, *Expeditions,* vol. 1, 270.

54 **put on thin-soled moccasins:** Ibid., 269.

54–55 **"I sprang upon the summit . . . the abyss below":** JCF, *Report on an Exploration;* Jackson and Spence, *Expeditions,* vol. 1, 269–70.

55 **and Preuss grumbled:** Preuss, diary entry, August 17, 1842, Gudde and Gudde, *Exploring with Fremont,* 45.

55 **"wave in the breeze . . . waved before":** JCF, *Report on an Exploration,* Jackson and Spence, *Expeditions,* vol. 1, 270.

55 **"This flag . . . I brought it to you"**: Autobiographical fragment, Herr and Spence, *Letters,* 12.

56 **she was devastated**: Phillips, *Jessie Benton Frémont,* 68.

57 **written in her hand**: Jackson and Spence, *Expeditions,* vol. 1, 168.

57 **"The horseback life . . . most happy life work"**: JBF, *Memoir,* 41.

57 **"in dictation . . . to the subject"**: JCF, *Memoirs,* 163.

57–58 **"The long mountain . . . glowing sky"**: JCF, *Report on an Exploration,* Jackson and Spence, *Expeditions,* vol. 1, 255.

58 **"Now and then one would dart . . . pot over the fire"**: Ibid., 226.

58 **"an isolated granite rock . . . and forty in height"**: Ibid., 247.

58–59 **"a black preparation of India rubber . . . wind and rain"**: Ibid., 273–74.

59 **"I rose this morning . . . opposite side of the Missouri"**: Ibid., 285.

59 **free black son of Benton family servants**: John described him as "a free young colored man of Washington city." JCF, *Report of the Exploring Expedition to Oregon and North California in the Years 1843–44,* reprinted in Jackson and Spence, *Expeditions,* vol. 1, 426.

59 **John's personal servant**: Ibid., 428.

59–60 **"of many nations . . . twenty-one years of age"**: JCF, *Report of an Exploring Expedition,* Jackson and Spence, *Expeditions,* vol. 1, 575.

60 **"a fine-looking old man and his son"**: Ibid., 428. Frémont clearly did not get to know the men well; his report misidentified the Shawnee men as Delawares.

60 **James Rogers, had named his son Thomas Jefferson Rogers**: Ibid.

61 **"Sir . . . your duties"**: Abert to Frémont, May 22, 1843, Jackson and Spence, *Expeditions,* vol. 1, 345–46.

61 **"peaceable expedition . . . report to this office"**: Ibid.

61 **"hostile expedition . . . Indian war"**: Abert to Benton, July 10, 1843, ibid., 351.

61 **suspected a political plot**: JBF, writing in forward to JCF's *Memoirs of My Life,* 15–16.

61 **It was probably too late to stop John anyway**: So it would seem from the late date of Abert's letter. The scholar Donald Jackson argued that Jessie overdramatized her role in "The Myth of the Frémont Howitzer" (*Bulletin of the Missouri Historical Society* 23, April 1967: 205–14).

62 **"Mr. Fremont . . . JESSIE ANN BENTON FREMONT"**: "News from Oregon," *Washington Globe,* December 15, 1843.

62 **"The parading of a lady's . . . wherefore of its publication"**: "For the Arkansas State Gazette, Number V," *Weekly Arkansas Gazette,* January 17, 1844.

63 **"To Adelaide Talbot . . . Jessie B. Fremont"**: JBF to Talbot, September 16, 1843, Herr and Spence, *Letters,* 13.

63 **"Mr. Fremont says that early in January 1844, he will be here"**: JBF to Adelaide Talbot, December. 3, 1843. I, ibid., p. 15.

63–64 **"your letter . . . I look for him"**: JBF to Adelaide Talbot, February 1, 1844, ibid, 16–7.

64 **"He cannot be here until the middle of April"**: JBF to Adelaide Talbot, March 3, 1844, ibid., 18–19.

64 **"He will not be here . . . Jessie Benton Fremont"**: JBF to Adelaide Talbot, April 21, 1844, ibid., 21.

64 "The old whaling days of Nantucket . . . its useless hopes": JBF, *Souvenirs of My Time*, 162.

CHAPTER FIVE: I DETERMINED TO MAKE THERE A HOME

67 "Leaving the valleys . . . known human being": "The Far West," *Sunbury American and Shamokin Journal*, March 25, 1843.

67–68 "romantic and thrilling . . . our enterprising officer": "Literary Notices" and "The Far West," *New York Herald*, September 10 and 18, 1843.

68 "a little book . . . many amusing and exciting adventures": "A Real Buffalo Hunt," *Democratic Standard*, October 10, 1843.

68 "It is very flattering . . . want to hear more": JBF to Adelaide Talbot, April 21, 1844, Herr and Spence, *Letters*, 22.

68 "the country gone over . . . the conquest of it": The Athenaum article was reprinted in the *Washington Globe*, June 6, 1844.

68 based on the journals and letters: Irving, *Astoria*.

69 Public meetings were organized in Missouri: Dorris, "The Oregon Trail."

69 In the spring of 1842: Ibid.

69 "all the houses . . . in the vicinity": "Oregon Emigration," *Niles' National Register*, May 3, 1845.

69 220 wagons: Ibid., 129.

69 "the hotels were crowded . . . arms and equipments": Paul, *Francis Parkman's The Oregon Trail*, 3.

69 "water broke alternately over her guards": Ibid.

69–70 "squibs and serpents . . . a stout lead pencil": Ibid., 223.

70 "nearly impenetrable barrier . . . peopled by freemen": *New York Tribune*, reprinted in *Niles' National Register*, vol. 65, October 28, 1843.

70 "The clouds . . . the thunder storms": JCF, *Report of the Exploring Expedition to Oregon*, Jackson and Spence, *Expeditions*, vol. 1, 447.

70–71 "and as she gave . . . excellent cup of coffee": Ibid., 470.

71 "Our cannon caused unnecessary alarm": Preuss, diary entry, August 23, 1843, Gudde and Gudde, *Exploring with Fremont*, 86.

71 "Shooting buffalo with the howitzer is a cruel but amusing sport": Preuss, diary entry, August 10, 1843, ibid., 84.

71 "the brass cover . . . future traveler": JCF, *Report of the Exploring Expedition to Oregon*, Jackson and Spence, *Expeditions*, vol. 1, 509–10.

71 "the first ever attempted on the interior sea": Ibid., 502.

71 "highly exaggerated and impossible": Ibid., 471.

71 He gave the region a name, the Great Basin: Ibid., 541.

72 "glowing in the sunlight this morning": Ibid., 557.

72 "Three unknown Indians . . . and myself": Ibid., 562.

72 "On a low broad point . . . tents of the emigrants": Ibid., 564.

72 "their land of promise": Ibid., 567.

72 nineteen-year-old named William: JCF, *Memoirs of My Life*, 287.

72 he was believed to have come from the related Wasco tribe: This is the tradition of both the Chinook Nation and the Wasco tribe. Tony Johnson, chairman,

Chinook Indian Nation, email to author, May 8, 2019; Valerie Switzler, manager, the Confederated Tribes of Warm Springs Reservation of Oregon, email to author, May 8, 2019.

73 **"every comfort . . . shelter could give"**: JBF to Adelaide Talbot, June 15, 1844, *Expeditions*, vol. 1, 361.

73 **"a charm for me . . . correct some old error"**: JCF, *Memoirs of My Life*, 485.

73–74 **"God only knows . . . move ahead slowly"**: Preuss, diary entry, December 16, 1843, Gudde and Gudde, *Exploring with Fremont*, 99.

74 **0 degrees Fahrenheit**: "Table of observations with the thermometer," Jackson and Spence, *Expeditions*, vol. 1, unnumbered appendix after 784.

74 **"the air was dark . . . green prairie country"**: Ibid., 591.

74 **"a magic view from above . . . promised land"**: Preuss, diary entry, December 16, 1843, Gudde and Gudde, *Exploring with Fremont*, 102.

74 **rolled downhill some five hundred feet**: Ibid.

74 **52 degrees Fahrenheit**: "Table of observations with the thermometer," Jackson and Spence, *Expeditions*, vol. 1, unnumbered appendix after p. 784.

74–75 **thousands of rabbits**: Preuss, diary entry, December 16, 1843, Gudde and Gudde, *Exploring with Fremont*, 102.

75 **571 miles since the Columbia River**: "Table of Distances," Jackson and Spence, *Expeditions*, vol. 1, unnumbered pages after 724.

75 **"We have been sitting here . . . instead of water"**: Preuss, diary entry, December 16, 1843, Gudde and Gudde, *Exploring with Fremont*, 103.

75 **stolen, the men believed, by Indians**: JCF, *Report of the Exploring Expedition to Oregon*, Jackson and Spence, *Expeditions*, vol. 1, 603.

76 **"furniture and farming utensils . . . machinery for a mill"**: Ibid., 430.

76 **"plenty to eat" and "grass in abundance"**: Quaife, *Kit Carson's Autobiography*, 14.

76 **delayed giving the order for nearly two more weeks**: Charles Preuss wrote on January 5 that "we shall probably cross over to California," proving that the idea was part of the men's discussions; but Frémont wrote that he did not make the decision until January 18.

76 **"My decision was heard with joy . . . new life through the camp"**: JCF, *Report of the Exploring Expedition to Oregon*, Jackson and Spence, *Expeditions*, vol. 1, 611.

76 **"scarlet cloth . . . country of the whites"**: Ibid., 621.

76 **"pointed to the snow on the mountain . . . impossible for them to get through"**: Ibid.

76 **"now scanty provisions"**: Ibid., 622.

76 **peas, flour, rice, and sugar**: Preuss, diary entry, Janurary 26, 1844, Gudde and Gudde, *Exploring with Frémont*, 105.

77 **urged the travelers not to cross**: JCF, *Report of the Exploring Expedition to Oregon*, Jackson and Spence, *Expeditions*, vol. 1, 624–25.

77 **"He was thinly clad . . . worn out"**: Ibid., 625.

77 **snow began to fall**: Ibid., 626.

77 **"We still do not know where we really are"**: Preuss, diary entry, January 26, 1844, Gudde and Gudde, *Exploring with Fremont*, 104.

77 **"six feet deep on the level for a distance of three leagues"**: Quaife, *Kit Carson's Autobiography*, 79.

77 **"Driven by hunger . . . meat for food":** Ibid.

77 **"old tall, thick fir trunks were set afire . . . and our kitchen":** Preuss, diary entry, February 3, 1844, Gudde and Gudde, *Exploring with Fremont*, 108–9.

77 **Another dog, named Clammet:** Ibid.

78 **"Rock upon rock—snow upon snow":** JCF, *Report of the Exploring Expedition to Oregon*, Jackson and Spence, *Expeditions*, vol. 1, 630.

78 **"Seated around . . . serious faces":** Ibid.

78 **they had made it over the divide:** Ibid., 637.

78 **"was clear and very long . . . silence and desolation":** Ibid.

79 **9,338 feet above sea level:** Ibid., 638.

79 **at 8,574 feet:** The elevation now appears on a highway sign on California State Route 88, which leads through what is today called Carson Pass.

79 **"We had with us . . . for famished people":** JCF, *Report of the Exploring Expedition to Oregon*, Jackson and Spence, *Expeditions*, vol. 1, 645.

79 **"became light-headed . . . knowing where he was going":** Ibid., 645.

79 **"not yet recovered his mind" . . . "as if it were summer":** Ibid., 646.

79 **"On a bench . . . the curiosity to measure":** Ibid., 643.

79 **"Never did a name sound more sweetly":** JCF, *Memoirs of My Life*, 350.

79 **"I am a vaquero . . . very rich man":** Ibid.

80 **"under his hospitable roof":** Ibid.

80 **1,142 meandering miles:** "Table of Distances," Jackson and Spence, *Expeditions*, vol. 1, unnumbered pages after 724.

80 **"were all on foot . . . emaciated as themselves":** JCF, *Memoirs of My Life*, 350–51.

80 **exceeded 60 degrees Fahrenheit and once even hit 75:** "Table of observations with the thermometer," Jackson and Spence, *Expeditions*, vol. 1, unnumbered appendix after 784.

80 **130 horses, 30 head of cattle:** Hurtado, *John Sutter*, 128.

80 **"silver plated bridle":** Financial records, January 1, 1843–December 31, 1844, Jackson and Spence, *Expeditions*, vol. 1, 382, fn 387.

80 **"buck-skin pantaloons & moccasins":** Ibid.

80 **he fled to avoid debtors' prison:** Hurtado, *John Sutter*, 13.

81 **kanakas . . . rented out to him:** Ibid., 45.

81 **"a very moderate compensation . . . of clothing":** JCF, *Report of the Exploring Expedition to Oregon*, Jackson and Spence, *Expeditions*, vol. 1, 654.

81 **"take payment in dried meat":** Sutter to Antonio Sunol, May 19, 1845, Sutter papers, Bancroft Library.

81 **the laborers were "innocent":** Sutter to Antonio Sunol, June 14, 1845, ibid.

81 **"obtains as many boys and girls as he has any use for":** JCF, *Report of the Exploring Expedition to Oregon*, Jackson and Spence, *Expeditions*, vol. 1, 654.

81 **sexually abused the girls:** Hurtado examines the stories heard and spread by Heinrich Lienhard, another Swiss settler, in *John Sutter: A Life on the North American Frontier*, 115–16.

81 **planned wool factory:** JCF, *Report of the Exploring Expedition to Oregon*, Jackson and Spence, *Expeditions*, vol. 1, 654.

81 **after killing their parents in war:** "Will send you young Indians after the campaign against the Horse-thieves," Sutter writes in one letter. Sutter to Sunol,

May 19, 1845. "Correspondence Between John A. Sutter and Antonio Sunol, 1840–46," Bancroft Library.

81 **he took his time:** Chaffin, *Pathfinder,* 221.

82 **take positions working for Sutter:** Dillon, *Fool's Gold,* 147. Some dropped off the expedition after Frémont accused them of stealing sugar, but Frémont left on civil enough terms that one went out of his way to meet him upon his return to California in 1845–46.

82 **"inspired with California ... make there a home":** JCF, *Memoirs of My Life,* 419.

CHAPTER SIX: THE MANIFEST PURPOSE OF PROVIDENCE

85 **August 15, 1843:** "Minutes of the National Convention of Colored Citizens," August 15–19, 1843. JCF records himself camping on the Green River on that date in *Report of the Exploring Expedition to Oregon,* Jackson and Spence, *Expeditions,* vol. 1, 466.

85 **public hall at the corner of Washington and Seneca streets:** "Minutes of the Convention of Colored Citizens," 4.

85 **Henry Highland Garnet called the meeting to order:** Ibid. "Garnet" is the common spelling of his surname, although the minutes of the convention spelled it "Garnit."

85 **"infused with tears ... we shall take it.":** Ibid., 13.

86 **"at first lacked the depravity indispensable to shutting me up in mental darkness":** Douglass, *Narrative,* 32.

86 **"insurrection ... better way":** "Minutes of the Convention of Colored Citizens," 13.

86 **broke his hand:** Douglass, *Life and Times of Frederick Douglass,* 198.

87 **activists could range more widely giving speeches:** The role of transportation in Frederick Douglass's rise is noted in Blight, *Frederick Douglass,* 123–24.

87 **campaigning to end the House gag rule:** Barker, "The Annexation of Texas."

87 **leaving behind a trail of clear smooth water:** The ship's ice cutting was described in "The Princeton," *Washington Globe,* February 17, 1844.

87 **smokeless coal called anthracite, and had a funnel that could be retracted:** Pearson, "The 'Princeton' and the 'Peacemaker.'"

88 **in collaboration with John Ericsson:** It is commonly written that Ericsson developed one of the *Princeton's* big guns and Stockton the other, but correspondence shows both men working on both weapons in concert with others. Ibid., 167.

88 **"the invention of gunpowder":** Washington *Daily Globe,* February 14, 1844, 3.

88 **the army's chief of ordnance, who warned:** Ibid., 171.

88 **anchoring within sight of the Capitol's green dome:** It anchored "a mile below Greenleaf's Point," the southern extremity of the city. Today the Capitol dome remains visible from locations near this point, such as Reagan National Airport across the Potomac. "The U.S. Ship Princeton," *National Intelligencer,* February 13, 1844, 3.

88 **On February 16, President Tyler boarded the ship:** "The Princeton," *Daily Globe,* February 17, 1844, 3.

88 **"I saw the hammer ... the shattered gun":** Benton, *Thirty Years' View,* vol. 2, 568.

88 **included a black man, a slave:** Holland, *The Invisibles,* 177.

89 **"It is almost as if . . . and charged it":** Child writing in the *Liberator,* April 5, 1844, 5.

89 **"a positive good":** "Speech on the Reception of Abolition Petitions, Delivered in the Senate," February 6, 1837, in Crallé., ed., *Works of John C. Calhoun,* 631.

89 **"There never has yet existed . . . the labor of the other":** Ibid.

90 **"deafness . . . insanity, and idiocy":** Calhoun to Pakenham, April 18, 1844, ibid., 337.

90 **"sudden, reckless, and monstrous course":** Benton speech, May 16, 18, and 20, 1844, Appendix to *Congressional Globe,* 28th Congress, 1st Session, 474–86.

90 **"I shall not engage in schemes . . . face was never seen":** Ibid.

90 **"the crime and infamy of unjust war":** Ibid.

91 **"the same extra compensation":** "Extra Compensation," *Washington Union,* September 28, 1850.

91 **a Grove battery:** Silverman, *Lightning Man,* 236.

91 **"He was so worn-out . . . brilliant hollow eyes startled one":** JBF, *Souvenirs of My Time,* 61.

92 FOREIGN CONSPIRACY AGAINST THE LIBERTIES OF THE UNITED STATES: "Foreign Conspiracy Against the Liberties of the United States," *New-York Observer,* September 20, 1834. The article is attributed to "Brutus," the author of a dozen such articles; Brutus is identified as Morse in Silverman, *Lightning Man,* 134.

92 **his "electro-magnetic telegraph":** The bill was H.R. 641, 27th Congress, 3rd session. American State Papers.

92 **"laughed at in Congress":** JBF, *Souvenirs of My Time,* 61.

92 **Congress should also subsidize mesmerism:** Silverman, *Lightning Man,* 221.

92 **from chestnut poles:** Morse posted recurring newspaper ads offering to buy "straight and sound Chestnut Posts, with the bark on." *Daily Madisonian,* multiple dates including April 11, 1844.

93 **"9¾ o' clock . . . hissed by some":** "Telegraphic Dispatch," *Whig Standard,* May 28, 1844.

93 **"Those attending . . . Baltimore!":** "Morse's Telegraph," *Whig Standard,* May 28, 1844.

93 **there was no news in Washington:** "Washington," *New York Herald,* May 30, 1844.

93 **"the annihilation of space":** The phrase appeared in both the *New York Tribune,* May 27, 1844, and the *Whig Standard,* May 28, 1844.

93–94 **"Professor Morse's telegraph . . . that has been":** "Washington," *New York Herald,* May 30, 1844.

94 **"Mr. Saunders declares . . . favor of annexation":** Ibid., May 29, 1844.

94 **along with "mutterings":** "Telegraphic Despatch," *Whig Standard,* May 30, 1844.

94 **rush the news of Polk's nomination into print:** "Telegraphic News," *Daily Madisonian,* May 29, 1844.

94 **"the manifest purpose . . . Rocky Mountains":** Bancroft letter August 15, 1844, reprinted in the *Cadiz Sentinel,* September 4, 1844.

94–95 **"Senators . . . War is war, whether great or small":** Appendix to *Congressional Globe,* June 1, 1844, 499, American State Papers.

95 **August 6, 1844:** JCF, *Report of the Exploring Expedition to Oregon,* Jackson and Spence, *Expeditions,* vol. 1, 724.

95 **Gabriel . . . Jessie was not home:** JBF, *Souvenirs of My Time,* 163.

95 **"in his uniform and thin as a shadow":** Ibid., 163.

95 **"was thronged with welcoming friends":** Ibid., 165.

95–96 **The throng apparently included a reporter:** The *Missourian* article from August 13 was reprinted in the *Whig Standard* of Washington, August 19, 1844.

96 **become part of the crowded Benton household:** JCF, *Memoirs of My Life,* 409; JCF, *Report of the Exploring Expedition to Oregon,* Jackson and Spence, *Expeditions,* vol. 1, 724.

96 **questions about . . . California:** JBF refers to this in a passage of *Memoir,* 74.

96 **"We were forced . . . Mr. Frémont rented":** JBF, *Memoir,* 74.

96 **"kept up the camp habit and very early brought me coffee":** JCF, *Memoirs of My Life,* 414.

96 **"Nine o'clock . . . could not be done":** JBF, *Memoir,* 74.

97 **"The narrative . . . positive observation":** JCF, "Notice to the Reader," reprinted in the *Washington Union,* May 20, 1845.

97 **"Carson sprang over . . . compressed among rocks":** JCF, *Report of the Exploring Expedition to Oregon,* Jackson and Spence, *Expeditions,* vol. 1, 641.

97 **"going off for . . . only a rain storm":** JBF, *Memoir,* 46–47.

98 **"twenty feet deep . . . seventeen thousand feet":** "Lieut. Frémont's Expedition," *Whig Standard,* August 19, 1844.

98 **"Fremont's Peak beyond the South Pass":** "To the Public," *Daily Madisonian,* December 10, 1844.

98 **"*Fremontia vermicularis* . . . you do not know":** JCF to John Torrey, March 23, 1845, Jackson and Spence, *Expeditions,* vol. 1, 402.

98 **named one *Sphenopteris Fremonti*:** Appendix B, "Report of the Exploring Expedition," Jackson and Spence, *Expeditions,* vol. 1, 744.

98 **Convention of American Geologists and Naturalists:** "Convention of American Geologists and Naturalists," *New York Tribune,* May 7, 1845.

99 **"peculiarly arduous . . . encounter and overcome":** "Report of the Secretary of War," *New York Herald,* January 12, 1845.

99 **reprinted in the *Daily Madisonian* in Washington:** "Report of the Secretary of War," *Daily Madisonian,* December 6, 1844.

99 **first lieutenant to captain:** *Senate Executive Journal,* January 21, 1845, American State Papers.

99 **"five thousand extra copies":** *Senate Executive Journal,* March 1, 1845, 226, American State Papers.

99 **ten thousand extra copies:** *Senate Executive Journal,* March 3, 1845, 249, American State Papers.

99 **accounts . . . appeared in the Nauvoo paper:** Arrington, *Brigham Young: American Moses,* 124.

99 **descriptions of the Great Salt Lake:** Baugh, "John C. Frémont's 1843–4 Western Expedition," 23–55.

CHAPTER SEVEN: A TASTE FOR DANGER
AND BOLD DARING ADVENTURE

101 **"better to harmonize ... new element of discord":** Clay to Peter Buel Porter, 1838, cited in Jones, "Henry Clay and Continental Expansion, 1820–1844," 260–61.

102 **Pennsylvania mandated the use of the Bible:** Lannie and Diethorn, "For the Honor and Glory of God."

102 **reserved their own railroad cars:** "Fourth of July Celebration in Philadelphia by the Native Americans," *New York Herald,* July 2, 1844.

102 **"watching the flashes ... against the sky":** Testimony of George S. Roberts, Schmandt, "A Selection of Sources Dealing with the Nativist Riots of 1844."

102 **"the scene of riot and bloodshed—of civil war":** "Terrible State of Affairs in Philadelphia," *New York Herald,* July 9, 1844.

102 **he rushed the latest updates to Secretary of State:** Silverman, *Lightning Man,* 238.

102–3 **"Native Americans!" . . . "liberally":** editorial signed "J.T.B.," *Boston Courier,* October 31, 1844.

103 **"Half past 2, p.m. . . . additional returns":** "Presidential Election Returns," *Whig Standard,* November 4, 1844.

103 **would be "shamefully defeated":** "Col. Polk's Election," *Daily Madisonian,* November 6, 1844.

103 THE DEMOCRACY GLORIOUSLY TRIUMPHANT: Ibid., November 12, 1844.

103–4 **"We have no regrets . . . triumphant":** "The Whig Standard," *Whig Standard,* November 16, 1844.

104 **"The design to send ... Thomas H. Benton":** Benton to Francis Preston Blair, January 12, 1845, Thomas Hart Benton Papers, LOC.

105 **"Texas Torch-Light Procession":** "Texas Torch-Light Procession," *Daily Madisonian,* March 3, 1845.

105 **the headline** LAND! LAND!: Ibid.

105 **"fearful . . . certainly were sustained":** "The Inauguration," *National Intelligencer,* March 5, 1845.

105 **"a large assemblage of umbrellas":** Diary entry, March 4, 1845, *Memoirs of John Quincy Adams,* vol. 12, 179.

105 **"in a firm tone . . . impressed by it himself":** "The Inauguration," *National Intelligencer,* March 5, 1845.

105 **"in other sections":** Polk inaugural, *Daily Madisonian,* March 4, 1845.

106 **his famous son-in-law:** JCF, *Memoirs of My Life,* 418–19.

106 **"I mentioned that I had, shortly before ... three great rivers":** Ibid., 418.

106 **settle there in such numbers that the result became inevitable:** Benton expressed this view directly to President Polk. Polk, diary entry, October 25, 1845, Quaife, *Diary of James K. Polk,* vol. 1, 71–72.

106 **fifty-nine stories during 1843 and fifty-three in 1844:** Author search of *New York Herald* 1843–44, Chronicling America: Historic American Newspapers database, Library of Congress.

107 invited Captain Frémont to dinner: JCF, *Memoirs of My Life,* 420.

107 "twenty times as valuable to us as all Texas": Daniel Webster to Fletcher Webster, March 11, 1845, Webster, *Private Correspondence of Daniel Webster,* 204.

107 called him Aunt Fancy: Baker, *James Buchanan,* 25.

107 Jessie wrote out translations: JCF, *Memoirs of My Life,* 421. Polk's diary corroborates this story to an extent; at a slightly later period, October 1845, it refers to Polk directing Buchanan to share confidential documents with Benton. Polk, diary entry, October 24, 1845, Quaife, *Diary of James K. Polk,* vol. 1, 68.

108 He was to work near Bent's Fort: Abert to Frémont, February 12, 1845, Jackson and Spence, *Expeditions,* vol. 1, 395–96.

108 hire a "Botanical Colourist": Abert to Frémont, March 5, 1845, ibid., 399.

108 "the military peculiarity of the Country . . . you shall examine": Abert to Frémont, April 10, 1845, ibid., 407.

108 "if any operations . . . may be at command": Ibid.

108–9 "EXPLORING EXPEDITION . . . now have a chance": "Exploring Expedition," *Niles' National Register,* vol. 68, May 3, 1845, 129.

109 "What we do not understand . . . right it is ordered": "Frémont's Expedition," *Boston Daily Atlas,* June 4, 1845.

109 "Some conversation occurred . . . before his return": Polk, diary entry, October 24, 1845, Quaife, *Diary of James K. Polk,* vol. 1, 71–72.

110 summer of 1846 returning: She referred to this in her letter to JCF, June 18, 1846. Herr and Spence, *Letters,* 24. John also referred in his letters to his hopes of returning at that time.

110 "he seems drooping . . . much attached": Physician Caspar Wistar to T. Hartley Crawford, May 5, 1845, Jackson and Spence, *Expeditions,* vol. 1, 417.

110 "been a Quaker all winter": JCF, *Memoirs of My Life,* 424.

110 May 30, 1845: Theodore Talbot to Adelaide Talbot, May 30, 1845, Hine and Lottinville, *Soldier in the West,* 10.

111 "name no wages at present . . . make everything satisfactory": Martin oral history, *With Frémont 1845–49,* 1.

111 establishing service . . . Galveston: "Texas Mail," *Niles' National Register,* vol. 68, June 21, 1845, 245.

112 ostensibly friendly visit . . . Veracruz: Ibid., May 31, 105.

112 plotted . . . to raise a private army: Stockton letter to Bancroft, reproduced in Merry, *A Country of Vast Design,* 154.

112 "The day cannot be distant . . . hastening year of the Lord 1945!": John L. O'Sullivan, "Annexation," *United States Magazine and Democratic Review* 17, July–August 1845.

112 "measurer of coal and salt": Meltzer, Milton. *Nathaniel Hawthorne,* 54–55.

113 "two bloody scalps, dangling from the end of Godey's gun": JCF, *Report of the Exploring Expedition to Oregon,* Jackson and Spence, *Expeditions,* vol. 1, 680.

113 "the former an *American* . . . the latter a Frenchman, born in St. Louis": Ibid., 681.

113 "The more noble Indian . . . brought along the entire scalp": Preuss, diary entry, April 27, 1844, Gudde and Gudde, *Exploring with Frémont,* 127–28.

113 "I believe . . . taken by his own hand": Ibid.

114 **Swanok and Jim Sagundai:** JCF, *Memoirs of My Life*, 424. JCF does not give the first name Jim, but Anderson does in "The Delaware and Shawnee Indians," 259.

114 **"principal objects... beyond the Rocky Mountains":** JCF, *Memoirs of My Life*, 425.

114 **Several quit the expedition:** Martin, *With Frémont 1845–49*, 2.

114 **the captain decreed that they must walk instead of ride:** Ibid., 3.

114 **"encountered a Cheyenne.... was imposing":** JCF, *Memoirs of My Life*, 425.

115 **the explosion startled the camp:** Martin, *With Frémont 1845–49*, 5.

115 **"Throwing off... stirred the blood pleasantly for the moment":** JCF, *Memoirs of My Life*, 425–26.

115 **"well-appointed compact party... willing to meet it":** Ibid., 428.

116 **a world apart:** A standard modern history of the state is Starr, *California*.

118 **"Charge . . . necessary and, even, urgent":** Rosenus, *General Vallejo and the Advent of the Americans*, 80.

CHAPTER EIGHT: THE SPANIARDS WERE SOMEWHAT RUDE AND INHOSPITABLE

121 **"a broken band several miles in length":** JCF, *Memoirs of My Life*, 448.

122 **"an interior lake ... the lofty cypress":** Frémont, *Geographical Memoir*, Senate Document 148, 30th Congress, 1st Session, 1848, 21.

122 **Chrysopylae, or the Golden Gate:** Ibid. Also JCF, *Memoirs of My Life*, 512.

122 **"one of the best among the few ... chill of the afternoons":** Ibid., 453.

122 **"considerable Negro blood":** Savage, "The Influence of William Alexander Leidesdorff on the History of California."

123 **ship was sold out from under him:** Ibid.

123 **thirty-five thousand acres:** Ibid.

123 **the United States's first-ever diplomat of color:** The State Department itself may not have realized who was serving in its name. Today, the Office of the Historian lists "the first African-American diplomat" not as Leidesdorff but as Ebenezer Don Carlos Bassett, appointed consul general to Haiti in 1869, almost a quarter-century after Leidesdorff.

123–24 **"so at variance. ... it is fair to consider ... I find the theory of our Great Basin ... et le bon temps viendra":** JCF to JBF, January 24, 1846, reprinted in the *Easton Star*, May 26, 1846.

124 **"the appearance of an extensive park":** Archibald H. Gillespie, quoted in Marti, *Messenger of Destiny*, 25.

125 **nail down redwood shingles:** Kirker, "The Larkin House Revisited," *California History*, vol. 65, No. 1, March 1986, 28.

125 **one of the two Americans who married into the family of General Vallejo:** Rosenus, *General Vallejo and the Advent of the Americans*, 10.

125 **sometimes lending money to California officials:** One, Gov. Micheltorena, never repaid him. Ibid., 56.

125 **refusing to reimburse $31.34:** This story is contained in three letters. Larkin told Buchanan he was "destitute" of seal or flag April 11, 1844 (Hammond, *Larkin Papers*, vol. 2, 92). He paid Parrott and Co. $31.34 for a flag and staff January 21, 1845 (ibid., vol. 3, 19). He complained that "my bill for a flag" and

other expenses were "cut off," Larkin to Buchanan, March 9, 1846 (reprinted in JCF, *Memoirs of My Life*, 462).

125 **"spent their leisure time ashore . . . fish every day in the year?":** "Upper California," *New York Herald*, May 18, 1843.

126 **"We have . . . not more happy than a Californian":** "Sketches of California," *New York Herald*, June 12, 1845.

126 **"I never make to the Government an unreasonable request . . . well disposed toward me":** Thomas Larkin to JCF, March 8, 1846, Jackson and Spence, *Expeditions*, vol. 2, 79.

127 **"very friendly relations grew up with us":** JCF, *Memoirs of My Life*, 456.

127 **"a severe horsewhipping":** JCF to Dolores Pacheco, February 24, 1846, Jackson and Spence, *Expeditions*, vol. 2, 68.

127 **war was "probable":** JCF to James Clyman, no date, approximately April 1846, Jackson and Spence, *Expeditions*, vol. 2, 131.

127 **"any intelligence you may have received from the States":** JCF to Thomas Larkin, March 5, 1846, ibid., 73.

128 **In later years he would give several explanations:** The writer Josiah Royce, who interviewed both Frémonts in 1884, reported that John made contradictory claims, including that he had been given permission by Castro to survey the coastal passes. The available record shows he neither requested nor received any such permission. Royce, *California*, 115.

128 **"I had before my mind the home I wished to make . . . wanted for my mother":** JCF, *Memoirs of My Life*, 457.

128 **After inspecting Santa Cruz he drifted southeastward:** Frémont's map of California traces this route, which is also described in his memoir and in Martin, *With Frémont 1845–49*, 6.

128 **passing time until the snow melted:** JCF to Thomas Larkin, March 5, 1846, Jackson and Spence, *Expeditions*, vol. 2, 73.

128 **"I therefore practice the selfdenial . . . society in your capital":** Ibid.

129 **"you and the party . . . this same Department":** José Castro to JCF, March 5, 1846, ibid., 74–75.

129 **"unfortunate" . . . "false reports, or false appearances":** Thomas Larkin to José Castro and Manuel de Jesús Castro, March 6, 1846, ibid., 76.

129 **"must now either blindly obey. . . . by his crime":** Manuel de Jesús Castro to Thomas Larkin, March 8, 1846, ibid., 77.

129 **"a band of robbers . . . lance the ulcer":** Castro proclamation, March 8, 1846, ibid., 81.

129 **"Captain said that he wd leave the country, but wd not be driven out":** Theodore Talbot to Adelaide Talbot, July 24, 1846, Hine and Lottinville, *Soldier in the West*, 41.

130 **John used his spyglass:** JCF to Thomas Larkin, March 9, 1846, ibid., 81–82.

130 **a note in pencil:** JCF, *Memoirs of My Life*, 463.

130 **"I am making myself as strong as possible" . . . "J.C. Frémont":** Ibid.

131 **"trouble hereafter to Resident Americans":** Thomas Larkin to JCF, March 8, 1846, Jackson and Spence, *Expeditions*, vol. 2, 78–79.

131 **he was near 40 degrees latitude:** JCF, *Memoirs of My Life*, 460.

131 **Two men asked permission to quit:** Theodore Talbot identifies the two as Joseph Walker and Charles Taplin, and says of Taplin, "The Captain wrote home by him." Talbot gave a slightly earlier date for this departure, but was likely mistaken; he was writing his account without reference to notes. Theodore Talbot to Adelaide Talbot, July 24, 1846, Hine and Lottinville, *Soldier in the West*, 41.

131 **"The Spaniards . . . a solitary act of hostility":** JCF to JBF, April 1, 1846, reprinted in *New York Herald*, November 11, 1846.

131 **he probably inflated the size of the Mexican force:** The reliable Larkin thought it was not "three or four hundred" men but two hundred, as did an officer whose US Navy ship *Cyane* visited Monterey soon after the incident. "From California," *New York Tribune*, June 13, 1846.

131 **of "hardy warriors":** JCF to James Clyman, approximately April 1846, Jackson and Spence, *Expeditions*, vol. 2, 131.

132 **"An Indian let loose is of all animals . . . inflicting suffering":** JCF, *Memoirs of My Life*, 502.

132 **"feathers on their heads, and faces painted black, their war color":** Ibid., 517.

132 **killed 175 Indians:** Martin, *With Frémont 1845–49*, 7.

133 **"We found . . . survivors fled in all directions":** Quaife, *Kit Carson's Autobiography*, 95.

133 **"Our arrival took them . . . their habit of hostility":** JCF, *Memoirs of My Life*, 483.

133 **"caught the faint sound of horses' feet . . . fatigued by long traveling":** Ibid., 486–87.

134 **his servant was Benjamin Harrison:** Marti, *Messenger of Destiny*, 35.

134 **fluency in Spanish:** Ibid., 6–7.

134–35 **"confidential agent" . . . paid six dollars per day:** James Buchanan to Thomas Larkin, October 17, 1845, Moore, ed., *Works of James Buchanan*, vol. 6, 275–78.

135 **"The future Destiny . . . People of the United States":** James Buchanan to Thomas Larkin, no date, Bancroft, *History of California*, vol. 5, 1846–48, 596.

135 **"any other European power":** Ibid., 597.

135 **Gillespie verbally repeated the instructions:** Gillespie's testimony to this effect in an 1848 inquiry is cited in Royce, *California*, 130.

135–36 **"The information through Gillespie . . . object of the President":** JCF, *Memoirs of My Life*, 488–89.

136 **asserted nearly the same:** Jackson and Spence, *Expeditions*, vol. 2, fn xxxi.

136 **"I received nothing":** JCF to Thomas Hart Benton, May 24, 1846, JCF, *Memoirs of My Life*, 499–500.

136 **"I sat by the fire in fancied security . . . among the animals":** Ibid.

137 **"What's the matter over there?":** JCF, *Memoirs of My Life*, 490.

137 **Carson shouted "Indians!":** Ibid.

137 **never fired a gun:** Martin, *With Frémont 1845–49*, 9.

137 **remains of Basil Lajeunesse:** Ibid.

138 **"seized [the ax] and knocked his head . . . scalped him":** JCF, *Memoirs of My Life*, 492.

138 **"With our knives we dug a shallow grave" . . . "creek where he died":** Ibid.

138 **"Very sick here":** Ibid., 493.

138 **At Sagundai's suggestion:** Ibid.
138-39 **"In one of them . . . we found an old Indian woman who had been shot":** Martin, *With Frémont 1845-49*, 11.
139 **"being dry . . . the fire was a beautiful sight":** Quaife, *Kit Carson's Autobiography*, 100.
139 **"His hand was still grasping . . . wore when he was killed":** JCF, *Memoirs of My Life*, 494.
139 **John fired at the attacker and missed:** Ibid., 495.
140 **"I owe my life to them two":** So Carson was quoted in the *Washington Union*, June 15, 1847.
140 **gave the reins to Jacob Dodson:** JCF, *Memoirs of My Life*, 495.
140 **"By Heaven, this is rough work . . . time enough to forget about this":** Ibid., 495.

CHAPTER NINE: I AM NOT GOING TO LET YOU WRITE
ANYTHING BUT YOUR NAME

143 **"I shall be outnumbered ten to one and be compelled to make good my retreat":** JCF to James Clyman, approximately April 1846, Jackson and Spence, *Expeditions*, vol. 2., 131.
143 **"I have but a faint hope . . . late in September":** JCF to Thomas Hart Benton, May 24, 1846, ibid., 138.
143 **apparently in the hands of Sagundai:** Sagundai volunteered to carry a letter from California to Benton (Connelley, *A Standard History of Kansas and Kansans*, 249-50). It is likely that this was the letter Sagundai carried. JCF was known to have sent only two letters to Benton during the period when Sagundai could have returned, and the other letter was sent by Commodore Sloat.
144 **faced "perplexing complications":** JCF to James Clyman, approximately April 1846, Jackson and Spence, *Expeditions*, vol. 2., 131.
144 **"You are aware . . . times to come":** Thomas Larkin to JCF, May 31, 1846, Jackson and Spence, *Expeditions*, vol. 2, 141.
144 **he worked his way through the crew:** Larkin told a story of doing this in one of his pseudonymous letters to the same newspaper. Letter from "Paisano," *New York Herald*, June 12, 1845.
144 **"I have been keeping some . . . published Books of Travels":** Larkin to JCF, May 31, 1846, Jackson and Spence, *Expeditions*, vol. 2, 140-2.
144-45 **"a native of South Carolina . . . person and features":** "Captain Frémont," biographical sketch by "A.R.C.," reprinted in *Alexandria Gazette*, December 31, 1845. Variously edited versions of the same sketch also appeared in the *Augusta Chronicle*, *Washington Examiner*, and *Norfolk Democrat*.
145 **written in Washington:** "Captain Frémont," *Alexandria Gazette*, December 31, 1845.
145 **"Mrs. Frémont and two sisters attended the court as witnesses":** Thomas Larkin to JCF, May 31, 1846, Jackson and Spence, *Expeditions*, vol. 2, 141.
145 **"always endeavor to do them justice" . . . "as lasting as it is enviable":** The papers that reprinted this account included the *Washington Semi-weekly Union*, November 6, 1845.

145 "the little one declined an introduction": Thomas Larkin to JCF, May 31, 1846, Jackson and Spence, *Expeditions,* vol. 2, 140–42.

146 **staged a public event:** Herr, *Jessie Benton Frémont,* 130.

146 **debate and approve the treaty:** Ibid.

146 **purchased their house from an early member of the global elite:** JBF, *Souvenirs of My Time,* 57.

146 **all the way to Philadelphia and New York:** The not fully operational line is discussed in a letter from B. B. French, of the telegraph company, in the *Washington Union,* June 18, 1846.

146–47 **"magnificent collection of valuable European oil paintings":** Ibid.

147 **"a very handsome variety"** . . . **"book-cases and couches":** Ibid.

147 **less than fully dressed:** Meigs, *Life of Thomas Hart Benton,* 515.

147 **"the disease seems to have expended itself, and she is quite well again":** JBF to JCF, June 18, 1846. Herr and Spence, eds., *Letters of Jessie Benton Frémont,* 25.

147 **"discovered a good wagon road to Oregon . . . any heretofore travelled":** "Captain Frémont—Interesting," *Washington Union,* April 16, 1846.

147 **reprinted in at least a dozen papers:** Author search of Chronicling America: Historic American Newspapers database, LOC, October 15, 2017.

147 **"Fremont at Monterey":** It was first in the New Orleans *Daily Picayune,* April 22, 1846.

147 **She arranged for its publication:** JBF to JCF, June 18, 1846, Herr and Spence, *Letters,* 26.

148 **General Castro's demand:** "Later from Mexico," *Washington Union,* May 26, 1846.

148 **"not the least apprehension for Captain Frémont":** Ibid.

148 **the very next day a letter arrived:** JBF to JCF, June 18, 1846, Herr and Spence, *Letters,* 24.

148 **Kentuckian who did business in New Mexico:** Jackson and Spence, *Expeditions,* vol. 2, 150fn.

148 **"I hope that as I write":** JBF to JCF, June 18, 1846, Herr and Spence, *Letters,* 24–7.

151 **"the imminent risk of invasion . . . Mr. N. [sic] Frémont":** Proceedings of council of war, April 11, 1846, reprinted in JCF, *Memoirs of My Life,* 500.

152 **"a multitude of foreigners"** . . . **"find it convenient":** Proclamation, April 30, 1846, reprinted in ibid., 503.

152 **"leave the country . . . on pain of death":** William B. Ide narrative, reproduced in Ide, *Conquest of California,* 78.

152 **"naturally humane and generous":** Ibid.

153 **"their common safety"** . . . **"the place of meeting":** JCF, *Memoirs of My Life,* 509.

153 **"a large body of Spaniards on horseback"** . . . **"come to his camp":** Ide, in his narrative, quoted the document, which he said he had in hand while writing, though it has since been lost. William B. Ide narrative, reproduced in Ide, *Conquest of California,* 81.

153 **"required"** . . . **"to promote the object of the President"** . . . **"take California":** JCF, *Memoirs of My Life,* 488–89.

154 **a barracks in which 250 rifles . . . were stored:** Rosenus, *General Vallejo and the Advent of the Americans,* 112.

155 **looked like "banditti":** Ibid., 110.

155 **a hundred pounds of gunpowder:** Ide to Commodore Stockton, June 15, 1846, reprinted in JCF, *Memoirs of My Life*, 523-4.

155 **"This day we proclaim California a Republic" ... "be protected":** Ibid.

156 **"We have determined to make this country independent ... long road back":** Ide, June 18, 1846, reprinted in Bancroft, *History of California*, vol. 5, 1846-48, fn 159.

156 **his "earnest desire":** Ibid., 161.

156 **gunmen arrived in Sonoma:** Ibid., 164.

156 **"the Spaniards are not only satisfied, but pleased":** Ide to Stockton, reprinted in JCF, *Memoirs of My Life*, 523.

156 **"you are the prisoner of these people":** Rosenus, *General Vallejo and the Advent of the Americans*, 135.

157 **Castro was organizing troops:** JCF, *Memoirs of My Life*, 522.

157 **"we went to the rescue":** Talbot to his mother, July 24, 1846, Hine and Lottin-ville, *Soldier in the West*, 42.

157 **their captors had killed them:** Ibid., 160-61.

158 **"Shall I take these men" ... "no room for prisoners":** Bancroft, *History of California*, vol. 5, 1846-48, 171.

158 **"Three of Castro's party ... no loss on either side":** JCF to Thomas Hart Benton, July 25, 1846, Spence and Jackson, *Expeditions*, vol. 2, 183-84.

158 **"My scouts, mainly Delawares ... messages":** JCF, *Memoirs of My Life*, 525.

158-59 **"Pulling across the strait ... at full speed":** Ibid., 526.

159 **six brass cannons:** JCF to Thomas Hart Benton, July 25, 1846, Jackson and Spence, *Expeditions*, vol. 2, 183.

159 **inflated the number to fourteen:** JCF, *Memoirs of My Life*, 526.

159 **"It had now become necessary ... desired me to take charge of it":** Ibid.

159 **"Its existence was due to my presence ... to the settlers":** Ibid.

159 **"I called the people together ... placed under my direction":** JCF to Thomas Hart Benton, July 25, 1846, Jackson and Spence, *Expeditions*, vol. 2, 184.

160 **about 250 sailors and Marines rowed ashore:** The operation was described in a letter "from an officer on board the United States frigate *Savannah*," reprinted in the (Washington) *Daily Union*, October 26, 1846.

160 **a twenty-one-gun salute:** Ibid.

160 **"There may be a necessity of one hundred men, well mounted":** John Sloat to JCF, July 9, 1846, Jackson and Spence, *Expeditions*, vol. 2, 169.

160 **waiting without explanation:** Mariano Vallejo to JCF, July 12, 1846, ibid., 170-71.

160 **General Castro was retreating ... toward Los Angeles:** JCF, *Memoirs of My Life*, 531.

160 **a single cannon:** JCF to Thomas Hart Benton, July 25, 1846, Jackson and Spence, *Expeditions*, vol. 2, 184.

160-61 **"Before us, to the right ... shade of the pine trees grateful":** JCF, *Memoirs of My Life*, 534.

161 **"I pleased myself ... this Savannah of the seas":** Ibid., 535.

161 **he resolved he would not seize California's ports:** John Sloat to George Bancroft, June 6, 1846, reprinted in JCF, *Memoirs of My Life*, 536.

161-62 **"I have determined to hoist the Flag ... doing too much than too little":** John Sloat to John B. Montgomery, July 6, 1846, Jackson and Spence, *Expeditions*, vol. 2, 164.

162 **"perhaps fearing some other foreign Officer might do it"**: Thomas Larkin to James Buchanan, July 10, 1846, "Documentary: The Frémont Episode," 84.

162 **"Commodore Sloat was glad to see me" . . . "terminated abruptly"**: Ibid.

162 **"which juts into the sea . . . an ideal rest"**: Ibid.

CHAPTER TEN: DO NOT SUPPOSE I LIGHTLY INTERFERE IN A MATTER BELONGING TO MEN

166 **"information, on which we place implicit reliance"**: "California," *Daily Union* (Washington), September 2, 1846.

166 **"a detachment . . . post called Sonoma"**: Ibid.

166 **John allowed Jacob Dodson to enroll**: Senate Bill 79, 34th Congress, 1st Session, American State Papers.

166 **San Diego, which they seized without opposition**: "From the Pacific," *Washington Union*, October 26, 1846.

166–67 **"flying at every commanding . . . the United States"**: "Report of the Secretary of the Navy," *Washington Union*, December 12, 1846.

167 **"our squadron in the Pacific, with the co-operation of a gallant officer of the army"**: Polk's annual message, excerpted in Proceedings of the Court Martial in the Trial of Lieutenant Colonel Frémont, Jackson and Spence, *Expeditions*, vol. 2 supplement, 287.

167 **"Fremont is Governor, pro tem, of California"**: "From Santa Fe," *Boon's Lick Times*, November 21, 1846.

167 **"where a slave's face was never seen"**: Benton speech, May 16, 18, and 20, 1844, Appendix to *Congressional Globe*, 28th Congress, 1st Session, 485.

167 **"a state of war exists"**: *Senate Journal*, May 12, 1846, 287.

167 **"I have no sympathy for the war . . . Fighting is not his aim"**: JBF to John Torrey, March 21, 1847, Herr and Spence, *Letters*, 30.

167 **"as if revenging a private insult"**: Ibid.

167 **"a wanton deliberate lie" . . . "the extension of slavery"**: "Fourth Annual Meeting of the Western New York Anti-Slavery Society," *North Star*, January 7, 1848.

168 **"Look there in the centre! . . . the Western side of this continent"**: The letter is attributed to "the Washington correspondent of the *Commercial Advertiser*," reprinted in the *North-Carolina Standard*, February 24, 1847.

168 **"There is a very brave young man named Charles Taplin"**: JBF to James Polk, February 16, 1847, Herr and Spence, *Letters*, 29.

169 **"a herd of loafers who thus annoyed me"**: Polk, diary entry, June 21, 1847, Quaife, *Diary of James K. Polk*, vol. 3, 69.

169 **"There were many visitors . . . office for themselves"**: Polk, diary entry, July 1, 1846, ibid., vol. 2, 1.

169 **"lazy-looking loafers" . . . "I may believe them to be"**: Polk, diary entry, September 18, 1848, *ibid.* vol. 4, 124–25.

169 **Taplin received his lieutenant's commission**: Herr and Spence, *Letters*, 30.

170 **escorted the bride**: Polk, diary entry, March 19, 1847, Quaife, *Diary of James K. Polk*, vol. 2, 427–78.

170 stayed to chat far into the evening: Ibid.

170 "I am sorry for her disappointment . . . not necessary to happiness": JBF to Elizabeth Blair Lee, April 15, 1847, Herr and Spence, *Letters*, 32.

170 "I have written you a raven's letter . . . I am not cheerful": Ibid.

170 "thin and sad" . . . "pining for her husband": Lee quoted in Herr, *Jessie Benton Frémont*, 157.

170 "Our country . . . right or wrong, our country": "The Illumination of Washington," *Washington Union*, May 8, 1847.

170 Fireworks burst over the Washington Navy Yard: Ibid.

170–71 "brilliantly illuminated" . . . "not fire-proof": Ibid.

171 "the first and only flag . . . August 15, 1842": Ibid.

171 Word had filtered back east: For example, in the *Pittsburgh Gazette* in May 1847. Jackson and Spence, *Expeditions*, vol. 2, 441.

171 he presumed that his white hosts would disapprove: JCF, *Memoirs of My Life*, 74.

171–72 "modest as he is brave" . . . "the advance of civilization": "Kit Carson, of the West," *Washington Union*, June 15, 1847.

172 "I have my reasons for thinking that 'tis written by Jessie": Herr, *Jessie Benton Frémont*, 156.

172 The small force was approaching San Diego: Henry S. Turner, an aide to Kearny, reported that they encountered Californian forces "about 50 miles" from San Diego. HST to his wife, December 21, 1846, "Glimpses of the Past." Copy in LOC Frémont papers, "Miscellaneous."

173 "I demand that you cease" . . . "by the President": Stephen Kearny to Robert Stockton, January 16, 1847, Jackson and Spence, *Expeditions*, vol. 2, 263.

173 "I cannot do anything . . . on your demand": Ibid., 264.

173–74 "You are aware that I had contracted . . . ashamed to meet him": JCF to Thomas Hart Benton, February 3, 1847, ibid., 283.

174 "I was named Governor . . . gratitude to myself": Ibid.

174 a crowd of job seekers: Polk, diary entry, June 7, 1847, Quaife, *Diary of James K. Polk*, vol. 3, 52.

174 "Mrs. Fremont . . . were to be sent": Ibid., 52–53.

174 "Mrs. Fremont seemed anxious . . . giving her an answer": Ibid.

175 "the error being corrected" . . . "Court Martial": Ibid.

175 "had a full conversation . . . that distant region": Ibid.

175 Carson departed Washington June 15: "Kit Carson, of the West," *Washington Union*, June 15, 1847.

175 Jessie accompanied him: Ibid.

175 "a cluster of frame and log buildings" . . . "weary days of suspense": JBF and F. P. Frémont, *Great Events in the Life of Major General John C. Frémont*, 51.

175–76 "the rapid trampling of many horses" . . . "thought for others": Ibid., 51–52.

176 "he could not put it into speech": Ibid., 52.

176 "escaped from notice into the coming night": Ibid.

177 "For a selfish reason I wish your stay" . . . "wishes you": JBF to Edward F. Beale, September 20, 1847, Herr and Spence, *Letters*, 34–35.

177 "You will see" . . . "Jessie Benton Frémont": JBF to James Polk, September 21, 1847, ibid., 35–36.

178 **"Thanks to Morse!... steam pursued them":** Benton speech in Senate executive session, July 1848, reprinted in the (Washington) *Daily Union*, September 12, 1848.

178 **chosen to show her optimism:** Herr, *Jessie Benton Frémont*, 167.

178 **"We thank the court... to the press thus far":** "The Court Martial of Lieut. Col. Frémont," *New York Herald*, November 4, 1847.

178 **"California desert rangers... of the Great Basin":** Ibid.

178 **John, with Jacob Dodson and a Californian, rode four hundred miles in four days:** "The Oregon Horses," *New York Herald*, November 25, 1847.

179 **"It is no part of my intention... technical point":** Court-martial proceedings, Spence and Jackson, *Expeditions*, vol. 2 supplement, 4.

179 **"I name as the counsel... William Carey Jones, esquires":** Ibid.

179 **"You will be justified, and exalted... it will have its Sweet":** Thomas Hart Benton to JCF, October 8, 1847, Spence and Jackson, *Expeditions*, vol. 2, 405.

179 **"the subject of an outrage"... career:** Ibid.

179–80 **"we have carried the points which command the issues of the case":** JCF to Henry H. Sibley, November 5, 1847, Spence and Jackson, *Expeditions*, vol. 2, 456.

180 **staring at General Kearny:** Ibid., 326–27.

180 **"to be dismissed from the service":** Ibid., 338.

180 **"circumstances... greater experience than the accused":** Ibid., 340.

180 **"beg[ged] leave to recommend him to the clemency of the President of the United States":** Ibid.

180 **"in consideration of the peculiar circumstances"... "and report for duty":** Ibid., 341.

180 **In the house at C Street:** So Frémont datelined the letter. JCF to Roger Jones, February 19, 1848, Spence and Jackson, *Expeditions*, vol. 2, 478.

180–81 **"I... hereby send in my resignation... J.C. Frémont":** Ibid.

181 **presented to local authorities in 1849:** It was announced in the *Daily Sanduskian*, October 23, 1849.

181 **was "substantially unanimous":** Hayes described the petition in a letter to historian Henry Howe, July 22, 1889. Frémont papers, LOC.

181 *Fremont Weekly Freeman*: Chronicling America: Historic American Newspapers database, LOC.

181 **thirteen days to deliver:** Nevins, *Fremont: Pathmarker of the West*, 342.

181 **"malice and envy":** "Another String of Resolutions Offered in Executive Session, by Col. Benton," *New York Herald*, August 17, 1848.

182 **eight dollars per day:** "Col. Frémont," *New York Herald*, July 24, 1848.

182 **a "geographical memoir":** Frémont, *Geographical Memoir*, Senate Document 148, 30th Congress, 1st Session, 1848.

182–83 **"For some months I have been unwell"... "not even to remember it":** JBF to John Torrey, May 29, 1848, Herr and Spence, *Letters*, 36–37.

183 **"It is understood... proceed at once to San Francisco":** "Intelligence by the Mails," *New York Herald*, April 12, 1848.

183–84 **"go to California with a view.... desert explorer himself":** Ibid.

184 **"lies against Col. Frémont"... "notorious":** Benton open letter to the people of California, reprinted in *New York Herald*, September 26, 1848.

184 **"In speaking of this railroad . . . run off the track, sir":** "Thirtieth Congress," *New York Herald,* August 8, 1848.

184 **three St. Louis businessmen:** They were Robert Campbell, a merchant; Thornton Grimsley, a saddler; and Oliver D. Filley, a Dutch oven manufacturer. Spence, *Expeditions,* vol. 3, xxii.

185 **"comforting presence . . . the bitter cup":** The traveler, one T. C. Peters, described his encounter in a letter published in the *Buffalo Daily Republic* and reprinted in the *New York Tribune,* July 8, 1856.

185 **"to entertain their friends in their own house":** Ibid.

185 **"Lieut. Col. Fremont and 35 of his men . . . Westport":** *Jefferson Inquirer,* reprinted in *Saturday Morning Visitor,* October 14, 1848.

186 **"that is not an irreparable loss":** JBF to Elizabeth Blair Lee, April 15, 1847, Herr and Spence, *Letters,* 32.

186 **"Grief was new to me . . . give him up":** JBF to Christopher Carson, May 1863, Herr and Spence, *Letters,* 352.

186 **On October 8, 1848, the steamboat crew tied up:** Spence, *Expeditions,* vol. 3, xxv.

186 **John had intended to start out:** Jessie wrote in May 1848 that John intended to leave in June. JBF to John Torrey, May 29, 1848. Herr and Spence, *Letters,* 37.

186 **wanted to prove that the railroad route would be passable:** Herr and Spence, *Letters,* fn 37.

186 **the ashes of his campfire:** JBF, *Year of American Travel,* 17.

186 **a federal Indian agent:** Jessie remembered him as "Major Cummings"; he is identified as Robert W. Cummins in Spence, *Expeditions,* vol. 3, xxiv.

187 **"pleasant change of ideas":** JBF, *Year of American Travel,* 17–18.

187 **"the creak of his wife's rocking-chair . . . break the silence":** Ibid.

187 **"a sound full of pain and grief . . . she-wolf hunting her cubs":** Ibid., 19.

187 **"nerves already overstrained":** Ibid.

187 **"a big dark object . . . a speaking wolf too":** Ibid., 20.

CHAPTER ELEVEN: WE PRESSED ONWARD WITH FATAL RESOLUTION

189 **Appalachians to Buffalo, Detroit, and Louisville:** *The Liberator,* January 7, 1848, refers to the "New York, Albany and Buffalo Telegraph Co." *Congregational Journal,* February 17, 1848, notes a plan to extend the Detroit line to "Ann Harbor" and Ypsilanti, Michigan. *The Christian Watchman,* February 18, 1848, refers to a telegraph line to Cincinnati and Louisville, soon to be extended to Florence, Alabama, and New Orleans.

189 **"By Electric Telegraph":** One of many such headlines was in the *Boston Evening Transcript,* February 18, 1848.

189 **"rumors of peace":** "Highly Important from Mexico," *Boston Daily Atlas,* February 7, 1848.

189 **a messenger had reached New Orleans:** "By Magnetic Telegraph," *Boston Evening Transcript,* February 18, 1848.

190 **bragged about it himself:** One of his biographers writes, "All the evidence points to Sutter as the first to reveal the gold discovery, but he blamed others." Hurtado, *John Sutter,* 220.

190 **he told was Mariano G. Vallejo:** Ibid., 219.

190 **both of whom had met John during the war:** Governor Richard Mason was an officer who had quarreled with John. William T. Sherman recounted being so interested in the famous explorer that in 1847 he rode out of Monterey to introduce himself; they had tea, but Sherman left "without being much impressed." Sherman and Fellman, *Memoirs,* 25.

190 **bit the gold and pounded it flat with an ax:** Ibid., 40.

190 **four thousand men:** President James K. Polk, Annual Message, December 5, 1848.

190 **digging holes and using water to sift the earth:** Sherman and Fellman, *Memoirs,* 54.

190–91 **"For a time it seemed as though somebody would reach solid gold":** Ibid., 46.

191 **an oyster can filled with gold:** Ibid., 58.

191 **Larkin, the US consul, added a letter:** Thompson, "Edward Fitzgerald Beale and the California Gold Rush," 202.

191 **Two messengers, by two different routes:** The other was Lieutenant Lucien Loeser of the US Army. Sherman and Fellman, *Memoirs,* 68.

191 **in his midtwenties, with eager, observant eyes and a fringe of beard:** Jackson and Spence, *Expeditions,* vol. 2, 387; illustration after 388.

191 **linger long enough to testify:** Beale testified beginning December 23, 1847. Jackson and Spence, *Expeditions,* vol. 2 supplement, 270.

191 **"nothing of importance occurred":** Polk, diary entry, September 18, 1848, Quaife, *Diary of James K. Polk,* vol. 4, 125. The date of Beale's visit, September 18, is reported in Thompson, "Edward Fitzgerald Beale and the California Gold Rush," 202.

191 **William Carey Jones . . . wrote it up:** Ibid. Thompson, "Edward Fitzgerald Beale and the California Gold Rush," 202.

191 **"Are there any flowers or plants peculiar to a gold region?":** JBF to John Torrey, December 8, 1848. Herr and Spence, *Letters,* 37.

191 **"I have had neither the quiet nor the strength":** Ibid.

192 **"I shall go by the isthmus . . . commence running":** JBF to John Torrey, May 29, 1848, ibid., 37.

192 **"a much less interesting . . . women & children":** Ibid.

192 **six had run aground:** Six of eight ships in one stretch had wrecked in 1848–49. "Very Late From the Isthmus," *Weekly Herald,* February 17, 1849.

192 **some were turned away:** "From Chagres and Panama," *Schenectady Reflector,* March 2, 1849.

192 **twelve thousand dollars' . . . "the gold stories are not at all exaggerated, but are rather below the truth":** Ibid.

192 *Fremont's Exploring Expedition:* "New Publications," *New York Commercial Advertiser,* March 13, 1849.

192 **piles of luggage:** These details were noted by other visitors of the era. Steen, "Palaces for Travelers," 269.

192–93 **"devoted to the single male guests" . . . "velvet, lace, satin, gilding, rich carpets and mirrors":** Ibid.

193 **three emeralds that she wanted to have set in gold:** *Southern Sentinel,* quoting the *New York Sun,* March 22, 1849.

193 **"Mexican and Peruvian Emperors":** *New York Sun,* quoted in *Trenton State Gazette,* February 28, 1849.

193 **"I was much in the position of a nun . . . starting made harder than ever":** JBF, *Year of American Travel,* 22.

193 **"He went off . . . against their will":** Ibid, 23.

193–194 **"the cry of 'carrying off a free colored girl' . . . alarm of fire":** Ibid.

194 **"colored mob" . . . "what could be done":** Ibid., 24.

194 **"It was true that we were Southerners . . . contrary directions":** Ibid., 24.

194 **March 15, 1849:** The departure is recorded in the *New York Herald,* March 16, 1849.

194 **newspapers took note of the famous explorer's wife on board:** Including the *New York Examiner,* March 21, 1849; the *New York Evangelist,* March 22, 1849; the Washington *Daily Union,* March 20, 1849; and the *Worcester Palladium,* March 21, 1849.

194 **"a larger number . . . heretofore gone in any steamer":** "Movements for California," *New York Herald,* March 16, 1849.

194 **5 of the 338 were female:** A list of the passengers is printed in ibid.

194 **Collis P. Huntington, was:** A "C.P. Huntington" is on the passenger list in ibid.

194 **hoped to set up a branch store:** This was his plan from the beginning. Lavender, *The Great Persuader,* 7.

194 **rifles, woolen socks, and medicine:** Ibid., 8.

194 **"I was too worn down and silenced to care to know strangers":** JBF, *Year of American Travel,* 28.

195 **his berth, "thoroughly seasick":** Ibid., 27.

195 **"made me go into the air":** Ibid.

195 **"I had never seen the sea" . . . "of freshness":** Ibid., 27–28.

195 **"the numbness of grief":** Ibid., 25.

195 **"morbid dwelling on what was now ended":** Ibid., 28.

195 **"Perhaps the sharpest lesson of life . . . 'When I died the first time . . .'":** Ibid., 29.

196 **he had worked for the previous expedition:** Favour, *Old Bill Williams Mountain Man,* 160.

196 **"a man about six feet one" . . . "all muscle and sinew":** The traveler was Albert Pike, quoted in ibid., 92.

196 **an eccentric horseman:** Micajah McGehee, a member of the expedition, described Williams this way in a short memoir published in *Century Illustrated Magazine,* March 1891.

196 **his knees nearly touched his chest:** Nevins, *Frémont: Pathmarker of the West,* 352.

196 **expressed doubt about the wisdom of a winter crossing:** McGehee, "Rough Times in Rough Places," 772.

196 **delivered documents to William Clark:** Favour, *Old Bill Williams Mountain Man,* 50.

197 **"The sight was beautiful" . . . "wall of high mountains":** McGehee's short memoir was printed with the headline "Rough Times in Rough Places" in *Century Illustrated Magazine.*

197 "We occupied more than half a month" . . . "waste time in searching": JCF to
JBF, January 27, 1849, JBF, *Year of American Travel*, 70.

197 must have "entirely forgotten": Ibid.

197 "It was obvious that Bill had never been here": Preuss, diary entry, December 15,
1848, Gudde and Gudde, *Exploring with Frémont*, 144.

197 "two trappers . . . had been frozen to death here the year previous": McGehee,
"Rough Times in Rough Places."

197 "with the willfully blind eyes . . . confidence he pushed on": Kern, journal
entry, December 9, 1848, Spence, *Expeditions*, vol. 3, 94.

197 "Usually the snow forms no obstacle . . . traveling": JCF to JBF, JBF, January 27,
1849, *Year of American Travel*, 70.

198 "We had to rise from our beds" . . . "in pursuit of them": McGehee, "Rough
Times in Rough Places."

198 sketched bare trees and vertical rock walls: Two paintings are reprinted in
Spence, *Expeditions*, vol. 3, 101–2.

198 "the most rugged, and impracticable . . . even in the summertime": JCF to JBF,
January 27, 1849, JBF, *Year of American Travel*, 70.

198 "Even along the river-bottoms . . . tree trunk at zero": Ibid., 71.

199 "For days in succession . . . previous day's work": McGehee, "Rough Times in
Rough Places."

199 "noses, ears, faces, fingers, and feet": Ibid.

199 the only item . . . inexhaustible supply was coffee: Weeks later, when all other
food had run out, Charles Preuss wrote in his diary that they were able to share
"our coffee" with an Indian who offered them food (January 14, 1849, Gudde
and Gudde, *Exploring with Frémont*, 148).

199 starving mules ate the blankets: McGehee, "Rough Times in Rough Places."

199 "Old Bill Williams . . . when we got into camp": Ibid.

199 "pack saddles and packs . . . strewed along": JCF to JBF, January 27, 1849, JBF,
Year of American Travel, 71.

199 "It was impossible to advance . . . inevitable ruin": JCF to JBF, January 27, 1849,
ibid., 71.

200 His story had begun: When she wrote her memoir of her California journey,
she included a reference to Díaz. JBF, *Year of American Travel*, 88.

200 "two or three hundred huts . . . leaves of the palm": Augustus Campbell to his
mother, April 2, 1849, reprinted in Campbell and Campbell, "Crossing the Isthmus of Panama, 1849."

200 "as small as a craft could well be . . . stepping down upon a toy": JBF, *Year of
American Travel*, 45.

200–201 "The scenery is delightful" . . . "cried like a child": Letter reprinted in the *Salem
Register*, May 17, 1849.

201 "The woods are alive with parrots, chattering away like so many demons":
Ibid.

201 "with all the sympathies of his kind nature" . . . "my comfort and security":
JBF, *Year of American Travel*, 14–15.

201 "to see that everything . . . home talk with a lady": Ibid., 49.

201 "being young and strong and a Kentuckian": Ibid., 50.

201 **"when suddenly his eyes . . . from sunstroke"**: Ibid., 51.

201 **doctor at Gorgona:** The name may confuse anyone looking at a modern map of Panama, which includes a Pacific seaside community called New Gorgona but no Gorgona inland on the Chagres River. Nineteenth-century maps of Panama did show such a town, which appears to have vanished later as the landscape was reshaped by the building of the Panama Canal after 1903. One older map is reprinted in Campbell and Campbell, "Crossing the Isthmus of Panama, 1849."

201 **another collection of bamboo huts, surrounding a handful of stone houses:** Augustus Campbell to his mother, April 7, 1849, reprinted in Campbell and Campbell, "Crossing the Isthmus of Panama, 1849."

202 **"There were hundreds . . . hill-slopes"**: JBF, *Year of American Travel*, 51.

202 **"There were many women . . . and already many had died"**: Ibid., 51–52.

202 **"It was more trough than trail"**: Ibid., 52.

202 **"The whole thing . . . in helpless silence"**: Ibid.

203 **"From here I see the jail . . . to make them march about"**: Elizabeth Benton Frémont to Thomas Hart Benton, April 27, 1849, Herr and Spence, *Letters*, 40–41.

203-04 **"is apparently completely in possession of our countrymen" . . . "knocked down by the inevitable hammer"**: Letter from a correspondent in Panama City, dated May 15, 1849, *New York Evening Post*, July 6, 1849.

204 **as Worcester, Massachusetts:** "California Items," *Worcester Palladium*, March 21, 1849.

204 **Charleston, South Carolina:** "News from California," *Milwaukee Sentinel and Gazette*, May 28, 1849.

204 **Tahlequah, the new capital of the relocated Cherokee:** A note of Mrs. Frémont's progress and the illness of her brother-in-law appeared in the *Cherokee Advocate* on May 28, 1849.

204 DREADFUL INTELLIGENCE . . . FREMONT'S PARTY: "Dreadful Intelligence from the Rocky Mountains," *New York Herald*, March 27, 1849.

204 **ate their macaroni and cooked the meat of dead mules:** Frémont still had a little macaroni left on one of his last days before the rescue. JCF to JBF, January 27, 1849, JBF, *Year of American Travel*, 72. Survivor Andrew Cathcart recorded eating mule meat in his letter to C. J. Colville, February 10, 1849. Spence, *Expeditions*, vol. 3, 91.

205 **"A few days were sufficient" . . . "discouraged by misfortune"**: JCF to JBF, January 27, 1849, JBF, *Year of American Travel*, 72.

205 **He had borrowed them from Senator Benton's library:** JCF to JBF, January 27, 1849, JBF, *Year of American Travel*, 73.

205 **Lincoln had read them twice:** Donald, *Lincoln*, 54.

205-06 **"In a sunshiny day . . . till he froze to death"**: JCF to JBF, January 27, 1849, JBF, *Year of American Travel*, 73.

206 **"by Frémont's harsh treatment"**: Richard H. Kern, journal entry, Spence, *Expeditions*, vol. 3, 96.

206 **Around January 8:** Author's calculation. They walked five days for aid before finding an Indian who could help them, and Preuss's diary reports that they finally reached the home of the Indian the morning after that, or January 14.

206 "a magnificent breakfast of corn mush and venison, together with our coffee": Preuss diary entry, January 14, 1849, Gudde and Gudde, *Exploring with Frémont*, 148.

206 a rifle and John's own two blankets . . . "wretchedly poor" horses: JCF to JBF, January 27, 1849, JBF, *Year of American Travel*, 74.

207 "We had to open our eyes . . . skinny and hollow-eyed did they look": Ibid., 149.

207 "entirely lost sight of the purpose of their expedition" . . . straps, gun cases: Ibid.

208 Manuel returned to camp to die: Richard H. Kern, journal entry, January 16, 1849, Spence, *Expeditions*, vol. 3, 96.

208 the men cried: JCF to JBF, January 27, 1849, JBF, *Year of American Travel*, 80.

208 eleven had died: By JCF's count. JCF to JBF, Janaury 27, 1849, JBF, *Year of American Travel*, 78. On his undated notes of the expedition, JCF made an incomplete list of the members of his party, including 11 who are marked with a cross as dead. Spence, *Expeditions*, vol. 3, 52.

208 "a perfect skeleton, snowblind, frostbitten and hardly able to stand": Cathcart to C. J. Colville, February 10, 1849, Spence, *Expeditions*, vol. 3, 91.

209 commander ordered rations distributed to John's men: Richard H. Kern, journal entry, Spence, *Expeditions*, vol. 3, 97.

209-10 "Taos, New Mexico, January 27" . . . "the remembrance of friends": JCF to JBF, January 27, 1849, JBF, *Year of American Travel*, 75–86.

210 they were left to buy their own meals: Richard H. Kern, journal entry, Spence, *Expeditions*, vol. 3, 97.

210 "It will not be necessary . . . already written": JCF to JBF, January 27, 1849, JBF, *Year of American Travel*, 78–79.

210 "friends and strangers . . . my going any farther": Ibid., 81.

210 "my forehead purple . . . anything said to me": JCF to JBF, January 27, 1849, JBF, *Year of American Travel*, 83.

211 combat her "brain-fever": Ibid., 84.

211 "They were an eager, animated set . . . there was no escape": Ibid., 85.

211 One of the men in the tents was Collis P. Huntington: Lavender, *The Great Persuader*, 14.

211 she sat on the barrel of an old brass cannon: JBF, *Year of American Travel*, 85.

211 "The sight of this discouraged . . . go home": Ibid., 86.

211 "Of course I was up" . . . "crib for a lady!": Ibid., 87.

212 less than two weeks in California: Thompson, Gerald, "Edward Fitzgerald Beale and the California Gold Rush," 206.

212 a watch newly encased in gold: Ibid., 207.

212 gold nuggets dangled from the watch chain: Ibid.

212 "I was not advised but ordered to go home": JBF, *Year of American Travel*, 87.

212-13 "In the chronicle of the conquest . . . could name this my saddest": Ibid., 88.

213 more than three hundred passengers: Jessie remembered four hundred, but did not record the number until many years later (JBF, *Year of American Travel*, 88). The author of a letter to the *New York Post*, who traveled on the ship, made a contemporaneous estimate of three hundred after some got off at San Diego. *New York Evening Post*, July 30, 1849.

213 **built with berths for something closer to two hundred:** Each of the steamers built for the Pacific Mail line contained 50 to 60 staterooms and steerage berths for an additional 150 to 200 people. Kemble, "The Genesis of the Pacific Mail Steamship Company," 250.

213 **"throng"** . . . **"was any thing but agreeable":** Unnamed newspaper correspondent, June 20, 1849, *New York Evening Post*, July 30, 1849.

213 **six feet out of the water:** Kemble, "The Genesis of the Pacific Mail Steamship Company," 250.

213 **"equatorial heat"** . . . **"heroism of that adventurer":** Unnamed newspaper correspondent, *New York Evening Post*, July 30, 1849.

214 **"Everybody had a Shakespeare and not much besides":** JBF, *Year of American Travel*, 92.

214 **"No one knows what business has brought him here":** "The Following Is an Extract," *New York Evening Post*, August 14, 1849.

214 **"a low, busy, grating, whispering . . . told me were unusual":** JBF, *Year of American Travel*, 91–92.

214 **Cadwalader Ringgold, took charge:** Ringgold is identified in Steel, *T. Butler King of Georgia*, 73; the story of avoiding the breakers is told in JBF, *Year of American Travel*, 92.

CHAPTER TWELVE: JESSIE BENTON FRÉMONT WAS THE BETTER MAN OF THE TWO

217 **on June 4:** It was said to be an early-morning arrival that day. "Correspondence of the Evening Post," *New York Evening Post*, July 30, 1849.

217 **a new name, San Francisco:** So the letter writer to the New York Post called it in June 1849 (ibid.). It would be formally incorporated as the city of San Francisco in 1850.

217 **"a bleak and meagre frontispiece . . . chilling mist":** JBF, *Year of American Travel*, 97.

217 **"swarmed"** . . . **"Deserted ships of all sorts were swinging with the tide":** Ibid.

217 **They lingered, ate:** "Correspondence of the Evening Post," *New York Evening Post*, July 30, 1849.

218 **"so hard was the work":** Ibid.

218 **"salt pork, tin kettles, tools, and India rubber contrivances":** Ibid.

218 **"The mere landing of the passengers . . . pretty sure not to come back":** JBF, *Year of American Travel*, 98.

218 **"the attacks of innumerable fleas"** . . . **"hills are all alive":** Taylor, *Prose Writings of Bayard Taylor*, 112.

218 **"wooden sheds, mud huts and streets"** . . . **"tin plate":** "Correspondence of the Evening Post," *New York Evening Post*, July 30, 1849.

218 **its crew brought back word that John was alive:** JBF, *Year of American Travel*, 95; Spence, *Expeditions*, vol. 3, xxiii.

219 **"club of wealthy merchants":** JCF, *Year of American Travel*, 100.

219 **"beautiful garden . . . Scotch gardener":** Ibid., 99.

219 **English brand name Broadwood:** Ibid.

219 **"there daily blows a hurricane"**: "Correspoondence of the Evening Post," *New York Evening Post*, July 30, 1849.

219 **"Every man carried his code" ... "in a state of chaos"**: Crosby, *Memoirs of Elisha Oscar Crosby*, 42.

219 **his proclamation called on Californians**: Crotty, "The California Constitutional Convention of 1849."

219–20 **Portsmouth Square ... at three o'clock**: "Large and Enthusiastic Mass Meeting," *Alta California*, June 14, 1849.

219 **a thousand feet from the house**: The Virtual Museum of the City of San Francisco identifies the location of Leidesdorff's former house as the corner of Montgomery and California streets, roughly two-tenths of a mile from Portsmouth Square.

220 **the two military officers who had traveled on the *Panama* were his aides**: Steel, *T. Butler King of Georgia*, 73.

220 **"with his accustomed eloquence and ability"**: "Large and Enthusiastic Mass Meeting," *Alta California*, June 14, 1849.

220 **speakers also included ... William M. Gwin**: Ellison, "Memoirs of Hon. William M. Gwin."

220 **dreamed of returning to Congress as one of California's first United States senators**: So reported a correspondent named Freaner, in the *New York Evening Post*, August 14, 1849. Gwin said he had revealed his goal to Stephen A. Douglas while the two men watched the inauguration of President Taylor in Washington on March 4, 1849 (Ellison, "Memoirs of Hon. William M. Gwin").

220 **"understand the wants and necessities ... patriotism and sacrifices"**: "Correspondence of the Evening Post," *New York Evening Post*, July 30, 1849.

220 **would have been delighted to become governor**: A newspaper report before John's departure named this as his goal ("Intelligence by the Mails," *New York Herald*, April 12, 1848). Once a state government was organized, Jessie wrote that "Mr. Frémont could have been either Governor or first Senator," but that he ultimately chose the Senate for reasons to be later explained (JBF, *Year of American Travel*, 151).

220 **named Fremont Street**: The exact date it was named is not known, but it appeared as the address for a lumberyard in the *Alta California*, May 27, 1850.

220 **"The Grand Californian Lottery"**: "The Grand Californian Lottery," *Alta California*, July 26, 1849.

221 **"whiskey, 4th proof brandy" ... "Penn[sylvania] cheese"**: "New Goods Per Brig Col. Fremont," *Alta California*, July 2, 1849.

221 **"The mosquitoes ... know them by experience"**: JCF to Benjamin D. Wilson, June 1, 1849, Spence, *Expeditions*, vol. 3, 111.

221 **"on my account"**: Ibid.

221 **from mid-February to mid-April**: He reached a California ranch by April 20, 1849. Spence, *Expeditions*, vol. 3, xxxii.

221 **known as Agua Caliente**: JCF to JBF, January 27, 1849, JBF, *Year of American Travel*, 81.

221 **a rancho controlled by an American**: Spence, *Expeditions*, vol. 3, xxxii.

222 **"Some of the Sonorians decide[d] to go ... told them would be found"**: JCF, notes on 1848–9 expedition, undated, Spence, *Expeditions*, vol. 3, 51–52.

222 "I had always intended . . . foothold in it": JCF to Jacob R. Snyder, December 11, 1849, Spence, *Expeditions*, vol. 3, 122.

223 sold to John for three thousand dollars: *Frémont v. United States*, US Supreme Court, 1854.

223 "I had never seen the place" . . . "nothing of its character or value": JCF to Jacob R. Snyder, December 11, 1849, Spence, *Expeditions*, vol. 3, 122.

223 contemplated suing Larkin: Nevins, *Frémont: Pathmarker of the West*, 371; Gates, "The Frémont-Jones Scramble for California Land Claims."

223 making arrangements to build a special traveling coach: JBF, *Year of American Travel*, 118.

223 many soldiers deserted: Crotty, "The California Constitutional Convention of 1849."

223 "long thin young": JBF, *Year of American Travel*, 109.

224 renting the Frémonts one wing of it: Herr, *Jessie Benton Frémont*, 203.

224 window overlooking the bay: JBF, *Year of American Travel*, 154.

224 "my name represented only invasion and defeat": Ibid., 107.

224 "every eatable thing . . . nothing raised": Ibid., 104.

224 arriving on a different ship in late August: Lavender, *The Great Persuader*, 18.

224 hacking down enormous redwood trees: Taylor, *Prose Writings of Bayard Taylor*, 70.

224 "Fleas swarmed there . . . language is spoken": JBF to Lydia Maria Child, July–August 1856, Herr and Spence, *Letters*, 122.

225 helped him obtain equipment and sent him off to Las Mariposas: JBF, *Year of American Travel*, 114.

225 "cook, washer, and ironer" . . . "helpless woman in town": JBF to Lydia Maria Child, July–August 1856, Herr and Spence, *Letters*, 122.

225 four thousand dollars: Ibid.

225 held up his eight-pound lump of gold: Thompson, "Edward Fitzgerald Beale and the California Gold Rush," 207.

225–26 "wearing a sombrero" . . . "keen as a hawk's": Taylor, *Prose Writings of Bayard Taylor*, 69.

226 "the mark of confidence bestowed upon me": Spence, *Expeditions*, vol. 3, 116.

226 "were put for safety under the straw mattress" . . . "trunks in our rooms there": JBF, *Year of American Travel*, 125.

226 "with scrupulous honor . . . their stipulated portion": Ibid., 126.

227 "hundreds—soon becoming thousands—crowded to the same place": JCF to John R. Snyder, December 15, 1849, Spence, *Expeditions*, vol. 3, 120.

227 1,512 . . . 43 women . . . 1,105 miners: United States Census for Mariposa County, 1850.

227 the ship called *Colonel Fremont*: Crotty, "The California Constitutional Convention of 1849."

227 "the culprit hall" . . . "gamblers, convicts, and tipplers": Ibid., 9, 356.

228 Sherman . . . sent as an observer: Sherman and Fellman, *Memoirs*, 85.

228 "a sort of ornamental appendage": Crosby, *Memoirs of Elisha Oscar Crosby*, 39.

228 daily hosting other delegates: Ibid., 46.

228 "The Spaniards . . . with what grace they could": Ibid., 38.

228 "tall and of commanding presence" . . . "dignified expression": Taylor, *Prose Writings of Bayard Taylor*, 157.

228 "carried an enormous bowie knife & was half drunk most of the time": Crosby, *Memoirs of Elisha Oscar Crosby*, 46.

229 "foundation of civilization": Stanley, "Senator William Gwin: Moderate or Racist?"

229 "Gwin, with good grace adopted the clause prohibiting slavery": Crosby, *Memoirs of Elisha Oscar Crosby*, 48.

229 "Neither slavery . . . in this State": Constitution of the State of California (1849), Section 18.

229 "The admission of California . . . every other consideration": Crosby, *Memoirs of Elisha Oscar Crosby*, 41.

229 prohibited the entry of any black people at all: "Further Particulars by the Empire City," *New York Tribune*, quoted in the *Portage Sentinel*, November 19, 1849.

229 "every white male citizen of the United States": Constitution of the State of California (1849), Article II, Section 1.

230 landowning Indians had previously enjoyed the franchise: Rosenus, *General Vallejo and the Advent of the Americans*, 203.

230 the legislature could, by a two-thirds vote, allow voting to select Indians: Constitution of the State of California (1849), Article II, Section 1.

230 "all property" . . . "shall be her separate property": Ibid.

230 by a single vote he was defeated: His biographer thinks Vallejo may have offered this addition to the crowded seal as a kind of joke, but his proposal was defeated by only a single vote. Rosenus, *General Vallejo and the Advent of the Americans*, 204.

230 **William T. Sherman saw him:** Sherman and Fellman, *Memoirs*, 84.

231 showing off samples of gold: Taylor, *Prose Writings of Bayard Taylor*, 110–11.

231 "that I really did not want slaves": JBF, *Year of American Travel*, 144.

231 "was made on the side of free labor . . . crowding into the country": Ibid., 146.

231 "Frémont was a very nice little gentleman . . . intelligent and comprehensive": Crosby, *Memoirs of Elisha Oscar Crosby*, 35.

231 Crosby denied that Jessie had influenced the convention: Ibid.

233 "I was induced to vote for him . . . extreme Southern man": Ibid., 41.

233 "so palpable a cut or insult to the South . . . chance of admission": Ibid., 42.

233 "What we had done in Monterey . . . continue the work": JBF, *Year of American Travel*, 151.

233 "our old home life to be restored": Ibid.

233 "By association" . . . "the two great parties": JCF to Jacob R. Snyder, December 15, 1849, Spence, *Expeditions*, vol. 3, 121.

233 "a central, national railroad" . . . "Asiatic races": Ibid.

234 "The result was entirely satisfactory" . . . "obstacles in the way of the road": Ibid., 122.

234 "The rains set in furiously . . . and heavily on the beach": JBF, *A Year of American Travel*, 154.

234 "tremendous rain" . . . "make him cross the pretty room": Ibid., 159.

235 "When we heard the steamer's gun" . . . "turned the way you wish to go": Ibid., 160.

235 **thinking it might take seven years:** Ibid., 150.
235 **"a timely and excellent donation for this state":** "Proceedings of the Legislature," *Weekly Pacific News,* January 31, 1850.
235 **one hundred volumes in all:** *Journal of the Senate of the State of California,* 1849–50, 96. Journal located by the California State Library, which, as of 2018, still possessed seven of the one hundred books.
235 **"treatise on field fortification":** Ibid.

CHAPTER THIRTEEN: WE THOUGHT MONEY MIGHT COME IN HANDY

239 **It was a Colt revolver:** Foote, *Casket of Reminiscences,* 339.
239 **mass-producing a small, five-shot weapon for civilian use:** Wilson, *Colt,* 42–43.
240 **feared a confrontation with . . . Thomas Hart Benton:** Foote, *Casket of Reminiscences,* 339.
240 **huddled in his cloak:** Peterson, *The Great Triumvirate,* 460.
240 **"great and primary cause" . . . "protecting us":** *Washington Union,* March 5, 1850.
240 **"pick a quarrel for a wicked purpose":** Chambers, *Old Bullion Benton,* 349.
240 **"a degenerate Roman senator":** Ibid., 357.
240 **"the oldest member of the Senate" . . . "calumniators":** "The Compromise Committee," *Weekly National Intelligencer,* April 20, 1850.
241 **"almost every Senator was on his feet":** Ibid.
241 **"I have no pistols! Let him fire! Stand out of the way, and let the assassin fire!":** Ibid.
241 **"locked it in his desk":** Ibid.
241 **to "assassinate" him:** Ibid.
241 **he wrote the United States attorney:** Benton letter to Philip Fendall, "U.S. District Atto," Thomas Hart Benton papers, LOC.
241 **interrupted by shouts from spectators:** *Congressional Globe,* 31st Congress, 1st Session, 115.
242 **"surrender" . . . was a "monster":** Benton, *Mr. Benton's Anti-Compromise Speech.*
242 **"a higher law than the Constitution":** Seward, *Seward at Washington, 1846–61,* 126.
242–43 **"dark and depraved" . . . "a new and powerful Northern party":** *Frederick Douglass' Paper,* April 5, 1850.
243 **"rambles much about the Parisian streets, unattended":** "Louis Napoleon," *North Star,* April 20, 1849.
243 **"were compelled to eat . . . before they became cold":** Ibid.
243 **"Col. Fremont is said to have fallen upon untold riches":** "More About the Californian Convention," *North Star,* November 23, 1849.
243 **his election to the Senate:** "California—the New Constitution," *North Star,* December 14, 1849.
243 **brick house . . . selected for its location:** So said his next-door neighbor Jane Marsh Parker in "Reminiscences of Frederick Douglass."
243 **turn waterwheels and dump waste:** Truesdale, "Historic Main Street Bridge."

243 a single room contained an iron printing press, a desk in the corner, and wooden type cases along the walls: Photo of Douglass's office, undated, Rochester Public Library, Local History and Genealogy Division.

243 Aided by an assistant and sometimes by his young daughter and son: Horace McGuire, "Two Episodes of Anti-Slavery Days."

244 "Colored newspapers ... are sometimes objected to" ... "professors and editors": "Colored Newspapers," *North Star,* January 7, 1848.

244 "volunteered in aid of the inhuman man-stealer": Ibid.

244 "the doctrine of NO UNION" ... "otherwise happy republic": Ibid.

244 Mary Hallowell, Maria E. Wilbur, Mary M'Clintock, and Amy Post: Ibid.

245 "gentlemen present in favor of the movement": Report of the Woman's Rights Convention, July 19 and 20, 1848.

245 "Anxiety was manifest" ... "nearly drowned them": "Woman's Rights Convention," *Frederick Douglass' Paper,* August 11, 1848.

245 "the omnipotency of right": Ibid.

245 "the faith ... the point of the bayonet": "The Southern Caucus," *Frederick Douglass' Paper,* January 12, 1849.

245 "it is the imperative duty of the Southern States ... at all hazards and to the last extremity": "Movements at the South on the Slavery Question," *Frederick Douglass' Paper,* January 19, 1849.

245 almost five whole columns: "Mr. Calhoun's Manifesto," *Frederick Douglass' Paper,* February 9, 1849.

245–46 "Those who cared nothing for the slave ... inheritance of the nation": Douglass, *Life and Times of Frederick Douglass,* 256.

246 "was hardly dry on the page ... to keep it alive and vigorous": Ibid., 255.

246 September 10, 1850, William M. Gwin presented his credentials: *Senate Journal,* September 10, 1850, 616.

246 His term was to end on March 3, 1851: Bigelow, *Memoir of the Life and Public Services of John Charles Fremont,* 409.

246 "Since the mission of Him who came into the world" ... "the real El Dorado": James Rhoads, "Colonel Frémont," *Sartain's Union Magazine of Literature and Art* 7 (October 1850): 241.

247 "F. Hultmann" ... loaned "Lieutenant Colonel J.C. Frémont" some $19,500: *Senate Journal,* January 13, 1851, 80.

247 actually spelled Huttmann: Spence, *Expeditions,* vol. 3, 349fn.

247 "Any slave" ... "liberated and free": Senate Bill 226, 31st Congress, Section 1.

247 "to run away from his, her, or their owner or lawful possessor": *Senate Journal,* September 14, 1850, 632.

247 "to prohibit the coming of free negroes to reside": Ibid., 633.

247 "the mustering of colored men into the service of the country": Dodson appealed to Congress for compensation in 1856. "Congress," *Daily National Intelligencer,* April 16, 1856.

247 John voted along with them: *Senate Journal,* September 12, 1850, 627.

248 because John faced reelection first, he would introduce the necessary legislation: Ellison, "Memoirs of Hon. William M. Gwin."

248 Foote struck him in the face: Foote, *Casket of Reminiscences,* 341.

248 "to preserve peace with the Indian tribes ... gold-mine districts": *Senate Journal*, September 11, 1850, 622.

249 "In California ... the strong hand alone": Bigelow, *Memoir of the Life and Public Services of John Charles Fremont*, 413.

249 "there has been no continuous effective policy" ... "white man": JCF, *Memoirs of My Life*, 27.

249 "moneyed capital" ... "courage and industry": JCF, "Address to the People of California," reprinted in *New York Evening Post*, February 14, 1851.

249 "shall have the authority to grant permits to American citizens": Senate Bill 343, 31st Congress, 1st session, 1.

250 "All our American population ... by foreigners": Ibid., 1366.

250 the first proposals to ban foreigners from the mines: Kanazawa, "Immigration, Exclusion, and Taxation."

250 tax that applied only to foreigners: Ibid.; Crosby, *Memoirs of Elisha Oscar Crosby*, 47.

250 "civilized Indians and inferior castes": *Congressional Globe*, September 24, 1850, 31st Congress, 1st Session, 1366.

250 "This brought into California ... to the exclusion of Americans": Ibid.

250 "not taking ... stipulated portion": JBF, *Year of American Travel*, 126.

251 "More than half ... born aliens": *Congressional Globe*, September 24, 1850, 31st Congress, 1st Session, 1366.

251 "presidential aspirant" ... "of foreign birth": Ibid.

251 numerous states in the nineteenth century allowed noncitizen residents to vote: Lyman, in "Our Inequalities of Suffrage" in 1887, lists Alabama, Arkansas, Colorado, Florida, Georgia, Indiana, Iowa, Kansas, Louisiana, Michigan, Minnesota, Missouri, Nebraska, North Carolina, Oregon, Texas, and Wisconsin. These states had various residency requirements of up to one year, and some excluded "paupers" from the vote, but did not require US citizenship (p. 306).

251 "they were voters in Wisconsin ... blast all their hopes": *Congressional Globe*, September 24, 1850, 31st Congress, 1st Session, 1366.

251 "I think Mexicans are a miserable people ... from the mines": Ibid.

251–52 "We know nothing" ... "gets all the gold": Ibid.

252 "But we do not want them at all": Ibid.

252 "persons from Europe who produce testimonials of good character": Ibid.

252 November 21 they were gliding through the Golden Gate: Herr, *Jessie Benton Frémont*, 219.

252 "over seven hundred paces" ... "good, long paces at that": "Long Wharf," *Alta California*, October 15, 1851.

252 grown ill on the voyage: Bigelow, *Memoir of the Life and Public Services of John Charles Fremont*, 428.

252–53 12,625 residents in San Francisco County: All census figures were reprinted by the *Sacramento Transcript*, October 31, 1850, and January 3, 1851.

253 take a house on Stockton Street: JBF and F. P. Frémont, *Great Events in the Life of Major General John C. Frémont*, 157.

253 capitalized at one million dollars: Spence, *Expeditions*, vol. 3, xlvi–xlvii.

253–54 **"Col. Frémont is now sojourning at San Jose"... "mingling freely with the members":** Untitled item, *Sacramento Transcript,* January 11, 1851; "San Jose Intelligence," *Alta California,* January 12, 1851.

254 **He was shocked:** So he seemed in his address "To the People of California," reprinted in *New York Evening Post,* February 14, 1851.

254 **the Frémonts would suggest that his opposition to slavery had caused his political trouble:** As in John's letter to Charles D. Robinson, reprinted in the *Washington Star,* April 10, 1856.

254 **in favor of slavery and tied to Southern interests:** Stanley, "Senator William Gwin: Moderate or Racist?"

254 **"If this bill passes"... "no pleasant residence for them":** "Frémont's Land Bill," *California Courier,* November 15, 1850. A rival newspaper, the *Alta California,* identified it as a Whig paper started by new arrivals.

254 **"senseless.... Fremont to the Senate":** Ibid.

254 **"we are not at all sorry":** "The News from the States," *Alta California,* November 30, 1850.

255 **"has been condemned in general terms for excluding foreigners":** JCF, "To the People of California," reprinted in *New York Evening Post,* February 14, 1851.

255 **"your delegation"... "held responsible":** Ibid.

255 **"sallow emigrants" from:** *Stockton Times,* November 16, 1850, quoted in Spence, *Expeditions,* vol. 3, xxxvii.

255 **"a tax upon American citizens to work in the mines":** "The Mining Bill," *Sacramento Transcript,* December 13, 1850.

255 **"Our people are already taxed enough":** Ibid.

255 **"the talented, urbane, and unsullied Fremont":** "Our San Jose Correspondence," *Daily Pacific News,* January 13, 1851.

255 **"I hope you will be at San Jose in time for the election":** JCF to Abel Stearns, December 1, 1850, Spence, *Expeditions,* vol. 3, 212.

255 **"the good things, which nourish and make glad the physical nature of man":** "Festive Entertainments at the Capital," *Daily Index* (Sacramento), February 20, 1851.

255 **a banquet thrown by one of John's Senate rivals:** Ibid.

256 **"suggested as a mode of getting along... 21st ballot":** "Proceedings of the Joint Convention," *Alta California,* February 21, 1851.

256 **"to sustain the nominee until the present Legislature ceases to exist":** "Arrival of the Columbia!" *Alta California,* February 24, 1851.

256 **"In Missouri, Mr. Geyer has been elected in place of Mr. Benton":** "United States Senators," *Sacramento Transcript,* March 6, 1851.

257 **offer to buy an immense rancho:** JCF to Abel Stearns, April 24, 1851, Spence, *Expeditions,* vol. 3, 224.

257 **"olives figs & grapes, as well as peaches & apricots":** JBF to Francis Blair, April 11, 1851, Herr and Spence, *Letters,* 43.

257 **an orchard in what would become the city's Mission District:** Spence, *Expeditions,* vol. 3, lxxi; JCF to Abel Stearns, December 12, 1851, ibid., 287.

257 **He had assigned seventeen leases:** Spence, *Expeditions,* vol. 3, xlv.

257 **"Mr. Frémont has had heavy losses in his gold experiments":** JBF to Francis Blair, August 14, 1851, Herr and Spence, *Letters*, 47.

258 **"Will you please write to Mr. Hoffman . . . a myth":** JBF to Charles F. Mayer, August 1, 1851, ibid., 44.

258 **cast suspicion on one another:** Hoffman sent Frémont a news clipping in which one agent, Thomas Denny Sargent, took out an advertisement saying Hoffman's leases after a certain date were "void" and "fraudulent." Spence, *Expeditions*, vol. 3, 289.

258 **"I have not been injured in body or mind":** Ibid., 85.

259 **anyone with a British accent was suspected of being a convict:** JBF and F. P. Frémont, *Great Events in the Life of Major General John C. Frémont*, 156.

259 **"said to be a Sydney man":** "Arrest of a Robber!" *Alta California*, June 11, 1851, 2.

259 **"pretty severe drubbing":** Ibid.

259 **"Committee of Vigilance" . . . "a dozen willing hands":** Ibid.

259 **"immediately ran him up":** Ibid.

259 **"swinging in the night air":** Ibid.

259 **"I was present when a man was hung" . . . "hold of the rope":** "Coroner's Inquest," *Alta California*, June 13, 1851.

260 **"I know that the sympathy . . . dear little boy":** JBF to Evey Heap, March 14, 1851. Herr and Spence, *Letters*, 41.

260 **Flames shot out of the windows of Baker and Messerve:** "The Fire of Yesterday," *Alta California*, May 5, 1851, 2.

260 **"Who could see the end?" . . . "raged and roared":** JBF and F. P. Frémont, *Great Events in the Life of Major General John C. Frémont*, 156–57.

260 **saved one million dollars' . . . by throwing it down a well:** "The Fire of Yesterday," *Alta California*, May 5.

260 **"burned like a furnace . . . headlong into the street":** "Reflections After the Event," *Alta California*, May 6, 1851.

260 **"I could not trust the man, but I did trust the child":** JBF and F. P. Frémont, *Great Events in the Life of Major General John C. Frémont*, 158.

261 **"I in my turn watched from that window the burning of my home":** Ibid., 159.

261 **English immigrants . . . build houses and a brewery:** Ibid., 156.

261 **"mirrors, china and glass . . . all our clothing":** Ibid., 160.

261 **with "cool method":** Ibid.

261 **"We thought money might . . . rent in advance":** Ibid.

261 **"silver and some gold":** Ibid.

261 **by "public ill-will":** Ibid.

CHAPTER FOURTEEN: ALL THE STUPID LAURELS
THAT EVER GREW

263 **"even in this month of August" . . . "this country just now":** JBF to Francis Blair, August 14, 1851, Herr and Spence, *Letters*, 45–46.

264 **"be in power":** Ibid.

264 **told it was time for their first real vacation:** Phillips, *Jessie Benton Frémont*, 178.

264 neither of the Frémonts had the patience to read all that he wrote them: When she finally met Hoffman in 1852, he asked her, "Have you read [my] letter?" Jessie answered, "Oh no! It's too long." Hoffman to JCF, April 29, 1852, Spence, *Expeditions*, vol. 3, 355.

264 "The mail has this moment arrived . . . is astounded": Hoffman to JCF, December 16, 1851, ibid., 289.

264 "not adapted to such business . . . business to which he is adapted": Spence, "David Hoffman: Frémont's Mariposa Agent in London."

265 "extensive frauds were about to be perpetrated in Europe": The *Daily Stockton Journal* allegations were reprinted in the *New York Evening Post*, February 28, 1851.

265 On February 1, 1852 . . . Panama: The *Alta California* of February 1, 1852, names John among the passengers on a ship departing San Francisco, reprinted in *New York Evening Post*, February, 28, 1851.

265 wrapped in a tablecloth and slung onto the back of a porter: JBF, *Souvenirs of My Time*, 210–11.

265 a ship called the *Africa*: Ibid., 213.

265 2.5 million people: Great Britain Historical Geographic Information System (GB Historical GIS), "A Vision of Britain Through Time."

265 "a great relief" . . . "remove the ugly suspicions": "Great Britain," *New York Times*, April 19, 1852.

265 "chintz and flowers and wood fire": JBF, *Souvenirs of My Time*, 213.

265 "becomes a millionaire fresh from California": "Great Britain," *New York Times*, April 19, 1852.

265 April 1850 to late 1851, a lecturer in London had premiered an art display on the explorations: Spence, "David Hoffman: Frémont's Mariposa Agent in London."

266 350,000 people . . . women's publications: Ibid.

266 "The leaders of fashion are ever on the watch for every fresh celebrity": "Great Britain," *New York Times*, April 19, 1852.

266 reception of the Duchess of Derby: Ibid.

266 shook the hand of the aged Duke of Wellington: JBF, *Souvenirs of My Time*, 216.

266 leader of the Barings banking house . . . Royal Geographical Society: Ibid., 217.

266 dressed in a gown of pink satin with blond lace: Ibid., 218.

266 policemen arrested John: Herr, *Jessie Benton Frémont*, 228.

266 "sponging house" . . . "ante-room to the jail": JCF to Thomas Hart Benton, April 13, 1852, Spence, *Expeditions*, vol. 3, 351.

267 "My husband is arrested" . . . "You are a great rascal" . . . "My father says so": All dialogue is from Hoffman to JCF, April 29, 1852. Spence, *Expeditions*, vol. 3, 354–59.

268 "The arrest, from all accounts, was outrageous": (*New York*) *Evening Mirror*, reprinted in *State Capital Reporter* (Concord, NH), May 4, 1852.

268 "I have reason to believe" . . . "my patriotism has been oozing out for the last five years": JCF to Thomas Hart Benton, April 13, 1852, Spence, *Expeditions*, vol. 3, 351.

268 "help pay expenses": Ibid.

268 **"a short, thick-set man"** . . . **"swaggering air of pretension":** "Uncle Tom's Cabin," *National Era,* June 5, 1851.

269 **UNCLE TOM'S CABIN:** Ibid.

269 **secretly coordinated a women's campaign in defense of Cherokee Indians:** Hershberger, "Mobilizing Women, Anticipating Abolition." 15–40.

269 **seemed to have been loosely based on earlier works:** One useful exploration of the book's sources is found in Nichols, "The Origins of Uncle Tom's Cabin."

269 **first edition sold out in four days:** Levine, "Uncle Tom's Cabin in Frederick Douglass' Paper."

269 **"The [book] has not yet reached us"** . . . **"we are not surprised at the delay":** Ibid.

269 **"rise up a host of enemies against the fearful system of slavery":** Ibid.

270 **he traveled from Rochester to Andover, Massachusetts:** Douglass, *Life and Times of Frederick Douglass,* 247.

270 **"as to what can be done"** . . . **"I am for no fancied . . . fair play":** Ibid., 247–49.

270 **"Exodus of the Jews from Egypt":** Delany, *Condition, Elevation, Emigration and Destiny of the Colored People of the United States,* 175.

270 **"The truth is, dear madam, we are here, and we are likely to remain":** Douglass, *Life and Times of Frederick Douglass,* 250.

270 **"an encouraging sign of the times":** "General Winfield Scott," *Frederick Douglass' Paper,* June 24, 1852.

270 **"destruction is necessary to the abolition of slavery":** Ibid.

270 **"new and powerful Northern party":** "Oath to Support the Constitution," *Frederick Douglass' Paper,* April 5, 1850.

270–71 **Douglass . . . held the floor:** Marshall, "The Free Democratic Convention of 1852."

271 **"Free soil, free speech, free labor, and free men!":** Ibid.

271 **"cordial welcome":** Ibid.

271 **easy path to citizenship:** Ibid.

271 **"a sin against God . . . make right":** Ibid.

271 **"I should dissolve the Union . . . a year to Congress":** JBF to Elizabeth Blair Lee, November 14, 1851, Herr and Spence, *Letters,* 52.

271 **"frenzy for building and speculating in city property":** JBF, *Souvenirs of My Time,* 254.

271–72 **"Give instructions . . . have to perform":** Lord Dundonald to JCF, July 2, 1852, Frémont papers, LOC.

272 **former Senate colleague:** JCF to William Gwin, December 20, 1852; JCF to P. G. Washington, July 11, 1853, Spence, *Expeditions,* vol. 3, 364, 374–75.

272 **John wrote Gwin a letter of thanks:** JCF to William Gwin, December 20, 1852, ibid., 364–65.

272 **"My counsel promised me the ratification . . . last several mails":** Ibid.

272 **the land commission confirmed John's title:** *Frémont v. United States,* 58 US 17, 1854.

272–73 **"Above every other consideration . . . I had been so long engaged":** JCF writing in *The American Journal of Science and Arts,* May 1854, reprinted in Spence, *Expeditions,* vol. 3, 381.

273 **midnight on June 16:** "Three Days Later from Europe," *New York Times*, June 16, 1853.

273 **a vast octagon:** "The Crystal Palace-Plan of the Interior," *New York Times*, July 15, 1853.

273 **fifty-cent admission . . . ten-dollar season tickets:** "Crystal Palace," *New York Herald*, August 22, 1853.

273 **"impossible to mistake" . . . "utilitarian characteristics":** "The Crystal Palace Opened to the Public," *New York Herald*, July 16, 1853.

273 **"Morse's patent electric telegraph apparatus in operation":** Association for the Exhibition of the Industry of All Nations, *Official Catalogue of the New-York Exhibition of the Industry of All Nations*, 50.

273 **a "printing telegraph":** Ibid.

273 **"while we . . . that ever shadowed American soil":** "Opening of the Crystal Palace," *New York Times*, July 14, 1853.

274 **a proposal that the United States should purchase Cuba:** "Cuba, Mexico, and the Spanish-American Republics," *New York Herald*, August 22, 1853.

274 **IS THE WHIG PARTY DEAD?:** Ibid., 3.

274 **"still attractive at the National . . . as full as ever":** Ibid., 4.

274 **studio on Broadway:** Spence, *Expeditions*, vol. 3, 403.

274 **carefully coiffed hair and a fringe of beard:** Carvalho portrait, LOC collection, reprinted in ibid., 374.

274 **founding the first Reform Jewish synagogue in the United States:** Elzas, *The Reformed Society of Israelites of Charleston*, 21.

274 **"A half hour previously" . . . "under similar circumstances":** Carvalho, *With Frémont*, reprinted in Spence, *Expeditions*, vol. 3, 383.

275 **"from freezing point to thirty degrees below zero":** Ibid., 385.

275 **dressed like white people . . . written laws:** Connelley, *The Provisional Government of Nebraska Territory*, x, 1–3.

275 **leading the movement to organize Nebraska Territory:** Ibid., 30–32.

275 **electing one of their own as a provisional governor:** He was William Walker, identified in newspaper reports as a Wyandot of mixed race. "A St. Louis Paper," *New York Spiritual Telegraph*, October 8, 1853.

275 **opposed by men linked with Senator David Atchison:** Connelley, *The Provisional Government of Nebraska Territory*, 32.

276 **pay the Indians two dollars per day:** Spence, *Expeditions*, vol. 3, 382.

276 **no one . . . should talk with reporters . . . keep a journal:** Ibid., liv.

276 **pain so intense that it spread to his chest, throat, and head:** JBF to Elizabeth Blair Lee, October 14, 1853, Herr and Spence, *Letters*, 53–54.

276 **in "undefined dread":** Ibid.

276 **"soothed the pain" . . . "'on his legs'":** Ibid.

277 **report suggesting he had already abandoned it:** *New York Spiritual Telegraph*, citing the *Washington Star*, October 8, 1853.

277 **"I can't say I am satisfied" . . . "anxieties to me":** Ibid.

277 **"a horrid, lurid glare, all along the horizon":** Carvalho, *With Frémont*, reprinted in Spence, *Expeditions*, vol. 3, 410.

277 **as "my journal":** Carvalho, undated letter, *With Frémont*, reprinted in ibid., 400.

277 **"with a decayed trunk on his shoulder"**: Carvalho, *With Frémont*, reprinted in ibid., 457.

278 **"We generally slept double . . . weight of the snow resting on me"**: Ibid., 388.

278 **"in a voice tremulous with emotion"**: Ibid., 427.

278 **on December 14, they reached their objective**: JCF to Thomas Hart Benton, February 9, 1854, Spence, *Expeditions*, vol. 3, 466.

279 **"Col. Frémont put out his hand . . . many more miles of travel"**: Carvalho, *With Frémont*, reprinted in Spence, ed., *Expeditions*, vol. 3, 455.

279 **"occultation" . . . "for hours"**: Ibid., 458.

280 **"That is not the point" . . . "how we can do it"**: Ibid.

280 **It was February 8, 1854**: Ibid., 464.

280 **a town of about four hundred**: JCF to Thomas Hart Benton, February 9, 1854, ibid., 471.

280 **only three years old**: Ibid.

280 **"the Delawares all came in sound . . . more or less frost-bitten"**: Ibid., 470.

280 **"three beautiful children . . . restored to embrace my own"**: Carvalho, *With Frémont*, reprinted in Spence, *Expeditions*, vol. 3, 463.

280 **pay with drafts against Palmer, Cook and Company**: Ibid., 469.

280 **Almon Babbitt . . . secretary and treasurer of Utah Territory**: John referred to him in a letter as "Mr. Babbitt, Secretary of the Territory" (JCF to Thomas Hart Benton, February 8, 1854, ibid., 469). His full name appears in various sources including Herr and Spence, *Letters*, 570.

281 **"the alternative of continuing on foot"**: JCF to Thomas Hart Benton, February 9, 1854, Spence, *Expeditions*, vol. 3, 468.

281 **"mental and moral greatness" . . . "the residence of freemen"**: Crafts, *An Oration, Delivered in St. Michael's Church*, 5–6.

281 **"well and so hearty that [I am] actually some 14 pounds heavier than ever before"**: JCF to *Alta California*, April 21, 1854, Spence, *Expeditions*, vol. 3, 474.

CHAPTER FIFTEEN: DECIDEDLY, THIS OUGHT TO BE STRUCK OUT

283 **"In midwinter, without any reason" . . . "Frémont and his party"**: JBF, *Far-West Sketches*, 30.

283 **"When I have no more anxious thoughts pressing on my heart it will not ache"**: JBF to Elizabeth Blair Lee, spring 1854, Herr and Spence, *Letters*, 58.

284 **reported to the Senate on January 4, 1854**: *Senate Journal*, January 4, 1854, 77.

284 **"measure of peace and compromise"**: *Washington Union*, January 8, 1854.

284 **"manly, noble or independent" . . . "honors and distinction"**: The *Tribune* article was reprinted in "The Nebraska Bill—Abolitionism," *Washington Union*, January 14, 1854.

284 **"willing to tolerate slavery" . . . "excluded"**: Douglass, *Life and Times of Frederick Douglass*, 256.

284 **"a broad belt of heavy timber" . . . "the richest verdure"**: JCF, *Report of an Expedition*, reprinted in Jackson and Spence, *Expeditions*, vol. 1, 172.

285 **"the peace of the country"**: Chambers, *Old Bullion Benton*, 401–2.

285 hiring a private express company instead: Ibid., 405.

285 "I am heart-sick being here" . . . "is very outspoken": Seward, *Seward at Washington 1846–61*, 216–17.

285 "Safety had come to him . . . his previous work": JBF and F. P. Frémont, *Great Events in the Life of Major General John C. Frémont*, 186.

286 "forget he has lots of wives": JBF to Francis Preston Blair, April 13, 1854, Herr and Spence, *Letters*, 58.

286 Babbitt, a Democrat: Harmon, Huefner, and Young, "Almon W. Babbitt, Joseph E. Johnson, and the Western Bugle."

286 "deprived of her companionship": JBF, *Year of American Travel*, 43.

286 "How great a loss this was . . . those who knew her": Ibid.

286 a "primary election": Chambers, *Old Bullion Benton*, 406.

286–87 "a riot was then taking place": "Telegraphic" news column, *Washington Sentinel*, August 10, 1854.

287 riot had started on election day: Primm, *Lion of the Valley*, 170.

287 at eleven o'clock in the morning: Benton gave the time in a card published in the *Washington Union*, February 28, 1855.

287 "standing in the crowd, looking, with others, on the blazing roof of his dwelling": "Fire," *Washington Sentinel*, February 28, 1855.

287 Jessie stood with him: JBF, *Souvenirs of My Time*, 105.

287 later froze in a hose: "The Late Fire," *Washington Sentinel*, March 1, 1855; JBF, "Some Account of the Plates," in JCF, *Memoirs of My Life*, xxi.

288 a looking glass sailed out of a third-floor window: "The Destruction of Colonel Benton's House," *Washington Sentinel*, February 28, 1855.

288 "Neither of us had slept" . . . "can talk after a calamity": JBF, "Some Account of the Plates," in JCF, *Memoirs of My Life*, xxi.

288 "It is well, there is less to leave now—this has made death more easy": Ibid.

288 "considerable rejoicing among the land claimants": "Later from California," *Evening Star* (Washington DC), April 24, 1855.

288 Mrs. Edward Carrington of Botecourt: "Mount Vernon Central Association," *Alexandria Gazette*, January 27, 1855.

288–89 onetime student . . . to practice law: Miller, "VMI Men Who Wore Yankee Blue, 1861–1865."

289 "indiscriminate immigration" . . . "American history and of their duties": Jessie attributes all ideas here to John in JBF and F. P. Frémont, *Great Events in the Life of Major General John C. Frémont*, 192.

289 in the country twenty-one years: The idea had been part of nativist discourse for many years; in 1844 the publisher of the *Boston Courier* endorsed it in a signed editorial. "Native Americans!," *Boston Courier*, October 31, 1844.

289 "he was a member of the Native American party": Ibid.

289 "It was a serious enterprise. . . . under twenty-one years of age": JCF, *Report of an Exploring Expedition*. Reprinted in Jackson and Spence, *Expeditions*, vol. 1, 575.

289 "making an offer" . . . "Democratic candidate for the Presidency": JBF and F. P. Frémont, *Great Events in the Life of Major General John C. Frémont*, 193.

290 Entry-level members . . . were not even told the name: Desmond, *The Know-Nothing Party*, 46.

290 **Order of Know-Nothings:** It is said that Horace Greeley's *Tribune* coined the term in December 1853, but some papers can be found that used the phrase earlier, deploying it without explanation as if it was already commonly understood; one example was the *Democrat and Sentinel,* September 2, 1853.

290 **"remove all foreigners, aliens or Roman Catholics from office":** Desmond, *The Know-Nothing Party,* 55.

290 **losing more than they gained:** Although no polling existed to prove it, the analyses that reach this conclusion include Sacher, "The Sudden Collapse of the Louisiana Whig Party."

290 **the Wide-Awakes:** Desmond, *The Know-Nothing Party,* 77.

290 **five thousand of them escorted an anti-Catholic preacher:** Ibid.

291 **burned in Maine:** Ibid., 75.

291 **stole a block of marble:** Ibid., 76.

291–92 **"That is a disputed point" . . . "base alloy of hypocrisy":** Abraham Lincoln to Joshua Speed, August 24, 1855, Fehrenbacher, *Abraham Lincoln: Speeches and Writings, 1832–1858,* 363.

292 **John B. Floyd . . . William Preston:** Jessie identified Floyd as a supporter in *Great Events in the Life of Major General John C. Frémont,* 192. Elizabeth Frémont identified Preston in *Recollections of Elizabeth Benton Frémont,* 75.

292 **In the summer of 1855, Floyd:** Elizabeth Benton Frémont indicates that this meeting took place shortly before John met with Jessie in Nantucket; Jessie's letters show that she was there in the summer of 1855 and John arrived there in August (Elizabeth Benton Frémont, *Recollections,* 75).

292 **Democrats met John . . . at the St. Nicholas:** JBF and F. P. Frémont, *Great Events in the Life of Major General John C. Frémont,* 193.

292 **"profusion of mirrors" . . . "Eastern prince":** William E. Baxter, who stayed at the St. Nicholas in 1853, quoted in Steen, "Palaces for Travelers," 275.

292 **velvet-pile carpets . . . marble tables:** Ibid.

292 **repeal of the Missouri Compromise:** The substance of this meeting is described by Jessie and Lily, neither of whom were present themselves. Jessie named the Fugitive Slave Act as the price for the Democrats' support, but seemed also to allude to the Compromise. Lily described a proposal to "permit alternate states to come into the Union as free and slave states," which was functionally what the Compromise repeal could allow. No matter what precisely was said, no Democrat could have won support in the South without supporting the repeal (Elizabeth Benton Frémont, *Recollections,* 75).

292 **"impossible . . . to accept":** JBF and F. P. Frémont, *Great Events in the Life of Major General John C. Frémont,* 193.

293 **"I . . . considered him very light metal . . . governed him were Abolition":** In a letter published in newspapers, Floyd denied that any such meeting had taken place, but then described his own participation in the meeting; apparently his disingenuous denial was limited to the way others had described it. "Gov. Floyd and Col. Frémont," *New York Times,* September 15, 1856.

293 **the conference failed:** JBF and F. P. Frémont, *Great Events in the Life of Major General John C. Frémont,* 193.

294 **"old sailors and whaling captains"** . . . **"whaling in their turn":** JBF to Elizabeth Blair Lee, August 17, 1855, Herr and Spence, *Letters,* 59–61.
294 **"I shall not begin to tell you how forlornly lonesome this island is":** Ibid.
294 **"'strong-minded' speech making woman":** Ibid.
294 **key politicos who had met in Philadelphia:** Bartlett, *John C. Frémont and the Republican Party,* 15.
294–95 **"My dear Mr. Blair . . . to promise your assistance":** JBF to Francis P. Blair, August 27, 1855, Herr and Spence, *Letters,* 71.
295 **drafting a platform of ideas:** Gienapp, *Origins of the Republican Party,* 322.
295 **"a little old gentleman"** . . . **"hat too big for his head":** Murat Halstead, quoted in Smith, *Francis Preston Blair,* 229.
295 **"The storms of faction beat around him"** . . . **"honor and eternal truth":** *Washington Globe,* May 10, 1832, quoted in Smith, "Francis P. Blair and the Globe."
296 **"I am told to tell you** . . . **your own library":** Ibid., 75.
296 **"I thank you from the bottom"** . . . **"may not be fully aware of":** Bradford R. Moore to Francis P. Blair, December 11, 1855, Blair Papers, LOC.
296 **a single article about John Charles Frémont:** Smith, *Francis Preston Blair,* 220.
296 **He drew Bigelow into the circle** . . . **members such as Thurlow Weed:** Gienapp, *Origins of the Republican Party,* 321–2. This interpretation seems most plausible, although half a century later Bigelow published an account that claimed a movement in the opposite direction, in which he drew Blair into the contest (Bigelow, *Retrospections of an Active Life,* vol. 1, 143).
297 **"water, fire, and gas all over":** JBF to Blair, November 3, 1855, Herr and Spence, *Letters,* 73–74.
297 **having the images developed:** JBF, "Some Account of the Plates," in JCF, *Memoirs of My Life,* xvi.
297 **the son of Irish immigrants:** R. Wilson, *Mathew Brady,* 6.
298 **he was introduced to** . . . **Morse:** Ibid., 10.
298 **weathered and strong** . . . **hidden:** The image of JCF is in the collection of the National Portrait Gallery.
298 **Seward had been supportive of Catholics and immigrants:** Bartlett, *John C. Frémont and the Republican Party,* 13–14.
298 **he must wait until 1860:** Gienapp, *Origins of the Republican Party,* 310.
298 **"a candidate must have a slim record in these times":** Ibid., 324.
299 **"Buchanan and his wife":** Baker, *James Buchanan,* 25.
299 **"obliged to apply to Mrs. Frémont** . . . **parentage":** Bigelow, *Retrospections of an Active Life,* vol. 1, 143.
299 **She traveled to Virginia:** JBF to Elizabeth Blair Lee, Herr and Spence, *Letters,* 112–13.
300 **"repulsive"** . . . **false claim that Anne divorced and remarried:** Bigelow, *Memoirs of the Life and Public Services of John Charles Fremont,* 20–21.
300 **"Her account of the colonel's origin** . . . **purpose very well":** Bigelow, *Retrospections of an Active Life,* vol. 1, 143.
300 **"Will Mr. Upham let my alterations** . . . **sober judgment on Mr. Frémont's":** JBF to Charles Upham, May 31, 1856, Herr and Spence, *Letters,* 102.

300 **did not directly mention that it was an elopement:** Upham, *Life, Explorations and Public Services of John Charles Frémont*, 20.

300-01 **"our friends ... to the Col. [on] 9th Street":** Isaac Sherman to Charles Upham, June 2, 1856, Hugh Upham Clark collection, LOC.

301 **"J.B." ... "the second section of the bill":** JBF to Charles Upham, June 24, 1856, Hugh Upham Clark collection, LOC.

301 **"Decidedly, this ought to be struck out":** Ibid.

301 **"This ended my old life" ... "dropped by every relative":** JBF and F. P. Frémont, *Great Events in the Life of Major General John C. Frémont*, 203.

301 **"not adapted to such business":** Spence, "David Hoffman: Frémont's Mariposa Agent in London."

301 **saying it had borne out Benton's vision:** "I congratulate you on this verification of your vision," wrote Frémont to Benton, February 9, 1854. Spence, *Expeditions*, vol. 3, 469–70.

302 **"I do not think I can go to Washington":** JBF to Elizabeth Blair Lee, April 18, 1856, Herr and Spence, *Letters*, 97.

302 **"I have made one thing a fixed resolve ... almost suicide":** Ibid.

302 **"I know both my people too well ... not had a line from him":** Ibid., 97–98.

302 **"a fair occasion":** Ibid., 97.

302 **just caught a train toward Missouri:** JBF to Elizabeth Blair Lee, June 9, 1856, Herr and Spence, *Letters*, 105–6; Herr, *Jessie Benton Frémont*, 250.

303 **Some Missourians wanted profit from real estate:** Andrews, "Kansas Crusade: Eli Thayer and the New England Emigrant Aid Company."

303 **It had been founded by Eli Thayer:** Ibid., 497–99.

303 **Robinson, an agent of the Emigrant Aid Company:** Gienapp, *Origins of the Republican Party*, 171.

303 **sometimes-violent battles over land ownership:** Bancroft, *History of California*, vol. 6, 330; Hurtado, *John Sutter*, 283–84.

303 **"We were defeated then ... your battle with them in Kansas":** JCF to Charles Robinson, reprinted in the *Washington Star*, April 10, 1856.

304 **"complete if it had given ... 'the equality of the races'":** Ibid.

304 **federal authorities arrested ... treason:** "Interesting from Kansas," *New York Herald*, May 23, 1856.

304 **threw its printing press in the Kansas River:** Andrews, "Kansas Crusade."

304 **burned ... the Free State Hotel:** Ibid.

304 **"devastated and burned to ashes by the Border Ruffians":** "The King Is Dead—Live the King," *New York Tribune*, May 26, 1856.

304 **"A few bare and tottering ... of Human Slavery":** Ibid.

305 **"incoherent phrases" ... "truth which he did not make":** Smith, *Francis Preston Blair*, 225.

305 **"hemmed in" ... "insensible on the floor":** "A Canadian Witness of the Assault on Mr. Sumner," *Congregational Herald*, June 5, 1856.

305 **"The telegraph has already spread" ... "incorrect":** "Washington Correspondence," *Charleston Courier*, May 26, 1856.

305 **"was beaten ... Southern men":** Ibid.

305 **"the hearty congratulations . . . the Abolitionist Sumner":** "Public Approval of Mr. Brooks," *Charleston Courier*, May 28, 1856.

306 **"handsome gold headed cane" . . . "chastise Abolitionists":** Ibid.

306 **"the slaves of Columbia" . . . "happiest laborers on the face of the globe":** Ibid.

306 **"chivalrous" . . . "poltroon Senator of Massachusetts":** "Southern Feeling on the Brooks and Sumner Affair," *New York Herald*, June 8, 1856.

306 **Democrats . . . turning to Republicans:** Gienapp, *Origins of the Republican Party*, 302–3.

306 **"Has it come to this . . . do not comport ourselves to please them?":** Ibid, 359.

CHAPTER SIXTEEN: HE THROWS AWAY HIS HEART

309 **On December 11, 1854, Jacob Dodson filed a petition:** *Senate Journal*, December 11, 1854, American State Papers.

309 **John had violated the law . . . enlist:** "Thirty-fourth Congress," *National Intelligencer*, April 16, 1856.

309 **"Jacob Dodson, a colored man" . . . "legally enlisted":** Senate Bill 79, 34th Congress, 1st Session, American State Papers.

309 **"in charge of the retiring rooms":** *New York Tribune*, reprinted in the *Daily Gate City*, September 2, 1865.

309 **Pierce signed the bill:** "A Bill Become a Law," *Washington Globe*, April 23, 1856.

310 **"anti-slavery Know Nothings and nigger worshipers":** "The Great Contest— the Northern Masses Moving for Frémont," *New York Herald*, June 12, 1856.

310 **"corrupt, imbecile and most wretched":** Ibid.

311 **"frighten Adopted Citizens into their net":** "The Free and Earnest Conferences," *New York Tribune*, June 14, 1856.

311 **a letter refusing the nativists:** Nevins, *Frémont: Pathmarker of the West*, 431.

311 **Apollo Rooms . . . birthplace of the New York Philharmonic:** Saerchinger, "Musical Landmarks in New York."

311 **"The dark lanterns . . . wide open to Broadway":** "The George Law Anti-slavery Know-nothing Convention—First Day," *New York Herald*, June 13, 1856.

311 **"a large proportion of sharp, hungry, and calculating politicians" . . . "finger in the pie":** Ibid.

311 **political "wire workers":** Ibid.

311 **thirty thousand dollars in cash payments:** Gienapp, *Origins of the Republican Party*, 330.

311 **Banks would refuse the Know-Nothings:** Various maneuvers in this intricate plan are described to Banks in letters and telegrams in the Nathaniel P. Banks collection, LOC.

311 **"like a farthing candle":** "The George Law Anti-slavery Know-nothing Convention—First Day," *New York Herald*, June 13, 1856.

311 **Messages snapped back and forth:** Some telegrams to Banks in Washington are in the Banks papers, LOC.

312 **"Long before the hour" . . . "able to gain admission":** "The Presidency," *New York Herald*, June 18, 1856.

312 **"the old fellow's big head" . . . "uproarious applause":** Journalist Murat Halstead, quoted in Smith, *Francis Preston Blair*, 229.

312 **"The delegates to this Convention . . . face of the earth":** "The Presidency," *New York Herald*, June 18, 1856.

312 **"received with loud cheering . . . the frontier heroes":** Ibid.

312–13 **"Gentlemen . . . I am opposed to Slavery . . . beyond its present limits":** "The People's Convention," *New York Tribune*, June 17, 1856.

313 **"the principles promulgated in the Declaration of Independence":** 1856 Republican Party platform.

313 **"have been deprived of life" . . . "condign punishment":** Ibid.

313 **"liberty of conscience and equality of rights among citizens":** Gienapp, *Origins of the Republican Party*, 336.

313 **"His three weeks' . . . worthy of imitation":** Upham, *Life, Explorations and Public Services of John Charles Frémont*, 305.

314 **"reputation has been marvelously made within six months for this emergency":** Gienapp, *Origins of the Republican Party*, 341.

314 **"indebted to Fremont . . . relations of the world":** "The Great Contest—the Northern Masses Moving for Fremont," *New York Herald*, June 12, 1856.

314 **"a deep and solemn conviction" . . . "unaccountable":** Halstead, *Trimmers, Trucklers and Temporizers*, 102.

314 **"chasms in logic":** Ibid.

314 **giant American flag bearing the explorer's name:** "The People's Convention," *New York Tribune*, June 19, 1856.

314 **a woodcut portrait of the nominee:** Ibid., 4.

314 **"desperate struggle" . . . "same terms as slaves":** Quoted in the *Western Democrat*, July 15, 1856.

315 **"Free Soil, Free Speech, Free Men and Frémont":** The many places this slogan can be found include the *New York Tribune*, July 11, 1856.

315 **A piece of the iron railing broke off and crashed down:** Abbott, *Reminiscences*, 108–9. The broken balcony is also alluded to in the *New York Times*, August 13, 1856.

315 **"He is cheered so much" . . . "what he is saying":** Abbott, *Reminiscences*, 108–9.

315 **"Mrs. Frémont!" . . . "Give us Jessie!":** Ibid.

315 **"For a lady to make her appearance . . . an innovation":** Ibid.

315 **"Such occasions as this are apt to disconcert ladies":** Ibid.

315 **"a universal shout":** Ibid.

315 **"The crowd are crazy with enthusiasm" . . . "in hand in the air":** Ibid.

315 **"a mere practice to train their voices":** Ibid.

316 **"Young America" . . . "Old Fogyism":** Undated editorial cartoon, Frémont papers, LOC.

316 **"GIVE 'EM JESSIE":** *New York Evening Mirror*, reprinted in *Frederick Douglass' Paper*, July 4, 1856.

316 **"The felicitous double entendre . . . can win over in a month":** Ibid.

317 **"taking away an old man's daughter" . . . "runaway lovers":** Ibid.

317 **The article was reprinted:** *Boston Daily Atlas*, June 27; *National Anti-Slavery Standard*, June 28; *Newark Daily Advertiser*, June 30; *Sentinel of Freedom*, July 1;

Frederick Douglass' Paper, July 4; *Portland Advertiser,* July; (Pennsylvania) *Weekly Miners' Journal,* July 12; *Washington Reporter (Pennsylvania),* July 23.

317 **"Freemen of the North awake! . . . Down with Slavery!":** Cleveland Republican Association, *Fremont and Dayton Campaign Songs for 1856,* 11, Fremont papers, LOC.

317 **"Oh Jessie is a sweet bright lady":** Ibid., 6.

317 **Women in some cities . . . gather to sing:** One such organization, in Fall River, Massachusetts, was described in the *Boston Evening Transcript,* July 19, 1856. Another, in New York, was described scornfully in the *Charleston Courier,* September 17, 1856.

317 **"Fire away, my gallant lads . . . 'give him Jessie'":** McClure and Hand, *Fremont Song Book,* 17, Frémont papers, LOC.

318 **"Southern lady" . . . institutions:** *Boston Courier,* reprinted in *Frederick Douglass' Paper,* July 4, 1856.

318 **"a new feature in political gatherings":** "Frémont and Freedom in Buffalo," *New York Tribune,* July 11, 1856.

318 **"the presence of some 400 ladies . . . 'our Jessie'":** Ibid.

318 **"attended all the great mass meetings" . . . "Tippecanoe battle ground":** "Female Stump Speaker," *Daily Dispatch,* October 27, 1856.

318 **"We must enlist music and ladies in our cause":** "The Cause in Ohio—the Town of Fremont," *New York Tribune,* July 11, 1856.

318 **"Over the River and Through the Wood":** The original title was "The New England Boy's Song About Thanksgiving Day." Child, *Flowers for Children,* 25.

318 **crediting her mother for her beliefs:** JBF to Lydia Maria Child, July–August 1856, Herr and Spence, *Letters,* 122–23.

319 **"the temper of children" . . . "influences of slavery":** Ibid.

319 **"The enquiry has repeatedly reached . . . your undivided support":** "Frémont and Dayton," *Frederick Douglass' Paper,* July 4, 1856.

319 **"we are Abolitionists . . . that very ground":** Ibid.

319 **"much less can Frémont himself be suspected . . . abolitionism":** Tinelli, *Frémont, Buchanan and Fillmore,* 10.

319 **"If white men were enslaved . . . the Republican party":** Ibid.

319 **"We would rather see this just man made President":** *Frederick Douglass' Paper,* August 15, 1856, reprinted in Douglass, *Speeches and Writings,* 339.

319 **"with whatever influence we possess":** Ibid.

319–20 **"Right Anti-slavery action . . . that particular time":** Ibid.

320 **"abandon a single Anti-Slavery Truth or Principle":** Ibid.

320 **"The present . . . a thousand fold in the future":** "Frémont and Dayton," *Frederick Douglass' Paper,* July 4, 1856.

320 **he had to write a letter of explanation:** Blight, *Frederick Douglass,* 276.

320 **"twenty-five of our leading men":** "Our Alabama Correspondence," *New York Herald,* August 24, 1856.

320 **ten years in prison or hanging:** Ibid.

321 **"kindness" . . . "St. Domingo revolution":** "The Mobile Development," *Richmond Dispatch,* August 27, 1856.

321 **"incendiary"** . . . **"fiendish aim"**: "The Emeute at Mobilei," *New York Herald,* August 24, 1856.

321 **"Let all who follow negro dictation . . . reasons for this course"**: "Reasons of the Negro Douglass for Supporting Frémont," *Star of the North,* September 24, 1856.

321 **"Frederick Douglass supports Fremont" . . . "crew supports Fremont"**: "Look On This Picture!," *Daily Iowa State Democrat,* September 3, 1856.

321 **"There was never half the reason . . . Frémont and Dayton"**: "What Will the Allies Do?" *Richmond Dispatch,* June 24, 1856.

322 THE FEARFUL ISSUE . . . ONE DESTINY: Democratic pamphlet cover, 1856, Frémont papers, LOC.

322 **"no Union with slaveholders"**: Ibid., 6.

322 BLACK REPUBLICAN . . . FRAUD UPON THE PEOPLE: "Black Republican Imposture Exposed!" 1856 pamphlet, Frémont papers, LOC.

322 **United States totaling $960,614:** Ibid.

322 **$107,875 worth of horses and supplies:** Ibid.

323 **formally requesting an investigation:** JBF to Elizabeth Blair Lee, August 12, 1856, Herr and Spence, *Letters,* 122; *National Era,* August 14, 1856.

323 **"I have no room for prisoners"**: Bancroft, *History of Caliifornia,* vol. 5, 1846–48, 171.

323 **"Quite at the beginning . . . courteous dignity"**: JBF and F. P. Frémont, *Great Events in the Life of Major General John C. Frémont,* 205.

323 **"As booksellers" . . . "regenerate the Government"**: "Great Sale of Booksellers," *Charleston Courier,* September 25, 1856.

323 **on "tremendous walks"**: JBF and F. P. Frémont, *Great Events in the Life of Major General John C. Frémont,* 205.

323 **coffee and fruit:** Ibid.

324 **"market baskets of mail matter"**: Ibid.

324 **Jessie cull the newspapers:** Elizabeth Benton Frémont, *Recollections,* 77.

324 **"could not have withstood" . . . "wanted a square fight"**: Ibid.

324 **"while the hearty laughs . . . rang up to the roof"**: JBF and F. P. Frémont, *Great Events in the Life of Major General John C. Frémont,* 205.

324 **"gave me all the pain intended"**: Ibid.

324 **"Jessie Circle" . . . "admirers of Mrs. Jessie Fremont"**: "The Jessie Circle," *Charleston Mercury,* August 15, 1856.

324 **"It is now admitted . . . regulate the affairs of the nation"**: Ibid.

324 **Elizabeth Cady Stanton was a mother of seven:** Ginzburg, *Elizabeth Cady Stanton,* 9.

325 **"taking my watch with the baby from midnight to six"**: JBF and F. P. Frémont, *Great Events in the Life of Major General John C. Frémont,* 205.

325 **"a small, swarthy individual" . . . "was never divorced"**: "Col. Frémont," *Richmond Enquirer,* June 27, 1856.

325 **"which by the way I have still managed to keep him ignorant of"**: JBF to Francis P. Blair, August 25, 1856, Herr and Spence, *Letters,* 132.

325 **"If, as alleged . . . disqualified from being President"**: "Frémont Not Eligible to the Presidential Office," *Ohio Democrat,* September 11, 1856. This article quotes the *New York Express,* which in turn quotes the *Richmond Whig.*

326 **FREMONT'S ROMANISM ESTABLISHED . . . MOST FOUL COALITION:** Undated campaign pamphlet, Frémont papers, LOC.

326 **mistakenly referred to him as Catholic:** Gienapp, *Origins of the Republican Party,* 368; "Items of Fact and Fancy," *Portage Sentinel,* March 27, 1856.

326 **"made no secret of it":** "Frémont's Romanism and Col. Russell," *Daily American Organ,* August 20, 1856.

326 **a Catholic rather than a Protestant symbol:** "The Romanism of Frémont," *Daily American Organ,* July 31, 1856.

326 **"doing much damage":** Gienapp, *Origins of the Republican Party,* 369.

326 **"we shall lose Pa., N.J., Inda., Conn., & the Lord knows how many other states":** Ibid., 370.

327 **MORE EVIDENCE; FREMONT A MOHAMEDAN!:** "More Evidence—Frémont a Mohamedan," *Demoine Courier,* September 25, 1856.

327 **"We bring this charge . . . Catholic and a Protestant":** Ibid.

327 **"but he never was at any time . . . that Church":** JBF to Elizabeth Blair Lee, July 23, 1856, Herr and Spence, *Letters,* 119.

327 **"The charge is losing votes for you":** Elizabeth Benton Frémont, *Recollections,* 78.

327 **"Then I must lose them . . . matter of politics":** Ibid.

328 **"With our knives we dug a shallow grave, and . . . left them among the laurels":** JCF, *Memoirs of My Life,* 492.

328 **decision was "a mistake":** Gienapp, *Origins of the Republican Party,* 371.

328 **"I would go with him . . . punishment to such slanderers":** JBF to Elizabeth Blair Lee, August 12, 1856. The letter refers to both the Catholic charges and the California-related charges. Herr and Spence, *Letters,* 125.

329 **"Mr. Frémont says . . . my confessional":** Ibid., 124.

329 **restore "family harmony":** Chambers, *Old Bullion Benton,* 421.

329 **"parties founded on principle . . . with which the name a member of my family is connected":** Ibid., 422.

329 **"order, law, and justice":** Ibid.

330 **"Father is very much changed I think" . . . "interest too in public affairs":** JBF to Elizabeth Blair Lee, September 16, 1856, Herr and Spence, *Letters,* 137.

331 **featured the state's governor:** George, "Mechem or Mack: How a One-Word Correction in the 'Collected Works of Abraham Lincoln' Reveals the Truth about an 1856 Political Event."

331 **"Fellow countrymen" . . . "this should not be the case":** Fehrenbacher, *Abraham Lincoln: Speeches and Writings, 1832–1858,* 376–82.

331 **"You who hate slavery and love freedom . . . principle of equality":** Ibid.

332 **THE LATEST NEWS . . . for gambling purposes:** "Received by Magnetic Telegraph," *New York Tribune,* October 17, 1856.

332 **alleged without evidence that the Democrats had stuffed ballot boxes:** "Board of Aldermen," *New York Tribune,* October 16, 1856.

332 **"Republican reader! is your township or ward organized . . . save this nation":** "Two or three months since," *New York Tribune,* October 21, 1856.

332–33 **"defeated . . . a little fishy on the Catholic question":** *New York Mirror,* quoted in *Washington Star,* November 3, 1856.

333 **"Clerk, Fred Douglas"** . . . **"'anti-slavery God'"**: *Washington Star,* November 5, 1856, reprinted in the *State Capital Fact* of Columbus, Ohio.

333 **"one of the largest and most enthusiastic"** . . . **"graced the meeting by their presence"**: "Workingmen's Mass Meeting at the Academy of Music," *New York Tribune,* November 1, 1856.

333 **had chosen to attend the event:** Ibid.

333 **"extended its refining . . . my whole life"**: Ibid.

333 **in the theater box sat Jessie Benton Frémont:** Jessie mentions her attendance in a letter to Elizabeth Blair Lee, November 2, 1856. Herr and Spence, *Letters,* 142.

334 **"the curse of human Slavery"** . . . **"the Republic shall cease to exist"**: "Workingmen's Mass Meeting at the Academy of Music," *New York Tribune,* November 1, 1856.

334 **"Post Master please send as soon as read"** . . . **"Telegraphs will do the rest"**: JBF to Elizabeth Blair Lee, November 2, 1856, Herr and Spence, *Letters,* 142.

335 **"marched around the town in procession"** . . . **"and the coffin burned"**: "Honors to Frémont," *Daily Dispatch,* November 11, 1856.

335 **HOW LIBERTY BEARS DEFEAT:** "How Liberty Bears Defeat," *New York Tribune,* November 11, 1856.

336 **an armistice between the sections:** The *New York Herald,* which had been promoting Frémont for 1860, printed the Charleston and Richmond reactions to it (April 17, 1857).

336 **"The audience included more *outre* specimens . . . the opposite sex"**: "Women's Rights Philosophy and Philosophers," *New York Herald,* November 27, 1856.

336 **"women were urged to attend . . . the party of progress"**: Herr, *Jessie Benton Frémont,* 277.

336–37 **"We are subsiding"** . . . **"I like here"**: JBF to Elizabeth Blair Lee, November 18, 1856, Herr and Spence, *Letters,* 146.

337 **"a fierce sleeting rain that makes man and beast go on their way with bowed heads"**: JBF to Francis Preston Blair, January 31, 1856, ibid., 148.

EPILOGUE

339 **"an emblem of national unity and power"**: "The Inauguratory Ceremonies," *New York Herald,* March 5, 1857.

339 **"I owe my election . . . hearts of the American people"**: James Buchanan, inaugural address, March 4, 1857, American Presidency Project.

339 **"speedily and finally settled"**: Ibid.

340 **"History shows . . . socially or politically"**: Roger Taney, *Dred Scott v. Sandford,* reprinted in *Washington Union,* March 11, 1857.

340 **"all men are created equal"** . . . **"would be so understood"**: Ibid.

340 **"too clear for dispute"** . . . **"flagrantly against the principles which they asserted"**: Ibid.

340 **"A house divided against itself cannot stand"** . . . **"ultimate extinction"**: Lincoln speech, June 16, 1858, Fehrenbacher, *Abraham Lincoln: Speeches and Writings, 1832–1858,* 426–34.

340–41 **"Why can we not have peace?"** . . . **"geographical lines"**: Ibid., 789–90.

342 **Senate "retiring rooms":** *New York Tribune,* reprinted in the *Daily Gate City,* September 2, 1865.

342 **"three hundred reliable"** . . . **"defence of the City":** Moore, *Sweet Freedom's Plains,* 88.

343 **"foundation of civilization" wrote:** Stanley, "Senator William Gwin: Moderate or Racist?"

344 **"known throughout the length and breadth of the land":** Benton, *Thirty Years' View,* vol. 1, iv.

344 **his great-nephew Thomas Hart Benton:** Their family relationship is described in Wolff, *Thomas Hart Benton: A Life,* 17.

344 **"mainly evolving him from my inner consciousness":** Theodore Roosevelt to Henry Cabot Lodge, June 7, 1886, Morison, ed., *Letters of Theodore Roosevelt,* vol. 1, 102.

345 **soldier with saber drawn guarded the door:** Sherman and Fellman, *Memoirs,* 180.

345–46 **"Now"** . . . **"decision against all listening":** JBF and F. P. Frémont, *Great Events in the Life of Major General John C. Frémont,* 270–71.

346 **"excellent company"** . . . **"done to the General":** Emerson, *Journals,* vol. 9, 382.

346–47 **"Passage to India!** . . . **The road between Europe and Asia":** Walt Whitman, *Leaves of Grass,* 322–23.

347 **de facto president of** . . . **the Memphis, El Paso, and Pacific:** Cardinal Goodwin, who extensively researched the railroad, found no evidence John formally held the title. Goodwin, *John Charles Frémont,* 242.

347 **convicted by a French court in 1871:** Chaffin, *Pathfinder,* 483.

347 **Thousands of newspaper articles:** A database search of selected US newspapers from 1875 to 1889 found 2,293 page references to "John C. Frémont," 1,049 to "General Frémont," 835 to "Gen. Frémont," 321 references to "Jessie Benton Frémont," and 692 to "Mrs. Frémont." The single word "Frémont" appeared 44,637 times. Chronicling America: Historic American Newspapers database, LOC, author search January 1, 2019.

347 **retelling of John's four-hundred-mile horse ride:** "Endurance of Mustangs," *Saturday Journal,* September 23, 1876.

347 **"GENERAL FRÉMONT . . . been without income":** "General Frémont," *Daily Intelligencer,* June 5, 1878.

347–48 **"It was no great disappointment"** . . . **"debarred her":** "Jessie Benton Frémont," *Vancouver Independent,* April 22, 1880.

348 **"deserves its name** . . . **great-hearted we have found it":** JBF to William Morton, October 7, 1878, Herr and Spence, *Letters,* 449.

348 **"for the death"** . . . **"life is hard on women":** JBF to Elizabeth Blair Lee, July 29, 1883, Herr and Spence, *Letters,* 497.

349 **"I close the page"** . . . **"conflict among men":** JCF, *Memoirs of My Life,* 602.

349 **voted for him in 1856 and felt he owed his fortune:** Lavender, *The Great Persuader,* 9.

349 **tickets, letters of introduction along the route, and expense money:** Herr, *Jessie Benton Frémont,* 428.

350 **"impossible"** . . . **"upon his defeat":** Bigelow also credited John's ties to Thomas Hart Benton for his large vote totals; he either misremembered Benton's

opposition or believed that the public considered Benton an asset to John regardless of that opposition. Bigelow, *Retrospections of an Active Life,* vol. 1, 144.

351 **"his wife"... "hanged himself":** JBF, unpublished memoir, 48–49.

351 **Preuss became "deranged":** "Death of Charles Preuss," *Washington Sentinel,* September 3, 1853.

SOURCES AND ACKNOWLEDGMENTS

355 **dismissive mentions of John in their memoirs:** Sherman and Fellman, *Memoirs,* describes JCF numerous times, particularly 42 and 179–81.

355 **"Kit Carson, King of Guides":** by Albert W. Aiken.

356 **burned by his sister, Lily ... housecleaning:** Chaffin, *Pathfinder,* 503.

356 **"a vagrant by instinct—one might almost say a vagabond":** Goodwin, *John Charles Frémont,* 259.

356 **"chastened in style and much enlarged in content":** Nevins, *Frémont: Pathmarker of the West,* vii.

356 **"used psychiatric techniques":** Rolle, *John Charles Frémont: Character as Destiny,* xiv.

Bibliography

ARCHIVES, BOUND LETTERS, MANUSCRIPT COLLECTIONS, AND OTHER DOCUMENTS

Adams, John Quincy. *Memoirs of John Quincy Adams.* 12 vols. Philadelphia: Lippincott, 1876.

American State Papers, 1789–1838. Library of Congress.

Annals of Congress. Library of Congress.

Association for the Exhibition of the Industry of All Nations. *Official Catalogue of the New-York Exhibition of the Industry of All Nations.* New York: Putnam, 1853.

Banks, Nathaniel. Banks papers. Library of Congress Manuscript Division.

Benton, Thomas Hart. Benton papers. Library of Congress Manuscript Division.

———. *Mr. Benton's Anti-Compromise Speech.* Washington, DC: June 10, 1850.

California State Senate Journal 1849–50.

College of Charleston. Attendance records, College of Charleston archives.

Constitution of the State of California (1849).

Crafts, William. *An Oration, Delivered in St. Michael's Church, Before the Inhabitants of Charleston, South-Carolina, on the Fourth of July, 1812.* Charleston, SC: W. P. Young, 1812.

Crallé, Richard Kenner, ed. *The Works of John C. Calhoun.* New York: Appleton, 1860.

Dawson, J. L., and DeSaussure, H. W. *Census of the City of Charleston, South Carolina, for the Year 1848, Exhibiting the Condition and Prospects of the City, Illustrated by Many Statistical Details.* Charleston, SC: J. B. Nixon, 1848.

Douglass, Frederick. *Selected Speeches and Writings,* Foner and Taylor, eds. Chicago: Chicago Review, Press, 1950.

Emerson, Ralph Waldo. *Journals, 1820–1876.* Edited by Edward Forbes. Cambridge, MA: Riverside Press, 1913.

Fehrenbacher, Don E., ed. *Abraham Lincoln: Speeches and Writings, 1832–1858.* New York: Library of America, 1989.

———, ed. *Abraham Lincoln: Speeches and Writings, 1859–1865.* New York: Library of America, 1989.

Frémont, Jessie Benton. Frémont papers. Library of Congress Manuscript Division.

Frémont, Jessie Benton, and Francis Preston Frémont. *Great Events in the Life of Major General John C. Frémont, F.R.G.S. Chevalier de l'Ordre pour le Merite; etc. and Jessie Benton Frémont.* Unpublished, Bancroft Library collection 1891.

Frémont, John C. Frémont papers. Library of Congress Manuscript Division.

Frémont v. United States, 58 (US) 542.

Great Britain Historical Geographic Information System (GBHGIS). "A Vision of Britain Through Time." University of Portsmouth, 2018.

Greeley, Horace. Greeley papers. Library of Congress Manuscript Division.

Gudde, Elizabeth and Gudde, Erwin, ed. *Exploring with Frémont.* Norman: University of Oklahoma Press, 1958.

Hammond, George P., ed. *The Larkin Papers.* 11 vols. Berkeley: University of California Press, 1951–68.

Herr, Pamela, and Spence, Mary Lee, ed. *The Letters of Jessie Benton Frémont.* Urbana, IL: University of Illinois Press, 1993.

Hine, Robert, and Savoie Lottinville, eds. *Soldier in the West: Letters of Theodore Talbot During His Services in California, Mexico, and Oregon, 1845–53.* Norman: University of Oklahoma Press, 1972.

Jackson, Donald, and Mary Lee Spence. *The Expeditions of John Charles Frémont.* 2 vols. Urbana and Chicago: University of Illinois Press, 1970, 1973.

Lee, Robert E. "Map of the Harbor of St. Louis, Mississippi River, 1837." Washington, DC: US Army Corps of Engineers, 1837.

Martin, Thomas S. *With Frémont to California and the Southwest 1845–1849.* Edited by Ferol Egan. Ashland, OR: Lewis Osborne, 1975.

Morison, Elting E., ed. *Letters of Theodore Roosevelt.* 4 vols. Cambridge, MA: Harvard University Press, 1951.

National Convention of Colored Citizens. *Minutes of the National Convention of Colored Citizens: Held at Buffalo, on the 15th, 16th, 17th, 18th and 19th of August 1843.* Pamphlet. New York: Percy and Reed, 1843.

Report of the Woman's Rights Convention, Held at Seneca Falls, N.Y., July 19th and 20th, 1848. Rochester, NY: North Star, 1848.

Sherman, William Tecumseh. *Memoirs.* Edited by Michael Fellman. New York: Penguin Classics, 2000.

Spence, Mary Lee. *The Expeditions of John Charles Frémont,* vol. 3. Urbana and Chicago: University of Illinois Press, 1984.

Sutter, John. John Augustus Sutter letters, 1840–46. Bancroft Library, University of California, Berkeley.

Tinelli, L. W. *Frémont, Buchanan and Fillmore; or, The Parties Called to Order.* Pamphlet. New York: Livermore and Rudd, 1856.

United States Census.

Webster, Fletcher, eds. *Private Correspondence of Daniel Webster.* Boston: Little, Brown, 1875.

MEMOIRS AND HISTORIES

Abbott, Lyman. *Reminiscences.* Boston and New York: Houghton Mifflin, 1915.

Adams, John Quincy. *Memoirs of John Quincy Adams.* Edited by Charles Francis Adams. Philadelphia: Lippincott, 1877.

Arrington, Leonard J. *American Moses.* Urbana, IL: University of Illinois Press, 1986.

Baker, Jean. *James Buchanan.* New York: Henry Holt, 2004.

Bancroft, Hubert H. *History of California,* vol. 4, 1840–45. San Francisco: The History Company, 1886.

———. *History of California,* vol. 5, 1846–48. San Francisco: The History Company, 1886.

Bartlett, Ruhl Jacob. *John C. Frémont and the Republican Party.* Columbus: Ohio State University, 1930.

Bay, William Van Ness. *Reminiscences of the Bench and Bar of Missouri.* St. Louis: F. H. Thomas, 1878.

Benton, Thomas Hart. *Thirty Years' View.* New York: Appleton, 1858.

Bigelow, John. *Memoir of the Life and Public Services of John Charles Fremont.* New York: Derby and Jackson, 1856.

———. *Retrospections of an Active Life,* vol. 1, 1817–1863. New York: Baker and Taylor, 1909.

Blight, David W. *Frederick Douglass: Prophet of Freedom.* New York: Simon & Schuster, 2018.

Bray, Martha Coleman. *Joseph Nicollet and His Map.* Philadelphia: American Philosophical Society, 1994.

Chaddock, Katherine E., and Matalene, Carolyn B., eds. *College of Charleston Voices.* Charleston, SC: History Press, 2006.

Chaffin, Tom. *Pathfinder: John Charles Frémont and the Course of American Empire.* Norman: University of Oklahoma Press, 2002.

Chambers, William Nisbet. *Old Bullion Benton.* Boston: Little, Brown, 1956.

Connelley, William E. *A Standard History of Kansas and Kansans,* vol. 1. Chicago: Lewis, 1918.

———. *The Provisional Government of Nebraska Territory and the Journals of William Walker.* Lincoln: Nebraska State Historical Society, 1899.

Crosby, Elisha Oscar. *Memoirs of Elisha Oscar Crosby: Reminiscences of California and Guatemala from 1849 to 1864.* Edited by Charles Albro Barker. San Marino, CA: Huntington Library, 1945.

Delany, Martin. *The Condition, Elevation, Emigration and Destiny of the Colored People of the United States.* Amherst, MA: Humanity Books, 2004.

Desmond, Humphrey J. *The Know-Nothing Party: A Sketch.* Washington, DC: New Century Press, 1904.

Dillon, Richard. *Fool's Gold: A Biography of John Sutter.* New York: Coward-McCann, 1967.

Donald, David Herbert. *Lincoln.* New York: Simon & Schuster, 1995.

Douglass, Frederick. *Life and Times of Frederick Douglass.* London: Christian Age, 1882.

———. *Narrative of the Life of Frederick Douglass.* Boston: Anti-slavery Office, 1849.

Easterby, J. H. *A History of the College of Charleston.* Charleston, SC: Trustees of the College of Charleston, 1935.

Egon, Ferol, ed. *With Frémont to California and the Southwest 1845–49.* Ashland, OR: Lewis Osborne, 1975.

Elzas, Barnett A. *The Reformed Society of Israelites of Charleston.* New York: Bloch Publishing, 1916.

Favour, Alpheus H. *Old Bill Williams Mountain Man.* Norman: University of Oklahoma Press, 1962.

Foote, Henry S. *Casket of Reminiscences.* Washington, DC: Chronicle Publishing, 1874.

Frémont, Elizabeth Benton. *Recollections of Elizabeth Benton Frémont.* New York: Hitchcock, 1912.

Frémont, Jessie Benton. *Memoirs.* Unpublished, Bancroft Library collection, undated.

———. *Far-West Sketches.* Boston: Lothrop, 1890.

———. *Souvenirs of My Time.* Boston: Lothrop, 1887.

———. *A Year of American Travel.* New York: Harper and Brothers, 1878.

Frémont, Jessie Benton, and Francis Preston Frémont. *Great Events in the Life of Major General John C. Frémont, F.R.G.S. Chevalier de l'Ordre pour le Merite; etc. and Jessie Benton Frémont.* Unpublished, Bancroft Library collection, 1891.

Frémont, John Charles. *Memoirs of My Life.* Chicago: Belford, Clarke and Co., 1887.

———. *A Report on an Exploration of the Country Lying Between the Missouri River and the Rocky Mountains on the Line of the Kansas and Great Platte Rivers.* Washington, DC: United States Senate, 1843.

———. *A Report on the Exploring Expedition to Oregon and North California in the Years 1843–44.* Washington, DC: United States Senate, 1845.

Gienapp, William E. *The Origins of the Republican Party 1852–1856.* New York: Oxford University Press, 1988.

Gillikin, Margaret Wilson. *Saint Dominguan Refugees in Charleston, South Carolina, 1791–1822: Assimilation and Accommodation in a Slave Society.* PhD diss., University of South Carolina–Columbia, 2014.

Ginzberg, Lori D. *Elizabeth Cady Stanton: An American Life.* New York: Hill and Wang, 2009.

Goodwin, Cardinal. *John Charles Frémont: An Explanation of His Career.* Stanford, CA: Stanford University Press, 1930.

Hague, Harlan, and David J. Langum. *Thomas O. Larkin: A Life of Patriotism and Profit in Old California.* Norman: University of Oklahoma Press, 1990.

Halstead, Murat. *Trimmers, Trucklers and Temporizers.* Madison: Wisconsin State Historical Society, 1961.

Herr, Pamela. *Jessie Benton Frémont: American Woman of the 19th Century.* New York: Franklin Watts, 1987.

Holland, Jesse. *The Invisibles: The Untold Story of African American Slaves in the White House.* Guilford, CT: Lyons Press, 2016.

Hurtado, Albert L. *John Sutter: A Life on the North American Frontier.* Norman: University of Oklahoma Press, 2008.

Ide, Simeon. *The Conquest of California: A Biography of William B. Ide.* Oakland, CA: Biobooks, 1944.

Inglis, Fred. *A Short History of Celebrity.* Princeton, NJ: Princeton University Press, 2010.

Irving, Washington. *Astoria: Or, Enterprise Beyond the Rocky Mountains.* Philadelphia: Carey, Lea and Blanchard, 1836.

Lavender, David. *The Great Persuader.* New York: Doubleday, 1970.

Mahan, Alfred Thayer. *Admiral Farragut.* New York: Appleton, 1901.

Marti, Werner H. *Messenger of Destiny: The California Adventures, 1846-1847.* San Francisco, John Howell, 1960.

Meigs, William Montgomery. *The Life of Thomas Hart Benton.* Philadelphia: Lippincott, 1904.

Meltzer, Milton. *Nathaniel Hawthorne: A Biography.* Minneapolis, MN: Twenty-first Century Books, 2007.

Merry, Robert W. *A Country of Vast Designs.* New York: Simon & Schuster, 2011.

Moore, John Bassett, ed. *The Works of James Buchanan.* 12 vols. Philadelphia: J. B. Lippincott, 1908-11.

Moore, Shirley Ann Wilson. *Sweet Freedom's Plains: African-Americans on the Overland Trails, 1841-69.* Norman: University of Oklahoma Press, 2016.

Nevins, Allan. *Fremont: Pathmarker of the West.* New York: Longmans, Green and Co., 1955.

Paul, Harry G., ed. *Francis Parkman's The Oregon Trail.* New York: Henry Holt, 1918.

Peterson, Merrill D. *The Great Triumvirate.* New York: Oxford University Press, 1987.

Phillips, Catherine Coffin. *Jessie Benton Frémont: A Woman Who Made History.* San Francisco: John Henry Nash, 1935.

Pool, David De Sola. *Portraits Etched in Stone: Early Jewish Settlers, 1682-1831.* New York: Columbia University Press, 1952.

Pred, Allan R. *Urban Growth and the Circulation of Information: The United States System of Cities 1790-1840.* Cambridge, MA: Harvard University Press, 1973.

Primm, James Neal. *Lion of the Valley: St. Louis, Missouri, 1764-1980.* St. Louis: Missouri Historical Society Press, 1981.

Quaife, Milo Milton, ed. *The Diary of James K. Polk During His Presidency, 1845 to 1849.* 4 vols. Chicago: A. C. McClurg, 1910.

———. *Kit Carson's Autobiography.* Lincoln: University of Nebraska Press, 1966.

Rolle, Andrew. *John Charles Frémont: Character as Destiny.* Norman: University of Oklahoma Press, 1991.

Rosenus, Alan. *General Vallejo and the Advent of the Americans.* Berkeley, CA: Heyday Books, 1995.

Royce, Josiah. *California: A Study of American Character.* New York: Knopf, 1948.

Seward, Frederick W. *Seward at Washington, 1831-46.* New York: Derby and Miller, 1891.

———. *Seward at Washington, as Senator and Secretary of State, 1846-1861.* New York: Derby and Miller, 1891.

Silverman, Kenneth. *Lightning Man: The Accursed Life of Samuel F. B. Morse.* New York: Alfred A. Knopf, 2003.

Smith, Elbert. *Francis Preston Blair.* New York: Free Press, 1980.

Starr, Kevin. *California: A History.* New York: Modern Library, 2005.

Steel, Edward M. *T. Butler King of Georgia.* Athens: University of Georgia Press, 1964.

Taylor, Bayard. *Prose Writings of Bayard Taylor.* New York: Putnam, 1862.

Trent, William P., and Hellman, George S., eds. *The Journals of Washington Irving.* Carlisle, MA: Applewood Books, 1919.

Upham, Charles Wentworth. *Life, Explorations and Public Services of John Charles Frémont.* Boston: Ticknor and Fields, 1856.

Wilson, Robert. *Mathew Brady: Portraits of a Nation.* New York: Bloomsbury, 2013.

Wilson, R. L. *Colt: An American Legend: The Official History of Colt Firearms from 1836 to the Present.* New York: Artabras, circa 1986.

Wolff, Justin. *Thomas Hart Benton: A Life.* New York: Farrar, Straus and Giroux, 2012.

WORKS OF POETRY AND FICTION

Aiken, Albert W. *Kit Carson, King of Guides.* New York: M. J. Ivers, 1899.

Child, Lydia Maria. *Flowers for Children.* New York: C. S. Francis, 1854.

Whitman, Walt. *Leaves of Grass.* Reprinted edition of 1891–92. New York: Random House, 1930.

CONTEMPORARY NEWSPAPERS AND MAGAZINES

Three newspaper databases were accessed through the Library of Congress: Chronicling America; America's Historical Newspapers; and Newspaper Archive. The publications below were accessed through these databases except where specified otherwise.

Alta California
American Republican
Arkansas State Gazette/Weekly Gazette
Boon's Lick Times
Boston Courier
Boston Daily Atlas
Cadiz Sentinel
California Courier
Century Magazine, Hathi Trust
Charleston Courier
Charleston Mercury
Cheraw Gazette
Cherokee Advocate
Congregational Herald
Daily American Organ

Daily Dispatch
Daily Gate City
Daily Index (Sacramento)
Daily Intelligencer (Seattle)
Daily Iowa State Democrat
Daily Madisonian
Daily Pacific News
Daily Picayune (New Orleans)
Democrat and Sentinel
Democratic Standard
Demoine Courier
Easton Star
Frederick Douglass' Paper/North Star
Gazette and Commercial Advertiser
Liberator
Louisville Messenger
Milwaukee Sentinel and Gazette
National Era
National Intelligencer
New York Commercial Advertiser
New York Evangelist
New York Evening Post
New York Examiner
New York Herald
New-York Observer
New York Spiritual Telegraph
New York Sun
New York Times
New York Tribune
Niles' National Register, Hathi Trust
North-Carolina Standard
Ohio Democrat
Portage Sentinel
Republican and Savannah Evening Ledger
Richmond Dispatch
Richmond Enquirer
Sacramento Transcript
Sartain's Union Magazine of Literature and Art, Hathi Trust
Saturday Journal (New York)
Saturday Morning Visitor
Schenectady Reflector
Southern Sentinel
Star of the North
State Capital Reporter
St. Louis Enquirer

Sunbury American and Shamokin Journal
Trenton State Gazette
United States Magazine and Democratic Review, Hathi Trust
Washington Globe
Washington Sentinel
Washington Star
Washington Union
Weekly Herald
Weekly Pacific News
Western Democrat
Whig Standard
Worcester Palladium

JOURNALS, ARTICLES, AND DISSERTATIONS

Anderson, H. Allen. "The Delaware and Shawnee Indians and the Republic of Texas, 1820–1845," *Southwestern Historical Quarterly* 94, no. 2 (1990): 231–60.

Andrews, Horace Jr. "Kansas Crusade: Eli Thayer and the New England Emigrant Aid Company." *New England Quarterly* 35, no. 4 (1962): 497–514.

Barker, Eugene C. "The Annexation of Texas." *Southwestern Historical Quarterly* 50, no. 1 (1946): 49–74.

Baugh, Alexander. "John C. Frémont's 1843–44 Western Expedition and Its Influence on Mormon Settlement in Utah." Republished in Esplin, Scott C., Bennett, Richard E., Black, Susan Easton, and Manscill, Craig C., eds. *Far Away in the West.* Salt Lake City: Deseret Book, 2015.

Brophy, Alfred L., and Douglas Thie. "Land, Slaves, and Bonds: Trust and Probate in the Pre–Civil War Shenandoah Valley." *West Virginia Law Review* 119, no. 1 (2016).

Campbell, Augustus, and Colin D. Campbell. "Crossing the Isthmus of Panama, 1849: The Letters of Dr. Augustus Campbell." *California History* 78, no. 4 (1999/2000): 226–37.

Crotty, Homer D. "The California Constitutional Convention of 1849." *Historical Society of Southern California Quarterly* 31, no. 3 (1949): 155–66.

Crouthamel, James L. "Tocqueville's South," *Journal of the Early Republic* 2, no. 4 (1982): 381–401.

"Documentary: The Frémont Episode." *California Historical Society Quarterly* 6, no. 3 (1927): 265–80.

Dorris, Jonathan Truman. "The Oregon Trail." *Journal of the Illinois State Historical Society* 10, no. 4 (1918): 473–547.

Ellison, William H., ed. "Memoirs of Hon. William M. Gwin." *California Historical Society Quarterly* 19, no. 1 (1940): 1–26.

Gates, Paul W. "The Frémont-Jones Scramble for California Land Claims." *Southern California Quarterly* 56, no. 1 (1974): 13–44.

George, Tom M. "'Mechem' or 'Mack': How a One-Word Correction in the 'Collected Works of Abraham Lincoln' Reveals the Truth about an 1856 Political Event." *Journal of the Abraham Lincoln Association* 33, no. 2 (2012): 20–33.

Harmon, Nicholas D., Huefner, Michael S., and Anderson Young, Shauna C. "Almon W. Babbitt, Joseph E. Johnson, and the Western Bugle: An LDS Frontier Newspaper at Kanesville." *Journal of Mormon History* 39, no. 3 (2013): 163–97.

Hershberger, Mary. "Mobilizing Women, Anticipating Abolition: The Struggle Against Indian Removal in the 1830s." *Journal of American History* 86, no. 1 (1999): 15–40.

Hunt, Gaillard. "South Carolina During the Nullification Struggle." *Political Science Quarterly* 6, no. 2 (1891): 232–47.

Jackson, Donald. "The Myth of the Frémont Howitzer." *Bulletin of the Missouri Historical Society* (April 1967): 205–14.

Jones, Thomas B. "Henry Clay and Continental Expansion, 1820–1844." *Register of the Kentucky Historical Society* (July 1975): 241–62.

Jortner, Maura L. "Playing 'America' on Nineteenth-Century Stages; or, Jonathan in England and Jonathan at Home." PhD diss., University of Pittsburgh, 2005.

Kanazawa, Mark. "Immigration, Exclusion, and Taxation: Anti-Chinese Legislation in Gold Rush California." *Journal of Economic History* 65, no. 3 (2005): 779–805.

Kemble, John Haskell. "The Genesis of the Pacific Mail Steamship Company." *California Historical Society Quarterly* 13, no. 3 (1934): 240–54.

Kirker, Harold. "The Larkin House Revisited." *California History* 65, no. 1 (1986): 26–33.

Lannie, Vincent P., and Bernard C. Diethorn. "For the Honor and Glory of God: The Philadelphia Bible Riots of 1840." *History of Education Quarterly* 8, no. 1 (1968) 44–106.

Leavitt, Judith Walzer. "Under the Shadow of Maternity." *Feminist Studies* 12, no. 1 (1986): 129–54.

Levine, Robert S. "Uncle Tom's Cabin in Frederick Douglass' Paper." *American Literature* 64, no. 1 (1992): 71–93.

Lyman, J. Chester. "Our Inequalities of Suffrage." *North American Review* 144, no. 364 (1887): 298–306.

Marshall, Schuyler C. "The Free Democratic Convention of 1852." *Pennsylvania History* 22, no. 2 (1955): 146–67.

McGehee, Micajah. "Rough Times in Rough Places." *Century Illustrated Magazine*, vol. 41 (March 1891): 771–80.

McGuire, Horace. "Two Episodes of Anti-Slavery Days." Read Before the Rochester Historical Society, October 27, 1916. Published in *Rochester Historical Society* 4 (1925): 218–20.

Miller, Edward A. "VMI Men Who Wore Yankee Blue, 1861–1865." *VMI Alumni Review* (Spring 1996): 1–13.

Missouri Historical Society. *Glimpses of the Past*. Pamphlet. December–January 1934–35.

Moore, Robert. "William Clark's Indian Museum." National Park Service paper, undated.

Nichols, Charles. "The Origins of Uncle Tom's Cabin." *Phylon Quarterly* 19, no. 3 (1958): 328–34.

Parker, Jane Marsh. "Reminiscences of Frederick Douglass." *Outlook* 51 (April 1895).

Pearson, Lee M. "The 'Princeton' and the 'Peacemaker': A Study in Nineteenth-Century Naval Research and Development Procedures." *Technology and Culture* 7, no. 2 (1966): 163–83.

Sacher, John M. "The Sudden Collapse of the Louisiana Whig Party." *Journal of Southern History* 65, no. 2 (1999): 221–48.

Saerchinger, César. "Musical Landmarks in New York." *Musical Quarterly* 6, no. 2 (1920): 227–56.

Savage, W. S. "The Influence of William Alexander Leidesdorff on the History of California." *The Journal of Negro History* 38, no. 3 (1953): 322–32.

Schmandt, Raymond H. "A Selection of Sources Dealing with the Nativist Riots of 1844." *Records of the American Catholic Historical Society of Philadelphia* 80, no. 2/3 (1969): 68–113.

Smith, Elbert B. "Francis P. Blair and the Globe: Nerve Center of the Jacksonian Democracy." *Register of the Kentucky Historical Society* 57, no. 4 (1959): 340–53.

Spence, Mary Lee. "David Hoffman: Frémont's Mariposa Agent in London." *Southern California Quarterly* 60, no. 4 (1978): 379–403.

Stanley, Gerald. "Senator William Gwin: Moderate or Racist?" *California Historical Quarterly* 50, no. 3 (1971) 243–55.

Steen, Ivan D. "Palaces for Travelers: New York City's Hotels in the 1850's As Viewed by British Visitors." *New York History* 51, no. 3 (1970): 269–86.

Swift, John W., Hodgkinson, P., and Woodhouse, Samuel W. "The Voyage of the Empress of China." *Pennsylvania Magazine of History and Biography* 63, no. 1 (1939) 24–36.

Thompson, Gerald. "Edward Fitzgerald Beale and the California Gold Rush." *Southern California Quarterly* 63, no. 3 (1981): 198–225.

Truesdale, Dorothy S. "Historic Main Street Bridge." *Rochester History* 3, no. 2 (1941): 1–24.

Credits

PART AND CHAPTER TITLE PAGES

Page xviii: Col. Fremont planting the American standard on the Rocky Mountains, by Baker & Godwin, 1856. Library of Congress, Prints and Photographs Division, LC-DIG-ppmsca-03212.

Page 1: George Catlin, *Prairie Meadows Burning*, 1832, oil on canvas, Smithsonian American Art Museum, Gift of Mrs. Joseph Harrison, Jr., 1985.66.374.

Page 2: The Miriam and Ira D. Wallach Division of Art, Prints and Photographs: Print Collection, The New York Public Library. "Charleston, S.C." The New York Public Library Digital Collections. 1851. http://digitalcollections.nypl.org/items /510d47d9-7ccf-a3d9-e040-e00a18064a99.

Page 17: View of St. Louis by Leon Pomarede, ca. 1832–1835. Crystal Bridges Museum of American Art, Bentonville, Arkansas, 2007.16. Photography by Dwight Primiano.

Page 34: View of Washington by Robert Pearsall Smith, 1850. Library of Congress, Prints and Photographs Division, LC-DIG-pga-03316.

Page 46: Art and Picture Collection, The New York Public Library. "Fremont On The Rocky Mountains." The New York Public Library Digital Collections. 1876 - 1877. http://digitalcollections.nypl.org/items/510d47e1-1fe4-a3d9-e040-e00a18064a99.

Page 65: Albert Bierstadt, *Among the Sierra Nevada, California*, 1868, oil on canvas, Smithsonian American Art Museum, Bequest of Helen Huntington Hull,

431

granddaughter of William Brown Dinsmore, who acquired the painting in 1873 for "The Locusts," the family estate in Dutchess County, New York, 1977.107.1.

Page 66: Map of Oregon and Upper California from the surveys of Frémont and other authorities. Drawn by Charles Preuss in 1848. From *The Expeditions of John Charles Frémont: Map Portfolio* edited by Donald Jackson and Mary Lee Spence, published by University of Illinois Press, 1970.

Page 84: Inauguration of President Polk – The Oath, 1845. Library of Congress, Prints and Photographs Division, LC-DIG-ppmsca-51565.

Page 100: Portrait of General John C. Frémont by George Peter Alexander Healy. The Athenaeum.

Page 120: *Forest Camp—Shastl Peak* from *Memoirs of My Life* by John Charles Frémont. Page 377. Published by Belford, Clarke & Company, 1887.

Page 141: Cascade, Nevada Fall on Left, View above Vernal Fall, 1861, by Carleton E. Watkins. The Metropolitan Museum of Art, Gilman Collection, Museum Purchase, 2005.

Page 142: *Sagundai* from *Memoirs of My Life* by John Charles Frémont. Page 491. Published by Belford, Clarke & Company, 1887.

Page 164: Mexican News, by Alfred Jones (engraver) and Richard Caton Woodville, 1853. . Library of Congress, Prints and Photographs Division, LC-DIG-pga-03889.

Page 188: From *The Expeditions of John Charles Frémont*, edited by Donald Jackson and Mary Lee Spence, published by University of Illinois Press, 1970.

Page 216: Charles Christian Nahl, August Wenderoth, *Miners in the Sierras*, 1851–1852, oil on canvas mounted on canvas, Smithsonian American Art Museum, Gift of the Fred Heilbron Collection, 1982.120.

Page 237: Union, engraved by Henry S. Sadd, copied after T.H. Matteson, 1852. National Portrait Gallery, Smithsonian Institution, NPG.87.253.

Page 238: San Francisco / S.F. Marryat, delt., by M. & N. Hanhart, and Frank Marryat, 1850. Library of Congress, Prints and Photographs Division, LC-DIG-pga-01463.

Page 262: Mrs. J.C. Fremont sitting on the porch of her house in Mariposa. 1867. Photographer unknown. Albumen print carte de viste. Collection of Oakland Museum of California. Gift of Mrs. Carolyn K. Louderback.

Page 282: Stump Speaking by George Caleb Bingham, 1853–54. Saint Louis Art Museum, Saint Louis, Missouri, United States.

Page 308: Political cartoon from 1856. Wisconsin Historical Society, WHS56967.

Page 338: John Charles Frémont, his wife Jessie Benton Frémont, and their daughter stand before a redwood tree. Photograph from the John Charles Frémont and Jessie

Benton Frémont papers, Library of Congress, Prints and Photographs Division, PR 13 CN 2011:212.

INSERT

Insert page 1 (top left): Portrait of Mrs. Jessie Benton Fremont, Wife of Gen. John Fremont, by Thomas Buchanan Read. 1856. Braun Research Library Collection, Autry Museum, Los Angeles; 81.G.2.

Insert page 1 (top right): John C. Frémont. LC-BH82-523. Brady-Handy Photograph Collection, Library of Congress, Prints and Photographs Division.

Insert page 1 (bottom): Letter from John C. Frémont to Joel Poinsett, Box 1, John Charles Frémont and Jessie Benton Frémont papers, 1828–1980, MSS1459, Manuscript Division, Library of Congress, Washington, D.C.

Insert page 2 (top): Tasayac, or the Half Dome, from Glacier Point, Yosemite Valley, Mariposa County, Cal, by Carleton E. Watkins. LC-DIG-stereo-1s01436. Library of Congress, Prints and Photographs Division.

Insert page 2 (bottom left): Christopher Carson, 1943. LC-USZ62-107570. Library of Congress, Prints and Photographs Division.

Insert page 2 (bottom right): Thomas Hart Benton. LC-DIG-DS-13456. Library of Congress, Prints and Photographs Division.

Insert page 3 (top left): From *Memoir of the Life and Public Services of John Charles Fremont* by John Bigelow. Published by Derby & Jackson, New York, 1856.

Insert page 3 (top right): From box 4, folder 1, John Charles Frémont and Jessie Benton Frémont papers, 1828–1980, MSS1459, Manuscript Division, Library of Congress, Washington, D.C.

Insert page 3 (bottom): From box 2, folder 9, John Charles Frémont and Jessie Benton Frémont papers, 1828–1980, MSS1459, Manuscript Division, Library of Congress, Washington, D.C.

Insert page 4 (top left): From box 2, folder 1, Horace Greeley Papers, Manuscript Division, Library of Congress, Washington, D.C.

Insert page 4 (top right): Francis Preston Blair. LC-BH83- 45 [P&P]. Brady-Handy Photograph Collection, Library of Congress, Prints and Photographs Division.

Insert page 4 (bottom): Astor House Broadway, 1867, Society of Iconophiles, 1909 / etched by S.L. Smith, from a photograph. LC-DIG-ds-01872. Library of Congress, Prints and Photographs Division.

Insert page 5 (top and bottom left): From the collection of the Local History & Genealogy Division, Central Library of Rochester & Monroe County, NY.

Insert page 5 (bottom right): Frederick Douglass, created between 1879 and 1900. LC-USZC4-3623. Library of Congress, Prints and Photographs Division.

Insert page 6 (top): "The Grand National Fight 2 Against 1 Fought on the 6th of Nov. 1856" by J. Childs and John L. Magee. 1856. LC-USZ62-92030. Library of Congress, Prints and Photographs Division.

Insert page 6 (bottom left): James Buchanan, fifteenth president of the United States, by N. Currier. LC-DIG-pga-09177. Library of Congress, Prints and Photographs Division.

Insert page 6 (bottom right): John Bigelow. LC-DIG-DS-13455. Library of Congress, Prints and Photographs Division.

Insert page 7 (top): Black Republican Imposture Exposed! Washington, 1856. LC-1041663032. Library of Congress.

Insert page 7 (bottom left and bottom right): From Box 2, John Charles Frémont and Jessie Benton Frémont papers, 1828–1980, MSS1459, Manuscript Division, Library of Congress, Washington, D.C.

Insert page 8 (top left): Opening page of Jessie Benton Frémont's memoir, Fremont Family papers, circa 1839–1927, BANC MSS C-B 397, The Bancroft Library, University of California, Berkeley.

Insert page 8 (top right): Jessie Benton Frémont. UtCon Collection / Alamy Stock Photo.

Insert page 8 (bottom): San Francisco History Center, San Francisco Public Library.

Index

910.92 INSKEEP
Inskeep, Steve.
Imperfect union.
01/14/2020